PENGUIN
STUDIO

In memory of
Charles L. Coleman

CHAMPIONS

THE ILLUSTRATED HISTORY OF
HOCKEY'S GREATEST DYNASTIES

DOUGLAS HUNTER

PENGUIN
STUDIO

A PENGUIN STUDIO BOOK
Published by the Penguin Group
Penguin Books Canada Ltd, 10 Alcorn Avenue, Toronto, Ontario, Canada M4V 3B2
Penguin Books Ltd, 27 Wrights Lane, London W8 5TZ, England
Viking Penguin, a division of Penguin Books USA Inc., 375 Hudson Street, New York, New York 10014, U.S.A.
Penguin Books Australia Ltd, Ringwood, Victoria, Australia
Penguin Books (NZ) Ltd, cnr Rosedale and Airborne Roads, Albany, Auckland 1310, New Zealand

Penguin Books Ltd, Registered Offices: Harmondsworth, Middlesex, England

First published 1997
10 9 8 7 6 5 4 3 2 1

Copyright © Douglas Hunter, 1997

Printed and bound in Singapore on acid neutral paper

Canadian Cataloguing in Publication Data

Hunter, Douglas, 1959—
Champions : the illustrated history of hockey's greatest dynasties

Includes index.
ISBN 0-670-86894-9

1. Hockey teams – History. 2. National Hockey League – History. 3. Hockey – History. I. Title.

GV846.5.H85 1997   796.962'64   C96-930654-7

American Library of Congress Cataloguing in Publication Data Available

Visit Penguin Canada's web site at **www.penguin.ca**

ACKNOWLEDGMENTS

In the course of writing three previous books on hockey history—*Open Ice*, *A Breed Apart* and *War Games*—I interviewed somewhere in the order of 100 individuals. The result was a filing cabinet full of tape transcriptions and notes from telephone conversations, all of which I have drawn on for this work. Some interview subjects, like Bob Davidson, are no longer alive, and I was fortunate to have had the privilege of meeting him. The names of all those who I have spoken to are far too many to list here, but I remain grateful to people like Jean Béliveau, Allan Stanley, Jim Schoenfeld, Chuck Rayner, Frank Brimsek and Maurice Richard for the help they have been. I re-interviewed a number of players for this book, and in particular I must thank Cal Gardner, Johnny Bower, Glenn Hall and Dave Keon for their time.

The main research source for this book was the Hockey Hall of Fame Archives. I cannot thank enough Craig Campbell and the rest of the archives staff for their cooperation and good humour. As with *A Breed Apart*, Craig did a superb job ferreting out the better photographs in the archives' collection, particularly ones that had not yet been published. I must also thank the staff at Corbis-Bettmann, the National Archives of Canada and Bruce Bennett Studios for their cooperation in rounding up the other photographs that appear here.

The library of the HHOF Archives provided a seemingly boundless supply of vertical clipping files, official team histories and other resources. Particularly valuable was the indexed microfiche archive of issues of *The Hockey New*s. Several published works merit mention: *Net Worth*, by Alison Cruise and David Griffiths; *Lions in Winter*, by Chris Goyens and Allan Turowitz; and *The Complete Historical and Statistical Reference to the World Hockey Association*, by Scott Adam Surgent.

Sorting out players' careers and trades and the periods of service of coaches and managers was aided by a number of reference books, most prominent among them: *Inside Sports Hockey*, edited by Zander Hollander; *The National Hockey League Official Guide and Record Book*; *The American Hockey League Guide and Record Book*, and a 1950 edition of *Hendy's Who's Who in Hockey* on loan to me by Sam Bettio. Materials in the Conn Smythe Papers at the Archives of Ontario and other documents at the National Archives of Canada (which I used in writing *War Games*) have been the source of information contained in the chapters dealing with the Leafs of the 1940s, 1950s and 1960s and the Montreal Canadiens of the 1940s.

My editor, Meg Masters, did another fine job of keeping pace with an author who also happened to be illustrating and designing the book and who was prone to moving abruptly and tangentially when one facet of the project captured his imagination more than another. Copy editor Catherine Marjoribanks made sure the text sounded like the Queen's English, and production editor Lori Ledingham (who like Meg has now been through four books with me) tackled checking the page proofs and making sure all the bits and pieces were where they should be. Production director Dianne Craig ran interference with the film house and printer and made sure I understood what deadlines are. Finally, I must thank Penguin Canada publisher Cynthia Good for her continued support of my work, and Penguin Canada president Brad Martin and publicity manager Scott Sellers for their general enthusiasm and input on what belonged between the covers.

I would also like to thank a man I will never meet, Charles L. Coleman, to whose memory this book is dedicated. Mr. Coleman compiled the three-volume history *The Trail of the Stanley Cup*. It was an exhaustive and impressive task, and he produced a reference work all modern hockey writers know to depend on. This book would not have been possible without his pioneering effort.

Finally, my thanks go out to my wife, Debbie, for her tea and sympathy, office management and (most onerous of all) pitching in with the indexing.

Douglas Hunter

CONTENTS

Maurice Richard and Toe Blake, the prolific wingers of Montreal's "Punch Line" in the 1940s, converse in the dressing room. With Blake as his coach, Richard participated in Montreal's record streak of five consecutive Stanley Cup victories from 55/56 to 59/60

WHAT MAKES A DYNASTY?

WINNING THE STANLEY CUP IS THE PINNACLE OF ACHIEVEMENT IN THE NHL. WINNING IT AGAIN AND AGAIN IS THE MARK OF A DYNASTY, SOMETHING TODAY'S GAME CANNOT TOLERATE

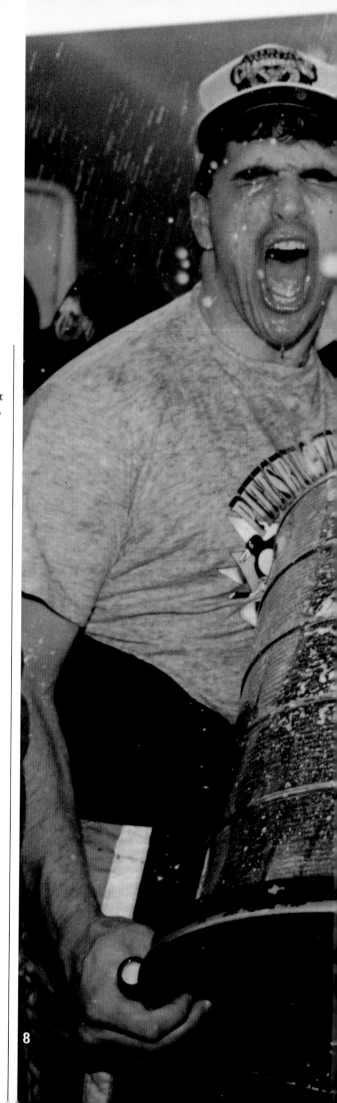

The history of professional hockey as experienced by the National Hockey League presents a panorama of change. The NHL has been around since 1917, and the game it plays has undergone a steady evolution—so much so that the hockey played in one era would be unrecognizable to the fans of another. The number of teams has ebbed and flowed. Only three teams completed the inaugural 17/18 season. They played 22 games, and the only team with artificial ice was the Toronto Arenas. Without artificial ice, the 96/97 season could not have featured an 84-game schedule with 26 teams, in locations like Phoenix, Los Angeles and Miami.

RIGHT: Kevin Stevens, Bryan Trottier and Ulf Samuelsson celebrate Pittsburgh's 91/92 Stanley Cup victory. It was Trottier's second Cup as a Penguin. He had already won four as a New York Islander. "I wish everyone who played hockey could know the feeling of winning the Stanley Cup," Trottier said after his second win, in 80/81. "You win it once and you get greedy. You want to keep on winning it." BELOW: Stanley Cup playoff tickets.

One thing that has not changed is the importance of the Stanley Cup. The trophy predates the league, having been presented in 1892 by the country's Governor General, Lord Stanley, Earl of Preston, as a challenge trophy between Canadian amateur clubs. The trophy's trustees later allowed it to be contested by professional clubs, and by 1915 it was in the exclusive domain of the professional game, the payoff to an end-of-season tilt between the champions of the National Hockey Association (which became the NHL in 1917) and the elite western league, the Pacific Coast Hockey Association. When the western professional game folded after the 1926 match, the Stanley Cup turned into the championship trophy of the NHL exclusively.

Winning—or losing—the Stanley Cup is the act that defines champions. Teams have always been able to win regular-season championships by compiling the best win-loss record (or before 26/27 by winning the O'Brien Cup, the NHL championship that advanced them into the interleague Stanley Cup finals), but this achievement has never carried the weight of a Cup win. Teams with indifferent regular-season records have gained immortality by pulling through in a championship series; teams with indomitable regular-season records have been cast as failures when the playoffs brought disappointment. If the dynasties chosen to be profiled in this

CHAMPIONS

8

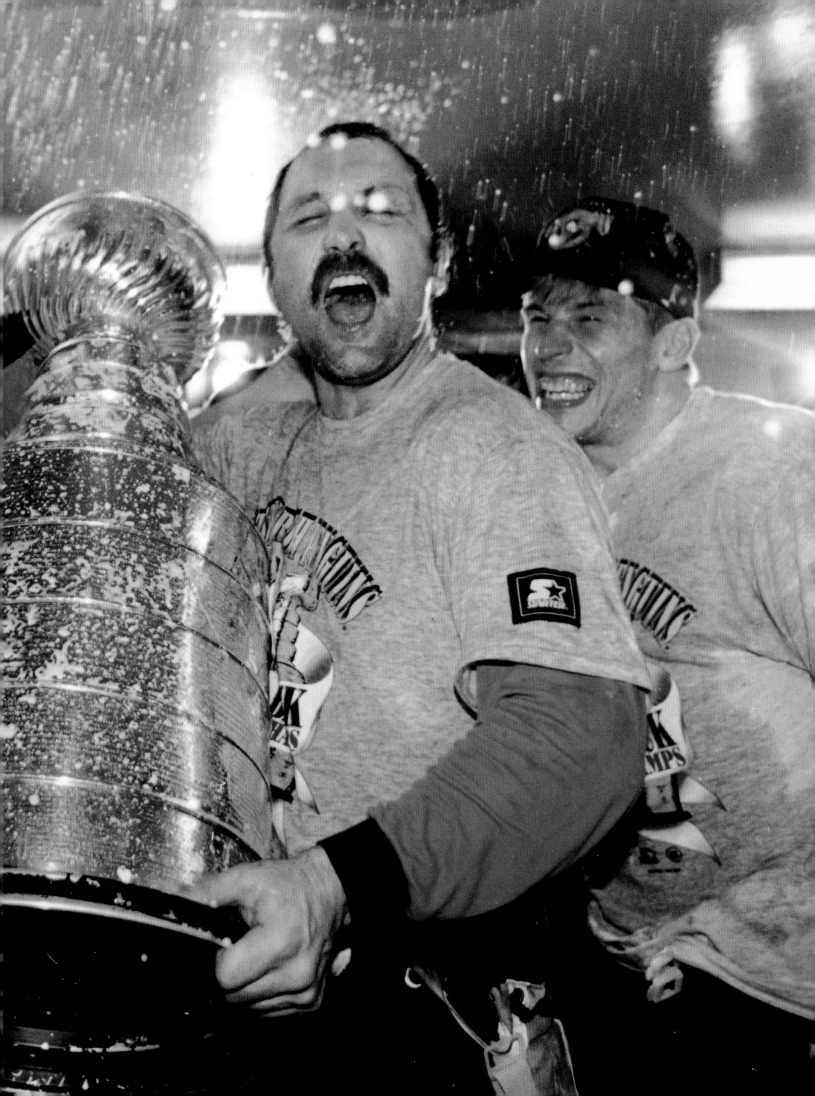

From 89/90 to 95/96, 13 different teams played in the Stanley Cup finals—the maximum possible was 14. Only the Pittsburgh Penguins made repeat appearances, winning in 90/91 and 91/92. The end—for now?—of dynastic domination of the Stanley Cup has been a boon to the NHL's overall health. In the 1990s, dynasties are bad for business. Everybody has to have a chance to win.

book were selected on regular-season achievement alone, some would not even have made the cut. The Toronto Maple Leafs, for example, in winning six Stanley Cups from 41/42 to 50/51, and another four from 61/62 to 66/67, only won two regular-season titles along the way. More than any other team, the Leafs demonstrated that winning Stanley Cups is about winning playoff hockey. It is a skill that has eluded some of the greatest regular-season teams in league history. The Blackhawks could distill only one Cup win from its 1960s campaigns; the Red Wings of 94/95 and 95/96 could not turn overpowering regular-season efforts into what would have been the first Detroit Cup win since 54/55.

This book is about the teams that won the Stanley Cup not once, but often enough to invite the description "dynasty." The research has been part detective work, part dissection, part social studies. The main questions to be answered were: What made a team great? What kept it on top? And what brought it down?

The teams explored here span the history of the NHL, and their achievements and failures touch on every aspect of the league's progress. The reasons for the rise and fall of team dynasties would seem to be straightforward: a great lineup is assembled through scouting, trades or drafting; a great coach guides the team to success; the dynasty ends with players ageing, new recruits not measuring up, or some other club beginning its own rise to greatness.

When it comes to building a great lineup, the different approaches general managers have taken over the years make for fascinating study. Many teams, particularly those operating before the universal amateur draft was introduced in 1969, were built from within, through shrewd scouting and amateur and minor-pro development systems that brought the new talent along. The Red Wings team of the 1950s was a textbook example of this approach. And after the universal draft, some teams were still able to build great teams from within, through clever drafting—or clever trading that earned them top draft picks. In this way the Montreal Canadiens of the 1970s and the New York Islanders of the early 1980s made their ascent.

But sometimes trading has played a dominant role. The 1960s Leafs were the first dynasty that can be said to have been engineered, as general manager Punch Imlach combined amateur talent from within the Leaf development system with a few established club players and a number of veterans from the championship lineups of the Red Wings and Canadiens. Imlach was the first general manager to build a new dynasty using large numbers of older players who had already served the bulk of their careers with other teams. The practice of building with proven winners was taken to its extreme in 93/94, when the New York Rangers won their first Stanley Cup since 39/40 with seven players who had already won Stanley Cups with the Edmonton Oilers.

Champions have been built using players other teams didn't want or need. The Bruins of the late 1960s and early 1970s benefited from a house-cleaning by the Chicago Blackhawks after they flopped in the 66/67 playoffs. Chicago's decision to unload Phil Esposito, Fred Stanfield and Ken Hodge was instrumental in the almost immediate resurgence of the ailing Bruins franchise. And after Boston came the Philadelphia Flyers, who were the first champions to build a winning lineup almost entirely out of professional hockey's spare parts. Nine members of the Flyers' winning 73/74 and 74/75 lineups once played on the margins of the Bruins system; about two-thirds of the Philadelphia club was composed of glorified journeymen, whipped into winning form by rigorous team discipline and an outlook even meaner than that of the Bruins club that provided their inspiration and so many of their players.

One factor, however, in the rise and fall of NHL dynasties is all too easy to overlook when counting up All Stars and measuring team scoring. And that is: the NHL is a business, and businesses can succeed and fail for reasons entirely other than the quality of their management, staff and product. The political and economic climate can change; owners can blunder or paint themselves into a financial corner. Things go wrong in business, and sometimes it is an unforeseen calamity striking a competitor that makes one business the market leader.

Professional hockey is no different. The fan likes to think of championship teams shaping their own destinies, of talent and perseverance carrying the day, and these are unquestionably the most important factors in shaping a dynasty. But whether or not a team can assemble and retain that talent has much to do with the business climate of the league and the financial circumstances of the franchise. Observers might be surprised to discover how often money or at least ownership issues are at the root of a dynasty's decline.

The model of decline many fans harbour probably derives from the 1960s Maple Leafs: the team roster ages, skills decline, rival clubs with rosters of younger stars take over. That model, in fact, seldom applies. The almost unbroken success of the Montreal Canadiens from 43/44 to 78/79, rolling through numerous successful lineup changes even as the league's dynamics shifted radically, demonstrated how a top-flight management could keep a good thing going for decades. But the end of the Canadiens' reign in 78/79 was due not only to the retirement of key players like Ken Dryden, Jacques Lemaire and Yvan Cournoyer. Fundamental was the franchise's sale by the Bronfman family to Molson

Breweries in the summer of 1978, which brought about a shake-up in the management of the team. Scotty Bowman, who had coached the Canadiens to five Stanley Cups since his arrival in 1971, decided his management future lay with the Buffalo Sabres and left after the 78/79 Cup win. So did director of player development Al MacNeil, who accepted the coaching job with the Atlanta Flames. After four consecutive Stanley Cups, the Canadiens were eliminated in the 79/80 quarterfinals by the unheralded Minnesota North Stars.

The Ottawa Senators of the 1920s and the Edmonton Oilers of the 1980s shared the same dynastic fate. Both teams crumbled because their owners could not withstand adverse financial circumstances. The Senators had won their fourth Stanley Cup since 1920 in the spring of 1927 and promptly began their decline. The NHL's aggressive expansion into the United States brought games against clubs from far-away addresses like Boston and Pittsburgh. Fan indifference to

this novelty led to poor regular-season attendance at Senators home games, and owner Frank Ahearn could not withstand operating losses. The arrival of the Great Depression in the fall of 1929 only exacerbated the problems of this small-market franchise. Ahearn began selling off the contracts of his most valued players to keep the team afloat, to no avail. After a one-season relocation to St. Louis in 34/35, the Senators disappeared entirely.

The Oilers were in the midst of a Cup-winning streak of their own when the recession of the late 1980s exacerbated the ongoing financial problems of franchise owner Peter Pocklington. Like Ahearn before him, he began unloading key players, the most famous being Wayne Gretzky, peddled to the Los Angeles Kings after the 87/88 Cup win. Ironically, it had been the financial difficulties of Nelson Skalbania in 1978 that had brought Gretzky to Pocklington's Oilers in the first place. Skalbania (who had sold the Oilers to Pocklington) needed cash to keep afloat his WHA franchise, the Indianapolis Racers. For $850,000, he sent 17-year-old

The Ottawa Senators (shown here during the First World War) won more Stanley Cups than any other team during the early days of professional hockey, but the franchise was doomed by NHL expansion in the 1920s. The club lost money even while winning because its fans wouldn't turn out for home games against expansion teams from places like Pittsburgh and Boston.

Gretzky and two other players to the Oilers, where Gretzky remained until Pocklington was compelled to liquidate key assets. Gretzky was expected to lead a charge on the Stanley Cup by the Los Angeles Kings, and with him the Kings made the 92/93 finals. After losing to the Canadiens, however, the Kings too fell on hard times as team owner Bruce McNall went to jail on a fraud conviction.

The New York Islanders, the toast of the NHL in the early 1980s, almost didn't happen as a dynasty because of the franchise owner's financial problems. General manager Bill Torrey and coach Al Arbour were steadily creating a genuine contender when the team's ownership crashed and burned in 1978. With principle owner Roy Boe having invested in a struggling basketball franchise, the New York Nets, and with $10 million in franchise start-up costs still burdening the Islanders, the operation was $22 million in the hole and teetering on bankruptcy. Torrey marshalled a refinancing and new ownership structure with one of the franchise's minority partners and got the debt down to $4 million in 1980. Had Torrey not acted, the Islanders dynasty we came to know never would have existed.

The most important factor in the fortunes of NHL teams in the late 1950s was not coaching or scouting but the attempt to form a players' association by leading figures such as Detroit's Ted Lindsay, Toronto's Jim Thomson and Montreal's Doug Harvey. The reaction of owners and management was swift, ferocious and ultimately self-destructive. Owners agreed that the bleak Blackhawks franchise would be the dumping ground of choice for the ringleaders. Toronto sent Jim Thomson and Tod Sloan there, the Red Wings Ted Lindsay and Glenn Hall. For the Wings, this punitive strike served only to hurry the end of its league domination; for the Leafs, the loss of Thomson and Sloan was more bad news for a once-great team on the skids. The Canadiens, by resisting the temptation to punish Harvey and others, kept a great team intact and made its continued successes possible. And Chicago quickly emerged as a new force in the league, winning a Stanley Cup in 60/61.

The most recent dynasty profiled in this book is that of the Oilers from 83/84 to 89/90. The new decade has not seen any club emerge with what could be called dynastic strength. The Penguins managed Cup wins in 90/91 and 91/92, but did so after only middling regular seasons and have not made the finals since. From 89/90 to 95/96, 13 different clubs played in the Stanley Cup finals—the maximum possible was 14. It was a far cry from the league of the 1950s, when the Montreal Canadiens played in ten consecutive finals and no team other than Montreal or Detroit won the Cup from 51/52 to 59/60. This has been good for the game—it means that half of the league's franchises have been in a Cup final in recent years. And in 94/95 and 95/96, three of the four finalists were some of the newest franchises: the New Jersey Devils (introduced in 82/83; originally the Kansas City Scouts and then the Colorado Rockies), the Colorado Avalanche (95/96; originally the Quebec Nordiques) and the Florida Panthers (93/94).

Free agency and expansion have changed the league tremendously. The employment pattern today is for players to win a Stanley Cup or two, demonstrate their marquee value and then take a job with the highest bidder. With so many teams and so many stars on the move it seems doubtful that any team will ever emerge to rival the accomplishments of the Canadiens of the late 1950s. Twelve players participated in all five consecutive Cup wins with Montreal, and four of them went on to win Cups again with the Canadiens in the late 1960s and early 1970s.

With the high salaries that come with star-packed rosters, windows of opportunity for Cup victories are narrowing for many clubs. The Leafs of the 1990s have demonstrated the financial realities of building a champion. After falling just short of making the Cup finals in 92/93 and 93/94, the franchise has seen its fortunes sink into the depths of the league. New ownership, strapped by takeover costs, cannot sustain the payroll of a potential champion. Across the league, there is concern that three different NHLs are taking shape. There will be the teams with the deepest pockets who can buy the lineups needed to win; there will be the teams that through sound management and inspired drafts and trades can build contenders; and there will be the teams in the poorer markets that will

serve as a de facto minor league, always drafting high because of their poor finishes, bringing along the new talents until they are too expensive for them to employ.

It seems too cynical, though, simply to say that money will decide who wins in the future. The history of professional sport is littered with owners who thought deep pockets could guarantee victory. But unquestionably the challenge for teams in today's volatile sports climate is not just to build a team that can win, but to hold a winning team together long enough to win more than once. Dynasties have not become impossible, but they have become a less likely component of the modern NHL. Future dynasties may in fact be loathed more than admired. They will be the teams with the biggest stars and the biggest salaries; there will be calls to have them broken up (the way the Canadiens of the 1970s were once assailed) in the name of league parity. In the modern NHL, a dynasty is an anomaly, a symptom of a league in trouble. In the

modern NHL, everyone must be a winner, or have the chance to be one.

The scenario for future Cup finals seems to have been set with the finals of 94/95 and 95/96. Three of four finalists were young teams with few brand-name stars. They were terrifically coached and the players were terrifically motivated. Such teams will likely continue to make their way to the finals, occasionally meeting juggernauts like the 93/94 Rangers or the 94/95 Red Wings, glittering machines stocked with brand-name players assembled in large part through trading and free agency. The young upstarts will make repeat trips to the finals if they can afford to hang onto the talents that have been turned into stars. The juggernauts will continue to win if winning continues to justify their massive payrolls.

The potential for dynasties today ultimately begins and ends at the bottom line. Can franchises afford dynasties? Even more crucial—can the league afford them? ○

One more time: Kevin Lowe, Mark Messier and Jari Kurri celebrate the Oilers' 89/90 Stanley Cup victory over the Boston Bruins. All but written off after the trade of Wayne Gretzky in 1988 and a poor 88/89 season, Edmonton's 89/90 performance, when the team no longer dominated the league in scoring or total wins, demonstrated the grit at the heart of a championship roster.

OTTAWA SENATORS
The Dawn of the NHL

CAPITAL GAINS

FROM THE SILVER SEVEN TO THE SILVER SIX: OTTAWA WAS HOME TO HOCKEY'S FIRST STANLEY CUP-WINNING DYNASTY

BELOW: The original Stanley Cup was purchased by Canada's governor general, Lord Stanley, Earl of Preston, in 1893 after he promised in 1892 to dedicate a challenge trophy for the country's amateur hockey clubs. The Ottawa Silver Seven, forerunners of the Senators, won it in four seasons from 1903 to 1906. The Senators won it in 1909 and 1911 in their pre-NHL days.

I n the mid-1920s, the Ottawa Senators were a dying breed, literally and figuratively. The hockey world was shocked by the death from acute peritonitis of the team's star right-winger, Jack Darragh, in June 1924. Darragh had been a Senator since 1910—seven years before the inception of the National Hockey League—when he had signed on for $20 a week and a new pair of skates. When Darragh died, the Boston Bruins and Montreal Maroons were a few months away from their first season of play. The proliferation of artificial-ice arenas, the death of the Western Hockey League after 25/26, and big money (some of it tainted) in the United States was about to take the NHL to a new level as the Roaring Twenties made professional sport a major-league entertainment.

The Senators, despite having the winningest record in Stanley Cup history, and despite capturing their fourth Cup in eight seasons in 26/27, were not going to be able to survive both expansion and the coming Depression. When the NHL left the Senators behind, it also left behind the last vestiges of the authentic community-based professional team. New champions would be built from a grab-bag of players who hailed from any old place. Overwhelmingly, the men who won Stanley Cups for Ottawa played as home-town heroes, and the franchise collapsed in part because those hometown fans could not get excited about buying tickets to see teams who hailed from much farther than Montreal. What did it matter when the Senators were playing a bunch of Canadians wearing uniforms of teams from places like Pittsburgh and Philadelphia? The franchise system made little sense to spectators who thought players and fans were one big family.

Ironically, in its bid to stay alive, the team would move to the most far-flung hockey outpost, St. Louis, and attempt to entertain uninitiated fans (racially

CHAMPIONS | 14

CHAMPIONS OF THE WORLD 1920-21

Jersey of Frank Nighbor, who starred with Ottawa from 15/16 to 29/30

divided by fencing in the stands) in an old cow palace. These Senators, renamed the Eagles, made about as much sense to the people of St. Louis as the Pittsburgh Pirates did to the citizens of Ottawa. After its one-season incarnation on the Mississippi in 34/35, the Ottawa Senators vanished from the league for some sixty years, the accomplishments of Jack Darragh and his teammates consigned to ancient history. So forgotten are their exploits that the *1995 National Hockey League Stanley Cup Playoffs Fact Guide* listed the Senators, reborn in 92/93, among franchises that "have not appeared in the Stanley Cup playoffs."

The original Senators did play a different brand of hockey, and unquestionably played it in an era far different from the one occupied by today's game. Ottawa's top club was once known as the Silver Seven, because in those days each team put seven men on the ice, including one in the "rover" position. The reduction of on-ice players from seven to six by the National Hockey Association for its 1911/12 season was meant to reduce team salaries, as the NHA was locked in a bidding war for stars with the Pacific Coast Hockey Association, whose champion began contesting the NHA's top club for the Stanley Cup in 14/15. With the rule change the Senators (as the Ottawa team was first called in 07/08) came to be described informally as the Silver Six. Right into the 1920s, they participated in the glory years of the "Sixty Minute Men," players who would be on the ice for an entire game. A few alternates were carried, but essentially the job of winning was done by one forward line, a pair of defencemen and a goaltender.

As the Silver Seven, Ottawa won the Stanley Cup in four consecutive seasons, from 1903 to 1906, in the years when it was a challenge trophy for Canadian amateur clubs like the Rat Portage Thistles and the Brandon Wheat Kings. As the Senators, Ottawa won its first Stanley Cup in 1909 by compiling the best record in the Eastern Canadian Hockey Association.

In the winter of 1910, a new league, the National Hockey Association, was founded, boiled down from general acrimony, spite and backstabbing among clubs in Ottawa, Montreal, Quebec City,

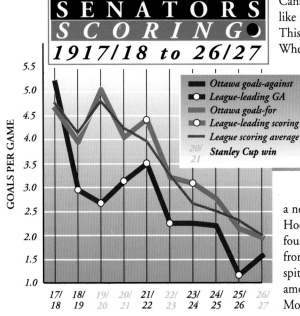

Clint Benedict

SENATORS
SCORING
1917/18 to 26/27

GOALS PER GAME

■	Ottawa goals-against
■○	League-leading GA
	Ottawa goals-for
○	League-leading scoring
	League scoring average
	Stanley Cup win

5.5
5.0
4.5
4.0
3.5
3.0
2.5
2.0
1.5
1.0

17/18 18/19 19/20 20/21 21/22 22/23 23/24 24/25 25/26 26/27

Ottawa, Renfrew (a lumber town upriver from Ottawa) and Cobalt and Haileybury (two booming silver mine centers at the headwaters of the Ottawa River).

The Senators began to assemble the lineup that would bring them success after the First World War. The opening game of the first NHA season was December 31, 1910, in Montreal between the Senators and a new team, the Canadiens. Georges Vezina was in goal for Montreal as Ottawa won 5-3. One of the Senators goals was scored by 20-year-old newcomer Jack Darragh, a left-handed shot on right wing who produced 17 more in the 16-game season. Darragh would play with the Senators, and only the Senators, for his entire 13-season professional career.

Darragh is, on record, the first Senators recruit among the players that won Stanley Cups with Ottawa in the NHL era, but he may have been preceded by fellow right-winger Harry "Punch" Broadbent. Broadbent wasn't signed as a Senator until the 12/13 season, but he would recall being paid at 16, in 1910, a handsome $600 while still an amateur so that the Senators could "use me when and wherever they needed me." He arrived officially in 12/13, at the same time as defenceman Horace Merrill and goaltender Clint Benedict, who gradually supplanted starting netminder Perce LeSueur.

Substitute Leth Graham played his first Senators games in 13/14, replacing Fred Lake. That season also saw the arrival of Eddie Gerard. The Senators had been pursuing Gerard since the NHA was founded three years earlier. He was an enormously gifted athlete—in addition to playing football for the Ottawa Roughriders, Gerard excelled in canoeing, lacrosse, golf, cricket and tennis. An educated, well-mannered young man, his only shortcoming was asthma. It's unclear whether he was with the Ottawa Victorias of the Federal Amateur Hockey League when they won the the 1908 Stanley Cup, but he definitely joined the Senators lineup midway through the 13/14 season, at first playing on left wing with Jack Darragh and center Skene Ronan. Ottawa badly needed offence; it finished fourth of six in the NHA that season, with the second lowest number of goals, 65 over 20 games.

In 14/15, the Senators improved greatly while playing a low-scoring defensive game. Clint Benedict had the starting goaltender's job as LeSueur was traded to the Toronto Ontarios for former Senator Fred Lake, who only played two games that season. Art Ross, who would later become coach and general manager of the Boston Bruins, was added on defence. The Senators tied for first with the Montreal Wanderers with 14 wins and six losses, defeated them in a two-game, total-goals playoff, and went west to play the Vancouver Millionaires of the Pacific Coast Hockey Association in the first Stanley Cup series held on the west coast.

The PCHA, formed by brothers Frank and Lester Patrick, accomplished players in their own right, had lured away many of the eastern game's best men. Among them were former Ottawa star Fred "Cyclone"

Ottawa Senators

The Dynasty of the 1920s

Featuring the players and management who participated in Ottawa's
Stanley Cup victories of 1919/20, 1920/21, 1922/23 and 1926/27

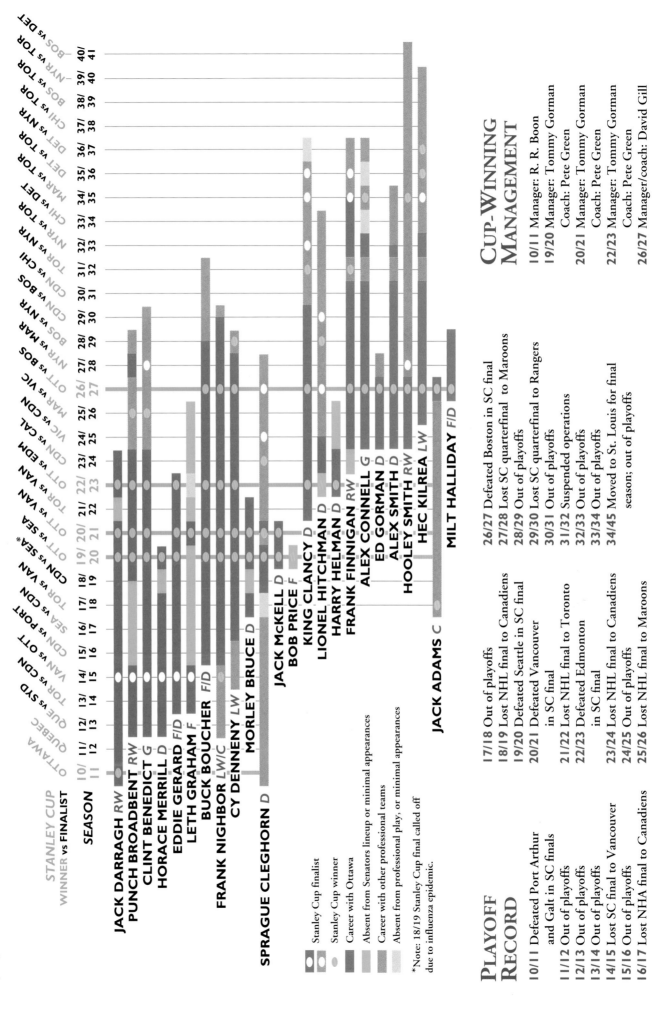

Cup-Winning Management

10/11	Manager: R. R. Boon
19/20	Manager: Tommy Gorman
	Coach: Pete Green
20/21	Manager: Tommy Gorman
	Coach: Pete Green
22/23	Manager: Tommy Gorman
	Coach: Pete Green
26/27	Manager/coach: David Gill

Playoff Record

10/11	Defeated Port Arthur and Galt in SC finals
11/12	Out of playoffs
12/13	Out of playoffs
13/14	Out of playoffs
14/15	Lost SC final to Vancouver
15/16	Out of playoffs
16/17	Lost NHA final to Canadiens
17/18	Out of playoffs
18/19	Lost NHL final to Canadiens
19/20	Defeated Seattle in SC final
20/21	Defeated Vancouver in SC final
21/22	Lost NHL final to Toronto
22/23	Defeated Edmonton in SC final
23/24	Lost NHL final to Canadiens
24/25	Out of playoffs
25/26	Lost NHL final to Maroons
26/27	Defeated Boston in SC final
27/28	Lost SC quarterfinal to Maroons
28/29	Out of playoffs
29/30	Lost SC quarterfinal to Rangers
30/31	Out of playoffs
31/32	Suspended operations
32/33	Out of playoffs
33/34	Out of playoffs
34/45	Moved to St. Louis for final season; out of playoffs

Taylor, and from Pembroke goaltender Hugh Lehman and center Frank Nighbor; these three were among the Millionaires who obliterated the Senators 6-2, 8-3 and 12-3 in the best-of-five series played in the spring of 1915. Ottawa goaltender Clint Benedict tended to drop the series from his career reminiscences, preferring to dwell on the Cups he and the Senators did win. In 1966 he allowed, "We were beaten so badly that we took the $147 share from the series and went to the World's Fair in San Francisco until the heat went off. I seldom talk about that team. Usually I cite the main reasons why we lost—and their names were Frank Nighbor, Frank Patrick and Cyclone Taylor, to mention a couple."

Nighbor's career had started when he went to Port Arthur, Ontario, with his buddy Harry Cameron to play Senior hockey for $25 a week in 1912; he scored six times in his first Port Arthur game. The next season he formally turned professional with the Toronto Blueshirts in the NHA. Nighbor scored 25 goals in 17 games for the Blueshirts, then jumped to the PCHA to star with the Millionaires in 13/14 and 14/15. After the 14/15 Cup drubbing Nighbor and the Millionaires laid on the Senators, Ottawa was able to lure him back east to play for them. He was an exceptional two-way player, a

Cy Denneny was purchased from the Toronto Blueshirts by the Ottawa Senators on January 31, 1917, for $750 and the rights to goaltender Sammy Hebert. It was considered an enormous sum for a hockey player, but Denneny's scoring touch helped the Senators win four Stanley Cups. Fifteen years after the Senators bought Denneny, the team sold Frank Clancy to the Maple Leafs for a cash-and-player package valued at $50,000.

master of the sweep and poke check, and in Ottawa he was converted from left wing to center.

The First World War made things difficult for professional hockey. Enlistments by players like Punch Broadbent and Leth Graham ate into rosters, and player shortages became even more dire after the draft was introduced in Canada in November 1917. But during the war the Senators added more key players, among them forward George "Buck" Boucher. The eldest of four hockey-playing brothers, Buck Boucher had played three years of professional football with the Ottawa Roughriders before joining the Senators in 15/16, initially as a forward.

The future of the Senators—and professional hockey in general in eastern North America—was bound up in the arrival and reception of Eddie Livingstone among the ownership ranks. In hindsight it is not easy to know who to blame for the complete breakdown in relations between Livingstone and his fellow NHA owners, even though Livingstone is traditionally portrayed as the guilty party. He simply may have been hard to get along with, but Livingstone also may have been doomed by holding too pivotal a position in the league, the Toronto franchise, with too little actual power.

Livingstone had arrived in the league in 14/15 by buying the Toronto Ontarios (originally the Tecumsehs) franchise and changing their name to the Shamrocks halfway through the season. Toronto then was also home to the Blueshirts, the 1913/14 Stanley Cup champions. Just before the 15/16 season, Livingstone bought the Blueshirts as well, only to have the team roster picked bare by a devastating PCHA raid. This may have seriously undercut his standing in the NHA, for the league overall suffered at the gate when an owner let some of the NHA's best players leave for the coast.

The league decided Livingstone could not own both Toronto operations and ordered him to sell the Shamrocks, but he couldn't find a buyer. At the same time he and the management of Toronto's Mutual Street arena, which had the only artificial ice in eastern Canada, could not come to terms on his use of the facility. Livingston closed down the Shamrocks, made noises about moving the Blueshirts to Boston, and ended up rebuilding his single team after the PCHA raid by using players he had under contract to the mothballed Shamrock operation.

The 16/17 season saw more feuding between Livingstone and his fellow team owners when a military team formed as the 228th Battalion, which was stacked with professional players, was allowed to enter NHA competition, based in Toronto. Coincidentally, the principal organizers of the 228th were the McNamara brothers, who had played for Livingstone's Shamrocks in 14/15. The McNamara boys were thought to be planning to take the Shamrocks off Livingstone's hands. Instead, George McNamara played on with Livingstone's Blueshirts while Howard went to the Canadiens and Harold left the game for a season. In 17/18, Howard was captain of the 228th and George was playing with him, competing directly with Livingstone's Blueshirts.

While the McNamaras' 228th rolled over the league, Livingstone was drawn into a spat with the Senators over Cy Denneny. Born in 1897 at Farrans Point (a hamlet obliterated by flooding in the creation of the St. Lawrence Seaway in the 1950s), Denneny was only 18 when he accompanied his older brother Corbett to Toronto midway through the 14/15 season to play for Livingstone's Shamrocks. Playing with center Duke Keats, the Denneny brothers' line was the most productive in the league in 15/16, producing 66 of Toronto's 97 goals. The teenage Cy tied for second in the league scoring race with 26 goals (assists were not recorded then), but Toronto finished last.

In the summer of 1916 Denneny came to Ottawa to play lacrosse and was invited to play for the Senators in 16/17. He decided he wanted to stay, but Livingstone wouldn't release him. Offers and counter-offers for Denneny's services flew while Denneny was under suspension by Livingstone for not having reported. It wasn't until January 31, 1917, that an agreement was finally reached, with the Senators giving Livingstone $750 and backup netminder Sammy Hebert. The Denneny deal was considered enormously expensive for the Senators, but they had just acquired the player who would be their all-time scoring leader for the equivalent of about one year's salary and a netminder Livingstone actually had no real use for—he immediately lent Hebert to the Quebec Bulldogs.

The controversies, meanwhile, mounted. The league that season introduced an unusual two-part schedule, with the winners of the first and second halves playing each other in the league championship. The Senators used Denneny on January 31, the first game of the second half, in defeating the 228th 8-0, but the McNamaras protested his use, noting that his formal release had not been made by the Blueshirts. This was technically correct, even though the actual trade deal was completed, and the Senators were ordered to forfeit the game. Then the 228th set off the biggest bomb of the season by withdrawing from league competition on February 10 to prepare to ship overseas. The fallout from that move revealed the team to be little more than a group of sporting ringers who were paid above and beyond their base pay to win hockey games. At least one player understood that the team was to share in gate receipts at the end of the season. Only two of them actually went overseas as soldiers.

The withdrawal of the 228th left the NHA's other teams scrambling to salvage a season schedule. Livingstone suggested that the league run a double schedule with the five remaining clubs for the rest of the season. His fellow team operators thought otherwise. Fed up with Livingstone, they acted decisively and capriciously, voting at a special meeting on February 11 to drop Livingstone's team from the remainder of the season and divvy up his players among the rest of the clubs. No indication was made of how or if they intended to compensate Livingstone for his loss, but they did say he could have his players back for the 17/18 season. From among Livingstone's six starters, Cy's brother Corbett was sent to the Senators. Ottawa lost the two-game total-goal playoff with the Canadiens for the league championship; the Canadiens then lost the best-of-five Stanley Cup final to the PCHA's Seattle Metropolitans, who became the first non-Canadian team to win the trophy.

After the excesses and confusion of 16/17, the owners of the Ottawa Senators, Montreal Canadiens, Montreal Wanderers and Quebec Bulldogs decided they no longer wanted to do business with Eddie Livingstone. The Toronto Arena Company directors had bought the Blueshirts franchise from Livingstone and asked the manager of their Mutual Street arena, Charlie Querrie, to run the team. Querrie, the original president of the Toronto Shamrocks (when they were still the Tecumsehs) was running the arena when Livingstone was at loggerheads with the company over the terms of his lease in 15/16. The league was also under pressure from the owners of the Montreal Arena Company, where the Wanderers and Canadiens played their home games. Unhappy with the quality of play, the owners were threatening to turn their arena exclusively into a skating venue if the two professional teams didn't improve.

The NHA's franchise owners—all of them, with one notable exception— resolved to form a new league, the National Hockey League. Livingstone, who still owned the mothballed Shamrocks, was deliberately left out in the cold, with the new league awarding its Toronto franchise to the Toronto Arena Company, which would ice a team called the Arenas. The Quebec Bulldogs were also awarded a franchise in the new league, even though the club's first act was to suspend operations indefinitely. It was obvious that the creation of a "new" league was nothing more than a manoeuvre by the participating owners to rid themselves of Livingstone.

The O'Brien family, flush with northern Ontario mining wealth, owned both the Renfrew Millionaires and Montreal Canadiens when the National Hockey Association was founded in 1910. The O'Briens dedicated the cup that bore their name in 1911 for the championship of the National Hockey Association. It continued as the championship trophy when the NHA became the NHL in 1917, and remained the symbol of league supremacy until the Stanley Cup became exclusively an NHL trophy in 1927.

Tommy Gorman (above) was sports editor of the Ottawa Citizen when Montreal Canadiens owner George Kennedy loaned him the $2,500 necessary to buy into the troubled Senators franchise in November 1917. After the team won three Stanley Cups, Gorman sold his share in January 1925 to Frank Ahearn (below) for $35,000 and a piece of the Connaught Park Jockey Club.

As a coach and general manager, Gorman went on to guide the Chicago Blackhawks, Montreal Maroons and Montreal Canadiens to Stanley Cup wins.

By this point an ambitious Ottawa newspaperman named Tommy Gorman had entered the picture. His father had died when Gorman was quite young, and he had found work as a page in the Canadian Parliament before entering his late father's trade by becoming a police, sports and general reporter with the *Ottawa Citizen.* Gorman was also an accomplished athlete, having won a gold medal with the Canadian lacrosse team at the 1908 Olympics.

Gorman worked all sides of the sports scene. In addition to editing the sports section of the *Citizen,* he was bringing in $10 a week as a press representative for George Kennedy, owner of the Montreal Canadiens franchise. In the troubled fall of 1917, Gorman was not long back from covering the catastrophic Halifax munitions explosion when George Kennedy (also known as Kendall, who was a wrestler and sports club operator) told him the Ottawa Hockey Association, which operated the Senators, was folding, and that the franchise and its players were available for $5,000. The Senators had already tried to withdraw from the league for the 16/17 season because of the war; when the league rejected their proposal, the franchise had been turned over to Edgar P. (Ted) Dey, manager of the city's Laurier Avenue arena.

The $5,000 asking price was far more money than Tommy Gorman had, but Kennedy wanted the Senators to stay afloat and in his corner if Livingstone was to be kept isolated by professional hockey interests, and he apparently believed his press rep was the man to run the shop. He lent Gorman $2,500 to buy into the team, with Martin Rosenthal and Ted Dey putting up the remainder as partners. Gorman was the only Ottawa delegate at the controversial November 22 meeting at Montreal's Windsor Hotel that locked out Livingstone and officially created the National Hockey League.

When the meeting was over, Gorman told Montreal sportswriter Elmer Ferguson, "Livingstone was always arguing. Without him we can get down to the business of making money." Within a year, Gorman and Dey had made enough money to buy out Rosenthal and for Gorman to pay back Kennedy.

The first season for the new league overall did not go well. On January 2, 1918 the Montreal arena burned down. The Canadiens moved to the cozy Jubilee rink and the Wanderers chose to fold. Thus, only three teams completed the second half of the schedule—the Canadiens, the Arenas and the Senators. Essentially Kennedy ran the league since he owned most of the Canadiens (he had sold a minority interest to the Brunswick Bulk Collender Company) and controlled half the equity of the Senators through his loan to Gorman.

Ottawa struggled through the first half of the 17/18 season, winning five and losing nine without Frank Nighbor, who was stationed briefly in Toronto with the Royal Flying Corps. Strings were pulled and Nighbor was sprung from the military, and with Cy

Denneny pursuing Montreal's Joe Malone for the scoring lead, Ottawa managed a 4-4 record in the second half. Malone scored a record-setting 44 goals in 20 games, while Denneny distinguished himself with 36. The NHL playoffs were between the Arenas and the Canadiens. Toronto won the first NHL title, and played host to the PCHA's Vancouver Millionaires in the best-of-five Stanley Cup final. By winning the Cup with a 2-1 victory in game five, the Arenas gave the new league a measure of sporting legitimacy.

On September 20, 1918, Ottawa's Gorman and Dey participated in the surreal fiction of an annual meeting of the inert National Hockey Association, the sole purpose of which was to have a show of hands (the attending Eddie Livingstone vigorously objecting) that voted to suspend the inactive league, and in the process squeeze Eddie Livingstone unequivocally out of the professional hockey racket.

Livingstone tried, without result, to reinvigorate the NHA that autumn and overthrow the Gorman-Dey-Kennedy-Querrie NHL that had supplanted it. There was a rumour that Livingstone, in concert with Percy Quinn (the original president of the Toronto Blueshirts who was supposed to buy the dormant Quebec Bulldogs), was intending to sue for conspiracy the Toronto Arenas, the Canadiens, the Senators and the NHA as controlled by Kennedy and accomplices. "It was alleged," as *The Trail of the Stanley Cup* put it, that the Mutual Street arena interests "had promised Ottawa and Canadiens some consideration for suspension of the NHA." The suit did not materialize, but at an NHL meeting on October 20 it was stated that only NHL teams would be permitted to play in Toronto's Mutual Street arena—the arena, of course, being owned by the Toronto Arena Company, which held the NHL Arenas franchise.

Quinn and Livingstone were thought to be planning to mount a separate league in the face of this cartel-like behaviour, and Quinn failed to follow through with his purchase of the Quebec club. As a result, only the Senators, the Arenas and the Canadiens played the 18/19 NHL season. To make the game faster and more exciting, the league introduced a center-ice neutral zone forty-feet wide in which forward passing was permitted, a concept adapted from the PCHA. Hockey was otherwise an "onside game," with no forward passing allowed, except by the goaltender in the PCHA. Already in 17/18 the NHL had taken the initiative of permitting the goaltender to fall to the ice, a strategy until then forbidden by all hockey rules. The motivator was said to be the Senators' Clint Benedict, who had been flaunting the regulation with a grab-bag of ruses that made his flops to the ice look accidental.

The league was so small and the rosters so compact that there were only about 18 starting players in the NHL in 18/19. Counting substitutes, the Senators had eight, and the team was very close to a championship lineup. Punch Broadbent, who had been awarded the

OTTAWA SENATORS 1917/18–26/27

Season	Finish	Record (W-L-T)	Points %	Awards (winners & runners-up)	All-Stars	Playoffs
17/18	3rd	9-13-0	40.9	ART ROSS: Denneny RU TOP GA: Benedict RU	*The NHL did not introduce All Star selections until 30/31*	Missed playoffs
18/19	1st	12-6-0	66.7	TOP GA: Benedict		Lost NHL final to Canadiens 4-1
19/20	1st	19-5-0	79.2	TOP GA: Benedict		Won SC final 3-2 over Seattle
20/21	2nd	14-10-0	58.3	ART ROSS: Denneny RU TOP GA: Benedict		Won SC final 3-2 over Vancouver
21/22	1st	14-8-2	62.5	ART ROSS: Broadbent, Denneny RU TOP GA: Benedict		Lost two-game total-goal NHL final to Toronto 5-4
22/23	1st	14-9-1	60.4	ART ROSS: Denneny RU TOP GA: Benedict		Won SC final 2-0 over Edmonton
23/24	1st	16-8-0	66.7	HART: Nighbor ART ROSS: Denneny TOP GA: Benedict RU		Lost two-game total-goal NHL final to Canadiens 5-2
24/25	4th	17-12-1	58.3	ART ROSS: Denneny RU LADY BYNG: Nighbor		Missed playoffs
25/26	1st	24-8-4	72.2	ART ROSS: Denneny RU LADY BYNG: Nighbor TOP GA: Connell		Lost two-game total-goal NHL final to Maroons 2-1
26/27	1st Div 1st OA	30-10-4	72.7			Won SC final 3-1 over Boston

NOTES
Awards: Few awards were available to NHL players from 17/18 to 26/27. The award for the league's leading scorer was introduced in the inaugural 17/18 season. (It wasn't actually called the Art Ross Trophy until 47/48.) The Hart, for the player most valuable to his team, was dedicated in 23/24. The Lady Byng, for sportsmanship and gentlemanly play, was first presented in 24/25. The Vezina, for the goaltender on the team with the lowest total goals against, arrived in 26/27. Before 26/27, this chart shows top GA performances according to the Vezina criteria.
Playoffs: Until 26/27, the Stanley Cup was contested between the championship clubs of the NHL and the professional western leagues.

Military Cross while in the Canadian artillery overseas, rejoined the Senators midway through the season. And Gorman made a striking and persistently controversial addition to the lineup when he acquired veteran defenceman Sprague Cleghorn from Kennedy.

Cleghorn was washed up in the winter of 1918 with a broken leg and a rocky marriage. His wife had sworn out a warrant for his arrest in January on assault charges after he hit her with a crutch, although the charges were later withdrawn. He was also without a team, as his Wanderers had folded that month when the Montreal arena burned down. As gifted a player as he was, Cleghorn was crazy-mean on the ice, a brawler at a time when brawling in hockey was for keeps, not a sweater-clutching ritual with a lot of off-balance punches glancing off helmets. Cleghorn had no compunction

about hacking at the faces of opponents with his stick, and he would boast of having been involved in at least 50 "stretcher-case" fights in his career.

As a young amateur, he had played on Montreal's Westmount Club team of 1906, a scrappy bunch that incurred 71 minutes in penalties in just one game. He went to New York as a ringer with his younger brother Odie in 1907 to play for the New York Wanderers of the nominally amateur city league, and was so pugnacious (as were the Canadian hirelings in general) that observers there feared for the future of hockey. He was still in the city league in 09/10 as a member of the Crescents Athletic Club team, but the following season officially turned professional with the Renfrew Creamery Kings (nicknamed the Millionaires) of the new NHA. Initially a forward, Cleghorn was converted

The Roaring (Boring?) Twenties

The neutral zone came to the National Hockey league in its second season, 1918/19, when it borrowed the concept from the Pacific Coast Hockey Association. The PCHA divided the rink into three equal zones, but the NHL chose to use a neutral zone defined by blue lines only forty feet wide. The neutral zone at center ice was the only place where forward passing was permitted. Teams could not make forward passes in their defensive zone (except for the goaltender, as far as the blue line, beginning in 21/22), in the attacking zone, or across the blue lines. Passes outside the neutral zone had to be lateral or back passes. In 26/27, the first season after the collapse of the professional western game, the NHL accommodated the flood of players coming into the league from the Western game to stock the new franchises in Detroit, Chicago and New York by increasing the neutral zone's size to 60 feet, a size it has remained to this day. But the passing restrictions remained in effect.

40 ft 60 ft

That sinking feeling...

Defence was the name of the game in the first decade of the NHL's existence and the average goals per team per game (shown in this chart) tumbled as the league tinkered with offensive-minded rule changes that only made its strategists stress defence even more. When the Canadiens' George Hainsworth (right) won the 28/29 Vezina with a goals-against average of just 0.98, the NHL knew it was in trouble.

Chart: GOALS PER GAME PER TEAM

4.8
4.6
4.4
4.2
4.0
3.8
3.6
3.4
3.2
3.0
2.8
2.6
2.4
2.2
2.0
1.8
1.6
1.4

17/18 19/20 21/22 23/24 25/26 27/28

Going it alone

Restrictive passing rules meant that playmaking was not a strong component of the star players' game during the 1920s. Top-ten scorers routinely accumulated far more goals than assists. Cy Denneny of the Ottawa Senators (right) won the 22/23 scoring race with only one assist in 21 games by scoring 22 times. But the collapse of the professional western league introduced exciting playmakers to the NHL. In 26/27, their debut NHL season, Dick Irvin recorded 18 goals and 18 assists for the new Chicago franchise and Frank Boucher amassed 13 goals and 15 assists for the new Rangers franchise in New York.

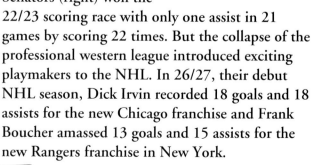

to defence to form a pair with Cyclone Taylor, whose electric rushing style rubbed off on Cleghorn and gave him some genuine skills to go with his psychopathic tendencies.

The O'Brien family, which backed the high-priced Creamery Kings and initially owned the Canadiens, decided to get out of hockey after the inaugural 10/11 NHA season. (After folding their Renfrew team they sold the Canadiens to George Kennedy.) The Renfrew players were divvied up among the remaining NHA teams by lottery, and the Montreal Wanderers drew Sprague Cleghorn. Odie was drawn by the Quebec Bulldogs but refused to report and found his way to the Wanderers as well.

Thus Sprague and Odie were on the ice together at Toronto's brand new Mutual Street arena on December 22, 1912, for an exhibition game between the Canadiens and the Wanderers that was meant to introduce the city's sports fans to professional hockey before the Blueshirts and Tecumsehs began playing for the first time in a few days. It was an exciting debut of the money game. The Canadiens' Newsy Lalonde ran Odie into the boards, which brought Sprague charging. He carved up Lalonde's forehead with his stick (somewhere between 12 and 18 stitches were required) in an attack so vicious that the horrified spectators insisted that more than the rulebook be thrown at Cleghorn. He was charged with assault and fined $50 in a Toronto court.

With the Wanderers having folded in January 1918, Sprague Cleghorn's rights were held by the Canadiens' Kennedy. Tommy Gorman asked Kennedy how much he wanted for Cleghorn. Kennedy considered the battered maniac and said he was Gorman's for the price of the train ticket that would get him to Ottawa.

It was one of the game's great steals. Far from washed up, Cleghorn was only halfway through an 18-season professional career. While he would play a vital role in the Senators' first two Stanley Cups as an NHL team, he ultimately contributed as much if not more in mayhem to the franchise's fortunes.

And if anyone thought the fortunes of professional hockey in eastern Canada could not worsen after the infighting of 16/17 and 17/18, they were wrong. On February 20, the Toronto Arenas folded after losing 9-3 to the Senators and the NHL became a two-team league. The remainder of the schedule was suspended—the teams had played only 18 games each—and the Canadiens, who had led with seven wins in ten starts in the first half of the season, entered a best-of-seven championship series against the Senators, who had dominated the second half with seven wins in eight starts. There was no one else to play a championship series, anyway. The best-of-seven was a significant departure from the two-game total-goals playoff used previously, and may have been chosen to increase gate receipts for the playoff participants in the shortened season.

The Senators were not at full strength. A death in the family had called away Frank Nighbor, who was the team's second-best scorer, with 17 goals that season. Jack Darragh moved over from right wing to center to fill in for him, and the Senators were down to two subs as Montreal handled them easily 8-4 in the opening game. The Canadiens won the next two games 5-3 and 6-3. Nighbor returned to the lineup for game four and, with his team facing elimination, helped assure a 6-3 win with a tenacious checking effort. Montreal won game five 4-2 to advance to play the Seattle Metropolitans in the Cup final.

For the first and only time in the Cup's history, there was no winner. With Seattle leading the series with two wins, one loss and a draw, the Canadiens gained a 4-3 win to tie the series after almost sixteen minutes of overtime. But Canadiens defenceman Joe Hall had left the ice feeling ill during the game. He was one of about half a dozen Canadiens, including owner George Kennedy, who were struck down by the influenza epidemic raging through North America. The series was called off. Just six days after the game, Hall died in a Seattle hospital.

After that dreadful season, the NHL found some footing in 19/20. The Quebec Bulldogs returned to play; Toronto got a new team, the St. Patricks; a new arena was built in Montreal (though it did not have artificial ice); and the regular-season schedule increased to 24 games. Ottawa's lineup solidified into a winning squad. Benedict was in goal, with Eddie Gerard and Sprague Cleghorn the main defensive pair. The starting line up front was Denneny, Darragh and Nighbor, with Broadbent also used effectively. Both Broadbent (called "Punch" and "Old Elbows") and Denneny could play the physical game, and they were called upon to protect the gentlemanly Darragh and Nighbor. Denneny was sensational as a scorer. He used a curved stick, which he created by stepping on the blade, and was probably the first player to deliberately use opposing defencemen as a screen when shooting. In nine of ten seasons, from 16/17 to 25/26, he was never worse than fourth in the scoring race.

By winning both the first and second halves of the 19/20 season, the Senators upset the odd NHA/NHL playoff format. They could not play themselves for the NHL championship, and so no championship series at all was held—an unsatisfactory turn of events from the perspective of ticket sales. The Seattle Metropolitans came to Ottawa for the Stanley Cup, and the Senators took a 2-1 lead in the best-of-five series in intolerable conditions. Warm weather meant the games were being played in glorified slush, and Ottawa had to concede that the series should be moved to Toronto's Mutual Street arena, still the only one with artificial ice in the NHL.

Seattle tied the series with an impressive 5-2 win, which prompted Jack Darragh to throw down his skates in the dressing room and declare, "I've had enough hockey for this winter. You will have to get along without me in the final game." Darragh grabbed a taxi to Union Station and hopped the first train back to Ottawa, where he could turn to his off-season job of breeding Rhode Island Reds. He was talked into hopping the first train back to Toronto, and on April 1, two days after bolting from Toronto, Darragh contributed a hat-trick as Ottawa won its first Stanley Cup of the NHL era with a 6-1 victory.

For 20/21, the Quebec franchise moved to Hamilton, where it became the Tigers. The Bulldogs had won only 4 of 24 games in 19/20, and for 20/21 Montreal and the St. Pats helped out by sending some additional talent to Hamilton. Ottawa didn't send anyone, its only player change coming when Sprague Cleghorn had a falling out with Gorman and was dropped after three games.

The Senators had a strong first half, winning it with an 8-2 record and outstanding goal figures. Its 49 goals-for were 10 more than any other team, while its 23 against were 15 better than the closest effort. The team faltered, though, in the second half, losing seven straight as it went 6-8, but by winning the first half of the season it reached the league finals against the St. Pats, who had been employing Sprague Cleghorn since the mid-season break.

The league was back to its two-game total-goals playoff format, and the Senators showed themselves to have recovered fully from their slump as they handled Toronto easily 5-0 and 2-0. The on-again off-again relationship between the Senators and Sprague Cleghorn was on again. Even though he played half of the regular season and the two playoff games against them as a St. Pat, Cleghorn was taken back on for the Stanley Cup series against the Vancouver Millionaires.

Western fans were utterly captivated by the spectacle. An estimated 11,000 people, the largest number ever to have watched a hockey game in Canada, saw Vancouver beat Ottawa 3-1 in the opening game, played under the seven-man western rules. By the time the five-game series was over, ticket sales had exceeded 51,000. The series, in keeping with tradition, switched between eastern and western rules with each game, and the Senators showed their skill by taking a 2-1 series lead with a 3-2 win under western rules. The Millionaires then tied it with a 3-2 win under eastern rules, and that brought up the deciding fifth game under western rules. It was a chippy, fight-filled game—Cleghorn personally collected four penalties—

and Jack Darragh scored twice as the Senators successfully defended the Cup with a 2-1 win.

With the 21/22 season, the NHL rid itself of the peculiar split schedule, settling on an undivided 24-game season that would see first and second place meet in a two-game total-goals series to determine the league champion. The league also adopted the PCHA regulation of permitting the goaltender alone to make forward passes as far as the blueline. While the league remained in its same four-team alignment, the death of George Kennedy resulted in the sale of the Canadiens. The price was said to be $11,000; the value of NHL franchises was soaring, and in 1921 Tommy Gorman left his sports editing job at the *Ottawa Citizen* to devote himself entirely to the Senators.

Ottawa's Stanley Cup-winning lineup of 19/20 and 20/21 (the Silver Six) was changing. Gorman didn't want to try another season with Sprague Cleghorn and essentially walked away from him, to Cleghorn's disgust. Since he had originally been a Wanderer, and because the Wanderers franchise had folded in 1918, the league decided that he belonged to the league itself and assigned him to the Hamilton Tigers. The Canadiens' desire to have Cleghorn as a hometown star produced one of the league's first big trades, as Montreal sent Harry Mummery, Cully Wilson and Amos Arbour to Hamilton in exchange for Cleghorn and Billy Couture, who were probably the nastiest pair of defencemen in the business.

In addition to Cleghorn, Ottawa lost Jack Darragh, who chose to retire. In Cleghorn's stead the Senators signed an 18-year-old local boy, Frank Clancy, whose exciting rushing style would earn him the sobriquet "King." They also signed another hometown talent, 20-year-old Frank Boucher, brother of George ("Buck").

When Cleghorn's Canadiens called on the Senators in Ottawa on December 24 for their first meeting of the new season, the Senators thrashed the Montrealers 10-0. Ottawa won the next three encounters as well. On their fifth meeting of the season, in Ottawa on February 1, Cleghorn resolved to settle the score with the Senators for having dumped him after the Stanley Cup win the previous spring. He went on a rampage, enlisting the aid of brother Odie as he injured Gerard, Nighbor and Denneny badly enough to sideline them for two games; one account has Sprague Cleghorn getting his licks in on Tommy Gorman as well. Referee Lou Marsh declared the Cleghorn brothers a disgrace to the game, Ottawa asked for Sprague Cleghorn's expulsion from the NHL, but Hamilton and Toronto wouldn't go along. The next time Cleghorn played in Ottawa with the Canadiens, he had to be smuggled into the arena through the furnace room to keep him out of the hands of enraged fans.

Ottawa won the regular-season title with 14 wins, with the most goals for and the fewest against. Punch

The stylish and well-mannered Jack Darragh joined the Senators lineup in 1910 for $20 a week and a pair of skates. He played all 13 of his professional seasons with Ottawa. His death from acute peritonitis in June 1924 was a shock to the hockey world.

Broadbent and Cy Denneny, hailed as the "Gold Dust Twins," finished first and second in the scoring race, together producing 59 of Ottawa's 106 goals. In the playoffs, the St. Pats edged them 5-4 in the opening game in Toronto. Playing on poor ice back in Ottawa, the Senators were stymied by the outstanding rookie goaltender John Ross Roach. When the game ended in a scoreless draw, Ottawa had been upset and the St. Pats were playing at home in the Stanley Cup finals against the Vancouver Millionaires.

In the roughly played third game of the Cup final, St. Pats defenceman Harry Cameron was lost with an injured shoulder. Trailing the best-of-five series 2-1, the St. Pats asked for the Millionaires' permission to use Eddie Gerard, who had become the Senators' captain in 20/21. It was a generous gesture by Vancouver manager Lester Patrick to allow the star to enter the series, and he immediately regretted it. With Gerard behind the St. Pats blueline, Toronto tied the series with a 6-0 walloping. Patrick now refused to allow Gerard on the ice. Cameron limped back into the lineup and the revived St. Pats won the deciding game 5-1 to keep the Cup on NHL turf. After the series, Charlie Querrie asked Gerard what his substitution effort was worth to him;

Gerard simply waved off the thought of compensation. In appreciation, the Pats presented Gerard with a diamond pin.

For 22/23, Gorman decided that with Frank Nighbor continuing as his main center, he could sell the rookie Frank Boucher to Vancouver (he would one day be coach and general manager of the New York Rangers). Jack Darragh was coaxed out of his one-season retirement to substitute for Broadbent, and Harry Helman arrived as a substitute defenceman. In their third-last game of the regular season, Ottawa introduced a future defensive star in Lionel Hitchman as they defeated the Tigers 6-3 to secure first overall, one win ahead of the Canadiens.

These Senators were not quite the indomitable Silver Six of two and three seasons back. The regular-season win was narrow, and while they led in goals against—from 14/15 to 22/23, Clint Benedict had the best goals-against average in eight of nine seasons—the Senators were outscored by Toronto and Hamilton.

The NHL finals between Ottawa and Montreal produced some of the most blatantly brutal hockey yet witnessed. As expected, the main offender was Sprague Cleghorn, operating in concert with defence partner

Ottawa's Frank "King" Clancy appears at far left in this undated photo, possibly taken in March 1930 during the Senators' quarterfinal series with the New York Rangers. An exciting rushing defenceman, Clancy was borrowed by the Toronto Maple Leafs in 31/32 when the Ottawa operation folded for one season. After he helped them win the Stanley Cup, the Leafs bought his contract.

Billy Couture. Couture sent Cy Denneny from the opening game with a concussion after cracking his stick over Denneny's head from behind; the attack got Couture thrown out of the game. Cleghorn knocked Lionel Hitchman unconscious with a cross-check to the face. When referee Lou Marsh tossed out Cleghorn as well, the Montreal fans erupted and went after Marsh. Canadiens general manager Leo Dandurand anticipated the actions of the league and barred Couture and Cleghorn himself from the second game of the playoffs.

Ottawa had won the opening game 2-0, and it took a goal from a bandaged Cy Denneny to close to within a goal in a 2-1 loss that gave the Senators a thin total-goals victory.

Out west, there had been many changes in the professional game. In 21/22 the Western Canada Hockey League was founded, playing the six-man game, with teams in Edmonton, Regina, Calgary and Saskatoon. In 22/23 the PCHA adopted the six-man game as well so that it could play an interlocking schedule with the new league. The two leagues were still distinct entities with their own season champions, which made for an unwieldy Stanley Cup format. The Senators went west, faced with having to meet and defeat the Vancouver Maroons before taking on the Edmonton Eskimos in a Cup final.

The Senators' performance in Vancouver, where all the games were played, defined true grit. The ageing Jack Darragh found his first season back from retirement more than enough hockey for one winter, and did not make the trip. The Senators took along Billy Boucher (brother of Senators defenceman George and Vancouver cen-

ter Frank) of the Canadiens as a substitute, using Eddie Gerard and George Boucher as their main defensive pairing. Frank Nighbor, Cy Denneny (whose brother Corbett was with Vancouver) and Punch Broadbent formed the starting forward line; Frank Clancy and Harry Helman were on hand as subs.

The Cup series still alternated between western and eastern rules, although with the switch by the PCHA that season to six-man hockey there wasn't much difference between the rulebooks any more. With Clint Benedict playing superbly, Ottawa won the opening game 1-0 on a Punch Broadbent goal logged with five minutes of play remaining.

In game two, the injuries began mounting in the Ottawa lineup. Benedict was hit in the mouth by the puck, and after the 4-1 loss the Senators were also contending with injuries to Gerard, Denneny and Helman. When Vancouver manager Frank Patrick refused to allow the use of Billy Boucher as a substitute in game three, all the injured Senators dressed and played, and won 3-2. The momentum was theirs; a 5-1 win that allowed them to advance to play Edmonton moved Patrick to say that this Senators club was the greatest team he had ever seen.

A dislocated shoulder kept Eddie Gerard out of the first game against the Eskimos in the best-of-three Cup final. Frank Clancy took his place ably, and an overtime goal by Cy Denneny gave the Senators a 2-1 win. Gerard dressed for the second game, and regularly had to return to the bench to have his shoulder shoved back into place. Punch Broadbent's lone goal gave Ottawa perhaps its most satisfying and most impressive Stanley Cup win.

Eddie Gerard's career was over with the final game against Edmonton—the culprit was asthma, not his shoulder—and Jack Darragh was almost finished. Having scored 24 goals in 22 games in 19/20, his production had slipped to 11 in 20/21. His 22/23 season, following his one-year retirement, produced just six. Darragh returned for 23/24, but he was no longer a key component of the Senators' game.

The Senators overall were still a powerful team, and were able to win another season championship in 23/24 as Cy Denneny earned his only scoring title. The franchise was also moving into the modern game with the construction of a new artificial-ice arena. Ted Dey and Tommy Gorman formed a new partnership with Frank Ahearn in the Ottawa Hockey Association, to which the Senators franchise was transferred; Ahearn and Gorman then bought out Dey.

In Ahearn, Gorman found a partner with deep pockets. He was the son of Thomas Franklin Ahearn, an Ottawa engineer who had become one of the city's richest men by electrifying the town. The Ahearns owned the streetcar system, the streetlights and now a modern hockey palace.

The new auditorium heralded the coming revolution in the professional game. The league schedule could not increase (and with it ticket revenues) without a guarantee of ice. Until all franchises had artificial ice, the league would be locked into a 24-game mid-December to early March season, and even then there were problems. The Canadiens were not able to play their home-opener in 23/24 because Mount Royal arena did not have proper ice—the game had to be moved to Hamilton's artificial-ice arena.

The construction of the Ottawa Auditorium gave the NHL artificial ice in every location except Montreal, and that was about to be addressed with the construction of the Forum. But the spread of artificial-ice arenas had larger consequences for the NHL and for the Senators. Their proliferation meant that professional hockey could move into larger markets—American markets—whose climate otherwise would not allow it.

With three Stanley Cups in four seasons, the Senators were easily the strongest club in the NHL, with an enthusiastic fan base who took pride in a roster stocked with talents overwhelmingly from the city and the surrounding Ottawa Valley region. Even minus Eddie Gerard, and with Jack Darragh no longer effective offensively, the Senators were able to win the 23/24 regular season. Frank Nighbor was the first recipient of the league's most valuable player award, the Hart Trophy, outpolling the hated Sprague Cleghorn by one vote, but he was unable to lead his team past Cleghorn's Canadiens, who won the two-game total-goal series with 1-0 and 4-2 wins. It was Jack Darragh's last grasp at a Stanley Cup. He retired as planned, then died of acute peritonitis that summer.

The league was now in the grip of expansion fever. In February 1924 the NHL board of governors agreed to grant its first American franchise to Boston grocery magnate Weston Adams for the new season. That summer, it was also decided, with the Montreal Forum under construction, to put a second team in Montreal, which chose the name the Maroons. The Senators sold the new Montreal club two veteran performers, Punch Broadbent and Clint Benedict, ostensibly to help strengthen a start-up operation, although Benedict in truth had disappointed in his performance in the spring playoffs against the Canadiens, and the Senators had a new goaltending star, Alex Connell, waiting to take his place.

The Senators underwent a complete overhaul for 24/25. In addition to Benedict being replaced by Connell, three new players appeared: defencemen Alex Smith and Ed Gorman and right-winger Reginald "Hooley" Smith.

Hooley Smith was an all-round athlete from Toronto; as a member of the Allan Cup-winning Granites of 1923, he won the 1924 Olympic hockey title. Gorman so pleased his employers that they felt confident enough to sell Lionel Hitchman to the floundering new Boston franchise, the Bruins. And from nearby Shawville, Quebec, the Senators signed an excit-

ing new right-winger, Frank "The Shawville Express" Finnigan.

Before the season had even begun, new franchise applications had been received from New York, Philadelphia and Pittsburgh. The New York and Pittsburgh applications were accepted; the teams, to be called the Americans and the Pirates, would join the league in 25/26. Both were backed by decidedly shady characters. The Americans, who would play at the new Madison Square Garden, were bankrolled by a notorious bootlegger, Bill Dwyer; the Pirates were the domain of an ex-boxer named Benny Leonard who believed teams should take their turns winning games.

The price of the new franchises of 24/25 and 25/26 was $15,000—that was $4,000 more than the Canadiens had sold for in 1921, player contracts included. In January 1925, Tommy Gorman sold his share of the Senators to Frank Ahearn for a whopping $35,000, plus Ahearn's interest in the Connaught Park Jockey Club. Two days later, Tex Rickard, president of Madison Square Garden, hired Gorman to assemble Bill Dwyer's Americans lineup. He was making little headway when the 24/25 league champions, the Hamilton Tigers, presented a golden opportunity. The Tigers were refusing to appear in the NHL playoffs unless they were paid another $200. The standoff occurred because some of the star Tigers had signed a two-year contract in 23/24 specifying a 24-game season. With the addition of the Bruins and Maroons in 24/25, the schedule had increased to 30 games. More games, more money—at least that's the way the Tigers saw it. League president Frank Calder suspended the entire team and ordered the second and third place St. Patricks and Canadiens to contest the NHL championship. (The Senators had missed third place by one tie.) The Canadiens won the series, then lost the Cup final to the Victoria Cougars. Tommy Gorman bought the entire Tigers dressing room for $75,000 and moved it to Madison Square Garden as the Hamilton franchise folded.

OPPOSITE PAGE: In 1925, Frank Nighbor inspired Lady Byng, wife of the Canadian governor general, to dedicate a new NHL trophy honouring sportsmanship and gentlemanly play. She made the first presentation herself to Nighbor at Government House in Ottawa. In 1926, the NHL again awarded him the Lady Byng Trophy. Nighbor was also the first recipient of the league's most valuable player award, the Hart Trophy, in 1924.

ABOVE: Appreciative fans in this undated photo welcome Nighbor home from a Senators' Stanley Cup win. The Senators won the 19/20, 20/21 and 21/23 Cups away from home.

At the end of the 24/25 season, Frank Nighbor was invited to Government House by Lady Byng, wife of the Canadian governor general. She showed him an ornate silver trophy and wondered if the league would accept it as a prize for its most sportsmanlike player. When Nighbor said he thought it would, she handed it to him, saying, "I present this trophy to Frank Nighbor as the most sportsmanlike player of 1925." The league now had the Lady Byng Trophy, and in 25/26 the league itself awarded it to Nighbor once more.

The Senators added another star for 25/26, 18-year-old Hec Kilrea, one of four hockey-playing Kilrea brothers in Ottawa. An extremely fast skater, the new left-winger formed a line with Finnigan and Nighbor. Ottawa won the regular season with 24 wins in 36 starts, four more wins than the second-place Maroons, who were being managed by former Senator Eddie Gerard.

Pittsburgh had done exceptionally well in its inaugural season, finishing third. Odie Cleghorn, who had left the Canadiens to serve as the Pirates' playing coach, was essentially using the roster of the Pittsburgh Yellow Jackets, a U.S. amateur team stocked with paid Canadians. The Maroons won the two-game total-goal playdown against the Pirates (3-1, 3-3), then met the favoured Senators.

With former Senators Benedict and Broadbent playing well and Gerard in charge, the Maroons scrapped to 1-1 and 1-0 scores that gave them the one-goal edge necessary to advance to meet the Victoria Cougars in a Cup series played in Montreal.

The Maroons won that best-of-five in four games. It was the last Stanley Cup to be played between clubs from rival professional western and eastern leagues. After the PCHA and WCHL merged to form the Western Hockey League in 25/26, the western game could not continue operating. The pressure on talent was too high, now that there were more NHL clubs in big-city markets crying out for players. In 26/27, the Stanley Cup became the exclusive domain of the NHL.

Three more American teams were added to the league in 26/27—the Chicago Blackhawks, Detroit Cougars and New York Rangers. Players from the defunct WHL were bought up, in some cases en masse, to fill the rosters of the new teams. Other WHL players were drafted by the existing NHL teams. Not the Senators, though; they didn't have to. For 26/27 they acquired veteran center Jack Adams from the St. Pats (who turned into the Maple Leafs in mid-season with their purchase by a group headed by Conn Smythe). And from within Ottawa the Senators signed Milt Halliday, who had gone to public school with Hec Kilrea and played with him right through Junior hockey and into the Ottawa Gunners of the city league. He was one of the Gunners' top scorers in 25/26, and the Senators signed him to a three-year contract at the start of 26/27. He played center and left wing, and defence when necessary.

Ottawa won its second consecutive regular-season title in 26/27 with a low-scoring team that allowed few goals. Connell was in net; Clancy and Boucher were the main defensive pair; Denneny, Hooley Smith and Nighbor were the regular forward line. They moved past the Canadiens with 4-0 and 1-1 efforts in the two-game total-goal Canadian division final, to meet the

Harry "Punch" Broadbent left the Senators during the First World War, and was awarded the Military Cross while serving with the Royal Canadian Artillery. He returned to the lineup during the 18/19 season, but was sold to the Montreal Maroons along with goaltender Clint Benedict in 1924 to help strengthen the new NHL franchise. Broadbent's Maroons upset the Senators in the 25/26 NHL championship, then won the Stanley Cup against Victoria of the Western Hockey League. He came back to the Senators for one season, 27/28, after Ottawa won the 26/27 Cup.

hugely improved Boston Bruins in the best-of-five Cup final. Ottawa was the better team—it had won 30 games to Boston's 21 in the new 44-game schedule—but the Bruins fought hard. Game one in Boston ended in a scoreless draw after 20 minutes of overtime. Ottawa won the next game 3-1 on goals by Clancy, Denneny and Finnigan. The series moved to Ottawa, and another draw resulted, with the teams tied at one after overtime had expired.

In the deciding game in Ottawa, neither team could score in the first period. The Senators went up in the second on goals by Finnigan and Clancy, with Boston's star right-winger Harry Oliver pulling the Bruins back to within a goal. Denneny scored in the third to put the game out of reach, and the contest ended in brawling. Hooley Smith inexplicably went after the mild-mannered Oliver, which brought Bruins defenceman Eddie Shore (who was one of the players to join the NHL from the western game) into the fray. Lionel Hitchman, who had been sold by Ottawa to Boston in 24/25, took on Buck Boucher, and when the game was over and the Cup was Ottawa's, Boston's Billy Couture (who was playing his last NHL season after being acquired from the Canadiens) attacked both on-ice officials.

League president Frank Calder, watching the fracas from a rinkside box, dispensed justice. Hooley Smith was fined $100 and suspended from the first month of the 27/28 season. Hitchman and Boucher were nicked for $50 each, and another $50 came from Boston's Jimmy Herberts for intimidating the referee.

Frank Ahearn responded to the spectacle by selling Hooley Smith to the Maroons, and received Punch Broadbent in return as part of the deal. But playoff discipline was not the only reason for Smith's banishment. Ahearn was losing money, and the sell-off of players had begun.

Frank Finnigan would recall how, even in a winning season like 26/27, the Senators still lost $50,000. Expansion was driving up player salaries, and Ahearn could not get the locals interested in games that didn't involve the Canadiens or the Maroons. (Montreal's proximity to Ottawa also probably helped sell tickets as Canadiens and Maroon fans followed their team to town.) Finnigan would remember playing in front of as few as 2,500 spectators at home games. Ahearn, however, was widely admired as the most solicitous owner imaginable. "Frank Ahearn was the greatest of gentlemen," Finnigan remarked in 1980. "There was nothing but the best for us wherever we travelled ... the best hotels and the best food was always ours. And they always had tickets for us to the best shows in New York, Chicago, Detroit ..."

Not even the Ahearn fortune could sustain a money-losing club. After the 26/27 Cup win, in addition to selling off Hooley Smith, Ahearn sent Ed Gorman to the Maple Leafs. Jack Adams quit to coach and manage the struggling Detroit franchise. After the

27/28 season, in which the Senators dropped into third place in the Canadian division with only 20 wins, Cy Denneny was sold to the Bruins, where he played part of the season and coached the team to the 28/29 Stanley Cup. Buck Boucher was shipped to the Maroons in 28/29, Punch Broadbent to the New York Americans. The day the stock market crashed in October 1929, Broadbent telephoned Bill Dwyer, told him he wasn't playing any more hockey and went into the air force. The last straw for the Senators was the unloading of Frank Nighbor in 29/30 to the Maple Leafs, where he played out his final season.

The Senators won only 14 games in 28/29, 21 in 29/30. In 1930 Frank Ahearn turned his mind to politics and was elected as a federal Liberal MP. After his Senators won only 10 games in 30/31, the team suspended operations for 31/32.

Toronto's Maple Leaf Gardens opened for the 31/32 season, and the Leafs had a new coach, Dick Irvin, the former star of the western game who had gotten the Blackhawks into the finals against the Canadiens the previous spring. With the Senators dormant, the Leafs were able to borrow two Senators stars, Frank Finnigan and Frank Clancy. The two men spent the season living at the Royal York Hotel as they helped the Leafs reach the finals against the New York Rangers, then cruise to the Cup with three straight wins. When it was over, Finnigan went back to Ottawa, where the Senators were being resurrected for 32/33. Conn Smythe could not allow Clancy to leave town, however, and he lavished $35,000 on Ahearn, plus the rights to Art Smith and Eric Pettinger, to keep the star defenceman. Smythe put

The most ferocious player during the Senators' glory years was Sprague Cleghorn. He played on the 19/20 and 20/21 Cup winning Senators, but was then let go by Tommy Gorman. Cleghorn could not forgive him, and as a vengeful Montreal Canadien he ruthlessly attacked his former Ottawa teammates. Gorman tried, and failed, to have him banned from the NHL.

29 | CAPITAL GAINS

A spry five feet, nine inches and 165 pounds, right-winger Frank "The Shawville Express" Finnigan was one of the last stars to shine with the Senators, joining the team full-time in 24/25. He was part of the final Stanley Cup-winning Ottawa team, in 26/27.

When the Senators folded for one season in 31/32, he and Frank Clancy were loaned to the Toronto Maple Leafs, with whom they won the Stanley Cup. The Leafs then bought Clancy's contract, but Finnigan returned to Ottawa as the Senators resumed play in 32/33.

In 34/35, the Senators franchise moved to St. Louis to play as the Eagles, and Finnigan went along, wearing the jersey at right. With the one-season experiment failing, however, Finnigan became a Maple Leaf again, this time for the remainder of his career, which ended in 1937.

the value of the total package at $50,000. This deal, made during the Depression, demonstrated how large the dollars had become in the professional game. Fifteen years earlier, the Senators had paid just $750 and a backup netminder for scoring ace Cy Denneny.

Frank Ahearn was running out of those dollars, at least out of dollars he was willing to lose in professional hockey. The Senators finished last in 32/33 and 33/34; by 33/34 the only player left from the 26/27 champions was The Shawville Express, Frank Finnigan, and he officially became a Maple Leaf in mid-34/35 after he and the Senators moved to St. Louis and tried playing as the Eagles that season. Eddie Gerard came along to St. Louis as manager, but his asthma forced him to quit halfway through the season. He was working as the Chief Clerk of the Department of Geodetic Survey in Ottawa when asthma claimed him in December 1937.

The Eagles won only 11 of 48 games in 34/35 and folded. In Montreal, Tommy Gorman was manager of the Maroons and Hooley Smith the captain as they defeated Clancy, Finnigan, Hec Kilrea (who had been sent to Toronto in 1933) and the rest of the Leafs for the Stanley Cup.

The Senators could not match the payrolls of larger centers, most of them American; the Ottawa market was simply too small. There were less than 30,000 people in Ottawa when the Senators closed shop, too few to allow a generous Frank Ahearn to come anywhere close to a break-even point. The city's travails were an early foreshadowing of the problems that would beset the Winnipeg Jets and the Quebec Nordiques in the 1990s, as their teams upped stakes and moved to greener pastures in Colorado and Phoenix.

Ottawa, however, could not be kept out of the NHL forever. In December 1990, the league's board of governors gathered in West Palm Beach, Florida, to hear pitches for the first expansion franchises since four ex-WHA teams had been admitted to the league in 1979. One of the contenders was an Ottawa group headed by real estate developer Bruce Firestone. On hand to press the case for a rebirth of the Senators was its last surviving player, Frank Finnigan.

Eighty-seven years old, tack sharp, with the mug of a former hockey professional and a full head of shock-white hair, The Shawville Express corralled league president John Ziegler at a gathering.

"You're going to give those boys in Ottawa a chance," he instructed Ziegler.

The next day, Ziegler did, and the Ottawa Senators were back in the NHL in 92/93. ○

Stars are Born: The Ascent of Playmaking

1918/19

Bluelines introduced to NHL, permitting forward passing in new 40-foot neutral zone at center ice. NHL begins awarding assists; Canadiens center Newsy Lalonde wins scoring race with 21 goals, 9 assists—the most assists of any top-ten scorer this season.

1921/22

Hamilton Tigers defenceman Leo Reise is first player to make top-ten scorers list with more assists than goals: 9 goals, 14 assists.

1924/25

Ottawa left-winger Cy Denneny, who won 1923/24 scoring title with 22 goals, 1 assist, finishes second this year with 27 goals, 15 assists.

1926/27

Collapse of the Western Hockey League brings stylish playmakers like Dick Irvin and Frank Boucher into the NHL. Bluelines repositioned 60 feet from goal lines, enlarging forward-passing neutral zone.

1929/30

Modern blueline offside rule appears and scoring soars. Bruins center Cooney Weiland wins scoring race with 43 goals. Ranger right-winger Frank Boucher is second with 36 assists.

1930/31

First season in which assists surpass goals in individual points production as the Maple Leafs' center Joe Primeau records league-leading 32 assists while linemate Leaf Charlie Conacher tops NHL with 31 goals.

1931/32

First NHL season in which top-ten scorers average more assists (0.49) than goals (0.48) per game.

1938/39

Assists reach 60.4% of average points production by top-ten scorers, entering the modern range. Pure playmakers come to the fore: Boston center Bill Cowley finishes fourth in scoring with 8 goals, 34 assists: Canadiens center Paul Haynes is ninth with 5 goals, 33 assists.

1934/35

First NHL season in which majority of top-ten scorers (7) have more assists than goals.

1935/36

New York Americans left-winger Sweeney Schriner becomes first player to win scoring race with more assists than goals: 19 goals, 26 assists.

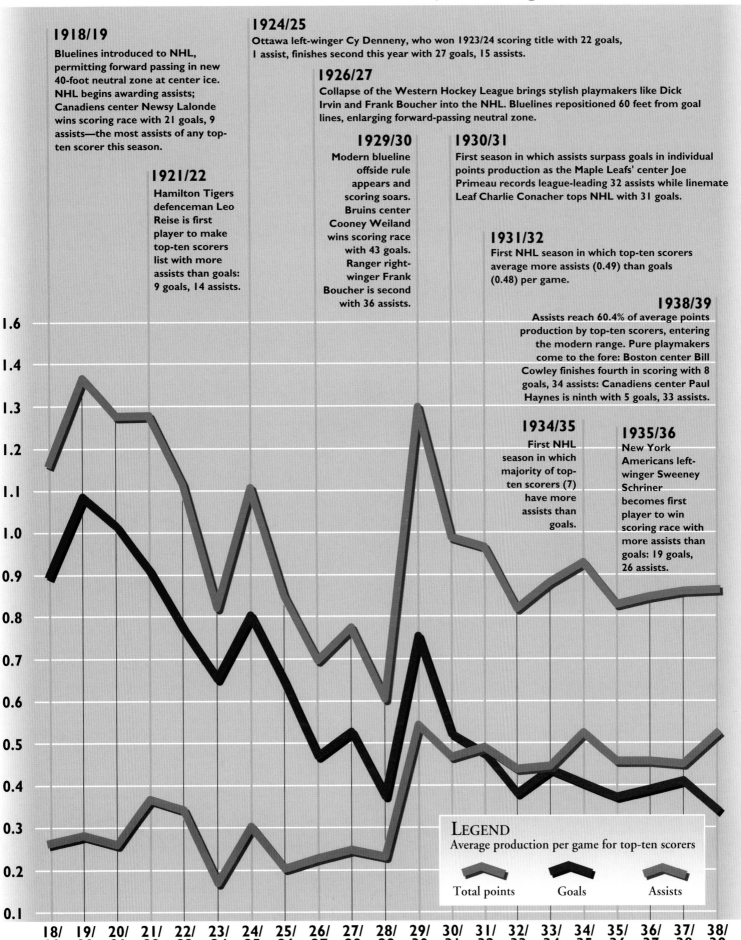

LEGEND
Average production per game for top-ten scorers

Total points   Goals   Assists

The curse of the championship season

After the Stanley Cup became the private domain of the NHL in 26/27, something curious happened. From 27/28 to 34/35, the NHL's top teams laboured under a discouraging curse: no club that posted the best regular-season record was able to win the Cup. In six of those eight seasons, the top club didn't even make it to the Cup finals. From this book's perspective, that drought meant that no club—no matter how powerful in the regular season—was able to mount what could be considered a truly dynastic performance, and it leaves a noticeable, albeit logical gap in this book's assessment of great teams after the reign of the Ottawa Senators from 19/20 to 26/27.

Why the drought? It had far less to do with the failure of top clubs to rise to the post-season challenge than it did with the peculiar playoff structure employed by the league.

The Stanley Cup became an all-NHL affair because of the collapse of the professional western game. With the addition of new NHL franchises in New York (the Rangers), Detroit (the Cougars) and Chicago (the Blackhawks), the league was divided

into two divisions, the Canadian (even though the New York Americans were part of it) and the American. Second- and third-place teams within each division played a two-game total-goal series to decide who met their division champion in another such series. The survivors of the divisional playoffs then met in the Cup final.

The divisional qualifying system meant that occasionally a club would finish fourth in its division and miss the playoffs, even though it had a better record than the third-place club in the other division. Thus Chicago failed to make the 32/33 playoffs, even though it had a better record than three of the teams in the Canadian division. This still goes on in hockey and other professional sports.

In 28/29, a cross-divisional playoff format arrived. The first-place Canadian team played the first-place American team, the second-place Canadian team the second place American team, and the third-place Canadian team the third-place American team.

Although the winner of the preliminary-round series between the divisional champions advanced directly to the finals, the system guaranteed that at least one top club was quickly out of Cup contention.

Compounding the playoff challenge for top clubs was that series were shorter than today's conventional best-of-seven. The NHL experimented with best-of-three, best-of-five and two-game total-goal formats. These quick series meant that a middling regular-season club could get hot and knock off a heavily favoured one. The league began with a best-of-five finals in 26/27, but in 29/30 switched to a best-of-three. The Canadiens managed a huge upset in downing a mighty Bruins club in two straight, and the Cup finals immediately went back to a best-of-five. In 37/38, Toronto lost a best-of-five final to the Blackhawks, the greatest underdogs in NHL history. Best-of-seven playoff hockey came to the NHL the next season, when the divisional format was scrapped after the collapse of the Montreal Maroons.

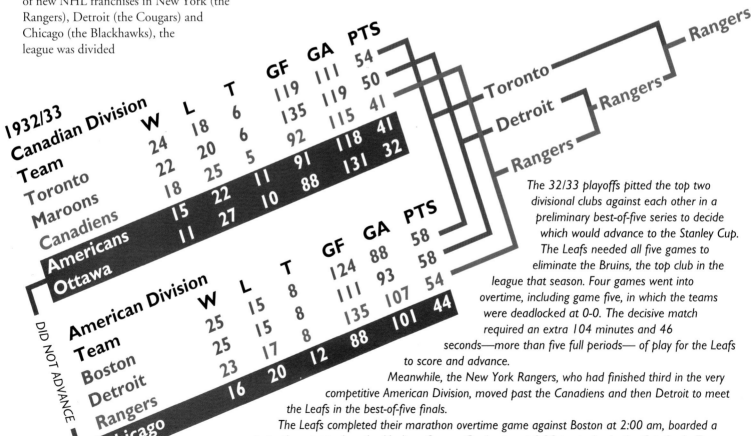

1932/33

Canadian Division

Team	W	L	T	GF	GA	PTS
Toronto	24	18	6	119	111	54
Maroons	22	20	6	135	119	50
Canadiens	18	25	5	92	115	41
Americans	15	22	11	91	118	41
Ottawa	11	27	10	88	131	32

American Division

Team	W	L	T	GF	GA	PTS
Boston	25	15	8	124	88	58
Detroit	25	15	8	111	93	58
Rangers	23	17	8	135	107	54
Chicago	16	20	12	88	101	44

DID NOT ADVANCE

The 32/33 playoffs pitted the top two divisional clubs against each other in a preliminary best-of-five series to decide which would advance to the Stanley Cup. The Leafs needed all five games to eliminate the Bruins, the top club in the league that season. Four games went into overtime, including game five, in which the teams were deadlocked at 0-0. The decisive match required an extra 104 minutes and 46 seconds—more than five full periods— of play for the Leafs to score and advance.

Meanwhile, the New York Rangers, who had finished third in the very competitive American Division, moved past the Canadiens and then Detroit to meet the Leafs in the best-of-five finals.

The Leafs completed their marathon overtime game against Boston at 2:00 am, boarded a train, then stepped on the Madison Square Garden ice at 8:30 pm to begin the Cup finals. Toronto lost the opening game and never recovered its wind as the Rangers won in four.

WINNING WAYS

NHL regular-season and Stanley Cup performances 1926/27-66/67

The charts over the next five pages reveal the regular-season performances of NHL clubs from 26/27, when the Stanley Cup became the exclusive domain of the league, to 66/67, the last season of the Original Six era. Divisional groupings are removed; teams are ranked according to their points percentage—the proportion of points earned in a regular season to total possible points—and organized according to which ones did and did not reach the playoffs. Stanley Cup winners and finalists are labelled.

Ottawa — *Senators*
Montreal — *Canadiens*
New York — *Rangers*
Boston — *Bruins*
Montreal — *Maroons*
Chicago — *Blackhawks*
New York — *Americans*
Toronto — *St. Patricks (1919–Feb. 1927)*
Maple Leafs (Feb. 1927–)
Pittsburgh — *Pirates*
Detroit — *Cougars (26/27–29/30)*
Falcons (30/31–31/32)
Philadelphia — *Quakers*

Reached Stanley Cup final
Team points percentage
Teams joined by green bar reached playoffs
Points percentage spread among playoff qualifiers
Won Stanley Cup
Teams in grey bar missed playoffs

In some seasons, non-qualifiers in one division had a regular-season record equal to or better than that of qualifiers in another division. In those seasons the bar linking non-qualifiers is offset.

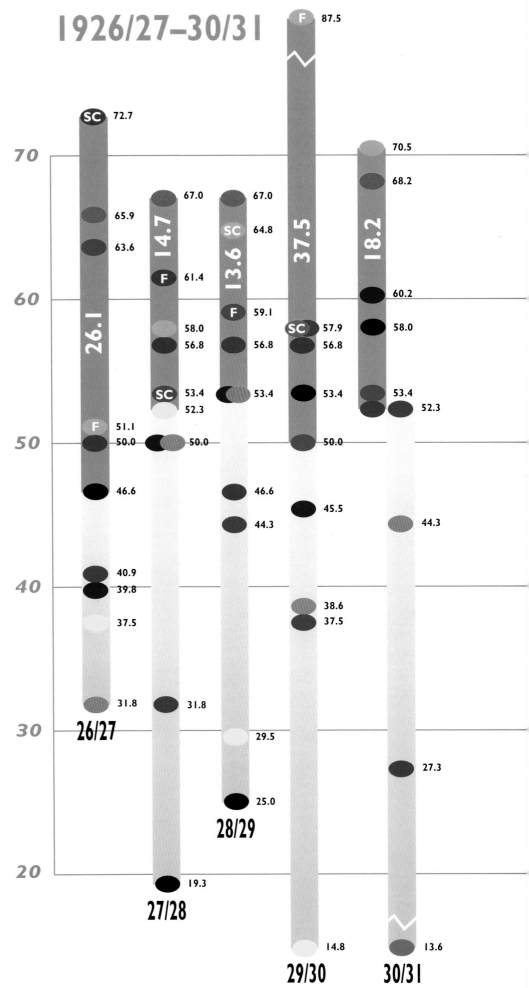

1926/27–30/31

WINNING WAYS
1931/32–39/40

The post-season drought for the league's best performers, which began in 27/28 (see page 32), began to lift in 34/35 when the Maple Leafs became the first top-performing regular-season club since 29/30 to reach the Stanley Cup finals. Like the Bruins of 29/30, though, the Leafs of 34/35 lost—in their case to the Maroons, in three straight. In 35/36, the

Detroit Red Wings put together back-to-back regular-season and Stanley Cup wins, and the drought was officially over.

The interdivisional playoff format continued to create inequities, however. The New York Americans, playing in the Canadian Division, qualified for the 35/36 playoffs, while their cross-town rivals, the Rangers, who had a far superior record in the powerful American Division, did not.

The divisional format was dropped after 37/38 and the death of the Montreal Maroons. The top six of seven teams then entered the playoff round.

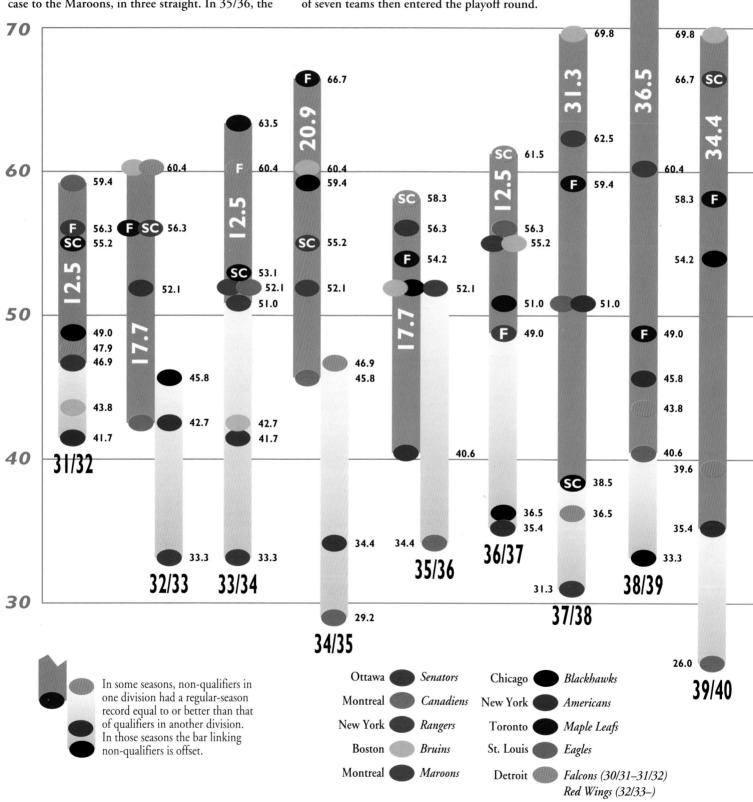

In some seasons, non-qualifiers in one division had a regular-season record equal to or better than that of qualifiers in another division. In those seasons the bar linking non-qualifiers is offset.

Ottawa	*Senators*	Chicago	*Blackhawks*
Montreal	*Canadiens*	New York	*Americans*
New York	*Rangers*	Toronto	*Maple Leafs*
Boston	*Bruins*	St. Louis	*Eagles*
Montreal	*Maroons*	Detroit	*Falcons (30/31–31/32)* *Red Wings (32/33–)*

CHAMPIONS   34

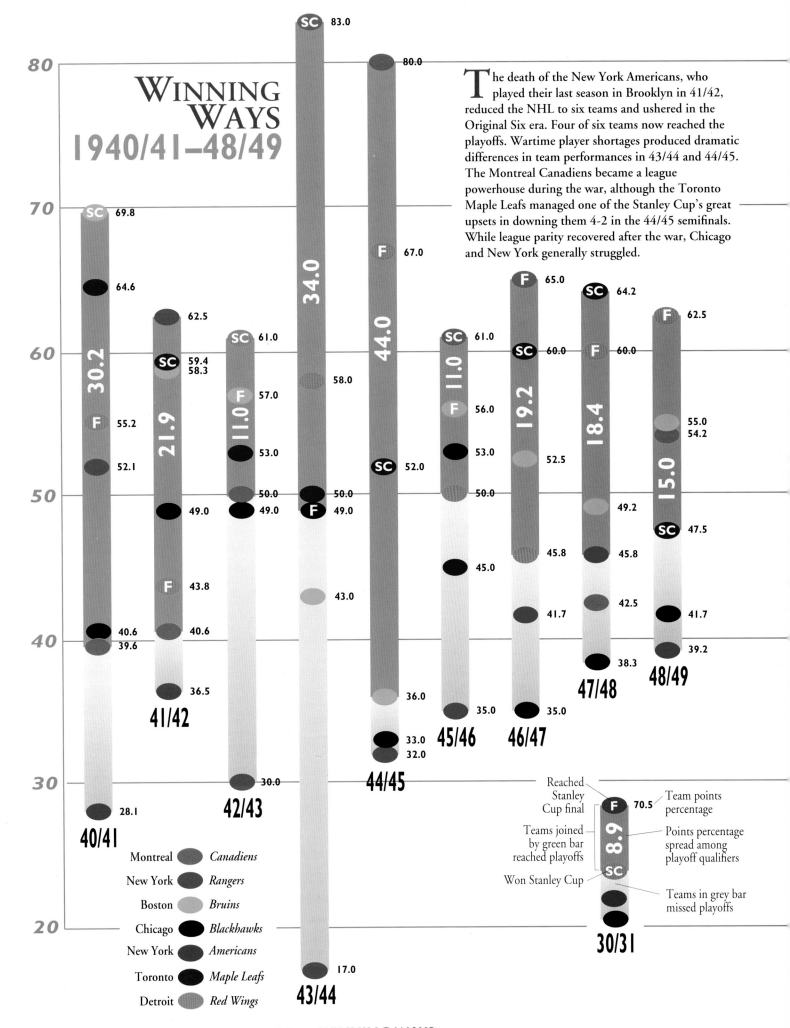

WINNING WAYS
1940/41–48/49

The death of the New York Americans, who played their last season in Brooklyn in 41/42, reduced the NHL to six teams and ushered in the Original Six era. Four of six teams now reached the playoffs. Wartime player shortages produced dramatic differences in team performances in 43/44 and 44/45. The Montreal Canadiens became a league powerhouse during the war, although the Toronto Maple Leafs managed one of the Stanley Cup's great upsets in downing them 4-2 in the 44/45 semifinals. While league parity recovered after the war, Chicago and New York generally struggled.

40/41
SC 69.8
64.6
55.2
52.1
40.6
39.6
28.1
30.2

41/42
62.5
SC 59.4
58.3
57.0
43.8
40.6
36.5
21.9
F

42/43
SC 61.0
53.0
50.0
49.0
30.0
11.0
F

43/44
SC 83.0
58.0
50.0
49.0
43.0
17.0
34.0
F

44/45
80.0
F 67.0
SC 52.0
50.0
36.0
33.0
32.0
44.0

45/46
SC 61.0
F 56.0
53.0
50.0
45.0
35.0
11.0

46/47
F 65.0
SC 60.0
52.5
45.8
41.7
35.0
19.2

47/48
SC 64.2
F 60.0
49.2
45.8
42.5
38.3
18.4

48/49
F 62.5
55.0
54.2
SC 47.5
41.7
39.2
15.0

Montreal — *Canadiens*
New York — *Rangers*
Boston — *Bruins*
Chicago — *Blackhawks*
New York — *Americans*
Toronto — *Maple Leafs*
Detroit — *Red Wings*

30/31
Reached Stanley Cup final — F 70.5 Team points percentage
Teams joined by green bar reached playoffs — 8.9 Points percentage spread among playoff qualifiers
Won Stanley Cup — SC
Teams in grey bar missed playoffs

80
70
60
50
40
30
20

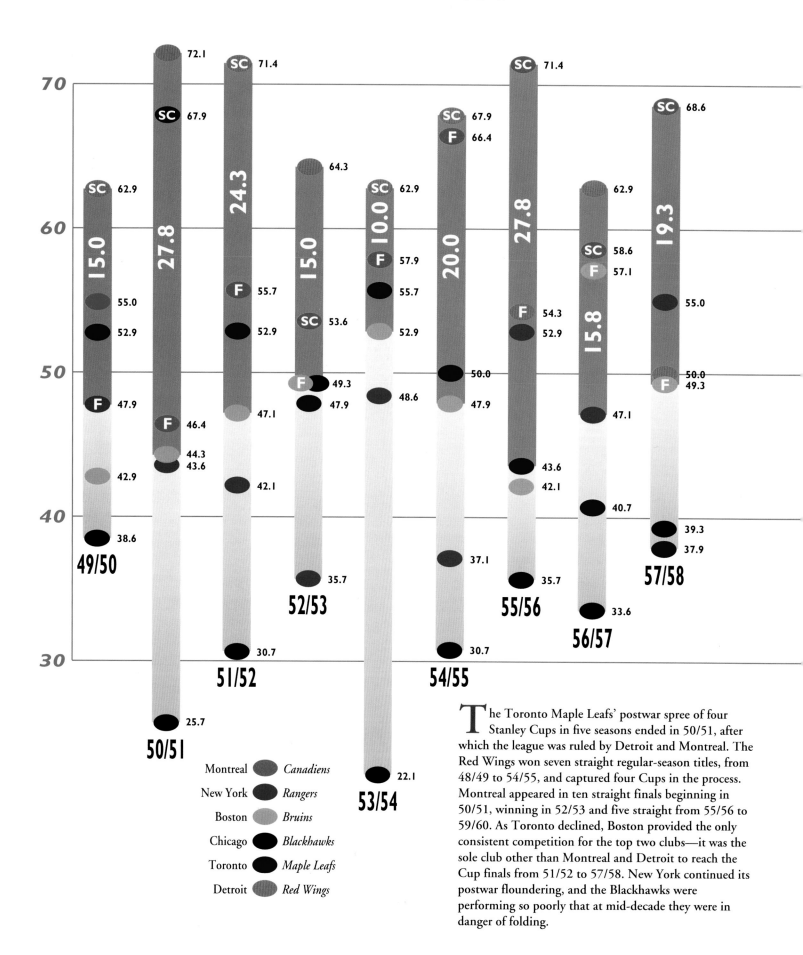

Montreal — *Canadiens*
New York — *Rangers*
Boston — *Bruins*
Chicago — *Blackhawks*
Toronto — *Maple Leafs*
Detroit — *Red Wings*

The Toronto Maple Leafs' postwar spree of four Stanley Cups in five seasons ended in 50/51, after which the league was ruled by Detroit and Montreal. The Red Wings won seven straight regular-season titles, from 48/49 to 54/55, and captured four Cups in the process. Montreal appeared in ten straight finals beginning in 50/51, winning in 52/53 and five straight from 55/56 to 59/60. As Toronto declined, Boston provided the only consistent competition for the top two clubs—it was the sole club other than Montreal and Detroit to reach the Cup finals from 51/52 to 57/58. New York continued its postwar floundering, and the Blackhawks were performing so poorly that at mid-decade they were in danger of folding.

WINNING WAYS
1958/59–66/67

Having established itself as the dominant club in the last half of the 1950s, Montreal continued to play superior hockey to the end of the Original Six era and beyond. The end of the 1950s was, however, marked by changes in the fortunes of other teams. Detroit stumbled, then recovered in the new decade, and while it reached four finals in the 1960s, it did not win another Cup. Boston collapsed after the 57/58 finals, and would not recover until the first expansion years. Toronto began its revival in 58/59 with the arrival of Punch Imlach as coach and general manager, and won four Stanley Cups in six seasons.

Chicago was resurrected at the same time, and while the team managed some regular-season successes, the Blackhawks were able to win only one Cup. New York continued to disappoint, its rejuvenation not coming until 66/67, under coach and general manager Emile Francis.

The revival of Toronto and Chicago, coupled with continued strength in Detroit and Montreal, made the last seasons of the Original Six era among the most competitive in league history. From 62/63 to 66/67, a team needed a points percentage of more than 50 to make the playoffs, a condition not experienced since 53/54. Toronto's Cup wins in the 1960s were produced with regular-season performances consistently lower than that of Detroit and Montreal in the 1950s.

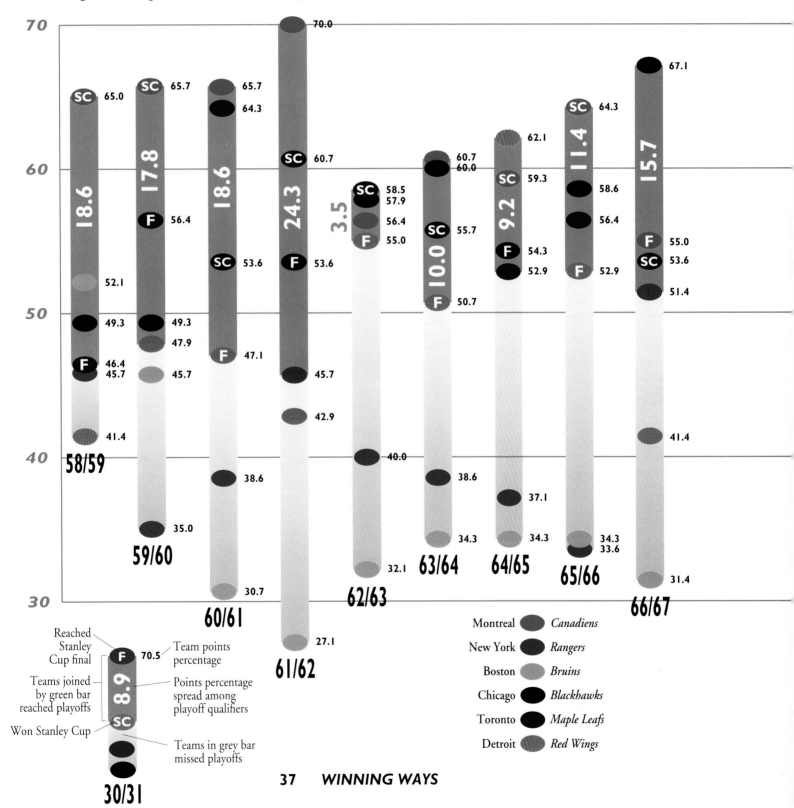

Montreal — Canadiens
New York — Rangers
Boston — Bruins
Chicago — Blackhawks
Toronto — Maple Leafs
Detroit — Red Wings

Reached Stanley Cup final — F
Team points percentage — 70.5
Teams joined by green bar reached playoffs — 8.9
Points percentage spread among playoff qualifiers
Won Stanley Cup — SC
Teams in grey bar missed playoffs

The Stanley Cup's biggest upsets

1937/38

Chicago Blackhawks defeat Toronto Maple Leafs

With a points percentage of just 38.5 (14 wins and 9 ties in 48 games), these Blackhawks are the poorest-performing team ever to win the Stanley Cup. Toronto, which finished first in the Canadian Division (with 24 wins and 9 ties, and a points percentage of 59.4), had the third-best record in the eight-team league. It was Toronto's fourth trip to the finals in six seasons, which also proved to be its fourth loss as the unlikely Blackhawks won the best-of-five series in four games. *(See opposite page.)*

1948/49

Toronto Maple Leafs defeat Detroit Red Wings

Although the Leafs had won the previous two Stanley Cups, the club turned in a poor regular-season performance. Its 147 goals were the second-lowest in the six-team league, and the club allowed 161. The Leafs scraped into the fourth and final playoff spot with 22 wins and 13 ties in 60 games for a points percentage of 47.5. Well out in front of the league, with 34 wins, 7 ties and a points percentage of 62.5, were the Red Wings. With their new offensive strike force, the Production Line of Ted Lindsay, Gordie Howe and Sid Abel, the Wings' 195-goal total was 17 more than the next-best effort, by second-place Boston, and its goals-against total was second only to that of third-place

Montreal. But in the finals, the Red Wings could not handle a Leafs squad that had rediscovered its championship form. Toronto became the first NHL team to win three consecutive Stanley Cups as it powered past Detroit in four straight. The 37/38 Blackhawks are the only other NHL club to have won the Cup after recording a regular-season points percentage of less than 50.

Other Overachievers: Stanley Cup winners with a low regular-season points percentage

1944/45 *Toronto 52%*
1933/34 *Chicago 53.1%*
1927/28 *N.Y. Rangers 53.4%*
1952/53 *Montreal 53.6%*
1960/61 *Chicago 53.6%*
1966/67 *Toronto 53.6 %*
1923/24 *Montreal 54.2%*
1992/93 *Montreal 54.3%*
1991/92 *Pittsburgh 54.4%*
1985/86 *Montreal 54.5%*
1990/91 *Pittsburgh 55%*

After winning just 14 of 48 regular-season games, the Chicago Blackhawks (seen hoisting coach Bill Stewart) upset the Toronto Maple Leafs in the 37/38 Stanley Cup finals.

Anatomy of an Underdog

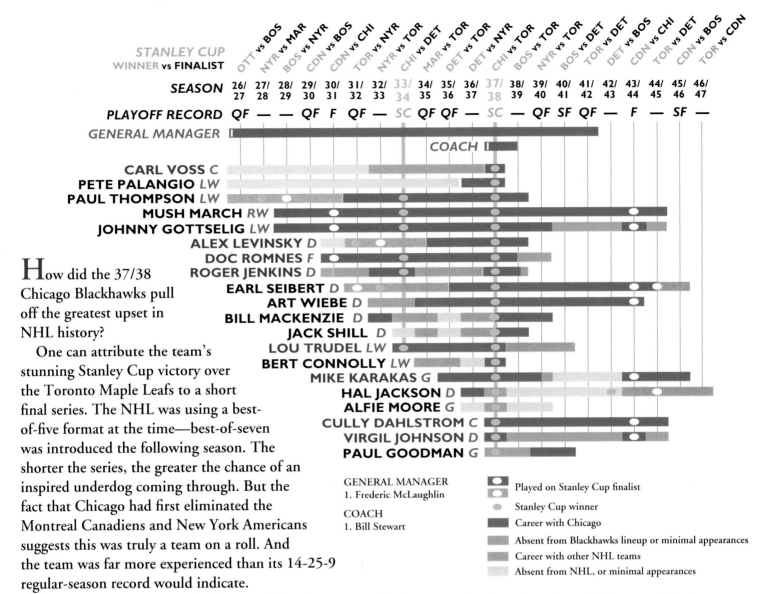

GENERAL MANAGER
1. Frederic McLaughlin

COACH
1. Bill Stewart

- Played on Stanley Cup finalist
- Stanley Cup winner
- Career with Chicago
- Absent from Blackhawks lineup or minimal appearances
- Career with other NHL teams
- Absent from NHL, or minimal appearances

How did the 37/38 Chicago Blackhawks pull off the greatest upset in NHL history?

One can attribute the team's stunning Stanley Cup victory over the Toronto Maple Leafs to a short final series. The NHL was using a best-of-five format at the time—best-of-seven was introduced the following season. The shorter the series, the greater the chance of an inspired underdog coming through. But the fact that Chicago had first eliminated the Montreal Canadiens and New York Americans suggests this was truly a team on a roll. And the team was far more experienced than its 14-25-9 regular-season record would indicate.

Chicago management made the use of **American-born players** a priority in the 1930s. As a result, 8 of 20 players to have their names inscribed on the Stanley Cup in 37/38 were Yanks. Some—like defenceman Alex Levinsky, forwards Doc Romnes and Lou Trudel and goaltender Mike Karakas—had already been around the team for a few seasons. For 37/38, Chicago beefed up its American quotient by reacquiring defenceman Roger Jenkins, bringing in journeyman forward Carl Voss from the Maroons, and signing two rookies, forward Cully Dahlstrom and defenceman Virgil Johnson.

Despite their poor regular season, the 'Hawks had a fairly talented, experienced lineup. Six players had been with the team when it won the 33/34 Cup, and of those, three—Mush March, Johnny Gottselig and Doc Romnes—were on hand when Chicago made the 30/31 finals against the Canadiens. In addition, star left-winger Paul Thompson had also won the Cup with the Rangers in 27/28, and reached the finals with them in 28/29. And in the back-to-back series between the Maple Leafs and the Rangers of 31/32 and 32/33, Earl Seibert and Alex Levinsky had squared off, each coming away with a Stanley Cup win.

Whatever magic was working for the Blackhawks in the spring of 1938 soon evaporated. The team won only 12 games and finished last in 38/39, encouraging a house-cleaning of veterans. Late in the season Paul Thompson hung up his skates to replace Bill Stewart as coach. Despite the overhaul, seven alumni of the storybook 37/38 team were still around, still being coached by Thompson, when the Blackhawks next reached the finals, in 43/44. They could not reignite the spark of 37/38, and were swept in four by the Canadiens.

TORONTO MAPLE LEAFS
The Forties

CONN GAME

WITH SIX STANLEY CUPS IN TEN SEASONS, THE MAPLE LEAFS FINALLY LIVED UP TO THE HIGH EXPECTATIONS OF TEAM IMPRESARIO CONN SMYTHE

RIGHT: Captain Ted Kennedy accepts the 48/49 Stanley Cup from NHL President Clarence Campbell as the Maple Leafs become the first NHL team to win three straight Cups.
BELOW: Kennedy's predecessor as captain, Syl Apps, graces the cover of a Maple Leaf Gardens programme of the early 1940s.

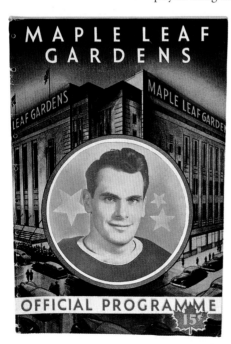

It took a world war to transform the Toronto Maple Leafs from (in team impresario Conn Smythe's analogy) a bridesmaid to a bride. After winning the Stanley Cup in 31/32 under new coach Dick Irvin (and in their new home, Maple Leaf Gardens), the Leafs made six Cup finals, from 32/33 to 39/40, and lost every one of them.

The Leafs weren't the only first-class club to struggle in the post-season in the 1930s, and the main reason for the shortfalls was the peculiar playoff structure used from 28/29 to 37/38 which called for the first-place teams in the Canadian and American Divisions to meet each other in the semifinals, thereby guaranteeing that one top club was knocked out of contention in the opening round. (See page 32.) But this happened to the Leafs only once, in 33/34, when they won the Canadian Division and were defeated in the semifinals by the Red Wings (who went on to lose to Chicago in the finals).

Conn Smythe didn't blame the playoff structure for the Leafs' failures in the Stanley Cup finals of the 1930s. Instead, he came to suspect that his club did not have the intestinal fortitude to win a championship, with some star players being content to earn bonus pay based on their scoring output in the regular season. The Leaf playoff failures also raised well-founded suspicions that Smythe dropped Irvin as his coach after the 39/40 series (Toronto's third straight finals defeat) because he had lost faith in Irvin's ability to ever deliver another championship.

There was no great shame, however, in Irvin's performance in that decade. The former star of the professional western game was a regular All Star selection as coach, and in six Stanley Cup losses his Leafs were only truly upset once, in 37/38. That season the Leafs, the Canadian Division champions, first dispatched the American Division champions, the Bruins, who had a much better regular-season record. The finals should

CHAMPIONS

have been a pushover for Irvin's Leafs, as they were facing the lowly Blackhawks, who had a points percentage of 38.5 (compared to the Leafs' 59.4) and had scraped into the playoffs in the last of six slots. But the Leafs lost to an inspired crew, going down in four games in the best-of-five series (see pages 38-39).

In the next two finals, however, the Leafs were up against more accomplished clubs. In 38/39 their opponents were the Bruins, who had finished well ahead of the rest of the league with a points percentage of 77.1, one of the best regular-season performances in league history. And in 39/40 the Rangers and their superior record were the Leafs' undoing.

Certainly Smythe may have felt that it was time for a change, that Irvin had taken the club as far as he was able to, but Irvin's removal after the 39/40 final was complicated by the fact that Hap Day, a Toronto mainstay from 24/25 to 36/37, had retired after playing his last professional season as a New York American in 37/38, and Smythe wanted his former Leaf captain (and minority partner in his sand and gravel business) to move up into coaching. Smythe killed two birds with one stone in the summer of 1940 when he suggested to Irvin and the struggling Montreal Canadiens that they would be good for each other.

Day delivered as Smythe hoped he would, returning the Stanley Cup to Maple Leaf Gardens after a gripping seven-game final against Detroit in the spring of 1942.

In the late 1930s, the Leafs were steadily evolving, moving away from the lineups that couldn't quite deliver a championship all through the 1930s—evolving even in the course of losing the three straight finals from 37/38 to 39/40. By 37/38, a number of storied names were gone from the roster. George Hainsworth had been replaced in goal in 36/37 by an unflappable former Red Wings property, Turk Broda, who Red Wings coach and general manager Jack Adams described as being able to "tend goal in a tornado and never blink an eye." The celebrated "Kid Line" of Joe Primeau, Busher Jackson and Charlie Conacher had dissolved with Primeau's retirement after 35/36;

Conacher was sent to Detroit for 38/39, Jackson to the New York Americans for 39/40. Hap Day had already moved on to the Americans for 37/38, and defensive greats King Clancy and Red Horner were making their exits, with Clancy retiring after a six-game outing in 36/37 to turn to officiating and later coaching, and Horner retiring after 39/40.

A new Leaf team was forming, up front around centers Syl Apps (who took over as captain from Horner in 1940), Pete Langelle and Billy "the Kid" Taylor, and standout wingers Bob Davidson, Nick Metz, Gord Drillon and Sweeney Schriner, acquired from the Americans for 39/40. Bucko McDonald, a veteran of two Red Wings Stanley Cup winners, was added to the team in 38/39, joining Bingo Kampman, a 37/38 addition, in the reargard. Other bright young talents coming on stream included defenceman Wally Stanowski and Nick Metz's younger brother Don on right wing. Change was unrelenting, and was capped by the replacement of Irvin with Day behind the bench for 40/41. The 41/42 Cup team had just 7 players who had been with the team since 37/38, 9 who went back to 38/39, and 13 who had been part of the 39/40 losing effort.

The 41/42 final was the first for Apps as captain and Day as coach. But even with the roster turnover, there was still a wealth of unhappy playoff experience in the Leaf lineup. Nick Metz and Bob Davidson had played in all five previous losing Leaf Cup appearances; Apps, Broda, Drillon and Kampman had endured the three straight losses at the end of the 1930s, while Bucko McDonald and Pete Langelle had been on hand for the last two. But since the 39/40 loss, the Leafs had made some important changes. A first-rate new defenceman, Bob Goldham, had joined the team in 41/42, and a veteran winger, Lorne Carr, had just been picked up from the Americans, where he had once played with Schriner and Day.

Nothing seemed to have changed in the general playoff fortunes of the club, however, as the 41/42 final series against the Red Wings unfolded. Down three games to none in a best-of-seven final, and losing the fourth game 2-0 in the middle of the second period, Conn Smythe's Leafs appeared assured of a particularly ignominious place in Cup lore. Instead, Day and his team mounted a comeback effort that had never been witnessed in league playoff history, and would not be repeated until 74/75, when the New York Islanders fought back from a three-game deficit to oust the Pittsburgh Penguins in the quarterfinals. The feat has, however, remained unduplicated in a final series.

The Leafs' Cup win has been handed down to us as a masterful triumph, but in the course of dealing out accolades it tends to be overlooked that the Leafs were almost humiliated by a far inferior club. Toronto finished the regular season in second, just three points behind the Rangers, while the Red Wings had struggled to make the playoffs, finishing fifth with only 19 wins in 48 games.

In reaching the finals Toronto had to eliminate the first-place Rangers, and perhaps that six-game series

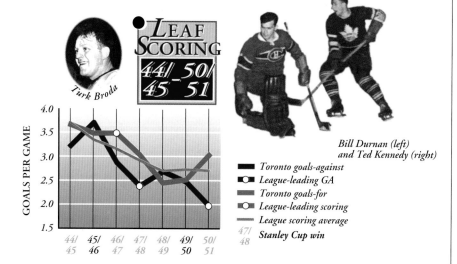

Turk Broda

LEAF SCORING 44/ 50/
45 51

Bill Durnan (left)
and Ted Kennedy (right)

GOALS PER GAME

4.0
3.5
3.0
2.5
2.0
1.5

44/ 45/ 46/ 47/ 48/ 49/ 50/
45   46   47   48   49   50   51

■ Toronto goals-against
●▬ League-leading GA
▬ Toronto goals-for
○▬ League-leading scoring
▬ League scoring average
47/
48
▬ Stanley Cup win

TORONTO MAPLE LEAFS

The Winning War Years

Featuring the players and management who participated in Toronto's
Stanley Cup victories of 1941/42 and 1944/45

GENERAL MANAGER   COACH
1. Conn Smythe   1. Hap Day
(from 1927)   2. Joe Primeau

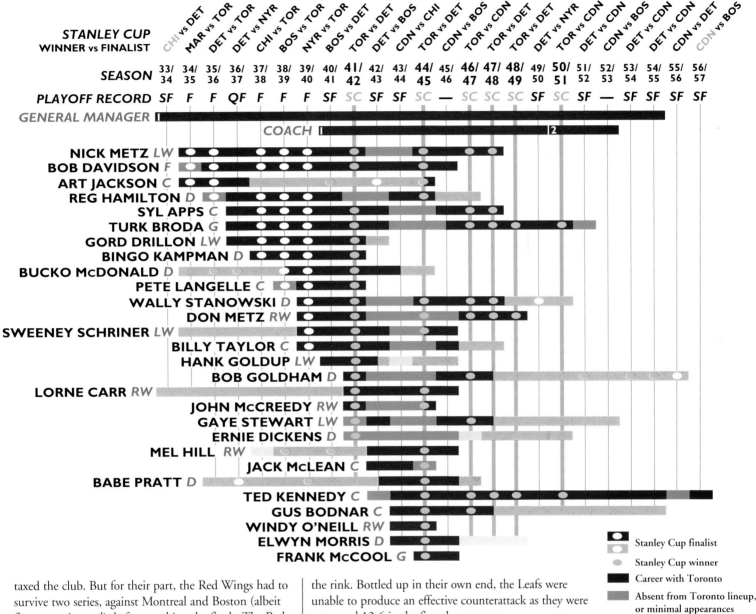

STANLEY CUP WINNER vs FINALIST	CHI vs DET	MAR vs TOR	DET vs TOR	DET vs NYR	CHI vs TOR	BOS vs TOR	NYR vs TOR	BOS vs DET	TOR vs DET	DET vs BOS	CDN vs CHI	TOR vs DET	CDN vs BOS	TOR vs DET	TOR vs CDN	TOR vs DET	DET vs NYR	TOR vs CDN	DET vs CDN	DET vs BOS	DET vs CDN	CDN vs DET	CDN vs BOS
SEASON	33/34	34/35	35/36	36/37	37/38	38/39	39/40	40/41	41/42	42/43	43/44	44/45	45/46	46/47	47/48	48/49	49/50	50/51	51/52	52/53	53/54	54/55	55/56	56/57
PLAYOFF RECORD	SF	F	F	QF	F	F	F	SF	SC	SF	SF	SC	—	SC	SC	SC	SF	SC	SF	—	SF	SF	SF	SF

Legend:

- Stanley Cup finalist
- Stanley Cup winner
- Career with Toronto
- Absent from Toronto lineup, or minimal appearances
- Career with other NHL teams
- Absent from NHL, or minimal appearances

---

taxed the club. But for their part, the Red Wings had to survive two series, against Montreal and Boston (albeit five games in total), before reaching the finals. The Red Wings won the first three games against Toronto 3-2, 4-2 and 5-2 by employing a grinding dump-and-chase style inspired by the offside rules of the era. At the time, a player couldn't make a forward pass across his own blue-line, which meant the only way a team could get the puck out of its own end, short of icing it, was for someone to stickhandle it out. The strategy of Jack Adams was to have his Red Wings fire the puck into the Leafs' end, flood the zone with all five skaters in what was known as a ganging attack, and keep hitting whichever hapless Leaf tried to escape with the puck. Watching in the stands as the Leafs were being herded toward a rout was 16-year-old future Leaf Ted Kennedy, who couldn't help but notice that all the skate marks were in Toronto's end of

the rink. Bottled up in their own end, the Leafs were unable to produce an effective counterattack as they were outscored 12-6 in the first three games.

On the cusp of defeat, Hap Day juggled his lineup, benching defenceman Bucko McDonald and star winger Gord Drillon, who at the time was the leading playoff goal-scorer in the league. Drillon's place on the line with Bob Davidson and Nick Metz was taken by Nick's brother Don, who had played 25 games with the Leafs that season and ridden the bench for most of the playoffs. (Substitute forward Hank Goldup also saw more ice time.) In McDonald's place Day employed Ernie Dickens, who had spent most of the 41/42 season with the Leafs' American league farm team, the Pittsburgh Hornets. While he didn't contribute a single goal or assist in the Leafs' post-season, Dickens was instrumental in solving Toronto's problems in its own end.

In game four the Leafs rebounded from their two-goal deficit to tie the score by the end of the second period. At 4:18 of the third period left-winger Carl Liscombe restored the Red Wings' lead; two minutes later Syl Apps tied the game again. At 12:45 Nick Metz, assisted by brother Don and Apps, put the Leafs ahead for the first time.

With about two minutes to go, Red Wings defenceman Eddie Wares was assessed a minor penalty. He cursed at a linesman and refused to leave the ice, a response that earned him a $50 fine and a game misconduct. Detroit then received a penalty for having too many men on the ice. Don Grosso was chosen to serve the bench penalty, but rather than head to the box he dropped his sticks and gloves, looking for a fight. This earned Grosso a $25 fine.

When the game was over and Toronto had won 4-3, Jack Adams took to the ice and punched referee Mel Harwood. League president Frank Calder, who was watching the farce unfold, banned Adams from the rest of the series and fined Grosso and Wares an additional $100 each.

Without their coach, the Red Wings played like a team that shouldn't even have made the playoffs. In game five Nick Metz scored at 9:24 of the first period while Red Wings tough guy Jimmy Orlando was in the penalty box. At 15:13, Detroit center Alex Motter accidentally put the puck in his own net, and the goal was awarded to Wally Stanowski. That set the tone for the rest of the Red Wings' effort as Don Metz contributed a hat-trick to a 9-3 demolition. Toronto then cruised confidently to its Cup victory with 3-0 and 3-1 wins. After staving off defeat in game four and seeing Adams banned from the series, the Leafs outscored Detroit 15-4 in their comeback drive.

It was a last hurrah for the confounded Leafs of the 1930s, for the war emphatically intervened in league affairs after that Stanley Cup. Canada had been at war since September 1939, but the United States did not join in fully until December 1941 and the Japanese attack on Pearl Harbor, making 41/42 the last NHL season before the full effect of mobilization would be felt. Either through the draft or voluntary enlistment, players began leaving the league in droves in 1942, and for the next three seasons the NHL took on a makeshift look, as clubs stocked their rosters with talents—many of them either young and untested or over the hill—beyond the reach of the draft.

Some teams suffered more than others. The Rangers and Bruins, league powerhouses at the beginning of the war, had their rosters gutted. The Rangers never really recovered from the loss of continuity when hostilities ceased, and while the Bruins put up a fight in the post-war years, they were not able to reestablish the form that brought them Stanley Cup wins in 38/39 and 40/41.

Toronto, Detroit and Chicago soldiered on through the war, while Montreal experienced a tremendous resurgence under Irvin's guidance and with new talent, such as Maurice Richard, Elmer Lach and goaltender Bill Durnan. In the 43/44 semifinals the Leafs were humiliated by the Canadiens in a 4-1 series loss that culminated in an 11-0 shelling at the Montreal Forum. It was, remarkably, the first time the Leafs and Canadiens had ever met in the playoffs, and the bitterness in Toronto's loss would help fuel the intensity of this new rivalry. Hap Day dismissed the loss as having been a series that pitted "kids against grownups," as the Leafs had relied on teenage recruits like centers Gus Bodnar and Ted Kennedy in meeting the challenge of the more mature Canadiens squad.

In 44/45, the makeshift Leafs had their revenge. Montreal had dominated the league in the regular season, losing only eight games and sewing up five of six positions on the first All Star team. But Toronto, which had finished third with 24 wins, was the only team to post a winning record (5-4-1) against Montreal in the regular season, and upset the Canadiens 4-2 in the semifinals. The Leafs then outlasted second-place Detroit in a low-scoring final that went all seven games. Only 18 goals were scored in the series, with three shutouts being recorded by Toronto's Frank McCool and two by the Red Wings' Harry Lumley. Day succeeded in this series, as he had against Montreal, by sticking to a close-checking game plan that relied mainly on only two forward lines: Kennedy, Davidson and Hill, and Bodnar, Schriner and Carr, with Nick Metz on hand to provide relief with Johnny McCreedy and Art Jackson.

The win thrilled Conn Smythe, who had gone to war with his own anti-aircraft battery and returned home in September 1944 after being seriously wounded at Caen. But the 44/45 Stanley Cup had been a victory of determination over talent, and the Leaf win bore no promise of dynastic greatness. Save for promising newcomers like Bodnar and Kennedy, the Leafs of 44/45 had been largely a quixotic mix of oldtimers and fill-ins. Bob Davidson, for one, had hung in to play on Kennedy's left wing, serving as captain in the absence of Syl Apps, who had enlisted in September 1943.

The team showed its lack of genuine strength in 45/46, missing the playoffs altogether as the league returned to a peacetime footing. Like other teams, the Leafs were reclaiming talents as demobilization continued into 1946. After completing his officer's training, Syl Apps had been waiting to participate in the land invasion of Japan when atomic bombs ended the war in the Pacific. Now Apps was back in the Leaf lineup for the

start of the 45/46 season, as were defenceman Bob Goldham and left-winger Gaye Stewart, who had been rookie of the year in 42/43. But their outstanding goaltender Turk Broda, who had been a sporting ringer in Canadian army hockey and softball teams overseas, did not rejoin the team until late January 1946, when he promptly displaced the team's netminding hero of 44/45, Frank McCool. Don Metz, who had gone into the army and then the air force after the 41/42 Cup win, had been discharged in time to participate in the 44/45 Stanley Cup win, but was now assigned to the Pittsburgh Hornets for most of 45/46; center Bud Poile, a standout rookie in 42/43, was only in the 45/46 lineup for nine games after returning from military service.

The anomaly of the war years is underlined by the fact that the 46/47 Leaf lineup had more members of the 41/42 championship team than of the 44/45 championship team. The 46/47 Leafs had seven veterans of 41/42—center Syl Apps, goaltender Turk Broda, defencemen Bob Goldham and Wally Stanowski, rightwinger Don Metz and left-wingers Nick Metz and Gaye Stewart. Only five members of the 44/45 team were on hand just two seasons later—41/42 members Nick and Don Metz and Stanowski, and new recruits Kennedy and Bodnar.

While Smythe was away at war, management of the Leafs had been left to a Maple Leaf Gardens executive committee, with long-standing employee Frank Selke serving as acting general manager. With the war over, Smythe resumed his general managership (officially he was called managing director) and ran Selke out of town; Selke promptly secured the general manager's position in Montreal for 46/47.

Why Selke was ousted has never been clear, and the

reasons are a convoluted amalgam of issues, beginning with the Leafs having traded away on February 10, 1943 the rights to Smythe's treasured defensive prospect, Frank Eddolls, in exchange for the rights to 17-year-old Ted Kennedy. Smythe would later assert that he had been outraged by the trading away of a player then serving his country (Eddolls had enlisted in the RCAF and was playing for the Montreal air force team in the Quebec Senior league), but in his distraught letters home from overseas in the spring of 1943 to Leaf scout Squib Walker, Smythe made no mention of such an issue.

After Smythe returned home and saw Kennedy in action with the Leafs, particularly as Kennedy led the team in scoring in the 44/45 playoffs, he had to concede that the teenager from Humberstone, Ontario, had been a wonderful find and that the trade had worked out to Toronto's advantage. And Smythe in his memoirs would acknowledge that punishing Selke alone for the trade would have made no sense, as the actual trade deal was signed by Hap Day, not Frank Selke—Day was a good friend of former NHL great Nels Stewart, who had been coaching Kennedy on the Port Colborne Sailors Senior club in 42/43 when he convinced Day of his worth. If anyone should have been punished by Smythe, then, overwhelmingly, it should have been Day.

On the other hand, while overseas, Smythe had come to suspect that Selke, in concert with board members Ed Bickle and Bill MacBrien, was plotting to have him ousted permanently from the team's general managership, or at least were acting as if he were never coming back. Smythe was offered the NHL presidency on his return from overseas in September 1944. He turned it down, and suspected that the Selke faction had arranged the job offer as a way to get him out of Maple

Turk Broda kicks away a Rangers scoring effort in game three of the 39/40 Stanley Cup finals. The Leafs won the game 2-1, but the Rangers went on to take the series 4-2. Three of New York's wins came in overtime, including the clinching 3-2 win on a Bryan Hextall goal. It was Toronto's third consecutive loss in the Cup finals.

This jacket belonged to stalwart forward Bob Davidson, whose Maple Leaf career began in 34/35. He was one of the few older players on the Leaf roster during the Second World War, and served as substitute captain while Syl Apps was in the Canadian army. He went on to become the Leafs' chief scout, securing rights to talent that would participate in the Leaf revival of the 1960s.

Leaf Gardens. In the spring of 1946, Smythe approached Selke (who was a minority shareholder) and asked for his support in making a run at securing the company presidency. It was undoubtedly a squeeze play by Smythe, for he had been publicly critical of Selke over the poor performance of the Leafs in the 45/46 season, knew well how the two of them felt about each other, and thus knew that Selke wouldn't cast his lot with him. Selke's equivocating allowed Smythe to deliver an ultimatum: if you're not with me, there won't be any place in the new organization for you. Selke accurately read the future, resigned his position and moved over to the Canadiens, where he replaced Tommy Gorman as general manager.

With Selke gone, Smythe reasserted control and tore apart the losing roster of 45/46 that Selke had left him. To what should have been Selke's everlasting credit, after Smythe had taken a leave of absence from his Gardens duties in January 1941 and left the challenge of winning in wartime to Selke, the Leafs had won two Stanley Cups. But the team now needed to be put on a peacetime footing, and Smythe moved to do so in concert with Day and scout Walker. Both men were old cohorts of Smythe's. Walker had played with Smythe on the University of Toronto team that won the Ontario Junior title in the spring of 1915, and enlisted with him right after. (Selke had opposed them in the lineup of the Union Jacks of Berlin, now called Kitchener.) Day had been a pharmacy student at the University of Toronto when Smythe was managing the Varsity Senior squad,

and left his studies in 1924 to turn pro with the Toronto St. Patricks. When Smythe levered a purchase of the Toronto NHL franchise in 1927 and renamed it the Maple Leafs, he made Day the team's captain.

The 46/47 rebuilding began with the retirement or removal of a number of older, draft-exempt veterans. With younger players returning, the veterans' age was beginning to show, particularly with the speed of the new game ushered in by the two-line offside. The Leafs no longer had scoring power up front, and a slew of forwards were cashiered. Bob Davidson, who had played his first games as a Leaf in 34/35, was a spent force at 34, having contributed only 18 points in 45/46. Smythe made him Day's assistant coach, then arranged for him a short hitch as coach of the St. Louis Flyers of the American league. A two-and-a-half season posting as coach of the Pittsburgh Hornets followed, after which Davidson took over as the Leafs' chief scout when Squib Walker died. Right-winger Lorne Carr was no longer effective at 36; from 43/44 to 45/46 his points production plummeted from 74 to 13. Mel "Sudden Death" Hill, 32, acquired from the defunct Americans for 42/43, had his points production fall from 35 to 12. And on left wing, Sweeney Schriner was scratched. Schriner had already retired once, in 1943, at 31, citing family illness and income tax burdens as the reasons. He spent one year in the navy, playing military hockey in his native Alberta, before manpower cutbacks led to his discharge. The Leafs brought him in for 26 games of 44/45, and he contributed 42 critical points. But in 45/46 Schriner just didn't have it anymore, having been held to 19 points over 47 games.

Defenceman Babe Pratt, who had been league MVP in 43/44 after being acquired from the Rangers by Selke, had embarrassed the club by being suspended for nine outings in January 1946 for gambling on league games. His points production as an offence-minded defenceman was also way down, dropping from 41 to 25 points in one season. In June 1946 Smythe sold Pratt to the Bruins, though he regretted having to do so. In hindsight, it was probably the right managerial move; the hard-living Pratt's major-league career was effectively over by then.

That summer, Smythe also offloaded center Billy the Kid Taylor in a one-for-one deal to Detroit in exchange for Harry Watson. A Brooklyn American in 41/42, Watson was signed by the Red Wings when the Americans franchise folded and won a Stanley Cup with them in 42/43. After two years in the Canadian military, Watson had returned to play with Detroit for 45/46.

Smythe's motivations for moving aside Davidson, Schriner, Hill, Carr and Pratt are straightforward, but the Taylor deal remains a puzzler. Outwardly, the Leaf slump

TORONTO MAPLE LEAFS

The Dynasty of the late 1940s

Featuring the players and management who participated in Toronto's
Stanley Cup victories of 1946/47, 1947/48, 1948/49 and 1950/51

GENERAL MANAGER	COACH
1. Conn Smythe	1. Hap Day
(from 1927)	2. Joe Primeau

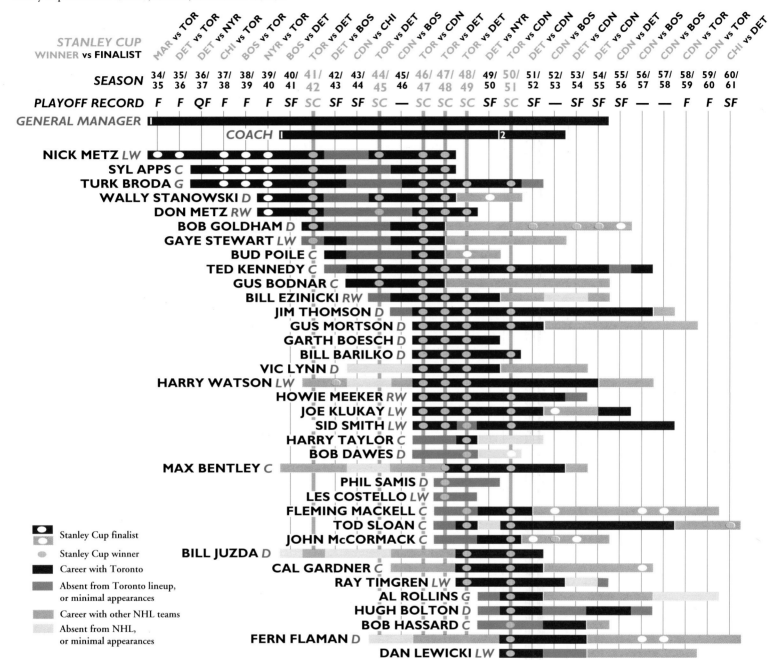

in 45/46 and Smythe's determination to give the lineup a revitalizing shakeup would seem to have been the motivator. Taylor had turned in a sub-par performance, with 41 points, compared to 60 in 42/43, before he went into the army; most important, as a playmaker his assists were way down, from 42 to 18. But then, Taylor did score 23 goals, the most in his career, and on the basis of raw numbers the Taylor-Watson swap would seem to have been tilted in Detroit's favour: Watson, in his first season back from the war, had only 24 points, and Taylor promptly led the league in assists with 46 as a Red Wing in 46/47. In Watson's favour were his size and checking ability (with a minimum of penalties), and he did prove to be a Maple

Leaf mainstay for more than eight seasons, during which he was regularly good for 30 or 40 points a season.

In truth, Smythe might have had a less obvious reason for offloading Taylor in such a simple deal: gambling. Wagering was the bane of all professional sports in the 1940s, and adding to Smythe's woes in 45/46 was the Pratt suspension. Smythe had also turned his energies to clearing Maple Leaf Gardens of what was known as the "bull pit" of bookies, and there were police raids to break up illegal operations in the Toronto area. Smythe's decision to sell Pratt and deal away Taylor might not have been coincidental. Two years later, Taylor, having bounced from Detroit to Boston to New York, was

RANGERS

BOSTON BRUINS

DETROIT REDWINGS

TORONTO MAPLE LEAFS

BROOKLYN AMERICANS

BLACK HAWKS CHICAGO

CANADIENS

TORONTO MAPLE LEAFS
WORLD CHAMPIONS
STANLEY CUP HOLDERS 1941-1942

COURTESY OF LOVE AND BENNETT

The Leafs were down three games to none in the 41/42 Stanley Cup final against the Detroit Red Wings when coach Hap Day juggled the lineup and guided the team to four straight wins. It was Toronto's first Cup victory in a decade. The comeback has never been repeated in a Cup final.

suspended for life from organized hockey, along with Bruins linemate Don Gallinger, for betting on his own team's games. (They were reinstated in 1970.) Smythe may well have known, when dealing with Pratt, that Taylor was trouble too, and chose to dump him as quickly and as efficiently as possible.

In the 46/47 rebuilding, ten returning members of the team's wartime editions were joined by ten brand new faces. Bill Ezinicki, a devastating bodychecker on right wing, had graduated from the Oshawa Generals Junior team to play eight games for the Leafs at the start of the 44/45 season, but the 20-year-old Winnipegger had then been called up by the draft. He was demobilized in time to join the Leafs for 24 games of 45/46, and was one of the few bright spots in the roster that season. He was the only person who played a significant part of 45/46 for the Leafs (without having been an established Leaf at some point during the war) to make the 46/47 team. Fellow Winnipegger Jim Thomson, a former star with the Leafs' Toronto Junior farm club, the St. Michael's College Majors, had been assigned to the Pittsburgh Hornets of the American league for 45/46. Appearing in five Leaf games that season, Thomson was the only newcomer other than Ezinicki not to have been doomed in Smythe's eyes by his participation in at least part of the Leafs' poor first postwar season.

The foundation of Smythe's rebuilding was an almost entirely new defence corps. Smythe had hoped

Frank Eddolls would be part of what he envisioned as his "soldier defence," as he put it in a letter home to Walker. It was an unelaborated description that suggested Smythe envisioned a defence lineup of actual war veterans, which may explain some of his dismay at losing Eddolls. In Eddolls' absence Smythe had to start with two returnees, Wally Stanowski and Bob Goldham, and go from there.

The NHL game had undergone a tremendous change during Smythe's wartime absence with the introduction of the two-line offside. It permitted a player to make a forward pass across his own blueline, provided the pass did not cross the new center-ice line. Designed to eliminate the tedious dump-and-chase style with which the Red Wings had almost triumphed in the 41/42 finals, it created an entirely new style of play, above all a faster-breaking game. Strategists like Hap Day reacted to this development by making defence an emphatically behind-the-blueline role. After all, if the defenceman could now pass the puck across his own blueline, there was no reason for him to carry it out of his own end and risk being caught up ice on a counter-rush. The Day playbook called for solid, dependable, stay-at-homers who could help Turk Broda keep pucks out of the net and give the forwards the confidence to deliver offence. Forwards, it must be said, were also expected to be complete two-way players, backchecking to make sure no man-advantage rushes descended on Broda and company. In this scenario, Ezinicki was one

TORONTO MAPLE LEAFS 1941/42-50/51

Season	Finish	Record (W-L-T)	Points %	Awards (winners & runners-up)	All-Stars	Playoffs
41/42	2nd	27-18-3	59.4	HART: Apps RU LADY BYNG: Apps, Drillon RU VEZINA: Broda RU	1ST TEAM: Apps (C) 2ND TEAM: Broda (G), McDonald (D), Drillon (RW)	Won SC final 4-3 over Detroit
42/43	3rd	22-19-9	53.0	CALDER: Stewart VEZINA: Broda RU	1ST TEAM: Carr (RW) 2ND TEAM: Apps (C)	Lost SC semifinal 4-2 to Detroit
43/44	3rd	23-23-4	50.0	HART: Pratt CALDER: Bodnar VEZINA: Bibeault RU	1ST TEAM: Pratt (D), Carr (RW) 2ND TEAM: Bibeault (G), Day (Coach)	Lost SC semifinal 4-1 to Montreal
44/45	3rd	24-22-4	52.0	CALDER: McCool VEZINA: McCool RU	2ND TEAM: Pratt (D)	Won SC final 4-3 over Detroit
45/46	5th	19-24-7	45.0	HART: Stewart RU ART ROSS: Stewart RU	1ST TEAM: Stewart (LW)	Missed playoffs
46/47	2nd	31-19-10	60.0	CALDER: Meeker LADY BYNG: Apps RU VEZINA: Broda RU		Won SC final 4-2 over Montreal
47/48	1st	32-15-13	64.2	LADY BYNG: Apps RU VEZINA: Broda	1ST TEAM: Broda (G)	Won SC final 4-0 over Detroit
48/49	4th	22-25-13	47.5	LADY BYNG: Watson RU		Won SC final 4-0 over Detroit
49/50	3rd	31-27-12	52.9	HART: Kennedy RU	1ST TEAM: Mortson (D) 2ND TEAM: Kennedy (C)	Lost SC semifinal 4-3 to Detroit
50/51	2nd	41-16-13	67.9	CALDER: Rollins RU VEZINA: Rollins	2ND TEAM: Thomson (D), Kennedy (C), Smith (LW)	Won SC final 4-1 over Montreal

of the most dangerous Leafs, an open-ice bodychecker who was wont to drift back across his own blueline and demolish any opponent on the opposing wing who was focused on splitting the defence. Around the league, hospitals became accustomed to Ezinicki's victims being wheeled in for x-rays.

In addition to Jim Thomson, three more defencemen were new to the Leaf starting lineup in 46/47. Garth Boesch, just turning 26, agreed to leave behind the 1,200-acre wheat farm he was running with his dad in Riceton, Saskatchewan, and played 35 of 60 games. Twenty-one-year-old Gus Mortson, who was from the northern Ontario mining town of New Liskeard, had starred with the St. Mike's Majors when they won the 44/45 Memorial Cup. He was assigned to the Tulsa Oilers of the U.S. league for 45/46, and in 46/47 with Toronto he displayed a fresh pugnacity, leading the NHL with 133 penalty minutes.

From the American league the Leafs also sprung 21-year-old Vic Lynn, who had come out of Saskatoon initially to play in the Rangers' development system. Acquired by Detroit, he had spent 32 games with Indianapolis of the American league in 43/44, with two

games as a Red Wing. In 44/45 he devoted a full season to the St. Louis Flyers of the American league, and in 45/46 turned in 53 games with the Buffalo Bisons of the American league and two games with the Canadiens. Lynn was an exception to the Hap Day playbook, being a defenceman with an offensive touch who collected 51 points in 53 games with the Bisons. Lynn played 31 games for Toronto in 46/47, with 20 points and 44 penalty minutes to show for it.

When injuries began to take their toll on the Leaf defence, Smythe called up a 19-year-old prospect from Timmins, Ontario who was playing for the Hollywood Wolves of the Pacific Coast league, a devastating bodychecker named Bill Barilko. "Hollywood Bill" played 18 regular-season games from February onward. The next season, he led the league in penalties with 147 minutes. Beginning in 46/47 with Mortson, the Leafs could brag about having the most penalized player in the league for five straight seasons. Mortson was followed by Barilko in 47/48, then Ezinicki in 48/49 and 49/50, then Mortson again in 50/51.

With so many retirements in the front lines, four new wingers also joined the club in 46/47. Twenty-two-year-old amateur prospect Howie Meeker graduated from Senior hockey in Stratford, Ontario to play right wing; with 45 points in 55 games, he was named the NHL's rookie of the year. Three new left-wingers were also brought in. In addition to Harry Watson, Joe Klukay and Sid Smith entered the lineup. Klukay had made a one-game appearance with Toronto in the 42/43 playoffs, then joined the navy, playing for its HMCS Cornwallis team in the Halifax defence league. After demobilization he played for the Pittsburgh Hornets in 45/46, and now became a full-time Leaf. Smith, just 21, came to the Leafs from the Quebec Aces Senior club. Center Harry Taylor, a 20-year-old product of the Winnipeg Monarchs Junior club, got a 9-game glimpse of the Leafs before being sent down to Pittsburgh; Smith managed a 14-game visit with Toronto before being sent down as well.

At the same time, Don Metz made his way back to the big league when he was called up from the Hornets on December 13, 1946. Though he had made a name for himself by scoring four goals and assisting on three others in the last four games of the 41/42 Cup, Don Metz's strength was as a backchecking, hard-nosed defensive forward, and in 46/47 he earned a Leaf starting position.

The Leafs of 46/47 led the league in goal-scoring (a rare turn for this two-way team) and vied all season with the Canadiens for first place. The Leafs were ahead by three points at mid-season, but ended up second, just six points back, in the spring. The balance of the 46/47 Leafs lineup is underlined by the fact that, while they led the league in scoring, only one player, Ted Kennedy, was a top-ten scorer. And Turk Broda was second only to Bill Durnan in goals-against.

The semifinals paired the Leafs with the fourth-place Red Wings, who had won only 22 games to Toronto's 31. The Leafs won the first game 3-2, but turned in one of their worst playoff performances in franchise history in game two, in which they outshot Detroit 29-24 but lost 9-1. Garth Boesch and Bill Barilko had a particularly poor game: the two defencemen were on the ice for six of the Red Wings' goals. From then on, however, the Leafs played like champions, cruising past Detroit with 4-1, 4-1 and 6-1 wins.

Montreal had defeated Boston in its semifinal pairing, which brought on the third playoff encounter between the Leafs and Canadiens in four seasons. It was, however, their first confrontation in the Stanley Cup, as the previous two meetings, in 43/44 and 44/45, had been in the semifinals. Montreal came out quickly at home, rocking the Leafs with a 6-0 defeat, but in game two the Leafs responded with a 4-0 win. Maurice Richard's explosive temper made a spectacular appearance in game two when he left Leaf defenceman Vic Lynn unconscious and bleeding on the Forum ice after smashing him on the head with his stick. Richard was fined $250 and suspended from game three for this outburst, and in his absence the Leafs took a 2-1 series lead with a 4-2 win at home. With Richard back, the

Canadiens continued to be stymied by Turk Broda, losing 2-1 to move a game away from surrendering the series. Elimination was staved off with a 3-1 win back in Montreal in game five, but Toronto secured its first post-war Cup victory with a 2-1 win on home ice.

Smythe consolidated his power at Maple Leaf Gardens in the fall of 1947 with a purchase of shares that made him both president of the Gardens and managing director of the Leafs. The Leaf victory the previous spring left him far from satisfied with the team's lineup. On November 2, 1947, only a few games into the new season, Smythe cut a blockbuster deal with the Blackhawks. The Chicago franchise had spent the better part of its history floundering, and there were few bright lights in the Blackhawks lineup. Foremost was center Max Bentley, a long-standing star who had won the last two scoring races while anchoring the "Pony Line" he formed with brother Doug and Bill Mosienko. Max Bentley was extremely marketable, but a one-for-one trade of stars would make no sense for the Blackhawks. Hawks general manager Bill Tobin needed a haul of players in exchange for Bentley, and the Leafs, coming off a Stanley Cup win, had enough surplus talent to cut a deal.

In the team's biggest trade to date, the Leafs sent five players to Chicago to get Bentley (and forward Cy Thomas, whose 14 games that season were his only NHL appearances). Smythe surrendered three young talents that had emerged during the war years—the entire forward line of Gus Bodnar, Bud Poile, and Gaye Stewart, all from Fort William, Ontario (now Thunder Bay) and so known as the "Flying Forts." Fort William was Squib Walker's home town, and securing the rights to these three young stars had been a considerable scouting coup.

In 45/46 Stewart had been runner-up for both the Hart and the Art Ross trophies, and had made the first All Star team. Like Poile and Bodnar, he'd had an indifferent 46/47 season as the Fort Line was broken up, although in the playoffs he came through with the second-highest Leaf offensive effort, behind Ted Kennedy. Bodnar had been sent down to Pittsburgh and only appeared in one Leaf playoff game; Poile appeared in seven of eleven playoff games as Day chose to go with Wally Stanowski when his injured knee allowed.

Smythe also surrendered two defencemen: Bob Goldham, who had been sent down to the Pittsburgh Hornets after being injured in 46/47, and Ernie Dickens, who had been left with the Hornets in 45/46. Smythe had been forced to add Goldham to the trade on the insistence of Blackhawks owner Jim Norris, and while he did so reluctantly, Goldham was expendable in a Leaf defence corps that had never been younger or tougher.

No great improvement resulted for the Blackhawks—through no fault of the Leafs shipped there—while Bentley proved a valued addition to the Leaf lineup. He was particularly effective on the point in the Leaf powerplay, and didn't have to bear the weight of the team's entire offensive effort the way he had in Chicago.

Other than the Bentley trade, the Leafs stuck with their championship lineup in 47/48. On the ice, the Leafs' goal production was down, as it was in the league overall, but Turk Broda became the only goaltender to win the Vezina while Bill Durnan was active in Montreal.

The Leafs won the regular season, five points ahead of Detroit, which had been building a contender with the addition of such new stars as Ted Lindsay and Gordie Howe, playing his second season. The Leafs opened their playoff drive with a semifinal series against fourth-place Boston. It took seventeen minutes and three seconds of overtime for the Leafs to win the opener 5-4; four goals by Kennedy and one by Bentley put the Leafs up by two games in a 5-3 win. A wild, brawling game followed in Boston, in which on-ice officials and coach Hap Day were attacked by Garden rowdies after the 5-1 Leaf win. A 3-2 Boston win extended the series, but the Leafs sent the Bruins packing in game five with a third-period goal by Kennedy that gave them a 3-2 win.

Detroit, meanwhile, had downed the Rangers in six games and advanced to a Cup showdown that proved the Red Wings were not yet ready to rule. Toronto swept them in four, with scores of 5-3, 4-2, 2-0 and 7-2.

Smythe considered it the greatest Leaf team to date, and after the commanding 47/48 Cup win, captain Syl Apps chose to retire. The charismatic star, who neither smoked, drank nor cussed beyond "By hum," was a model of the good-citizen athlete that would never be surpassed. He went out on top, a Stanley Cup champion who had just turned in the best season of his career, with 53 points in 55 games. Apps had been with the team since 36/37, and apart from his two-and-a-half season absence from 1943 to 1945, which began with a broken leg in January 1943 and was extended by his stint in the Canadian army, he had been a mainstay of the Leaf game.

The captaincy shifted appropriately to Ted Kennedy, who had become a Leaf as a 17-year-old in 1943 to help shore up the wartime gap left by Apps. Kennedy would be a charismatic team leader, another non-smoker and non-drinker who just couldn't get the hang of not cursing. But as a scorer and playmaker Apps still had to be replaced, and the retirement of the Leafs' other veteran forward, Nick Metz, strained the club's talent system, since they had traded away two young star centers, Bodnar and Poile, to get Max Bentley. In retrospect, Smythe felt that Apps's retirement placed too great a load on Kennedy and ended up shortening his career by several seasons.

After retiring to take a position with the department-store empire Eaton's, Apps apparently had a change of heart over the summer of 1948, and Smythe was sure he had talked him into coming back. But he did not show up at training camp as

promised, and Smythe learned that Hap Day had told Apps firmly that the captaincy had already been turned over to Kennedy; if Apps came back, he would no longer wear the "C." That ended any hope of an Apps comeback, and left Smythe and Day straining to find two new players to fill the skates of Apps and Metz.

Center Harry Taylor, who had played 9 games with Toronto in 46/47 before being sent down to Pittsburgh, now came up from the Hornets for 42 games, but it was his only significant spell in the majors. Smythe made a more long-term addition to his assembly of centers by trading defenceman Wally Stanowski to New York for Cal Gardner and an add-on to the deal, defenceman Bill Juzda, who turned out to be a pleasant surprise for Smythe. After seven games down in Pittsburgh the hard-hitting Juzda wound up earning a starting position in the talent-rich Leaf defence. Finally, Smythe called up from Pittsburgh for 29 games center Tod Sloan, a former star with the St. Mike's Majors. With the manpower problem at center addressed, Smythe decided to leave in Pittsburgh left-winger Sid Smith, who

Clarence "Hap" Day looks as happy as possible in this publicity photo taken on his wedding day. After starring with the Leafs in the 1920s and 1930s, Day took over as coach from Dick Irvin in 1940. He guided the Leafs to Stanley Cups wins in 41/42, 44/45, 46/47, 47/48 and 48/49.

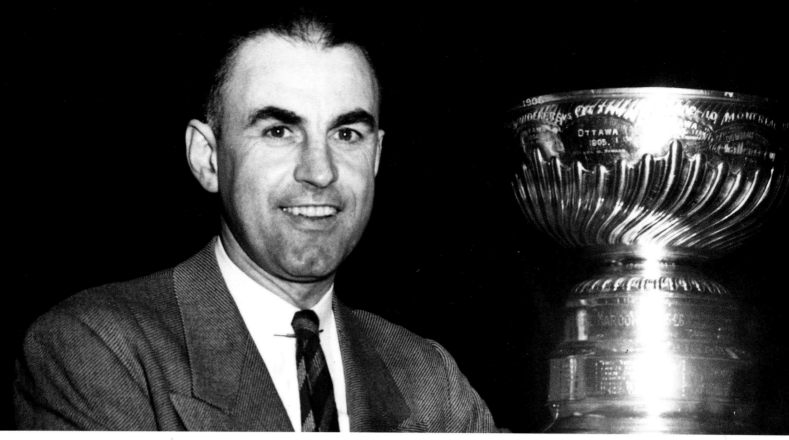

had spent half of the 47/48 season in the minors; in his stead Ray Timgren, a Toronto Marlboros graduate, played his first 36 games as a Leaf.

Statistically, it was not a good Leaf season. Wins dropped from 32 to 22 as the Leafs finished fourth. Scoring was down for the second straight season. From 209 goals back in 46/47, Toronto's offensive production in 48/49 slipped to 147, the second-worst output in the league; in the process the Leafs' goals per game had fallen from about 3.5 to 2.5. For the first time since 45/46, the Leafs had allowed more goals than they scored.

The Leafs struggled with new combinations up front resulting from the retirements of Apps and Nick Metz, and injuries caused regulars Cal Gardner, Howie Meeker, Vic Lynn, Joe Klukay and Garth Boesch to move in and out of the lineup. Hap Day even confirmed for the press that the Leafs were interested in acquiring Maurice Richard, a deal beyond consideration in Montreal. From this chaos, however, a strong club emerged in time for the playoffs, reinforcing Smythe's conviction that the only important thing about the regular season was that the team emerged from it with enough healthy players and a playoff berth from which to take a run at the Stanley Cup.

In the 48/49 playoffs the Leafs coalesced in a way few teams with such spotty regular seasons have managed. Detroit, the regular-season champions, fought through their semifinal with third-place Montreal, winning in seven games. Toronto might have finished nine points back of second-place Boston during the season, but the Leafs had a slight edge in their 12 meetings, winning six and tying one. It took Toronto only five games to get by the Bruins, and in the finals the Red Wings, so dominant in the regular season with 34 wins,

could not rise to the challenge of the focused Leafs. Toronto won the opener 3-2 in overtime and went on to sweep Detroit in four games for the second straight season. In the process, the Leafs became the first NHL team to win three consecutive Stanley Cups. (The Ottawa Silver Seven won it in four straight pre-NHL seasons from 1903 to 1906.) Their regular-season points percentage of 47.5 is the second lowest in the ranks of Stanley Cup winners, exceeded only by the 38.5 recorded by the unlikely Blackhawks of 37/38.

There were no sweeping changes in the Leaf lineup for 49/50. After the 48/49 Cup win, Don Metz retired to join his brother Nick in operating the family farm in Wilcox, Saskatchewan. Smythe did decide, however, he could live without Tod Sloan, whom he had once called the greatest amateur prospect he had ever seen. Though Sloan played 29 regular-season games in 48/49, he wasn't dressed for the playoffs (his regular-season participation put his name on the Stanley Cup). Smythe's eye was caught instead by Bob Solinger, the American league rookie of the year in 47/48, who was playing for the Cleveland Barons. To get him, Smythe sent Sloan, center Harry Taylor (who had appeared in one playoff game in 48/49) and Ray Ceresino to Cleveland, then assigned Solinger to Pittsburgh.

Fleming Mackell, a right-winger who had led the Ontario Junior league in scoring while at St. Mike's in 46/47, and who had played 11 regular-season and 9 playoff games in 48/49, moved toward a full-time NHL career when Hap Day inserted him in the lineup for 36 games. Center John McCormack, another St. Mike's product, also got his first regular Leaf shift, appearing in

34 games. And left-winger Sid Smith finally made the Leaf lineup full-time after winning the American league scoring title as a Hornet in 48/49.

One roster change arose from tragedy. At the first day of training camp in September 1949, Turk Broda's heir apparent, Hornets star Baz Bastien, lost an eye when struck by a screen shot from the point. When Broda needed to be relieved for two games in the new season, the Leafs brought in Al Rollins, who had been playing for Kansas City of the U.S. league.

The wisdom of Smythe and Day in leaving the championship Leaf lineup alone appeared suspect as the season progressed. The Leafs were devolving into a sub-par scoring team. The league moved to a 70-game season in 49/50 and the Leafs scored 176 goals while permitting 173. Detroit meanwhile continued to evolve into a dynamic postwar club with a powerful offence and stingy defence. Its "Production Line" of Gordie Howe, Sid Abel and Ted Lindsay swept the top three places in the scoring race as the Red Wings led the league in total goals (229), wins (37) and points (88). In Smythe's and Day's defence, Montreal, Toronto and New York, which took the three remaining playoff spots, were all low-scoring teams, while Boston and Chicago, which scored more than every club but Detroit, missed the playoffs. Toronto's regular season record, it must be said, was an improvement over the chaotic 48/49, and in this outing they finished third, three points behind Montreal. This set up a semifinal with Detroit, which very quickly turned into an ugly grudge match, with fists flailing and a constant parade in and out of the penalty box.

Having been swept by Toronto in the past two Stanley Cup finals, the Red Wings were eager to avenge their losses. In the opening game in Detroit, however, the Leafs blanked the Red Wings 5-0, and it did not help the tone of the series when Gordie Howe crashed into the boards after a collision with Ted Kennedy. No penalty resulted from the mishap, but Howe suffered a broken nose and cheekbone and had to undergo emergency surgery to relieve pressure on his brain from a broken blood vessel. The Red Wings had lost their star right-winger for the rest of the playoffs, and in game two the brawling resulted in 19 penalties as Detroit evened the series with a 3-1 win.

The players were on much better behaviour from then on, and the series seesawed between the two clubs. A 2-0 win gave Toronto a 3-2 series lead, but Detroit rebounded with a 4-0 win in Toronto to force a seventh game back in Detroit. No one could score in regulation time, and 8 minutes and 39 seconds into overtime Leo Reise converted a George Gee pass into the game and series winner, bringing the Leafs' Cup streak to an end before they could advance to the finals.

Conn Smythe's reaction to the near-miss of 49/50 was to delegate as much as he was capable. He promoted Hap Day to assistant general manager, and hired as the new Leaf coach Joe Primeau, star of the Kid Line of the 1930s, who had been masterfully coaching the St.

Mike's Majors and Toronto Senior Marlboros. A few key player changes were made. After the war the Rangers had tried splitting netminding duties between "Sugar" Jim Henry and Chuck Rayner, even though league regulations only required teams to carry one dressed-to-play goaltender. Smythe and Day now decided to use Rollins as their main netminder, with the 36-year-old Broda spelling him off. They executed one major trade, sending defenceman Vic Lynn and right-winger Bill Ezinicki to Boston to get standout defenceman Fern Flaman as well as utility center Phil Maloney.

The Leafs had lost defenceman Garth Boesch, who had decided to follow the Metz brothers' example and return to farming in Saskatchewan after four seasons with the Leafs. Defenceman Hugh Bolton and left-winger Dan Lewicki came up from the Senior Marlies, who had just won the national Senior championship, the Allan Cup, while being coached there by Primeau. And in one of the off-season's most important moves, Conn Smythe admitted to himself that he had made a huge mistake in dealing away Tod Sloan to get Bob Solinger. Solinger would have an off-and-on NHL career, while Sloan had immediately become a star with the Cleveland Barons. He tied for the scoring lead in the 1949/50 American league playoffs while the Leafs were tangling with the Red Wings, and in the middle of the playoffs he was sure he was going to be picked up by the Blackhawks, where ex-Leaf Charlie Conacher was coaching. He was happy to be free of the Leaf talent system, which he viewed as unhealthily monolithic, so he was somewhat distressed when he found his contract being reacquired by Smythe for 50/51.

With these few critical changes, the Leafs were a completely revitalized club in 50/51. Goal scoring, which had been sagging for the last few seasons, erupted dramatically. Only Detroit scored more goals, and five Leafs made the top-ten scorers' list—Max Bentley third, Ted Kennedy tied for fourth, Tod Sloan eighth, and Cal Gardner and Sid Smith tenth. In scoring 212 goals, the Leafs allowed only 138, as Al Rollins (who played 40 games to Broda's 30 with a personal GA of just 1.77) won the Vezina Trophy. Detroit won the regular season again, with 44 wins, and Toronto was close behind with 41. It looked like a two-team race, with the next-best effort, by Montreal, producing only 25 wins.

The playoffs, however, held their usual surprises. Montreal upset Detroit in six games to gain the finals. In the Toronto-Boston semifinal, things began badly for the Leafs, as they lost the opener at home 2-0, during which Rollins strained some knee ligaments and had to be replaced by Broda. Game two ended 1-1, as it was being played on a Sunday night and Toronto the Good's curfew law put an end to play at 11:45 p.m. The Leafs then found their form and, with Broda handling the series, downed the Bruins easily, winning 3-0, 3-1, 4-1 and 6-0.

The 50/51 Stanley Cup finals became a classic of Cup lore. The Leafs required just five games to defeat the Canadiens, but every game ended in overtime. Broda drew the starting assignment for the first two games, and with the series tied at one apiece Rollins was brought back. The Leafs were losing game five 2-1 in the dying minutes when Primeau pulled Rollins for an extra attacker. After Ted Kennedy won a face-off to the right of Canadiens netminder Gerry McNeil, the draw went back to Max Bentley at the point. He worked his way in and let a shot go that hit a skate in a tangle of legs in the slot. A second shot from that tangle by Sid Smith hit the left goalpost and ricocheted behind McNeil through the Canadiens' crease. Tod Sloan was waiting, and rapped in the tying goal that sent the game into overtime.

About two and a half minutes of overtime had been played when one of the most famous goals in hockey was scored. After a scramble around the Canadiens' goal involving wingers Harry Watson and Howie Meeker, Bill Barilko dashed in from his post at the blueline to intercept a clearing pass from Butch Bouchard intended for Maurice Richard. Abandoning your defensive assignment, above all in overtime in a Stanley Cup game, was a cardinal sin for a Leaf blueliner, and Barilko had come to exasperate Joe Primeau with his calculated gambles. Ted Kennedy has recalled how Primeau had told Barilko that he was going to get a rope with a hook so that he could haul Barilko back into position whenever he wandered. After Barilko's overtime dash sent the loose puck over the shoulder of the fallen McNeil to win the game and the series, Barilko and Primeau embraced on the ice. "You didn't want the hook on me that time!" Barilko crowed to his coach.

It was Barilko's third goal of the 50/51 playoffs. His first two had come in the Boston series: he had scored the only Leaf goal in the 1-1 tie in game two and another in the Leaf's 3-1 win in game four. He had played solid, even brilliant playoff hockey. It was his fifth consecutive spring in the NHL playoffs, and he had four Stanley Cups to show for it.

What followed was the stuff of legend. In August 1951, only weeks before Leaf training camp opened, a float-plane carrying Barilko back to Timmins from a fishing trip went missing north of Cochrane, Ontario. The plane, and Barilko's remains, were not found until the summer of 1962, not until the Leafs had won another Stanley Cup that spring. The Leafs endured an 11-season Cup drought in Hollywood Bill's absence. Once the Cup was recovered, so was Barilko.

There was more to the Leafs' Cup drought than the loss of Barilko, although Ted Kennedy believes the hard-hitting defenceman would have become an All Star had misfortune not intervened. Foremost was the Leafs' failure to adjust to the new flavour of the NHL. Detroit and Montreal were excelling with high-powered offences, and while the Leaf team of 50/51 was one of the most productive in terms of goals for and against in franchise history, the formula slipped away. Joe Primeau stayed as coach only two more seasons after winning the 50/51 Cup—it was said he could not stand having Smythe second-guessing him. And Smythe and Day executed a

number of trades that some felt served only to dismantle a great club with years of success still left in it.

Tod Sloan was particularly embittered by trade decisions, coming to feel that they broke up a championship club, and that his ensuing seasons with the Leafs were wasted years as far as his own career were concerned. Sent to Chicago in the summer of 1958 after angering Smythe by spearheading the stillborn players' association movement, Sloan was at least able to end his career with one more Stanley Cup win, as a Blackhawk in 60/61.

Johnny McCormack, whose relationship with Conn Smythe was soured by his decision to marry in mid-season (a no-no that had also landed Bill Ezinicki in hot water before he was dealt to Boston), was traded to Montreal after the 50/51 Cup win. After 51/52, left-winger Dan Lewicki, a star prospect, was sent down to Pittsburgh for two seasons and then dealt to the Rangers, where he immediately made the top-ten scorers' list, the second All Star team, and was runner-up in Lady Byng voting. On January 9, 1952, Fleming Mackell was dealt to Boston for defenceman Jim Morrison; there, Mackell played in three Stanley Cup finals with the Bruins.

Leaf wins fell from 41 to 29 in 51/52, and in the semifinal Detroit swept them in four games. Smythe and Day responded to the playoff debacle with another blockbuster trade with the Blackhawks. They gambled a bevy of first-class players—Al Rollins, Gus Mortson and Cal Gardner, as well as minor pro prospect Ray Hannigan—on one Blackhawk, goaltender Harry Lumley, who had been so impressive against the Leafs in the playoffs while a Red Wing. Lumley did play well for the Leafs, but the team never recovered from the trade, missing the playoffs altogether in 52/53.

At the start of 52/53, Joe Klukay was sold to the Bruins; two seasons later, the Leafs were cutting a deal to get him back. Max Bentley, once a scoring champion, was so discouraged by his performance that he simply quit the team in mid-52/53 and went home to Saskatchewan. The Leafs coaxed him back to complete the schedule, and after he produced only 23 points in 36 games Toronto traded him to New York, where he played his last season.

Perhaps the strangest deal of Toronto's lost decade was the offloading of defenceman Fern Flaman. Having acquired him from Boston in 50/51, after the 53/54 season, the Leafs dealt him back to Boston for center Dave Creighton, who was coming off a 40-point effort. But the Leafs simply sold Creighton to Chicago in November as part of a league-wide effort to revitalize the down-and-out Blackhawks (and ended up dealing for him back again in 1958). Though the Flaman deal was a dead-end trade for the Leafs, Boston made out like bandits. Flaman played in two Cup finals for the Bruins and made the second All Star team three times in a career that continued to 60/61.

At the same time, the Leafs were baffled by their inability to convert into Maple Leafs the prospects who were playing so well in Pittsburgh. The Hornets had become a perennial American league contender, losing a seven-game league final to Cleveland in 50/51, defeating Providence in six games in 51/52, and losing to Cleveland again in seven games in 52/53. Yet from those teams, only two players became Maple Leaf mainstays—defenceman Tim Horton and right-winger George Armstrong—and even they initially struggled to establish themselves in the NHL.

With less than two weeks to go in the 54/55 season, Hap Day shared his frustration with a reporter. "Frank Selke told me he thought the Canadiens were well stocked for years to come with the talent they have now on their minor teams. It looks that way too. But you never can tell. We've felt at times we were in the same position, with championship contenders from Pittsburgh right down the line. But when the time comes that you need a fellow to plug a hole, you suddenly discover the fellow you had in mind can't do the job in the NHL. That could happen in Montreal."

It didn't happen, as Montreal began a record streak of five straight Stanley Cup wins the next season. There was tremendous irony in the circumstances of the two clubs, as the architect of the Canadiens powerhouse, Frank Selke, had been run out of Maple Leaf Gardens by Smythe in 1946. In an apoplectic letter home to scout Squib Walker in the spring of 1943, following the Eddolls-Kennedy swap, Smythe had disparaged Selke's skills as a deal-maker, complaining that Selke was "a very poor judge of hockey players." On the basis of this outburst, Smythe himself appeared to be a very poor judge of managers. In his memoirs, Smythe conceded that Selke "did well" running the Canadiens, one of the great understatements ever unleashed on the sport. In Montreal, Selke built the greatest team the game may ever see, and while Smythe's own accomplishments with Day were considerable with the postwar Leafs, by the mid-1950s Smythe's hockey sense was fading while Selke's seemed as omniscient as ever.

The Leaf successes in the immediate postwar years were based on the club's mastery of playoff hockey. The club's regular-season performances were most often fair to good, or just good enough to make the playoff round. The talent Smythe had assembled attracted minimal accolades. Remarkably, in the course of winning three straight Stanley Cups from 46/47 to 48/49, with 12 victories in 14 final-series games, only one Maple Leaf, Turk Broda, was voted to an All Star team in those years.

After being dropped by the Red Wings in four games in the 54/55 semifinals, the Leafs were forced to contend with the retirement of captain Ted Kennedy, who had just won the Hart Trophy. Smythe admitted to himself that his hockey sense was fading and made good on his plans to leave the general manager's job to Day alone when he reached 60, which came in early 1955. Day struggled through two more increasingly poor Leaf seasons, then walked away from the job after 56/57 when he sensed Smythe's public lack of confidence in him.

The once-proud Leaf franchise, so ably resurrected by Day with the 41/42 Cup victory, awaited another saviour. When he arrived in 1958 in the guise of new coach and general manager Punch Imlach, another Leaf dynasty quickly emerged from the confounding misfortunes of the 1950s. ◯

Bill Barilko was wearing this jersey when he scored the overtime goal that won the Maple Leafs the 50/51 Stanley Cup. A few months later, Barilko went missing on a fishing trip when the float-plane he was aboard failed to return to his home town of Timmins, Ontario. The Leafs didn't win another Cup until the spring of 1962. Soon after that victory, the crash site and Barilko's body were discovered.

DETROIT RED WINGS
The Fifties

MASS PRODUCTION

UNDER GENERAL MANAGER JACK
ADAMS, THE DETROIT RED WINGS
EXEMPLIFIED EXCELLENCE IN THE
EARLY POSTWAR NHL GAME

For nine seasons, from 47/48 to 55/56, the Detroit Red Wings were a Stanley Cup fixture, playing in seven finals and winning four of them. They were also the kings of the regular season: from 48/49 to 54/55 they won seven straight regular-season titles. Only the Montreal Canadiens have ever come close to challenging the Red Wings feat, as they managed five season titles in a row from 57/58 to 61/62. From 74/75 to 81/82 the Canadiens won eight straight Norris division titles, but in overall league play the late-1970s Canadiens were regularly denied the top spot by the Philadelphia Flyers and the New York Islanders—the best that celebrated team could do was three straight, from 75/76 to 77/78.

Detroit's legendary team differed significantly from the great Canadiens clubs of the late 1950s and late 1970s in that it was not truly one team. A close look at the winning streak reveals a club in transition, with age and experience rapidly giving way to youth. Only six players on the 49/50 Cup team were still around when Detroit won its last Cup to date, just five seasons later, in 54/55. In comparison, twelve Montreal Canadiens played on all five Cup-winning teams from 55/56 to 59/60, with two more playing on four of them. Part of the marvel of this Detroit streak, then, is that the Red Wings were able to pull off such massive rebuilding and maintain a winning formula.

Ironically, it was also this penchant for ruthless roster shuffling that brought the dynasty to an abrupt end. General manager Jack Adams figured that a winning hockey club had about five years in it, and Detroit's record would pretty much back him up: the core team of the Motor City era lasted about four seasons, from 51/52 to 54/55, during which it won three Cups. However, it might have won more had Adams not gutted it with a blockbuster trade to Boston,

RIGHT: Tony Leswick, Terry Sawchuk and Ted Lindsay congratulate each other on their "perfect" Stanley Cup win of 51/52: eight straight victories, over Toronto and then Montreal.
BELOW: the team jacket crest of Terry Sawchuk celebrates Detroit's first postwar Stanley Cup win, in 49/50

CHAMPIONS | **56**

then rubbed salt in his own wounds by dealing away two franchise players in response to the players' association drive of 1957. Detroit never recovered, and Red Wings fans have never ceased looking back, now for some 40 years, to a time when their club had no equal.

The architect of the Red Wings was "Jolly Jack" Adams; the same age as his nemesis, Leaf impresario Conn Smythe, the Fort William, Ontario native had broken into the major professional game with the Toronto Arenas of the NHL in 17/18, the league's first season. As a right-winger, Adams appeared in eight games and didn't score once. While he did contribute a goal in the first game of NHL championship, a two-game total-goal affair against the Canadiens, Adams did not travel west with the Arenas when they defeated the Vancouver Millionaires in the Stanley Cup match against the top Pacific Coast Hockey Association team.

After another season with the Arenas, Adams went west to play in the Pacific Coast league for Vancouver. He excelled in the seven-man western game, leading the league in scoring in 21/22 with 25 goals in 24 games. Although the Millionaires lost to the Toronto St. Patricks in the Stanley Cup final that year, Adams was a series standout with six goals in five games. The St. Pats signed him for the very next season, and Adams played with them for four years before moving over to the Ottawa Senators for 26/27.

Adams scored only 5 goals in 40 games as a Senator, but he was able to end his professional career that spring as a Stanley Cup champion when Ottawa defeated Boston. It was the first Cup championship that didn't require a playoff between the NHL and a professional western league, as the western game had folded after 1925/26 and player contracts had been bought up en masse by the latest NHL franchises. In 26/27 the Detroit Cougars, New York Rangers and Chicago Blackhawks brought the NHL to ten teams.

While playing in the 26/27 Cup finals, Adams caught wind of the fledgling Detroit club's need for fresh talent behind the bench and in the front office to avoid collapse. He pitched himself as their saviour, and the very next season, he joined the Cougars as coach and general manager. The team con-

tinued to stumble, missing the playoffs four times in its first five seasons. Renamed the Falcons in 30/31, they made the quarterfinals in 31/32. The franchise's fortunes truly improved when Chicago grain magnate Jim Norris bought the team in 1932, changed the name to the Red Wings and gave Adams the financial backing necessary to create a contender. In Norris's second year as owner, Detroit reached the 33/34 Cup finals after finishing on top of the American Division, but lost the final to the Blackhawks, who had finished seven points behind them. In 35/36, Detroit ended an eight-season drought in the league, in which the team with the best regular-season record could not convert the performance into a Cup win. The Red Wings won both the regular season and the Stanley Cup in 35/36 and 36/37, then lost their way. The team won only 12 of 48 games in 37/38, and struggled for the next few seasons to reclaim its greatness.

In wartime, the Red Wings were able to convert mostly indifferent regular seasons into three straight appearances in the Cup finals from 40/41 to 42/43. After winning 21 of 48 games, Detroit met the Bruins in the 40/41 Cup finals, but went down in four straight. In 41/42, the Red Wings won only 19 of 48 games, but made the finals against the Leafs and almost stole the series. Leading three games to none, Adams and the Red Wings fell apart in game four. Though they only lost the game 4-3, penalty calls late in the third period caused the volcanic Adams to take to the ice after the last whistle and punch referee Mel Harwood. The assault got Adams banished for the rest of the series, and the Leafs regrouped to win three straight games and the Cup.

If nothing else, the fiasco of game four showed how instrumental Adams was to his team's performance. With Adams back for 42/43, the Red Wings led the league with 25 wins in a closely contested season and downed the Bruins in four to win their first Cup in six seasons, albeit with star defenceman Ebbie Goodfellow spelling off Adams as player-coach. In 44/45 the Red Wings were back in the finals again, this time in a defensive gridlock against Toronto that produced only 18 goals in 7 games. Detroit trailed three games to none, then recovered to force a seventh game in a reversal of fortune that recalled the 41/42 final against the Leafs. But with a 2-1 win in Detroit the Leafs again prevailed, in the last championship to be played in wartime. When hostilities ceased that summer, the Red Wings, the Leafs, and the other four NHL clubs to have survived the war, embarked on rebuilding programs designed to put behind them the makeshift rosters of wartime and adjust to the new game introduced by the two-line offside of 43/44.

The Red Wings came out of wartime to begin building a powerful club with a handful of veterans, who gave it stability while the professional game was caught up in a tremendous youth drive. That drive was inspired by two events: the end of the Second World War, which

Terry Sawchuk and Sid Abel • 51/52

RED WINGS
scoring
47/48 to 55/56

GOALS PER GAME

3.5
3.0
2.5
2.0
1.5

| 47/ | 48/ | 49/ | 50/ | 51/ | 52/ | 53/ | 54/ | 55/ |
| 48 | 49 | 50 | 51 | 52 | 53 | 54 | 55 | 56 |

■ *Detroit goals-against*
▭ *League-leading GA*
▬ *Detroit goals-for*
▢ *League-leading scoring*
─ *League scoring average*
53/
54
Stanley Cup win

Detroit Red Wings

The Dynasty of the Early 1950s

Featuring the players and management who participated in Detroit's Stanley Cup victories of 1949/50, 1951/52, 1953/54 and 1954/55

GENERAL MANAGER
1. Jack Adams (from 1927/28)

COACHES
1. Tommy Ivan
2. Jimmy Skinner

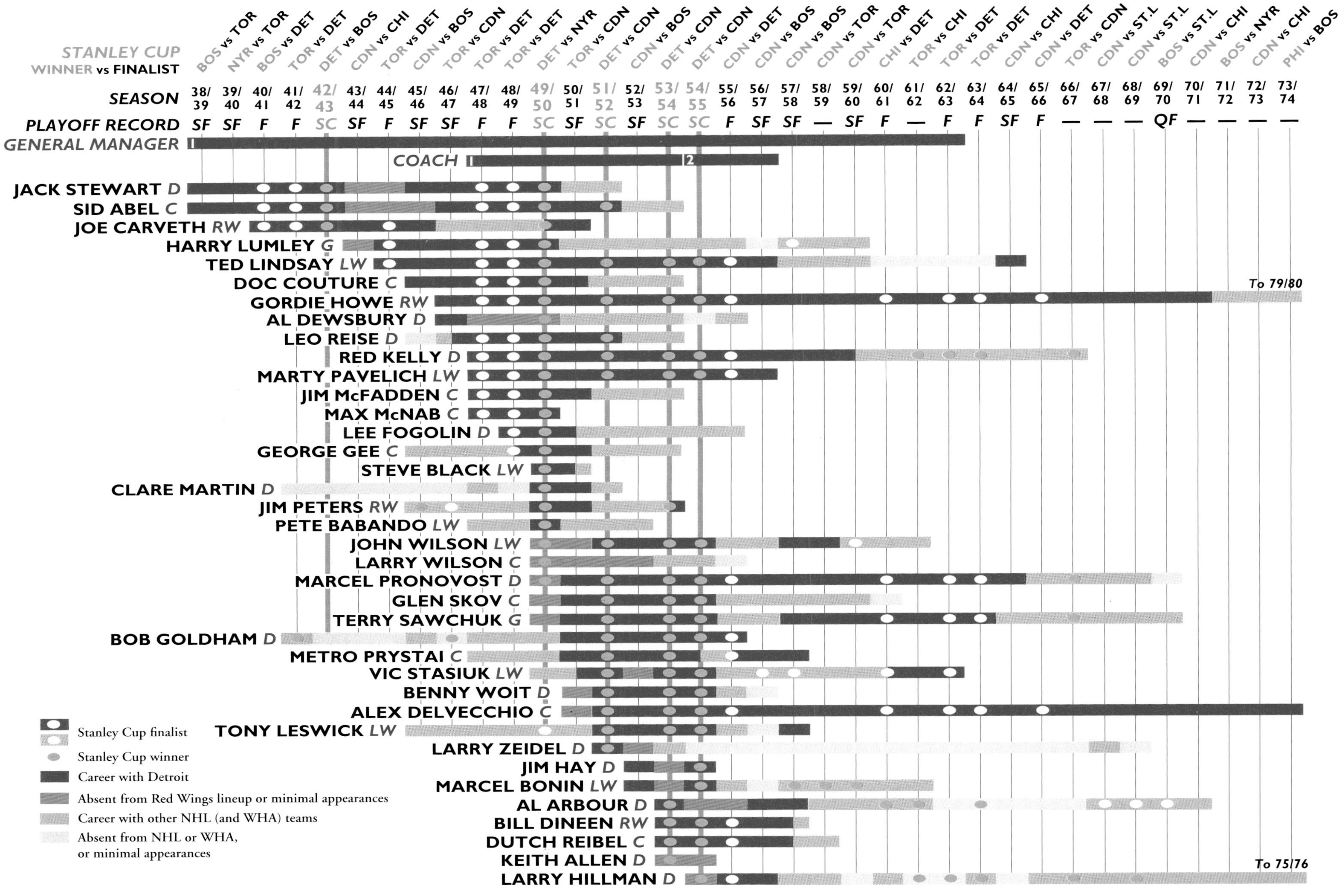

STANLEY CUP
WINNER vs FINALIST
BOS vs TOR, NYR vs TOR, BOS vs DET, TOR vs DET, DET vs BOS, CDN vs CHI, TOR vs DET, CDN vs BOS, TOR vs CDN, TOR vs DET, TOR vs DET, DET vs NYR, TOR vs CDN, DET vs CDN, CDN vs BOS, DET vs CDN, DET vs CDN, CDN vs DET, CDN vs BOS, CDN vs BOS, CDN vs TOR, CDN vs TOR, CHI vs DET, TOR vs CHI, TOR vs DET, TOR vs DET, CDN vs CHI, CDN vs DET, TOR vs CDN, CDN vs ST.L, CDN vs ST.L, BOS vs ST.L, CDN vs CHI, BOS vs NYR, CDN vs CHI, PHI vs BOS
SEASON
38/39, 39/40, 40/41, 41/42, 42/43, 43/44, 44/45, 45/46, 46/47, 47/48, 48/49, 49/50, 50/51, 51/52, 52/53, 53/54, 54/55, 55/56, 56/57, 57/58, 58/59, 59/60, 60/61, 61/62, 62/63, 63/64, 64/65, 65/66, 66/67, 67/68, 68/69, 69/70, 70/71, 71/72, 72/73, 73/74
PLAYOFF RECORD
SF SF F F SC SF F SF SF F F SC SF SC SF SC SC F SF SF — SF F — F F SF F — — — QF — — — —
GENERAL MANAGER 1
COACH 1 2
JACK STEWART D
SID ABEL C
JOE CARVETH RW
HARRY LUMLEY G
TED LINDSAY LW
DOC COUTURE C
GORDIE HOWE RW
To 79/80
AL DEWSBURY D
LEO REISE D
RED KELLY D
MARTY PAVELICH LW
JIM McFADDEN C
MAX McNAB C
LEE FOGOLIN D
GEORGE GEE C
STEVE BLACK LW
CLARE MARTIN D
JIM PETERS RW
PETE BABANDO LW
JOHN WILSON LW
LARRY WILSON C
MARCEL PRONOVOST D
GLEN SKOV C
TERRY SAWCHUK G
BOB GOLDHAM D
METRO PRYSTAI C
VIC STASIUK LW
BENNY WOIT D
ALEX DELVECCHIO C
TONY LESWICK LW
LARRY ZEIDEL D
JIM HAY D
MARCEL BONIN LW
AL ARBOUR D
BILL DINEEN RW
DUTCH REIBEL C
KEITH ALLEN D
LARRY HILLMAN D
To 75/76
Stanley Cup finalist
Stanley Cup winner
Career with Detroit
Absent from Red Wings lineup or minimal appearances
Career with other NHL (and WHA) teams
Absent from NHL or WHA, or minimal appearances

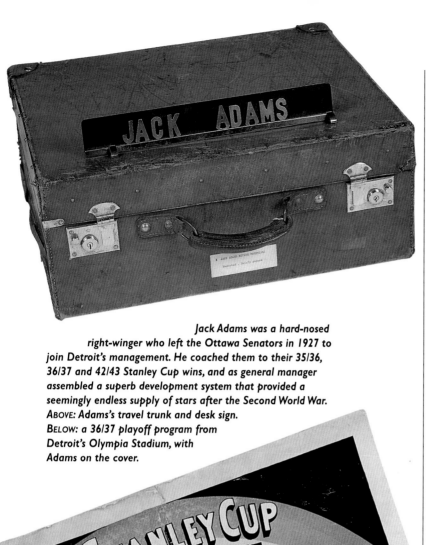

brought an end to drafts and military service for players in Canada and the United States, and the arrival of the two-line offside, which created the modern high-speed head-manning game. That game brought new defensive and offensive roles to all players on the ice, and youth, in addition to having the advantage of fresh legs, also were trained in their amateur days to play in the new style.

Only three players from the 44/45 team were still around when Detroit won the Cup in 49/50, just five seasons later: right-winger Joe Carveth, who had joined the Red Wings in 40/41, goaltender Harry Lumley, and left-winger Ted Lindsay, a St. Michael's College Junior graduate who joined the lineup at 19 in 44/45. (Regulars Sid Abel and Jack Stewart were temporarily absent in 44/45.) The Red Wings had not been an offensive machine before 43/44—players on the top-ten scorers' list were rare. And while the club had been strong defensively, no Red Wings goaltender had ever won the Vezina, introduced in 1927 and awarded to the goaltender on the team with the fewest total goals against. The club had enjoyed first-class goaltending from Johnny Mowers from 40/41 to 42/43, the three straight seasons in which it reached the finals, and when Mowers departed for the Royal Canadian Air Force in 1943, the club appeared to have a transitional netminding star in Joe Turner, who was named a first-team All Star with Detroit's American league farm club, the Indianapolis Capitols, when the Caps won the league championship in 42/43. Mowers, a Canadian, decided to join the U.S. Marines, and the game lost a future great when he was killed in action in northern Europe in early 1945. The Red Wings, though, seemed to have an indefatigable supply of goaltending talent. In 43/44, they brought in 17-year-old Harry Lumley for a three-game inspection, and in 44/45 the teenager called "Apple Cheeks" was a starting NHL goaltender and a standout in the Stanley Cup finals. And before the war was even over, a 14-year-old prospect from Winnipeg named Terry Sawchuk had come down for an assessment that led to his being signed by Adams and moved to Ontario to play Junior hockey.

The Red Wings quickly began assembling a dynamic new lineup in front of Lumley. In addition to the ferocious Lindsay, a left-winger right out of the Adams mould whose father, Bert Lindsay, had tended goal in the PCHA and the NHL's forerunner, the National Hockey Association, Adams brought in two young Saskatchewan prospects in 1945/46: 20-year-old center Doc Couture from Saskatoon, who split his season between Detroit and Indianapolis, and 17-year-old center Gordie Howe from Floral, who was assigned to the Omaha Knights of the

Jack Adams was a hard-nosed right-winger who left the Ottawa Senators in 1927 to join Detroit's management. He coached them to their 35/36, 36/37 and 42/43 Stanley Cup wins, and as general manager assembled a superb development system that provided a seemingly endless supply of stars after the Second World War.
ABOVE: Adams's travel trunk and desk sign.
BELOW: a 36/37 playoff program from Detroit's Olympia Stadium, with Adams on the cover.

DETROIT RED WINGS 1947/48–55/56

Season	Finish	Record (W-L-T)	Points %	Awards (winners & runners-up)	All-Stars	Playoffs
47/48	2nd	30-18-12	60.0	CALDER: McFadden VEZINA: Lumley RU	1ST TEAM: Quackenbush (D), Stewart (D), Lindsay (LW)	Lost SC final 4-0 to Toronto
48/49	1st	34-19-7	62.5	HART: Abel LADY BYNG: Quackenbush VEZINA: Lumley RU	1ST TEAM: Quackenbush (D), Stewart (D), Abel (C) 2ND TEAM: Howe (RW), Lindsay (LW)	Lost SC final 4-0 to Toronto
49/50	1st	37-19-14	62.9	ART ROSS: Lindsay, Abel RU LADY BYNG: Kelly RU VEZINA: Lumley RU	1ST TEAM: Abel (C), Lindsay (LW) 2ND TEAM: Reise (D), Kelly (D), Howe (RW)	Won SC final 4-3 over New York
50/51	1st	44-13-13	72.1	ART ROSS: Howe CALDER: Sawchuk LADY BYNG: Kelly VEZINA: Sawchuk RU	1ST TEAM: Sawchuk (G), Kelly (D), Howe (RW), Lindsay (LW) 2ND TEAM: Reise (D), Abel (C)	Lost SC semifinal 4-2 to Montreal
51/52	1st	44-14-12	71.4	HART: Howe ART ROSS: Howe, Lindsay RU LADY BYNG: Kelly RU VEZINA: Sawchuk	1ST TEAM: Sawchuk (G), Kelly (D), Howe (RW), Lindsay (LW)	Won SC final 4-0 over Montreal
52/53	1st	36-16-18	64.3	HART: Howe ART ROSS: Howe, Lindsay RU LADY BYNG: Kelly VEZINA: Sawchuk	1ST TEAM: Sawchuk (G), Kelly (D), Howe (RW), Lindsay (LW)	Lost SC semifinal 4-2 to Boston
53/54	1st	37-19-14	62.9	HART: Kelly RU ART ROSS: Howe CALDER: Reibel RU LADY BYNG: Kelly VEZINA: Sawchuk RU NORRIS: Kelly	1ST TEAM: Kelly (D), Howe (RW), Lindsay (LW) 2ND TEAM: Sawchuk (G)	Won SC final 4-3 over Montreal
54/55	1st	42-17-11	67.9	VEZINA: Sawchuk NORRIS: Kelly RU	1ST TEAM: Kelly (D) 2ND TEAM: Sawchuk (G), Goldham (D)	Won SC final 4-3 over Montreal
55/56	2nd	30-24-16	54.3	ART ROSS: Howe RU CALDER: Hall LADY BYNG: Reibel VEZINA: Hall RU	1ST TEAM: Lindsay (LW) 2ND TEAM: Hall (G), Kelly (D), Howe (RW)	Lost SC final 4-1 to Montreal

U.S. league with 19-year-old defenceman Al Dewsbury from the Toronto Young Rangers.

Adams augmented the dividends of his first-class scouting and amateur development system with deal-making. Though he cultivated a reputation for savvy trades, they didn't always work out. For 46/47, Adams dealt Joe Carveth to the Bruins for left-winger Roy Conacher. A star with Boston when they won the 38/39 and 40/41 Stanley Cups, Conacher was returning from four years in the Canadian army. After a season in Detroit he decided (as he put it) that it was time to get a real job, and refused to report to Detroit for

47/48. When he balked at being traded to New York, Conacher was sold to Chicago on November 1, 1947, and Adams ended up trading Calum MacKay to Montreal to get Carveth back in November 1949. Another star acquisition with no long-term payoff was playmaking center Billy Taylor, brought from the Leafs for 46/47. Taylor set a league record for assists and finished third in the scoring race as a Red Wing, but was unloaded to Boston after only one season. Not every deal was a washout, though. Twenty-four-year-old defenceman Leo Reise (whose father, Leo Sr., played for the Hamilton Tigers, New York Rangers and New York

It's over: Rangers defenceman Allan Stanley and goaltender Chuck Rayner confront the heartbreak of Pete Babando's game seven overtime goal, which won the Red Wings the 1949/50 Stanley Cup. Pete Babando, who is out of the picture, was fed the puck from a faceoff by George Gee, who is between Stanley and Rayner. Detroit's Doc Couture (18), playing in his third straight Cup final, finally sees victory.

Americans) was picked up from Chicago in 46/47 and provided solid blueline skills.

Perhaps Adams's most important acquisition was someone to take over from him behind the bench in 47/48. Tommy Ivan had been a key figure in the powerful hockey program at the army training base in Cornwall, Ontario, during the war, and came out of the military to coach Detroit's U.S. league farm team in Omaha in 45/46. The next season he moved up to run the Capitols in Indianapolis. The team played in the Western Division, which was far more competitive than the Eastern Division. Indianapolis compiled a 33-18-13 record, scoring more goals than any other team in the league. Its 79 points would have put them comfortably in second place in the East, but in the West they missed third place, the final playoff spot, by one point. Ivan nonetheless had proven his worth, and he moved up to Detroit to take charge of the Red Wings.

Ivan was a rarity in that he had never actually played in the NHL, a head injury having cut his own career short. At the time, Boston was being coached by Dit Clapper, Toronto by Hap Day, Montreal by Dick Irvin, and Chicago by Johnny Gottselig and then Charlie Conacher. Proven NHL veterans who could speak to players from experience were the norm; that someone could run a tier-one professional team based on general smarts was unheard of. Ivan also defied his military background by being a player's coach, someone who could empathize with their lot and offer a kind and encouraging word when required. He was the antithesis of Punch Imlach, who had served in Cornwall with him and would be seen as one of the game's great taskmasters when he took over the Leafs in 1958.

There was a good cop, bad cop quality to the Red Wings management, with Jolly Jack Adams providing the terror and Ivan the positive reinforcement. Between the two of them, Detroit was made a contender. With Ivan's arrival, Detroit appeared in three straight Cup finals. The team was fourth overall with 55 points the season before he took control; in 47/48, his first season in charge, Ivan squeezed out eight more wins for a total of 72 points and moved the Red Wings into second. The team blended tried-and-true veterans with a large roster of young recruits. Up front he had the "Production Line," centered by veteran captain Sid Abel, with youngsters Ted Lindsay on the left and Gordie Howe on the right. In goal was Harry Lumley, and his defence was first rate. The experienced Bill Quackenbush and Jack Stewart were accompanied by the previous season's addition, Leo Reise, and a fresh signing, Leonard "Red" Kelly from the St. Michael's College Majors, which was part of the Leaf farm system (see page 96). The Majors had just lost the Memorial Cup finals and the Leafs didn't think Kelly had an NHL future. It was a tremendous oversight by Toronto, who had also missed out on Lindsay when he was playing for the Majors. Kelly arrived in Detroit just as Doug Harvey was appearing in the Canadiens lineup,

and the pair would be the most productive defencemen offensively through the 1950s. Kelly and Bill Gadsby, who was playing in Chicago and then New York, were the only two defencemen to make the top-ten scorers' list in the decade.

Kelly had just turned 20 when he made the Red Wings, and another two seasons would pass before he ignited as an offensive threat. Gordie Howe was similarly slow to establish himself as a marquee player: like Kelly, his breakthrough season was 49/50. Lindsay had already blossomed in 46/47, his third season, and Lumley, though only 21, was starting his fourth full season. While he had already proved his worth back in the 44/45 finals, when he was just 18, the 47/48 season provided him with his regular-season breakthrough: his average fell from 3.06 to 2.46 (as he missed the Vezina by just five goals) and his shutouts improved from three to seven.

In 46/47, two Red Wings were selected as second-team All Stars—old hands Jack Stewart and Bill Quackenbush on defence. In 47/48, Detroit took three of the first-team positions, with Stewart and Quackenbush joined by Lindsay, who led the league with 33 goals and finished ninth in the scoring race, having only 19 assists. Lindsay's performance was telling—his future as a scoring star depended on his linemates Abel and Howe scoring more, which would give him more assists. Once this trio was firing on all cylinders, the Red Wings would be virtually unstoppable.

They were still stoppable in 47/48, though. It took them six games to eliminate the Rangers, who squeezed into the final playoff spot four points ahead of a momentarily dishevelled Canadiens squad. Now they were facing the Leafs, regular-season winners and defending Cup champions. The polished Leafs over-

whelmed the Red Wings, executing a four-game sweep that concluded with a 7-2 shellacking on Detroit's home ice. Center Jimmy McFadden, at 27 a rather mature rookie who had just won the Calder, was a playoff standout, finishing fourth in post-season scoring just behind the team's top producer, right-winger Pete Horeck, who had been acquired from Chicago in 46/47. And defenceman Red Kelly had turned in the next best Detroit effort, with five points. But Detroit's big guns failed to hit their targets as the Leaf checking game shut down the Production Line. Lindsay produced three goals in ten games, Howe one and Abel none. The line was outproduced by three defencemen, Kelly, Reise and Stewart, who combined for six goals. And the team had surrendered 30 goals in 10 games, compared to 20 in 9 by Toronto. It was a young team, though, with much promise. Marty Pavelich had just completed his first season on left wing, and so had Max McNab, Jim

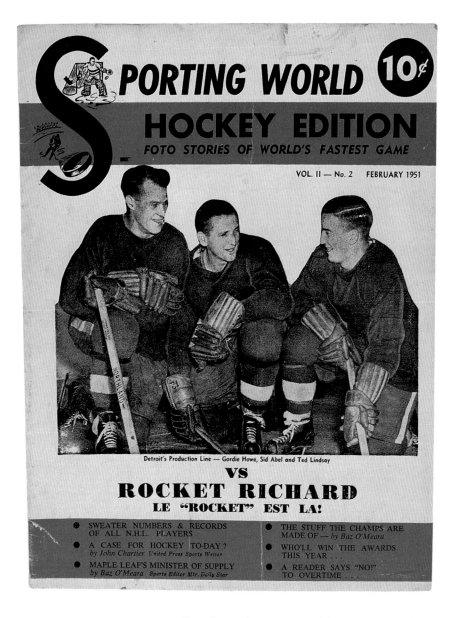

SPORTING WORLD 10¢

HOCKEY EDITION
FOTO STORIES OF WORLD'S FASTEST GAME

VOL. II — No. 2   FEBRUARY 1951

Detroit's Production Line — Gordie Howe, Sid Abel and Ted Lindsay

VS
ROCKET RICHARD
LE "ROCKET" EST LA!

- SWEATER NUMBERS & RECORDS OF ALL N.H.L. PLAYERS
- A CASE FOR HOCKEY TO-DAY?
  by John Chartier United Press Sports Writer
- MAPLE LEAF'S MINISTER OF SUPPLY
  by Baz O'Meara Sports Editor Mtr. Daily Star
- THE STUFF THE CHAMPS ARE MADE OF — *by Baz O'Meara*
- WHO'LL WIN THE AWARDS THIS YEAR . . .
- A READER SAYS "NO!" TO OVERTIME . . .

The rivalry between Detroit and Montreal may have been the greatest in NHL history, fuelled by proud, high-scoring personalities. ABOVE: the Red Wings Production Line of Gordie Howe, Sid Abel and Ted Lindsay takes on Maurice Richard, according to Sporting World in February 1951. The line had swept the top of the scoring race ahead of Richard in 49/50. In 50/51, Howe outscored Richard 43 goals to 42 and beat him to the scoring title, with 20 points to spare.

second-best goals-against effort. Abel won the Hart Trophy and joined defencemen Jack Stewart and Bill Quackenbush on the first All Star team, while Howe and Lindsay made the second team.

In the semifinals, the Red Wings had their hands full with the Canadiens, who had finished the season strongly back in third. Almost 45 minutes of overtime were needed for Detroit to win the opener at home, and it took the full seven games for the Red Wings to prevail. This brought on another final against the Leafs, who had struggled through the regular season into fourth and had won five and tied two against Detroit in their 12 meetings. The Leafs showed the franchise's instincts for playoff hockey were still knife sharp. To the dismay of their fans and management, the Red Wings were swept in four by the Leafs again.

Adams decided he could not stand pat after two straight finals losses to Toronto. In August, he made a shake-up trade, sending his veteran defenceman Bill Quackenbush to Boston with right-winger Pete Horeck. Quackenbush had been with the team since 42/43, and in addition to making the first All Star team last season had won the Lady Byng Trophy after playing all 60 regular-season games without a single penalty. Horeck had been acquired in 46/47 from Chicago for left-winger Adam Brown, and in 11 playoff games in 48/49 he had plainly disappointed, held to one goal and one assist, after leading the team in playoff points, with ten, in 47/48. Horeck had also sinned by serving four minutes' worth of penalties in the final series, during which the Leafs scored three goals. In the second game Sid Smith scored twice while Horeck was off serving a minor, and in the deciding game the Leafs had been able to tie the score while Horeck was serving another one.

In return for Quackenbush and Horeck, Adams received a slate of Bruins veterans. Defenceman Clare Martin, approaching 28, had first played with Boston in 41/42, but had spent 48/49 with Hershey in the American league. Right-winger Jim Peters, who was turning 27, was a Montreal native who had been acquired from the Canadiens by the Bruins in 47/48. Finally, left-winger Pete Babando had just completed his second NHL season at age 24. Also included in the deal was prospect Lloyd Durham, who never made the NHL. A few other minor adjustments were made. George Gee had proved his worth in 48/49, and with Sid Abel, Jim McFadden, Doc Couture and Max McNab around, Detroit had no shortage of players who could play center. As a result, Bud Poile was sold to Boston. Finally, in November, Adams brought the old Roy Conacher trade full circle by reacquiring right-winger Joe Carveth, whom he had sent to Boston for Conacher in 1946.

Despite the complexity of these deals, the essential Red Wings team was unaffected, and in 49/50 it took flight, winning 37 and tying 14 in the new 70-game season to finish 11 points ahead of Montreal. It again pro-

Conacher and Jimmy McFadden at center, making for three rookies at the pivot point of forward lines.

The Red Wings returned to play in 48/49 with almost no changes. But less than two weeks into the season "Trader Jack" was cutting a deal, sending center Jim Conacher, left-winger Bep Guidolin and defence-man Doug McCaig to Chicago for two more experienced centers: Bud Poile, who had broken in with Toronto in 42/43, and George Gee, who had made the Blackhawks in 45/46. In addition, Lee Fogolin, who had subbed for Stewart for two games when he was injured in the 47/48 finals, came up from Indianapolis for 43 games on the Detroit defence. Otherwise, Adams and Ivan went with the same team that had fallen short against Toronto. And in this new season, the Production Line began to produce. Although Howe was limited to 40 games by knee surgery, the line was together long enough to demonstrate their true potential. Abel and Lindsay each produced 54 points; by outscoring his winger 28 to 26, Abel finished one position ahead of Lindsay, in third, in the scoring race. The Red Wings comfortably finished first overall, nine points ahead of Boston. They outscored Boston, which had the second-best output, by 17 goals, and posted the

duced the most goals and allowed the second fewest against. The Production Line locked up the top of the scoring race in the order of Lindsay, Abel and Howe. No forward line had ever swept the first-team All Star selections when Montreal's Punch Line of Elmer Lach, Toe Blake and Maurice Richard did it in 44/45, and no line had done it since. The Production Line came awfully close in 49/50, with Abel and Lindsay making the first team, but Richard bumped Howe down to the second team after comfortably leading the rest of the league with 43 goals, 8 more than Howe. In 50/51 Howe was able to supplant Richard and join Lindsay on the first team, after edging Richard 43 to 42 in goals and leading him in the scoring race by 20 points, but Abel was left back on the second team when Milt Schmidt of Boston polled the most votes at center. Howe and Lindsay were back on the first team together in 51/52, 52/53, 53/54 and 56/57, but Abel's career in Detroit ended in 51/52 without a return to any All Star team.

It was appropriate that in 51/52, when Abel was 34 and completing his final Detroit season, an original Punch Liner, Elmer Lach, would secure the first-team berth at center. Montreal and Detroit were tremendous rivals in these years, and they guarded their records jealously and ferociously. Particularly sacred was Richard's achievement of 50 goals in one season, set in 44/45. Howe, his rival for the league's right-wing bragging rights, came close to the mark in 51/52, with 47, and then seemed certain of matching or exceeding Richard in 52/53, when he had 49 with two games to go. In the second-last game, against Chicago, Howe was held scoreless as the Blackhawks won, 4-3. The Canadiens and the Red Wings then met for their final match of the season. The only thing that mattered that night for Detroit players was setting up Howe; the only thing that mattered for Montreal players was stopping him. Richard's teammates came through for him: Howe was kept off the scoreboard as Montreal won 2-1. By then the league consensus, as expressed in All Star voting, was that Howe was the greater player—he also won the Hart Trophy that year in addition to the scoring race. But Richard's record had held, and that's what mattered in Montreal.

In 49/50, when the Production Line ruled the league, Detroit could do no wrong. After dominating

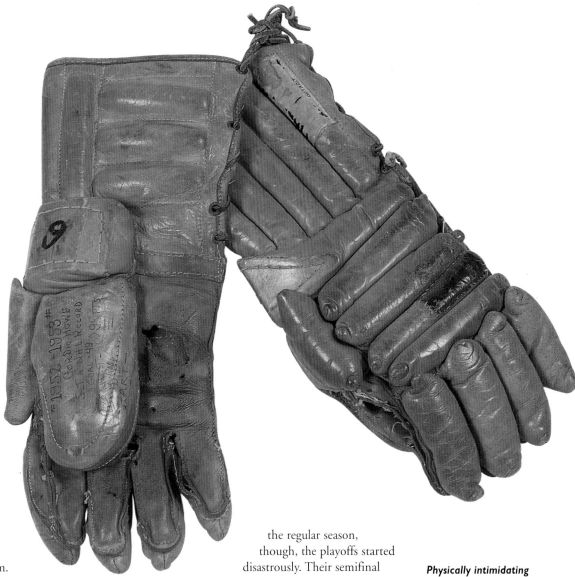

the regular season, though, the playoffs started disastrously. Their semifinal opponent was Toronto, which had given them so much grief over the years. In their opening match in Detroit, Toronto blanked the Wings 5-0, but far worse was the outcome of a collision between Howe and Ted Kennedy. Howe was rushed to hospital with facial fractures and a concussion and had to undergo surgery to remove life-threatening pressure on his brain. Staggered in their opening game, the Red Wings now had to face the rest of the playoffs without their greatest star.

Down three games to two in their 49/50 semifinal, Detroit regrouped with a 4-0 win at Maple Leaf Gardens that brought on a showdown seventh game back at the Olympia. The teams played a thrilling scoreless match, and it was left to defenceman Leo Reise to knock a ten-footer past Broda at 8:39 of overtime and send Detroit into the finals against an inspired Rangers crew.

Detroit was not through with Toronto—at least, not with Maple Leaf Gardens. The Rangers' home ice, Madison Square Garden, was booked by the circus (a consistent annoyance for the Rangers at playoff time), and so the club chose Toronto as its "home" site. The fourth-place Rangers had upset the second-place Canadiens 4-1 in their semifinal. After finishing last

Physically intimidating and ambidextrous, Gordie Howe was a 1950s scoring machine; either of the above gloves could deliver the power and accuracy of his shot. He won four straight scoring titles from 50/51 to 53/54, and in 52/53 fell one goal shy of matching Maurice Richard's then-unmatched feat of scoring 50 times in one NHL season.

with 18 wins in 48/49, the Rangers had hauled themselves out of the league cellar with an inspired lineup. They had no big guns, but scoring wasn't a guarantee of success, as the last-place Blackhawks had demonstrated, with players finishing sixth, seventh, ninth, tenth, eleventh and thirteenth in the scoring race. The best Ranger offensive effort came from center Edgar Laprade, who had just completed one of his finest seasons, with 44 points, and won the Lady Byng. The Rangers had also picked up center Bud Poile, who had been sent to Boston by Detroit at the start of the season. Right-winger Ed Slowinksi, with 37 points, was having a standout season, and the defence included Allan Stanley, the Calder Trophy runner-up in 48/49. But foremost the Rangers had Chuck Rayner, whose goaltending made them contenders. Rayner had the fourth-best goals-against record that season—indifferent, perhaps, for a six-team league, but it was widely acknowledged that his brilliance was winning games the Rangers otherwise wouldn't. He won the Hart Trophy in 49/50, and made the second of three consecutive appearances on the second All Star team.

The Rangers came so close to winning the Cup. After taking a 3-2 series lead they were leading game six 3-1 when Detroit tied it. The Red Wings fell behind by a goal again at the beginning of the third period, then tied it again and finally won the game 5-4 on a Sid Abel goal, to force a seventh game. The Rangers also led in that game, by 2-0 in the first period, but Detroit fought back to tie it at three apiece and send the Cup into overtime. George Gee won a faceoff in the Rangers' end, got the puck to Pete Babando, and Babando's quick shot was sufficiently screened to elude Rayner. After three finals in three years, the Red Wings could finally lay claim to the Stanley Cup.

The response of Jack Adams to this triumph was to cut himself a whopper of a deal. Concerned to the point of paranoia about complacency in his team, Adams was determined to show that a Cup win was no reason to think that the club actually had a winning lineup. On July 13, three months after winning the Cup, Adams engineered a nine-player deal with Chicago. Off to the Windy City went goaltender Harry Lumley, left-winger Pete Babando, veteran defenceman Jack Stewart, defensive fill-in Al Dewsbury and center Don Morrison, a minor pro property. And into Motor City came goaltender "Sugar" Jim Henry, center Metro Prystai, left-winger Gaye Stewart and defenceman Bob Goldham.

The murky ownership structure of NHL clubs at the time made any trade between the Red Wings and the Blackhawks—or between either team and the Rangers—more a shuffling of a business's assets than an actual swap. This was because, despite the NHL constitution's injunction against any one interest owning more than one franchise, the Norris family actually owned three. In addition to the Red Wings, the Norrises had owned the Blackhawks since 1944 (with

Bill Tobin fronting for them as a paper owner) as well as the Rangers, through a controlling block of Madison Square Garden stock. (For that matter, the Norris family had an unknown degree of sway in Boston through mortgages it underwrote for the cash-strapped ownership during the Depression.)

Detroit was the pride of the Norris family—Chicago and New York were, as a rule, neglected—so it is not surprising that Trader Jack's July 1950 asset swap worked out entirely in Detroit's favour. Gaye Stewart and Bob Goldham were former Cup winners with the Leafs who had gone to Chicago (with Bud Poile, among others) in the 1947 monster trade that brought Max Bentley to the Leafs. With that trade, Chicago had broken up its own powerful Pony Line. In this deal, by surrendering Prystai, the Blackhawks dismantled the line he formed with Bep Guidolin and Bert Olmstead that produced 66 of the team's 203 goals in 49/50. The Red Wings also picked up a first-rate goaltender in Sugar Jim Henry, who had formed the first tag-team netminding

pair with Chuck Rayner in New York until the Rangers decided they couldn't afford two NHL salaries in the crease and sent Henry to Chicago. Henry was not yet proven as a goaltender who could carry a team single-handedly, and Detroit flipped him to the Bruins.

Had they been more patient with Henry, Chicago would have found itself with a quality netminder and would not have had to make such a costly trade to get Lumley. But Chicago was feeling the heat after the great Frank Brimsek, who had come to Chicago for 49/50 following a distinguished career in Boston, decided to retire. And Detroit, for their part, could afford to move Lumley to acquire such a package of standouts, and then toss aside Henry, who would become a star in Boston, because they had a secret weapon idling in Indianapolis: Terry Sawchuk.

Sawchuk was nothing less than a phenomenon, and in his prime he was probably the greatest goaltender the game will ever see. Frank Boucher, coach and general manager of the Rangers, had no doubts

about him. "Terry Sawchuk is the greatest goalie in the history of league hockey," he pronounced in 1952.

Sawchuk had begun playing Junior hockey in his native Winnipeg at just 15; Detroit scouted him, signed him, brought him east to play in the Ontario Junior A, and by the time he was 17 had his signature on a professional contract. He went to the Omaha Knights of the U.S. league in 1947; after winning rookie of the year honours, he moved up a notch to Indianapolis of the American league in 1948 and won another rookie of the year award. He was playing in Indianapolis in 49/50 when Lumley was forced to sit out a few games after injuring his foot while playing forward in a charity game. It was just the kind of misfortune that made for abrupt career changes in professional hockey. In 7 games with the Red Wings, Sawchuk allowed only 16 goals and recorded one shutout; his GA of 2.29 was even better than Lumley's first-rate 2.35 over the season. Sawchuk was only 20 years old when Adams handed him the starting assignment for a championship team.

And Trader Jack wasn't through trading. On December 10, 1950, he pulled off another swap with Chicago, surrendering defenceman Lee Fogolin and left-winger Steve Black for left-wingers Bert Olmstead and Vic Stasiuk. Fogolin was the third defenceman Adams had traded away since winning the Cup the previous spring, but he could make the Fogolin deal with confidence because he had a great new blueline talent, Marcel Pronovost, playing full-time this season. And this trade, too, worked in Detroit's favour. Olmstead and Stasiuk were quality players who had long careers ahead of them; while Fogolin played on with Chicago through 55/56, he was made expendable by Pronovost's arrival, and Black's NHL career was over that season. But having almost robbed the Blackhawks blind, Adams bungled. Though Olmstead was Metro Prystai's productive linemate in Chicago in 49/50, Adams mysteriously did not attempt to make use of the pair. Nine days after landing Olmstead, Adams sent him to Montreal for right-winger Leo Gravelle. Gravelle played his last NHL games that season; Olmstead proceeded to play in ten straight Stanley Cup finals—eight with Montreal (of which they won four), two with Toronto—then capped his career in 61/62 with a Stanley Cup win as a Maple Leaf.

Swaps like the Olmstead-Gravelle deal undercut Adams's self-proclaimed reputation as a savvy deal-maker. Rearranging assets within the Norris empire was one thing; doing business with someone as shrewd as Montreal's Frank Selke was another. And not even the deals involving the hapless and helpless Blackhawks always went the right way. But the Red Wings' own development system (which Adams deserves credit for creating) was so productive that this talent pipeline could fill in most any gap a bad deal created. And no one exemplified the nose for talent of the Detroit scouting system more than Terry Sawchuk.

Red Kelly (left) and Marty Pavelich reign in a rush by Montreal's Paul Masnick in game seven of the 53/54 Stanley Cup final. One of the era's great rushing defencemen, Kelly tied the game at one apiece in the second period. Detroit won the game and the Cup on a fluke overtime goal by Tony Leswick, whose dump-in shot was accidentally redirected over Canadiens goaltender Gerry McNeil's shoulder by All Star defenceman Doug Harvey when he tried to glove the puck. The Canadiens were so disgusted with the loss that they left the ice of the Detroit Olympia without shaking the victorious Red Wings' hands.

Sawchuk did not betray Adams's confidence in him. He was brilliant in his rookie NHL season, winning the Calder (his third rookie award in three leagues) and missing the Vezina by just one goal. Sawchuk so pleased the team that Jim Norris paid him the $1,000 bonus he would have received had the Leafs' Al Rollins not edged him by one goal.

The Red Wings overall were impressive, finishing first with a points percentage of 72.1, outscoring every other team as Howe won the scoring race. The upset that followed, however, was one of the greatest in playoff history, as the loathed Canadiens, which had finished 36 points back in third, downed Detroit in six and went on to lose to second-place Toronto in the finals.

Trader Jack's response to the loss was entirely predictable. Another house-cleaning was in order to deal with the bogeyman named Complacency. That summer, Gaye Stewart was sent to the Rangers for left-winger Tony Leswick—a good deal, as Leswick would be around for three Detroit Cup wins, while Stewart had only a season and a half of NHL hockey left. Veteran center Doc Couture was moved to Montreal for left-winger Bert Hirschfield—not much of a deal for either party. Hirschfield, who had played only 33 games over two seasons for the Canadiens, never played for Detroit, or any other NHL team again, while Selke eked 10 games out of Couture in 51/52 before sending him to the Blackhawks.

Adams's big deal of the summer of 1951 was a typically oddball one with the Norris family's Blackhawks. Adams dumped six players in Chicago—Jim McFadden, George Gee, Jim Peters, Clare Martin, "Rags" Raglan and Max McNab—for essentially nothing in return. The trade did give Detroit $75,000 and defenceman Hugh Coflin, but this was just cash moving from one Norris pocket to another, an almost meaningless exercise, and Coflin, who had played 31 games with Chicago in 50/51, never played another NHL game.

The deal did little more than deposit players Adams no longer had use for in the poor corner of the Norris hockey empire. McNab hadn't played at all for Detroit during the 50/51 season and appeared in only two playoff games, and never played at all for Chicago; McFadden hadn't contributed a single point in the six-game semifinal with Montreal; Raglan, who had put in 33 games on defence in 50/51, did play 67 games over the next two seasons with Chicago; Gee, who had contributed one point in the disastrous semifinal, gave three solid seasons to Chicago; Peters, who didn't get any points in the semifinal, still had some seasons left in him; and Martin would be sent to New York in 51/52, his last NHL season.

There were other shuffles, mostly minor, but the talent pool did provide some important new faces. Alex Delvecchio, not yet 20, who would play more than 22 seasons at center for the Red Wings, came into the line-up; already Detroit had brought in a promising young center, Glen Skov, in 50/51. Both were important addi-

tions, as captain Sid Abel was embarking on his last season. And 23-year-old Benny Woit made the defence corps.

Detroit's offence had been carried on the shoulders of Gordie Howe, Sid Abel and Leo Reise in the calamitous 50/51 semifinal; Ted Lindsay was held to one assist. In 51/52 Lindsay was back with a vengeance, finishing second to his linemate, Hart winner Gordie Howe, in the scoring race as Howe stung the league for 47 goals, 16 more than any other player. Detroit led in team scoring, while Sawchuk won his first Vezina with 24 goals to spare. The club again dominated regular-season play, finishing with 100 points, 22 points ahead of Montreal, with a points percentage of 71.4.

There would be no repeat of the 50/51 playoff collapse. Detroit produced a perfect post-season, racking up eight straight wins as they swept first Toronto and then Montreal to win the Cup. It was an almost effortless performance; had there been a most valuable player award then in the playoffs, it almost certainly would have gone to Sawchuk, whose GA was 0.63, as he posted four shutouts. Detroit outscored its opponents 24-5 and concluded the playoff win streak with back-to-back 3-0 shutouts of the Canadiens. Lindsay, so ineffective offensively in the 50/51 semifinal, led on goals, with five, as many as the Leafs and Canadiens combined managed on Sawchuk.

It was as close to a perfect season as the NHL might ever see. Naturally Adams couldn't resist tinkering with the formula, although he showed uncharacteristic restraint. Standout defenceman Leo Reise was sent to the Rangers for right-winger Reg Sinclair, a sideshow deal as Sinclair only lasted one season in Detroit while Reise, who had just turned 30, managed two more with New York. On balance, it had the look and feel of a mercy trade to another neglected corner of the Norris hockey world, as the poverty of the Rangers' 51/52 performance had been exceeded only by that of Chicago. The only other major lineup change came as Sid Abel decided to take up the opportunity to serve as player-coach of the Norris empire's floundering Blackhawks, and the captaincy moved to Lindsay. In Reise's absence Jim Hay broke into the lineup; Marcel Bonin joined the team on left wing.

Detroit was not quite the runaway success it had been in 51/52, but 52/53 was still a fine season. Detroit recorded its fifth straight season championship, and outscored all other teams; Howe and Lindsay again finished 1-2 in the scoring race (with Delvecchio, Prystai and Kelly joining them in the top ten), and Sawchuk won another Vezina and earned his third straight first-team All Star appearance. The playoffs began with the club firmly on track as third-place Boston went down 7-0 in the opening semifinal match. With outstanding goaltending from Jim Henry, though, Boston rebounded to take a 3-1 series lead. Detroit stayed alive with a 6-4 win at home, but Boston delivered on its upset promise with a 4-2 victory that sent them into the finals against

No hard feelings: Montreal Canadiens captain Butch Bouchard dumps Red Wings captain Ted Lindsay in the third period of game two in the 54/55 final. Lindsay had set a modern playoff record by scoring four times in the first two periods as the Red Wings romped to a 7-1 win. It was Detroit's fifteenth consecutive win, another league record.

Montreal—a match the Canadiens won in five games.

Much of the blame for the semifinal collapse fell on Sawchuk's shoulders. After only three seasons, the league's pre-eminent goaltender, as moody as he was talented, was beginning to show some of the strain that claimed so many other netminding greats at this time. The job carried enormous pressures: a 70-game season with no backup to provide relief, and a new weapon called the slapshot that had just been introduced by Montreal's Bernie "Boom-Boom" Geoffrion. Bill Durnan had quit at the top of his game in 49/50; his replacement, Gerry McNeil, asked to be replaced by understudy Jacques Plante in the 52/53 semifinals. A bright new talent, Jack Gelineau, who won the Calder in the Boston goal in 49/50, quit after one more season. It was a profession with, it seemed, little prospect of long-term employment.

Sawchuk also had a disturbing weight problem. Nearly six feet tall, he had reported to training camp in 51/52 at a beefy 220 pounds, and after working down to 195 at Adams's request that season, he went into a weight-loss free-fall, dipping below 170 pounds. Sawchuk turned in another outstanding performance in 52/53, but a broken bone in his foot gave him a forewarning of the fate awaiting most every goaltender who is forced to make way, even temporarily, for a hot young prospect. Harry Lumley's sprained ankle in 49/50 had given Sawchuk the opportunity to show enough of his stuff in the big league for Adams to deal Lumley away in his favour. Three seasons later, the injured Sawchuk sat out seven games as 21-year-old Glenn Hall was called up from Detroit's Western league affiliate, the Edmonton Flyers, for six of them. Hall shut out Boston 4-0 and produced a GA of 1.67, then dutifully returned to Edmonton. Adams put Sawchuk back in goal, but did not put Hall out of his mind.

The league was turning into a two-team affair. Toronto had been slipping since last winning the Cup in 50/51. Chicago, momentarily competitive under Sid Abel in 52/53, sank to 12 wins in 53/54; New York at the same time managed a one-season burst of competence in 53/54, though it still missed the playoffs. Boston was a middling club entering some difficult seasons.

That left Detroit and Montreal. The Red Wings were still a first-class operation, and they won another season championship in 53/54. The club had been able to make another mercy shipment of talent to Chicago (Larry Zeidel, Lou Jankowski and Jim Hay) with no discernible effect as it brought in three more sparkling talents from its development system: defenceman Al Arbour, right-winger Bill Dineen and center Dutch Reibel. Detroit also retrieved Jim Peters from Chicago in January in exchange for the rights to two Junior players.

At the same time, Montreal was steadily improving, benefited by the arrival of Jacques Plante and Jean Béliveau. Gordie Howe comfortably won another scoring title in 53/54, with Lindsay third, but Richard, Geoffrion and Olmstead were second, fourth and fifth as Montreal outscored Detroit by four goals—no one

had outscored Detroit since 47/48. The Vezina eluded Sawchuk, again by the slimmest margin, as Toronto's Harry Lumley (acquired from Chicago in a blockbuster 1952 trade) allowed one less goal. Lumley also took the first All Star team spot from Sawchuk.

Detroit was still the reigning regular-season and Stanley Cup champion and conducted itself accordingly in the playoffs. It opened its semifinal against Toronto with a 5-0 pasting and went on to win a closely played series with a Ted Lindsay goal in the second period of overtime in game five. The Canadiens were waiting, having swept Boston in four. Detroit built a 3-1 series lead, but Montreal rebounded to force a seventh game. At the end of regulation time the teams were tied at one on goals by Red Kelly and Floyd Curry. The winner was a fluke, as Tony Leswick dumped in a high shot and turned to go to the bench. When Montreal's Doug Harvey tried to glove the puck, it glanced off his thumb and over Gerry McNeil's shoulder. Montreal was so disgusted by the loss that the players followed coach Dick Irvin to the dressing room without even bothering to shake hands with the Red Wings.

Adams chose to stand pat with his winning lineup in 54/55, making only one significant change. It began with an innocuous Norris empire swap in October, as right-winger Lorne Davis, who had just been acquired from Montreal by Chicago, was sent to Detroit in November for defensive standout Metro Prystai. It was little more than an in-house loan of Prystai, who would be retrieved the very next season. The Prystai deal was part of a greater emergency airlift of talent from around the league to shore up the crumbling Blackhawks, which, despite the proximity of the Norris fortune, was in danger of folding.

Sid Abel had had his fill of coaching the Hawks, and quit after 53/54. Unfortunately for the Red Wings, the strange lure of the Blackhawks worked its magic on Tommy Ivan. Detroit's outstanding coach longed to move up the corporate ladder but knew he had no hope of a general managership with the Red Wings with Jack Adams so firmly installed. Ivan accepted the opportunity to serve as Chicago's general manager in July 1954, and Adams brought in Jimmy Skinner to coach.

Like Ivan, Skinner had never played in the NHL. Born in Selkirk, Manitoba, he had been the last man cut at the Red Wings training camp in the fall of 1944. He was sent to Omaha of the U.S. league, where he served as captain of the Knights while playing under Ivan. Adams saw Skinner's potential as a coach and encouraged him in that direction as an alternative to ending his career as a minor pro. He coached the Red Wings' OHA Junior A affiliate in Windsor and then Hamilton for six seasons, and along the way nearly 30 Red Wings of the 1950s played their Junior hockey under his tutelage, among them Sawchuk, Pronovost, Skov, Wilson and Reibel. His promotion to the Red Wings came as a surprise to those who thought Bud Poile would have been chosen—Poile was a former

Terry Sawchuk was the focal point of a blockbuster nine-player deal between the Red Wings and the Bruins after Detroit's 54/55 Stanley Cup win. He is in top form above as the Bruins defeat the Canadiens in Montreal 3-1 on November 10, 1956. A month later, Sawchuk was in a Boston hospital with mononucleosis. When his nerves gave out in January, his Bruins career of one-and-a-half seasons was over. Detroit sent Boston Johnny Bucyk to get him back.

NHLer, after all, and he was behind the bench of the WHL's Edmonton Flyers, which was a more senior coaching rung than Junior A. But Skinner was experienced, knew the Red Wing lineup intimately and was well respected as a player's coach.

The closeness of the seven-game Red Wings-Canadiens final in 53/54 foreshadowed the neck-and-neck battle between the two clubs in 54/55. Detroit logged another season championship, two points ahead of Montreal, surviving a ten-day suspension of Ted Lindsay after he clubbed with his stick a Toronto spectator who had taken a swing at Howe during play. The misdemeanor did not prevent him from winning the Hart.

The regular-season title came in a home-and-away series with Montreal that closed the season for both clubs. Maurice Richard had just been suspended for the remainder of the season and the playoffs; the infamous Montreal riot over Richard's sentence cut the first game short while Detroit was leading 4-1. The Red Wings were awarded the game by default and then defeated Montreal easily at home 6-0 to take their seventh straight league title. Sawchuk won another Vezina, edging out Harry Lumley of Toronto by one goal. Montreal outscored Detroit for the second straight season, this time by a comfortable 24 goals as Geoffrion, Richard and Béliveau locked up the top of the scoring race, relegating Dutch Reibel and Gordie Howe to fourth and fifth. The rivals were in a league of their own, with 42 wins for Detroit and 41 for Montreal; Toronto trailed in third with 24.

Detroit made short work of Toronto in their semi-final, sweeping them in four. Montreal also had little trouble with Boston, downing them in five. Another seesaw battle, at times brutal, unfolded between two very proud clubs. When Detroit won game two 7-1 to take a 2-0 series lead, two records were set by the Red Wings: most consecutive wins (15) and most goals (4) in two periods of playoff hockey, by Ted Lindsay. The Canadiens then tied the series with wins at home. And when Detroit won game five to take a 3-2 series lead, a

treasured Canadiens record was surpassed as Gordie Howe's hat-trick exceeded the 43/44 playoff performance of Toe Blake in amassing 8 goals and 11 assists in just 9 games. A 6-3 win at home by Montreal sent the series back to Detroit for a decisive seventh game. Detroit built a 3-0 lead that Montreal could not overcome. With a 3-1 win, the Red Wings had their fourth Stanley Cup in six years; the last three had come against the Canadiens.

Jack Adams celebrated by tearing the championship club apart. He cut two major deals in June, leaving only nine players untouched. Chicago was again on the receiving end of a league charity airlift, and from the Red Wings came center Glen Skov, defenceman Benny Woit and left-wingers Johnny Wilson and Tony Leswick. In return, Adams accepted right-winger Jerry Toppazzini, defenceman Gord Hollingworth and centers Dave Creighton and Johnny McCormack. Only Hollingworth played any role in the Red Wings' future, albeit a minor one as he played about half of the next three seasons. Creighton went to New York at the beginning of the season, McCormack never played, and in January 1956 Toppazzini was sent to Boston.

The big deal in the summer of 1955 was with the Bruins, who thought they could do better than Jim Henry in goal. When Adams allowed that he had a goaltender to move, the Bruins assumed it was Glenn Hall, parked in Edmonton. To their amazement, it was Sawchuk. Adams had concluded his moody netminder was a burnt-out case after just five seasons, and with Hall stewing in the minors he had no qualms about unloading Sawchuk. But Sawchuk was just the beginning of the deal. Adams threw in two left-wingers—Vic Stasiuk, a veteran of three Red Wings Cup wins, and Marcel Bonin—and minor-pro right-winger Lorne Davis. In return he received five Bruins: left-wingers Ed Sandford and Réal Chevrefils, minor-league center Norm Corcoran, goaltending prospect Gilles Boisvert and defenceman Rocky Godfrey. Of the five players acquired in the Sawchuk deal, only one, Godfrey, had a long-term future with the Red Wings. Chevrefils was packaged with Toppazzini in the January deal that brought Detroit center Murray Costello and left-winger Lorne Ferguson—a swap that favoured Boston. Corcoran was sent to Chicago that season, and so was Ed Sandford so that Metro Prystai could be retrieved.

After (most of) the shuffling was through, Detroit was a poor facsimile of its so recent greatness. Midway through the season the Red Wings were struggling even to make the playoffs, with just 12 wins, while Montreal was far out in front with 24. Skinner's crew ended the season in second with just 30 wins, 12 fewer than in 54/55 and 15 fewer than first-place Montreal. The much improved Rangers won more games than Detroit, with 32, but a surplus of ties gave Detroit a two-point edge over New York.

Despite the debilitating trades, the Red Wings stayed in the Cup race with the help of several key rookies. Hall, with the league's second-best GA of 2.11, recorded 12 shutouts, won the Calder and made the second All Star team; left-winger Johnny Bucyk and center Norm Ullman had moved up with him from Edmonton; and teenage defenceman Larry Hillman, who would play on six Stanley Cup winners, began his first full season after participating in the 54/55 win.

Toronto fell to Detroit in five in their semifinal, and that brought on the third straight Cup final between the Canadiens and the Red Wings and their fourth in five seasons. The tide clearly had turned in league fortunes. Montreal pronounced itself the dominant club by winning comfortably in five. Trader Jack had traded himself into a corner.

Detroit had seemed capable of the sort of lengthy reign at the peak of the league that the Canadiens were pulling off. Some of the blame for the demise of the Red Wings dynasty rests with the Norris family. After patriarch Jim Norris died in December 1952, son Jimmy took firm charge of the Blackhawks and daughter Marguerite the Red Wings. By all indications Marguerite was a shrewd manager of Red Wings affairs, and her dislike and mistrust of Jack Adams—she would recall him as "Rotten, just really evil," for the authors of Net Worth—kept his managerial excesses somewhat in check. But Marguerite lost a powerplay within the family trust that delivered the Red Wings to her far less competent brother Bruce in 1955. Under Bruce, Adams all but ran amok.

After the deals that shipped half the 54/55 championship lineup out of town, Adams and Bruce Norris exacerbated the team's circumstances by reacting with vindictive outrage to the effort spearheaded by captain Ted Lindsay to form a players' association. At the time, Detroit's circumstances were far from hopeless, as the club won the 56/57 regular season, but Boston downed them in five in the semifinal. Adams helped crush the association drive by punishing Detroit's two chief organizers, Lindsay and Hall. He sent them to Chicago, receiving in return left-winger Johnny Wilson (who had

gone to Chicago in the big deal of June 1955), center Forbes Kennedy and minor-pros Bill Preston and Hank Bassen. It was a ridiculously one-sided deal. Wilson and Kennedy were journeymen players, and while Bassen would provide backup netminding, Preston never played in the NHL. Lindsay had just finished second to Gordie Howe in the scoring race, made the first All Star team for the second straight season and the eighth time in ten seasons, and had led his team to another regular-season championship. Hall had just earned his first appearance on the first All Star team, with six more to come in his illustrious career. Adams also made an example of long-serving left-winger Marty Pavelich by sending him to the minors. Pavelich's points production had fallen considerably in the past two seasons, but he also happened to be Ted Lindsay's partner in a plastics company. Pavelich quit the game altogether to run the business.

With Hall gone, Adams needed a new goaltender, and he now decided Sawchuk, of all people, was his man. The former Red Wing great had hit rock bottom in his second season in Boston, quitting the game altogether after a mid-season nervous collapse that followed a bout of mononucleosis. (The Bruins had knocked off the Red Wings in the 55/56 playoffs with Don Simmons in goal.) To get Sawchuk back, Adams sent Boston Johnny Bucyk, who became their long-serving captain.

Sawchuk did have many fine years left in him, but the Red Wings did not. After earning a regular-season title with 38 wins in 56/57, the team did not win 30 games again until 62/63, or another season title until 64/65. By then Sid Abel was coach and general manager. Jimmy Skinner had quit in the middle of the 57/58 season, unable to withstand any longer the pressure of the job. While he respected and admired Adams, as a coach close to his players, he was evidently traumatized by the fallout of the players' association drive.

While the Red Wings did make four Cup finals from 60/61 to 65/66, the club could not convert the appearances into a victory. On October 14, 1964, Abel bought back from Chicago the contract to the indomitable Lindsay. It would be his last hurrah as a Red Wing. Only three others were left from the last Cup team of a decade earlier: the ageless Gordie Howe, Alex Delvecchio and Marcel Pronovost.

Lindsay attempted to hide on the retired list after the 64/65 season to avoid being left unprotected in the intraleague draft, but the ruse, which would have seen Lindsay un-retire for the 65/66 season with Detroit, was vetoed by Toronto's board of governors member Stafford Smythe. And so Lindsay was retired for good when the club reached the 65/66 finals and lost in six to the Canadiens—nor was Pronovost on hand, having joined Sawchuk in Toronto.

Pronovost and Sawchuk (along with Red Kelly, who had been traded in 59/60, and Larry Hillman, acquired by Toronto in 1960) won one last Cup together as Maple Leafs in 66/67. The once-mighty Red Wings missed the playoffs that season. They missed the playoffs 14 times in the next 16 seasons. ○

Bluelining in the early Fifties

In the early years of the Original Six era, championship clubs were built on solid defensive foundations, and those foundations differed greatly between successful teams. On the opposite page, the defence corps of three Stanley Cup winners—the Toronto Maple Leafs of 50/51, the Detroit Red Wings of 51/52, and the Montreal Canadiens of 52/53—are analyzed, based on their performances in their respective championship seasons. Each team brought its own formula to winning. The Leaf defencemen of 50/51 filled the team's enforcer roles, as both Bill Barilko and Gus Mortson led the league in penalty minutes during their careers. The Red Wings of 51/52 were far less penalized and made a greater overall contribution to goal scoring, led by the rushing example of Red Kelly. The Canadiens of 52/53, an older, more experienced team, were moderate in their penalty minutes and contributed only a minimum of offence, with the exception of Doug Harvey, the triggerman of the Montreal powerplay.

Jim Thomson

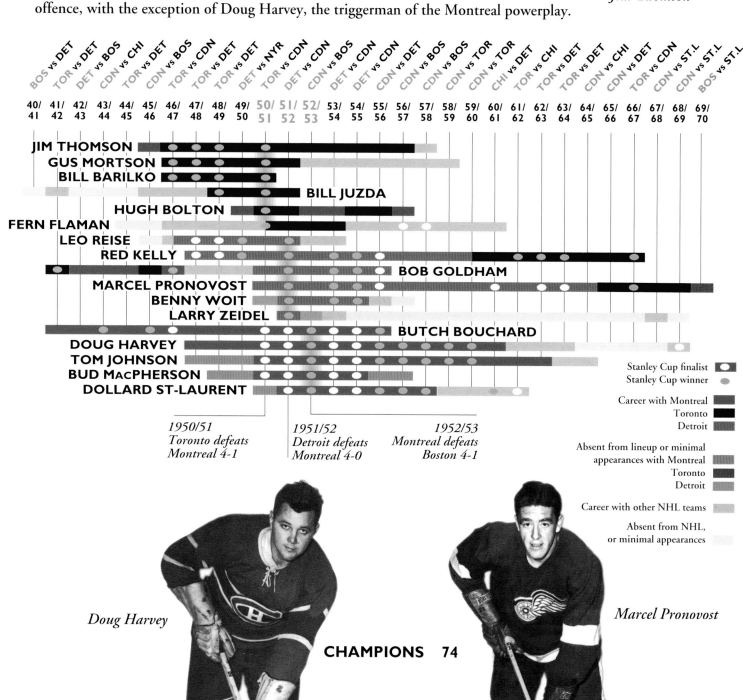

40/41 BOS vs DET	
41/42 TOR vs DET	
42/43 DET vs BOS	
43/44 CDN vs CHI	
44/45 TOR vs DET	
45/46 CDN vs BOS	
46/47 TOR vs CDN	
47/48 TOR vs DET	
48/49 TOR vs DET	
49/50 DET vs NYR	
50/51 TOR vs CDN	
51/52 DET vs CDN	
52/53 CDN vs BOS	
53/54 DET vs CDN	
54/55 DET vs CDN	
55/56 CDN vs DET	
56/57 CDN vs BOS	
57/58 CDN vs BOS	
58/59 CDN vs TOR	
59/60 CDN vs TOR	
60/61 CHI vs DET	
61/62 TOR vs CHI	
62/63 TOR vs DET	
63/64 TOR vs DET	
64/65 CDN vs CHI	
65/66 CDN vs DET	
66/67 TOR vs CDN	
67/68 CDN vs ST.L	
68/69 CDN vs ST.L	
69/70 BOS vs ST.L	

JIM THOMSON
GUS MORTSON
BILL BARILKO
BILL JUZDA
HUGH BOLTON
FERN FLAMAN
LEO REISE
RED KELLY
BOB GOLDHAM
MARCEL PRONOVOST
BENNY WOIT
LARRY ZEIDEL
BUTCH BOUCHARD
DOUG HARVEY
TOM JOHNSON
BUD MacPHERSON
DOLLARD ST-LAURENT

1950/51
Toronto defeats
Montreal 4-1

1951/52
Detroit defeats
Montreal 4-0

1952/53
Montreal defeats
Boston 4-1

Stanley Cup finalist
Stanley Cup winner

Career with Montreal
Toronto
Detroit

Absent from lineup or minimal appearances with Montreal
Toronto
Detroit

Career with other NHL teams

Absent from NHL, or minimal appearances

Doug Harvey

Marcel Pronovost

CHAMPIONS 74

POINTS PRODUCTION PER GAME

- Red Kelly — 0.701
- Jim Thomson — 0.521
- Doug Harvey — 0.493
- Hugh Bolton — 0.307
- Marcel Pronovost — 0.261
- Gus Mortson — 0.216
- Bill Barilko — 0.206
- Leo Reise — 0.204
- Bob Goldham — 0.202
- Benny Woit — 0.19
- Fern Flaman — 0.189
- Butch Bouchard — 0.172
- Tom Johnson — 0.157
- Dollard St-Laurent — 0.148
- Bill Juzda — 0.138
- Bud MacPherson — 0.085
- Larry Zeidel

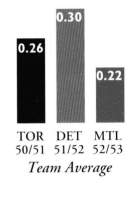

TOR 50/51	DET 51/52	MTL 52/53
0.26	0.30	0.22

Team Average

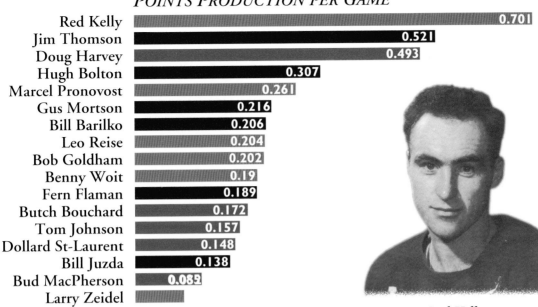

Red Kelly

PENALTY MINUTES PER GAME

- Gus Mortson — 2.37
- Fern Flaman — 1.91
- Bill Barilko — 1.66
- Bud MacPherson — 1.14
- Jim Thomson — 1.10
- Bill Juzda — 0.98
- Doug Harvey — 0.97
- Butch Bouchard — 0.95
- Tom Johnson — 0.90
- Larry Zeidel — 0.74
- Marcel Pronovost — 0.72
- Dollard St-Laurent — 0.63
- Leo Reise — 0.63
- Bob Goldham — 0.35
- Benny Woit — 0.34
- Red Kelly — 0.24
- Hugh Bolton — 0.15

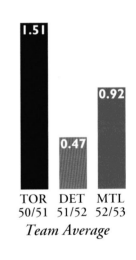

TOR 50/51	DET 51/52	MTL 52/53
1.51	0.47	0.92

Team Average

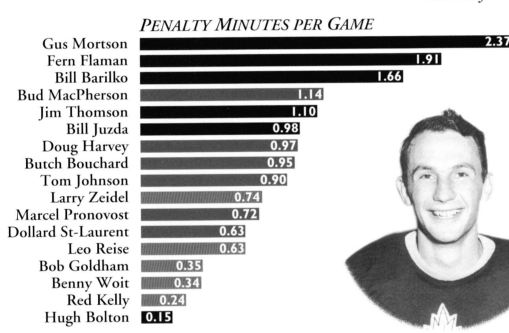

Gus Mortson

PLAYER AGE

- Butch Bouchard — 33
- Bill Juzda — 30
- Bob Goldham — 29
- Leo Reise — 29
- Doug Harvey — 29
- Gus Mortson — 26
- Bud MacPherson — 26
- Tom Johnson — 25
- Red Kelly — 24
- Benny Woit — 24
- Jim Thomson — 24
- Bill Barilko — 24
- Fern Flaman — 24
- Dollard St-Laurent — 23
- Larry Zeidel — 23
- Marcel Pronovost — 21
- Hugh Bolton — 21

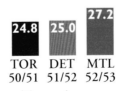

TOR 50/51	DET 51/52	MTL 52/53
24.8	25.0	27.2

Team Average

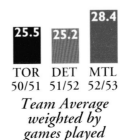

TOR 50/51	DET 51/52	MTL 52/53
25.5	25.2	28.4

*Team Average
weighted by
games played*

Butch Bouchard

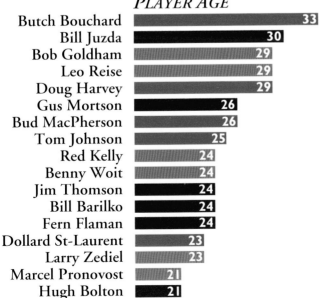

MONTREAL CANADIENS
Wartime to the Fifties

ROCKET MEN

MAURICE RICHARD PERSONIFIED A NEW ERA OF CANADIENS GREATNESS, PLAYING A FEROCIOUS GAME OF SPEED AND SKILL

RIGHT: Montreal Forum fans cope with the tear-gas a spectator unleashed during the riot of March 17, 1955. The Canadiens boosters ran amok after the suspension of their beloved Maurice "the Rocket" Richard on March 16.
BELOW: The jersey worn by Richard while captain of the Canadiens from 56/57 to 59/60.

T here really is no contest: the greatest team ever to play in the National Hockey League is the Montreal Canadiens. Its post-season dry spells have been few and far between, and its hot streaks remain unmatched. If you include their National Hockey Association days, Les Canadiens have won 24 Stanley Cups. The Toronto franchise ranks a distant second, with 14, and while the Leafs have not won one since 1967, Montreal has won ten since then.

The club's most productive period ran from 43/44 to 78/79, a 36-season span in which it won 18 Cups and the finals were breached another six times. Since then, the club has made three more trips to the finals, and won twice, in 85/86 and 92/93. At the very height of its prowess, the 1950s, Montreal was in ten straight finals and won six times, including a record five straight from 55/56 to 59/60. Of Montreal's eight trips to the finals during its NHL history that have *not* resulted in Cup wins (leaving aside the 18/19 final, called off because of the great influenza epidemic and the death of Canadiens defenceman Joe Hall), five came from 46/47 to 54/55. Thus, from 55/56 to 92/93, Montreal reached the finals 19 times and won 17—a success rate of almost 90 percent.

This book focuses on the run from 43/44 to 78/79, a period of nearly seamless transitions from one championship lineup to another. The club unquestionably has lived up to the motto (taken from John McCrae's First World War poem "In Flanders Fields") painted on the dressing room wall: "To you from failing hands we throw/ The torch; be yours to hold it high."

Before there was a National Hockey League, there was a club called the Montreal Canadiens. It was founded in November 1910 as part of the National Hockey Association, and won its first Stanley Cup in 1916. The Canadiens were particularly strong in the 1920s, and after back-to-back Cup wins in 29/30 and 30/31 seemed prepared for a lengthy reign. But the Depression nearly destroyed the team, as it did

CHAMPIONS | 76

the Canadiens' in-town rivals, the Maroons, which folded in 1938. From 32/33 to 39/40, the Canadiens missed the playoffs twice, were knocked out in the quarterfinals five times and reached the semifinals just once. In the spring of 1940, with the world at war, the Canadiens franchise was in tatters, having won only 10 of 48 games in the last season.

A most unlikely saviour arrived in the person of Toronto Maple Leafs impresario Conn Smythe. The Leafs' managing director knew that the NHL's overall health could be read in the vital signs of the Canadiens. The league had shed too many good clubs to withstand a final failure in Montreal. In addition to the Maroons, the Depression had claimed the Pittsburgh Pirates (which operated in their last gasp as the Philadelphia Quakers in 31/32) and the storied Ottawa Senators (reincarnated for one season as the St. Louis Flyers in 34/35). As well, the New York Americans had turned into a league charity case, and would not survive beyond 41/42, when the team was based in Brooklyn. The NHL was down to seven teams in the summer of 1940, and with the death of the Americans looming, would soon be at six. Were Montreal to fold as well, the league's status as the game's premier major-league operation would be in question, given that the American league, formed in 1936 (as the International-American league), was well established in prime U.S. markets and during the war was making moves to compete directly with the NHL by attempting to lessen its dependence on NHL prospects so that teams would no longer be just NHL farm operations.

Toe Blake was the lone star of the Canadiens when Dick Irvin became coach in 1940. He played on the famous Punch Line with Maurice Richard and Elmer Lach and served as team captain from 40/41 to 47/48. A bad ankle fracture forced his retirement in January 1948; he replaced Irvin as coach in 55/56.

Smythe's reaction to the Canadiens' woes was to send them a first-class coach, perhaps the best coach in the league at the time. Dick Irvin, a former star of the professional western game, had been coaching the Leafs since 31/32, when they won the Stanley Cup. The Leafs since then had reached the Cup finals six times in eight seasons, including the last three straight finals, but had lost every one of them. Smythe had concluded that Irvin, as talented as he was, had taken the Leafs as far as he could, and that it was time to hand the reins over to the Leafs' former captain, Hap Day.

To make room for Day, Smythe played matchmaker between Irvin and the Canadiens. It was a match that lasted 15 seasons, an eon in the world of NHL coaching, and it was a match that almost immediately jump-started a once-proud franchise.

Irvin was the first, but not the last, factor in the Canadiens' revival during the Second World War. The others were fresh talent, a change in passing rules, and the war itself. In the space of just a few seasons, the

unique hockey climate of the early 1940s brought forth one of the most powerful clubs the NHL has ever seen.

Irvin had little first-rate talent to work with when he took over in Montreal; a notable exception was Hector "Toe" Blake, a veteran who had come out of the Sudbury, Ontario, amateur system. After making his first NHL appearance as a Maroon in 32/33, Blake joined the Canadiens in 35/36 and won the league scoring title in 38/39, and the Hart Trophy to go with it. Blake was the only top-ten scorer in the Canadiens lineup in 39/40, and Irvin promptly made the left-winger, one of the game's great all-round players, his captain. The only other long-term player Irvin had to work with when he showed up was center Ray Getliffe, acquired from the Bruins after they won the 38/39 Stanley Cup. But beginning in the fall of 1940, two more important players entered the lineup: defenceman Ken Reardon, who came out of the Montreal Junior scene, and playmaking center Elmer Lach, from Nokomis, Saskatchewan.

As the team improved in the war years, it acquired many of the players who would build its legend. Foremost were defenceman Butch Bouchard and right-winger Maurice Richard. Bouchard made the team in 41/42; Richard moved up from the Canadiens' local Senior farm club, the Royals, in 42/43 and was given a two-year contract. He also joined with Lach and Blake to create a new forward unit that became known as the Punch Line. But only 16 games into the 42/43 season, the line crumbled when Richard broke his ankle. It was the third consecutive season in which Richard was knocked out of a team lineup by a fracture—first an ankle, then a wrist, and now an ankle again. He was considered so brittle that Richard would credit his two-year contract for giving him the chance ever to have a career—had he only signed for one year, the Canadiens might not have been willing to give him another try in 43/44.

To their enduring good fortune, the Canadiens did give Richard another try. With the Punch Line reunited in 43/44, the Canadiens went on a tear through the league, losing only five of 50 games and sweeping the Blackhawks in the Cup final.

The success of the 43/44 Canadiens went far beyond the performance of the Punch Line, which had yet to reach its peak of efficiency. Certainly a decisive factor was the arrival of the two-line offside rule that season, which created overnight the modern, high-speed, head-manning game for which Montreal was tailor-made. As well, the team's lineup had been greatly bolstered from 41/42 to 43/44, when Richard was joined up front by Buddy O'Connor (a future Hart and Lady Byng winner with New York), Gerry Heffernan, Fern Majeau and Bob Fillion. The club also had the old warrior Phil Watson on right wing, albeit temporarily. Beginning in 42/43, the league permitted teams to lend players to each other, to help shore up those franchises most debilitated by the loss of manpower entering military service. The most desperate team was the New

MONTREAL CANADIENS

The Champions of the 1940s

Featuring the players and management who participated in Montreal's
Stanley Cup victories of 1943/44 and 1945/46

GENERAL MANAGER	COACH
1. Tommy Gorman	1. Dick Irvin

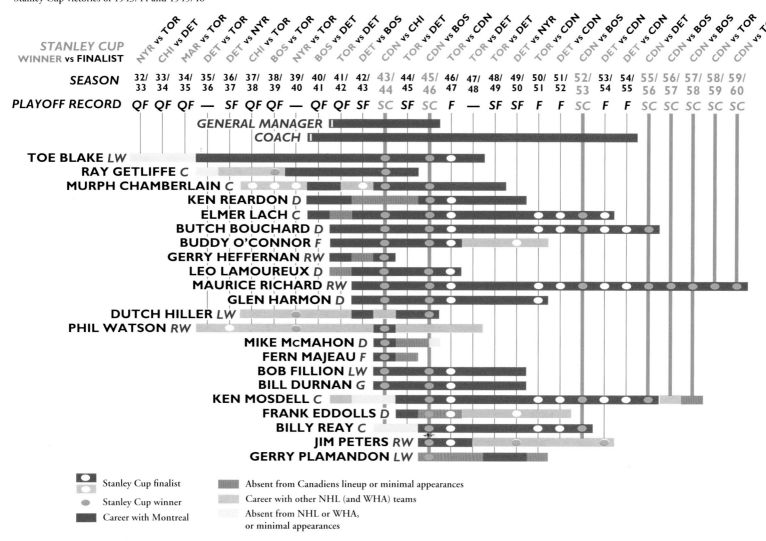

STANLEY CUP WINNER vs FINALIST

	NYR vs TOR	CHI vs DET	MAR vs TOR	DET vs TOR	DET vs NYR	CHI vs TOR	BOS vs TOR	NYR vs TOR	BOS vs DET	TOR vs DET	DET vs BOS	CDN vs CHI	TOR vs DET	CDN vs BOS	TOR vs DET	TOR vs DET	DET vs NYR	TOR vs CDN	DET vs CDN	CDN vs BOS	DET vs CDN	CDN vs CDN	CDN vs DET	CDN vs BOS	CDN vs BOS	CDN vs TOR	CDN vs TOR
SEASON	32/33	33/34	34/35	35/36	36/37	37/38	38/39	39/40	40/41	41/42	42/43	43/44	44/45	45/46	46/47	47/48	48/49	49/50	50/51	51/52	52/53	53/54	54/55	55/56	56/57	57/58	58/59	59/60
PLAYOFF RECORD	QF	QF	QF	—	SF	QF	QF	—	QF	QF	SF	SC	SF	SC	F	—	SF	SF	F	F	SC	F	F	SC	SC	SC	SC	SC

Legend:

- ▢ Stanley Cup finalist
- ● Stanley Cup winner
- ▬ Career with Montreal
- ▬ Absent from Canadiens lineup or minimal appearances
- ▬ Career with other NHL (and WHA) teams
- Absent from NHL or WHA, or minimal appearances

York Rangers, which had lost virtually its entire starting lineup. To help round out its roster, Montreal sent New York Fern Gauthier, John Mahaffy and Dutch Hiller, and secured the use of Watson in return.

Montreal also loaned goaltender Paul Bibeault to Toronto, as the Leafs' star netminder, Turk Broda, was overseas with the Canadian army. The Canadiens were able to do so because of the promotion from the Royals of Bill Durnan, an ambidextrous Senior league veteran (who was also a first-class softball pitcher and for a spell in the 1930s had given up the rink for the diamond). In Durnan the Canadiens found a goaltending star who would shine just as brightly once the league was back at peacetime strength. Though he was outpolled by the Leafs' teenage center Gus Bodnar in the Calder voting in 43/44, Durnan won the Vezina by allowing only 109 goals over 50 games—65 fewer than the next-best effort, by Toronto. In his seven-season NHL career, Durnan won the Vezina six times, yet as a Canadiens netminding star he has been, sadly, almost forgotten.

The home front had changed drastically with America's full entry into the war following the Japanese attack on Pearl Harbor in December 1941. There was serious doubt after the 41/42 season that the NHL could continue operating—less because of the loss of players than the loss of fans, who wouldn't be able to drive their cars to games because of restrictions on vital war materials such as oil and rubber. In 1940 Canada had initiated a home-defence draft, but the league was able to carry on with little initial effect on rosters. Players who completed 30 days of basic training at the beginning of the 40/41 season fulfilled their home-defence obligations and avoided the necessity of answering a draft call-up. No Canadian player in the NHL received a draft notice until January 1942, when the Leafs' Don Metz was summoned. Hockey players began entering military service predominantly through military camp teams, as players were actively recruited to play on Canadian armed forces clubs that were now vying for the Allan Cup in Senior league play. Boston's Kraut Line of Woody Dumart, Bobby Bauer and Milt Schmidt, stars of the Bruins' 40/41 Cup win, joined the

RCAF Flyers in time to help them win the 1942 Allan Cup, and over the summer of 1942 Rangers coach Frank Boucher participated in the creation of an army All Star team, the Ottawa Commandos, which won the 1943 Allan Cup. Among those many NHL talents who joined the Commandos were Montreal's Ken Reardon, and Dick Irvin pitched in with the coaching.

But the Canadiens by and large were untouched by the manpower losses suffered by other NHL clubs. This was mainly because general manager Tommy Gorman cleverly exploited a Canadian draft deferral provision for men who held vital-industry jobs. Hockey was not a vital industry—it had been pronounced of "low labour priority" at the start of the 42/43 season—but players who had jobs arranged for them in vital industries held draft deferrals that allowed them to keep playing. By early 1944, Dick Irvin was openly complaining to the Toronto press about having to send players back home on road trips to work in other jobs, jobs that were plainly arranged to secure draft deferrals.

The Canadiens steamrollered the Leafs in the semifinals in the spring of 1944, a series that culminated in an 11-0 whitewash. Toronto was so humiliated and outraged by the experience that the club successfully lobbied the NHL to amend its constitution for 44/45, forbidding use of players who had secured vital-industry

draft deferrals. But if the Leafs or any other club thought this measure would gut the Canadiens lineup they were deeply disappointed. The 44/45 Canadiens were little changed from the 43/44 dynamo. The only significant difference was the loss of Phil Watson, who insisted on returning to the Rangers. As a result, Montreal retrieved Gauthier, Hiller and Mahaffy, and used Gauthier and Hiller in the new season.

Many Canadiens undoubtedly continued to play because they had secured medical deferrals for sports-related injuries, but they were hardly unique in hockey or professional sports—major-league baseball operated in 1944 with about 40 percent of its players holding medical deferrals from the American draft. Nonetheless, Conn Smythe blamed the use of medical deferrals for the continued strength of Les Canadiens. With three fractures in three years, Maurice Richard was almost certainly playing on such a deferral (the authors of *Lions in Winter*, who interviewed Richard, reported that he was turned away by the army in 1940 and 1943). There is also circumstantial evidence that Bill Durnan was able to play in 44/45 on a medical deferral, based on an injury received at the 1944 training camp. (None of this can be confirmed because all deferral records were destroyed by the Canadian government in 1964.)

However the Canadiens were able to ice a team, the 44/45 lineup dominated the league like no other team until then, or since then. While it did not win as many games as in 43/44, losing eight after dropping three of its last eight matches, the club swept almost every major award. Durnan won another Vezina; the Punch Line swept the top three places in the scoring race (in the order of Lach, Richard and Blake); Lach won the Hart as he became the first NHL player to register more than 50 assists (54); and Richard became the first NHLer to score 50 goals in a season (and did it in 50 games). An unprecedented five of six positions on the first All Star team were claimed by Canadiens, with the Punch Line up front, Durnan in net and Bouchard on defence. As well, Irvin was named the first-team coach for the second straight season, and defenceman Glen Harmon made the second team.

The tremendous season had only one weak link. The Canadiens had dominated every team in the league but the Leafs, who, with their mix of teenagers and ageing veterans, won five, lost four and tied one against Montreal. When they met in the semifinals, the rigidly close-checking Leafs avenged their humiliation of the previous spring and upset the Canadiens in six games, then defeated the Red Wings in a seven-game final.

Montreal rebounded from the ignominy in 45/46. With the clouds of war no longer casting shadows on the game, the Canadiens ceased to be an overwhelming power, but unlike the inspired Leafs of 44/45, who missed the playoffs altogether in 45/46, the Canadiens proved that the lineup they had assembled in the war years was genuinely strong. The team won the 45/46 regular season and made short work of its playoff opponents, eliminating Chicago in four and downing Boston in five to win the Cup. Durnan, Bouchard and Richard made the first All Star team, while Reardon, back from military service, joined Lach and Blake on the second team. In 46/47, the Canadiens won their fourth consecutive regular season, Durnan became the first goaltender to win four consecutive Vezinas, and four Canadiens—Durnan, Bouchard, Reardon and Richard—made the first All Star team. In the Cup finals that spring, however, this celebrated lineup met its match in a rebuilt Leafs club. Bill Durnan made the fatal mistake of gibing in the press, "How did these guys get in the playoffs, anyway?" after he shut out Toronto 6-0 in the opening game. The roused Leafs proceeded to lay on a demonstration, winning four of the next five games to take the Cup.

It was the first of three straight Stanley Cup wins for Toronto, and with a young Red Wings team in rapid ascent, the Canadiens' greatness might well have faded away. The man who made sure that did not happen was Frank Selke, Sr.

Selke was an outcast of the Toronto Maple Leafs. He had been with the Leafs all through the years Dick Irvin had coached there, and had done a fine job in bringing two Stanley Cups to Maple Leaf Gardens as acting general manager while Conn Smythe was overseas with the Canadian army. But Smythe doubted Selke's loyalty, and when Selke didn't respond with sufficient enthusiasm to Smythe's plans to make a run at the Gardens presidency in the spring of 1946, Smythe indicated to him that his days with the Leaf organization would be numbered should Smythe succeed. Selke wisely did not doubt Smythe's ability to pull off his power play, and he resigned that May, 18 months before his adversary secured the Maple Leaf Gardens presidency.

Selke was immediately hired by the Canadiens as a replacement for Tommy Gorman, who was returning to his home town to manage the Ottawa Auditorium, in which he had bought a controlling interest.

Selke arrived to run a club that was more francophone in name than in fact. Though captain Toe Blake was fluently bilingual (his mother was French Canadian), his linemate Elmer Lach couldn't speak a word of French, while initially Maurice Richard's English was limited to "Yes" and "No." Coach Dick Irvin couldn't speak French, for that matter. English was the official language of the dressing room, and the club did not seem to have any enthusiasm for developing a francophone talent system, despite the fact that in 35/36 the Canadiens had been granted for three years right of first refusal on all French-Canadian talent bound for the NHL, a privilege extended to them in hope of buttressing the ailing franchise. When Gorman had taken on the general manager's duties in 1941 (having been manager of the Montreal Forum since 1936), his sporting claim to fame in the city was his management of the Canadiens' local anglophone rivals, the Maroons, until their demise in 1938. Thus, while the war years brought about the revival of the Canadiens as a hockey powerhouse, the club's emergence as a true cultural icon of Quebec had to wait until two Stanley Cups had been won and a critical change in management occurred.

Under Selke, the Canadiens acquired their modern character. The club did not become exclusively French Canadian by any means, but it now paid far more attention to developing its talent potential in Quebec, while also expanding and improving its amateur feeder system in anglophone centers like Winnipeg and Edmonton. Selke secured the assistance of an able young Montrealer, Sam Pollock, in revamping the system, and when Ken Reardon (an Edmonton native) retired after 49/50, he also played a vital role as he rose to become a club vice-president.

According to the authors of *Lions in Winter*, Selke "looked for three essentials in his players: a strong hockey background; a deep commitment to winning or an equally strong aversion to losing; and the sense of self-confidence, self-direction and self-motivation necessary in a player who would be asked to accept the team's regimentation. He wanted his players to adopt a shared perspective, rather than just an individual one. Personal expectations, attitudes and motives had to become team expectations, team attitudes and team motives."

The Canadiens were not an oasis of bliss in an otherwise embattled league—there were contract holdouts (including Richard) at the start of some seasons, Canadiens players were just as fearful as members of other teams of losing their starting jobs to new talent if they were injured, and the roster readily participated in the abortive union drive of 1957. But it is to the great credit of Selke that he managed to impose such a regimen of self-sacrifice and discipline on the team's roster without incurring the destructive resentments experienced so broadly under Jack Adams in Detroit and Conn

Gerry McNeil was wearing the catching glove at top when Bill Barilko scored the overtime goal on him that won Toronto the 50/51 Stanley Cup. He had something to cheer about in 52/53, when he triumphed in a goaltending duel with Boston's Sugar Jim Henry, as Montreal won its first Cup since 45/46.

Smythe in Toronto. In the initial postwar years, it may have appeared that, after the Canadiens' success of 45/46, the new game was going to belong to the Red Wings and the Leafs. Both teams did have their successes, but neither club was able to achieve the lengthy productivity of Montreal. Building on the initial successes of the war years, Selke's management shaped a string of championship teams reaching right to the end of the 1970s, long after Selke himself had retired.

There were adjustments to be made in the early postwar years. From 47/48 to 49/50, the Canadiens did not make the finals. The 47/48 season was the most bleak. On January 11, captain Toe Blake suffered a double ankle fracture that brought an end to the Punch Line and his playing career. Bill Durnan took over as captain for the rest of the season—the last NHL goaltender to serve as official team leader. The Canadiens finished fifth and missed the playoffs; they would not miss them again until the spring of 1970. In 48/49 they trailed Detroit and Boston in the regular season, but took Detroit to the full seven games in their semifinal before bowing out.

The 49/50 season was a great improvement as the club finished second to Detroit, with 77 points, compared with 65 in 48/49. The Canadiens were confronted by an inspired crowd of New York Rangers in the semifinal. Anchored by their great goaltender, Chuck Rayner, the fourth-place Rangers built a 3-0 series lead that brought about the collapse of the celebrated Durnan. Even while winning his sixth Vezina that season, Durnan had experienced heckling by Forum crowds, and had resolved that this season would be his last. Facing elimination by New York, Durnan went to Irvin and told him that he could not play. Irvin was forced to dress his alternate, Gerry McNeil, who could not turn the series around single-handedly. New York won in five and then lost the Cup final in a seventh-game overtime heartbreaker to Detroit. Durnan never played another NHL game.

McNeil was a fine goaltender—as was anyone who could hold down a starting position in the Original Six era, when teams were required to dress only one goaltender—and he was capable of taking the Canadiens to a Cup win. Despite the disappointments

of the past few seasons, the Canadiens were building a bright future. The Montreal Junior Canadiens farm club won the Memorial Cup in 49/50. The Blackhawks and Rangers were for the most part floundering, the Bruins were seeking in vain a return to the unequivocal greatness they had enjoyed at the beginning of the war, and the successful Red Wings and Leafs were toying with disaster by executing daring blockbuster trades—but the Canadiens were building upon a profitable past with new faces drawn overwhelmingly from Selke's new development system.

The team drew stability from veterans like Lach, Bouchard, Richard and Harmon, and centers Ken Mosdell and Billy Reay, who had joined the lineup in 44/45 and 45/46. Trades and cash deals were rare. Exceptions were Buddy O'Connor, who went to New York after 46/47 with Frank Eddolls in exchange for Hal Laycoe, Joe Bell and George Robertson and played against his old teammates in the Rangers' semifinal upset of 49/50; right-winger Jim Peters, who had joined the lineup in 45/46 and was dealt to Boston in 47/48 with minor-league center John Quilty for right-winger Joe Carveth, a Red Wings fixture during the war years; and left-winger Calum MacKay, acquired from the Detroit minor pro system in 49/50.

The club's development system meanwhile was paying handsome dividends. Three new defencemen—Bud MacPherson, Tom Johnson and the superlative Doug Harvey—were coming on stream as Leo Lamoureux retired after 46/47, Reardon after 49/50 and Harmon after 50/51. By 51/52 the club had a new defence corps, a mix of bright new talent and proven veterans: Bouchard (who became captain in 48/49), Harvey, Johnson, MacPherson and (playing his first three games in 50/51) Dollard St. Laurent. Up front as the new decade began were centers Lach, Mosdell, Reay and (beginning in 50/51) Paul Masnick; right-wingers Richard, Busher Curry (who had joined in 47/48) and (beginning in 50/51) Bernie Geoffrion; and left-wingers MacKay, Bert Olmstead (acquired from Chicago in 50/51 for right-winger Leo Gravelle) and Dick Gamble (who joined full-time in 51/52).

The Canadiens had an indifferent regular season in 50/51. They finished a distant third with a points percentage of 46.4. With 25 wins in 70 games, the club was far off the pace set by Detroit (44 wins) and Toronto (41). But with Richard providing a pair of overtime goals, the Canadiens dumped the apparently invincible Red Wings in six in their semifinal and advanced to meet the Leafs. While Toronto took the Cup in five games, Montreal pressed the Leafs into overtime in every game.

Bill Barilko's winning overtime goal marked the end to his career—he would be dead in August in a plane crash—and to Toronto's Stanley Cup spree, which stopped at four in five seasons. For the Canadiens, the 50/51 series heralded the arrival of a new era: they had made the finals, and would be in every one for ten straight seasons, a performance that remains unmatched.

A few player adjustments were made following the

Maurice Richard

CANADIENS SCORING 1950/51–1959/60

	Legend
▬	Montreal goals-against
▬◻	League-leading GA
▬	Montreal goals-for
▬◻	League-leading scoring
—	League scoring average
● 58/59	**Stanley Cup win**

GOALS PER GAME

4.0
3.5
3.0
2.5
2.0
1.5

50/51 51/52 52/53 53/54 54/55 55/56 56/57 57/58 58/59 59/60

Season	Finish	Record (W-L-T)	Points %	Awards (winners & runners-up)	All-Stars	Playoffs
43/44	1st	38-5-7	83.0	CALDER: Durnan RU VEZINA: Durnan	1ST TEAM: Durnan (G), Irvin (Coach) 2ND TEAM: Bouchard (D), Lach (C), Richard (RW)	Won SC final 4-0 over Chicago
44/45	1st	38-8-4	80.0	HART: Lach, Richard RU ART ROSS: Lach, Richard RU VEZINA: Durnan	1ST TEAM: Durnan (G), Bouchard (D), Lach (C), Richard (RW), Blake (LW), Irvin (Coach) 2ND TEAM: Harmon (D)	Lost SC semifinal 4-2 to Toronto
45/46	1st	28-17-5	61.0	LADY BYNG: Blake VEZINA: Durnan	1ST TEAM: Durnan (G), Bouchard (D), Richard (RW), Irvin (Coach) 2ND TEAM: Reardon (D), Lach (C), Blake (LW)	Won SC final 4-1 over Boston
46/47	1st	34-16-10	65.0	HART: Richard ART ROSS: Richard RU VEZINA: Durnan	1ST TEAM: Durnan (G), Reardon (D), Bouchard (D), Richard (RW)	Lost SC final 4-2 to Toronto
47/48	5th	20-29-11	42.5		1ST TEAM: Lach (C), Richard (RW) 2ND TEAM: Reardon (D)	Missed playoffs
48/49	3rd	28-23-9	54.2	HART: Durnan RU VEZINA: Durnan	1ST TEAM: Durnan (G), Richard (RW) 2ND TEAM: Harmon (D), Reardon (D)	Lost SC semifinal 4-3 to Detroit
49/50	2nd	29-22-19	55.0	VEZINA: Durnan	1ST TEAM: Durnan (G), Reardon (D), Richard (RW)	Lost SC semifinal 4-1 to New York
50/51	3rd	25-30-15	46.4	HART: Richard RU ART ROSS: Richard RU	2ND TEAM: Richard (RW)	Lost SC final 4-1 to Toronto
51/52	2nd	34-26-10	55.7	HART: Lach RU CALDER: Geoffrion	1ST TEAM: Harvey (D), Lach (C) 2ND TEAM: Richard (RW)	Lost SC final 4-0 to Detroit

50/51 loss. In 51/52 Johnny McCormack, who was in Conn Smythe's bad books for having married in mid-season, was acquired from the Leafs. Dickie Moore joined the lineup, giving the Canadiens attacking balance on the left wing to its scoring power on the right, which had Curry, Geoffrion (who had brought the full slapshot to the NHL the previous season when he played his first 18 games) and Richard. Geoffrion led the Canadiens' right-wingers in 51/52 with 30 goals and finished sixth in the scoring race. Across the league, Boom-Boom Geoffrion was outperformed on right wing only by Gordie Howe, who won the scoring race, and on his own team he was bettered only by Lach, who finished third in the scoring race on the strength of 50 assists. Geoffrion's performance earned him the Calder.

Injury limited Richard to 48 games in 51/52, but he was on hand when necessary. The team struggled with the fourth-place Bruins in the semifinals, prevail-ing when Richard scored the tie-breaking goal with four minutes to play in the seventh game. The finals brought on Detroit, but this season the Red Wings were not going to be upended. Detroit swept the Canadiens in four, giving them the Cup with eight straight playoff victories. Two straight finals for the Canadiens had produced two straight losses.

In 52/53 the Canadiens made one truly significant adjustment in personnel: Jacques Plante was called up from the American league farm club, the Buffalo Bisons, for a three-game inspection, and impressed by allowing only four goals. The club was in no great need of goaltending, as Gerry McNeil was playing his way onto the second All Star team. But having Plante available proved critical to Montreal's playoff fortunes as history repeated itself in the semifinals.

As in 49/50, the Canadiens came up against an inspired underdog. Then, it was the Rangers; now, it

was the Blackhawks, who hadn't been in the playoffs for the last six seasons. Chicago had found new life under player-coach Sid Abel, who had been traded from Detroit at his own request to fulfill the role. Though the Blackhawks had finished fourth to Montreal's second this season, they had only won one less game, and had outscored the Canadiens, 169 to 155. Chicago had an excellent lineup of experienced veterans gathered from other championship clubs: in addition to Abel, the Blackhawks had a slew of Stanley Cup-winning Leafs gathered over the past few seasons in monster trades: Al Rollins in goal, Gus Mortson on defence, and Vic Lynn, Gus Bodnar and Cal Gardner up front.

Defence and goaltending was supposed to be Montreal's edge: the team had allowed 148 goals to Chicago's 175, the league's second-worst record. But after Montreal won the first two games, Chicago rolled up three straight wins. Richard didn't even score until game five, a 4-2 loss that put the Canadiens at the brink of

elimination. Just as Bill Durnan went to Irvin in 49/50 and asked for McNeil to replace him, McNeil now asked Irvin to use Plante in his stead. It was the right move. Montreal rallied to win the necessary two games 3-0 and 4-1, and advanced to the finals against Boston.

Montreal won the opening game at home 4-2 with Plante in goal, and the 23-year-old newcomer let loose with a spout of characteristic self-congratulation. "They had 27 breakaways on me this season before they scored on me," Plante bragged after the win. "Gerry is a great goaltender, but he's so small that he has to move twice as fast as me to cover the same area."

In game two, Plante was made mortal by a 4-1 loss. Irvin decided to switch back to McNeil. Playing on an ankle deadened by freezing, McNeil anchored three straight wins of 3-0, 7-3 and 1-0, the clinching win coming on an overtime goal by Lach.

McNeil was not finished as the Canadiens' starter, but the weight of winning was bearing down on him.

Though Plante had disappointed in game two of the finals, he was McNeil's evident successor, and was able to play 17 games in 53/54 after McNeil was injured on February 11. The team was ageing—Bouchard and Lach had played for 12 seasons, Richard for 11. All Star voting preferences had shifted to the Red Wings, a young, dynamic team. From 44/45 to 49/50, Maurice Richard locked up the right-wing position on the first team. In 50/51, Gordie Howe took it over and held it for three seasons, consigning Richard to the second team. Bill Durnan had held the first-team goaltending berth for six of seven seasons; in 50/51, with Durnan's retirement, Terry Sawchuk took over for three straight seasons. In 51/52, four of six first-team players were Red Wings—Howe, Sawchuk, Red Kelly and Ted Lindsay—leaving two positions for Doug Harvey and Elmer Lach.

Center ice was where Montreal was most vulnerable in 53/54. Lach was reaching the end of the line, Mosdell had just completed his ninth season, and Reay had decided to retire after eight seasons, thereby beginning and ending his Montreal career with Stanley Cup wins. Frank Selke wasn't letting the matter go unattended. He'd had the perfect replacement center waiting in the wings for several seasons—Jean Béliveau.

Selke probably would have had the big, durable scoring star in the lineup already, were it not for the stubbornness of Béliveau's father. The standard device for securing amateur talents up until 1966 was the C-form, which was a contractual promise of professional services. In exchange for a signing fee (generally $100), the player agreed to be called up to play professionally within one year's time at an agreed-upon salary. Renewed annually, it was a notorious device that, in the postwar enthusiasm for fresh young talent, caused many young men to be hauled up into the professional game while still in their teens, when they were emotionally unprepared and financially poorly compensated.

The Canadiens tried to get Béliveau to sign a C-form, but his father would not budge: his attitude was that when the hockey season was over, Jean belonged to him, not to some professional hockey club. After keeping him on the Canadiens negotiating list for three years, Selke finally had to be satisfied with young Béliveau's signature on a B-form. This far more benign document (not often used) paid a large one-time bonus (about $1,000) and only held the player to the promise that, if and when he chose to turn professional, he would do so with that club.

At the time, the difference between "professional" and "amateur" was nearly indistinguishable, a matter of hockey's organizational structure rather than remuneration. Béliveau graduated from Junior hockey to play for the Quebec Aces of the Quebec Senior league. The league was part of the Canadian Amateur Hockey Association, but like other Senior leagues (and Junior leagues) it routinely paid players to play—some Senior league players were under contract with NHL clubs and were being paid by them, making the Senior circuit essentially a minor-pro development loop. Béliveau was being paid to play for Quebec, and handsomely so. His compensation package was in the $25,000 range, at a time when Tim Horton was making about $4,400 as a Maple Leaf. Béliveau was a franchise player, beloved by the fans of Quebec City, a star who packed the new Colisée with paying customers.

The few glimpses NHL fans had of Béliveau made it clear he could be a dominant force in the tier-one professional game. At 19, Béliveau was brought up for two games in 50/51 and produced a goal and an assist. In 52/53, he scored five times in just three games, the maximum number of permitted visits for a protected amateur. Selke wanted Béliveau desperately, but under the terms of the B-form he had no grounds to compel him to turn "professional" with the Canadiens.

Selke's solution was to make him turn professional by default. If the entire Quebec Senior league became a de facto professional league, then Béliveau would be a de facto professional as well, and under the terms of the B-form he would have to sign with Montreal. To engineer Béliveau's signing, the Canadiens bought the entire Quebec Senior league, made it a minor-pro circuit, and so brought Jean Béliveau into the Canadiens lineup for 53/54.

The 22-year-old had a rough introduction to the NHL. He didn't sign a contract until October 4, four days before Montreal's first game of the season. In Chicago on October 22, a slash cracked a bone in his ankle and took him out of the lineup until December 9. The day after he rejoined the team, he broke his cheekbone on a goalpost. When he returned to play on December 30, he was sporting a protective mask.

Béliveau's rookie season totaled 44 games, with 13 goals and 21 assists. Camille Henry of the Rangers won the Calder, with Dutch Reibel of Detroit runner-up. But Béliveau had amply demonstrated his worth, and in 54/55, with Elmer Lach having retired, he contributed 73 points in 70 games and finished third in the scoring race. In 55/56, he set a new scoring record for centers when he potted his 45th on March 15 (he finished the season with 47) and also earned the league scoring title, the Hart Trophy, and the first-team All Star berth.

Béliveau joined the Canadiens when the NHL was in its wildest seasons. Bloody on-ice confrontations, complete with nasty stick-swinging, were par for the course, and the Canadiens were seen by some as the least disciplined club. Maurice Richard's temper was truly explosive, and his penalty minutes steadily mounted. Having attracted only 46 minutes in 50 games when he scored 50 goals in 44/45, he incurred 112 minutes in 70 games in 53/54. Along the way he gathered a string

Bernie Boom-Boom Geoffrion brought the first fully developed slapshot to the NHL when he joined the Canadiens in 50/51. His stick appears below. He won the league scoring title by one point over Maurice Richard in 54/55 after his teammate was suspended, and won it again in 60/61.

MONTREAL CANADIENS

The Champions of the 1950s

Featuring the players and management who participated in Montreal's Stanley Cup victories of 1952/53, 1955/56, 1956/57, 1957/58, 1958/59 and 1959/60

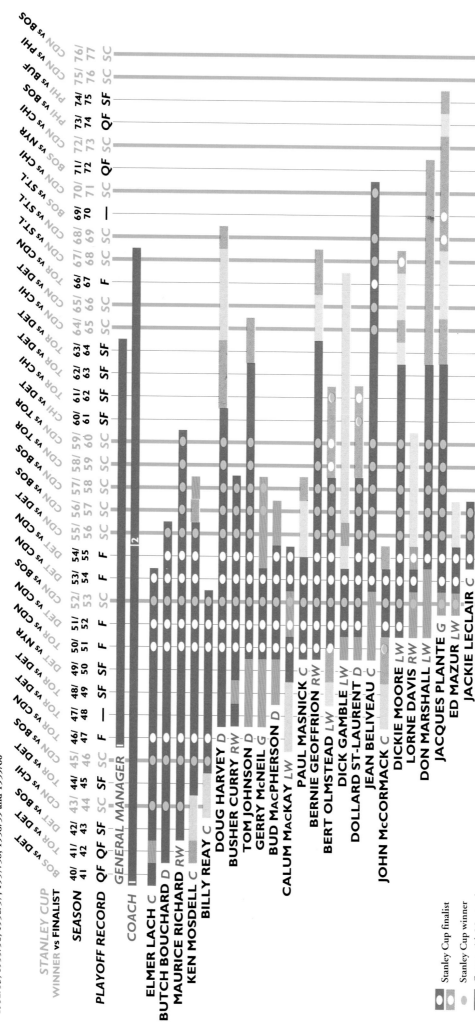

GENERAL MANAGER
1. Frank Selke

COACHES
1. Dick Irvin
2. Toe Blake

Stanley Cup finalist
Stanley Cup winner
Career with Montreal
Absent from Canadiens lineup or minimal appearances
Career with other NHL (and WHA) teams
Absent from NHL or WHA, or minimal appearances

of misconducts and fines for incidents involving both rival players and on-ice officials. They were often provoked by a fury over an injustice, whether perceived or real. Back in the 46/47 semifinals against Boston, for example, Richard was cut in the face by the checker assigned to him, left-winger Ken Smith. The infraction earned Smith a minor, which Richard felt did not go far enough, and to indicate his displeasure he banged his stick on the ice. That simple gesture earned him a misconduct penalty. In the finals against Toronto that spring, Richard responded to Vic Lynn's close checking by whacking him over the head, sending him unconscious and bleeding from the game. When he returned to the ice from serving his penalty, Richard replied to the goading of Bill Ezinicki by hacking Ezinicki's head as well, and received a one-game suspension.

The outbursts became more spectacular. In a game against the Bruins in Boston on January 18, 1948—one week after Toe Blake's career was ended by a double ankle fracture—Richard was sent off for breaking his stick on the arm of Milt Schmidt. To register his disapproval of the call, Richard threw his own stick and that of Murph Chamberlain (who was off for roughing) onto the ice, then left the penalty box to chew out referee Bill Chadwick. He was given a match misconduct and a policeman to take him to the Canadiens' dressing room.

Conn Smythe would recall in his memoirs a wild game at Maple Leaf Gardens in which Richard was sent to the dressing room. Smythe was in the corridor when suddenly

the door flew open and he charged out again, his eyes blazing the way he sometimes got, in what somebody once called the Rocket's red glare, so mad he was not seeing anything. I stepped in front of him and said, "Rocket! Where are you going! Won't do you any good...Get back!"

He seemed to come to. He stared at me. Then without a word, he turned and stomped back into the dressing room. I admired that man tremendously, would have given anything to have him play for me ...

Richard was by no means the lone miscreant. A few weeks before Richard's outburst in Boston, Ken Reardon was given a ten-minute misconduct when he punched a linesman who attempted to intervene in a fight between Butch Bouchard and Bill Ezinicki. And Bernie Geoffrion received a game misconduct and $250 fine when he shoved the referee into the boards after being assessed a minor penalty in a home game against Chicago on November 11, 1953. After a brawl led to

Geoffrion knocking Ranger Ron Murphy unconscious with his stick on December 20, Geoffrion was suspended from the remaining seven games between the two teams, Murphy from the remaining four games. Other teams had their share of hotheads and dangerous characters: Detroit had Ted Lindsay, for one, and the Leafs had the most penalized player in the league from 46/47 to 50/51, an honour passed between Gus Mortson, Bill Barilko and Bill Ezinicki. The game overall was bloody, brutal, and often dirty. On December 9, 1953, a match between the Leafs and Rangers produced a record 36 penalties, with $375 in fines.

Richard's sense of personal outrage, however, seemed to know no limits. As a scoring star subject to relentless, often dirty checking, his temper was often sorely tested. He led the league in penalty minutes in 52/53; on December 29, 1954, he both thrilled and appalled Toronto fans by scoring his 401st goal against the Leafs and by earning a major penalty and two misconducts for swatting a linesman with his glove in his determination to get at Bob Bailey, who had run him heavily into the boards.

Richard's ultimate demonstration of pure rage came on March 13, 1955, in a game in Boston. Around the 14 minute mark of the third period, Richard was cut with a high stick by Bruins defenceman Hal Laycoe. The referee signalled for a penalty, and Richard confronted Laycoe, who had dropped his gloves and stick. Richard clubbed him on the shoulder and face. A linesman intervened and got Richard's stick away, but Richard got free, retrieved a loose stick and broke it over Laycoe's back. He then collected another stick and hit Laycoe with it as well. A linesman held Richard down, but a teammate pushed the official away, and Richard managed to get in two solid punches to the

linesman's face before at last being removed from the ice.

Richard was given a match penalty for deliberately injuring the linesman, while Laycoe received a major penalty for the high-sticking incident and then a ten-minute misconduct for refusing to go to the penalty box. Laycoe claimed he had high-sticked Richard because Richard had hit him first in the glasses he wore. Richard asserted he thought the linesman was one of the Bruins when he began slugging him.

League president Clarence Campbell didn't buy Richard's excuse. The Canadiens star had already per-turbed Campbell with a ghost-written article that appeared in the Montreal paper *Samedi Dimanche* in January 1954, in which he called Campbell a dictator as he criticized his suspension of Geoffrion that season. Campbell was confident Richard knew he was punch-ing out a linesman and, citing the Bailey incident in December, noted in the inquiry held March 16 that "At

that time he was warned there must be no further inci-dent." Campbell was in a combative mood—he had suspended Ted Lindsay for ten days in January after the Red Wings captain struck with his stick a Toronto fan who had taken a poke at Gordie Howe. On the Richard incident Campbell ruled, "The time for probationary lenience has passed, whether this type of conduct is the product of temperamental instability or wilful defiance of the authority of the game does not matter. Richard will be suspended from all games both league and play-off for the balance of the current season."

There were three games left in the regular season, beginning with a match at the Forum against Detroit, with whom the Canadiens were vying for first place over-all, the first day after the Richard suspension. Detroit raced to a 4-1 first-period lead, and during the first inter-mission the crowd turned ugly, crowding around Campbell's box, tossing rubbish, and generally defying

MONTREAL CANADIENS 1952/53–59/60

Season	Finish	Record (W-L-T)	Points %	Awards (winners & runners-up)	All-Stars	Playoffs
52/53	2nd	28-23-19	53.6	VEZINA: McNeil RU	1ST TEAM: Harvey (D) 2ND TEAM: Olmstead (LW), McNeil (G), Richard (RW)	Won SC final 4-1 over Boston
53/54	2nd	35-24-11	57.9	ART ROSS: Richard RU NORRIS: Harvey RU	1ST TEAM: Harvey (D), Mosdell (C) 2ND TEAM: Richard (RW)	Lost SC final 4-3 to Detroit
54/55	2nd	41-18-11	66.4	ART ROSS: Geoffrion, Richard RU NORRIS: Harvey	1ST TEAM: Harvey (D), Béliveau (C), Richard (RW) 2ND TEAM: Mosdell (C), Geoffrion (RW)	Lost SC final 4-3 to Detroit
55/56	1st	45-15-10	71.4	HART: Béliveau ART ROSS: Béliveau LADY BYNG: Curry RU VEZINA: Plante NORRIS: Harvey	1ST TEAM: Plante (G), Harvey (D), Béliveau (C), Richard (RW) 2ND TEAM: Johnson (D), Olmstead (LW)	Won SC final 4-1 over Detroit
56/57	2nd	35-23-12	58.6	HART: Béliveau RU VEZINA: Plante NORRIS: Harvey	1ST TEAM: Harvey (D), Béliveau (C) 2ND TEAM: Plante (G), Richard (RW)	Won SC final 4-1 over Boston
57/58	1st	43-17-10	68.6	ART ROSS: Moore, H. Richard RU LADY BYNG: Marshall RU VEZINA: Plante NORRIS: Harvey	1ST TEAM: Harvey (D), H. Richard (C), Moore (LW) 2ND TEAM: Plante (G), Béliveau (C)	Won SC final 4-2 over Boston
58/59	1st	39-18-13	65.0	ART ROSS: Moore, Béliveau RU CALDER: Backstrom VEZINA: Plante NORRIS: Johnson	1ST TEAM: Plante (G), Johnson (D), Béliveau (C), Moore (LW) 2ND TEAM: Harvey (D) H. Richard (C)	Won SC final 4-1 over Toronto
59/60	1st	40-18-12	65.7	VEZINA: Plante NORRIS: Harvey	1ST TEAM: Harvey (D), Béliveau (C) 2ND TEAM: Plante (G), Geoffrion (RW)	Won SC final 4-0 over Toronto

the police. When someone tossed a tear-gas bomb, it was evident a full-scale riot was what some fans had come for. The game was called off (and forfeited to Detroit), and a mob went on a rampage through downtown Montreal.

In the Rocket's absence, Geoffrion edged out Richard for the scoring title by one point, an act that made him almost as hated among some fans as Campbell. Without Richard, the Canadiens advanced to the finals against the Red Wings, which they lost in the seventh game. In 53/54, Montreal had also lost to Detroit, on an overtime goal in game seven, when Doug Harvey tried to glove a routine dump-in shot and had the puck glance off his thumb and over Gerry McNeil's shoulder. In the last five seasons, Montreal had been in every final, but had won only one of them.

The 54/55 Cup proved to be the last Red Wings victory to date, but it was also the last Cup series in which Dick Irvin coached. More than the Cup losses, the Richard suspension and resulting riot seemed to spell the end of Irvin's 15-season run with Les Canadiens. Richard had become almost unmanageable in his on-ice rage; Irvin was a coach who was said to know how to motivate players by placing burrs under their saddles, who looked on with approval when stick-swinging erupted in his own practices. The Canadiens needed someone behind the bench who could get the most out of Richard (and other temperamental players) without risking suspensions and civil disobedience from the fans. Irvin had also caused some consternation at NHL head office during the Cup finals, when he took to task one of the linesmen who had testified at the Richard hearing, accusing him of not having told the truth. Campbell's opinion, expressed in his decision to suspend Richard, was that the Canadiens had exacerbated Richard's behaviour by not restraining him: "It

Dickie Moore and Bernie Geoffrion hoist rookie coach Toe Blake as Jacques Plante helps celebrate the 55/56 Stanley Cup victory over Detroit following a 3-1 win in game five. The victory avenged Montreal's bitter losses to the Red Wings in the 53/54 and 54/55 finals, both of which lasted seven games.

was too bad that his teammates did not assist officials instead of interfering with them." As with Fred Shero and the Philadelphia Flyers of the mid-1970s, Irvin was seen by some as an orchestrator of on-ice mayhem.

Irvin was out, and Maurice Richard's old linemate, Toe Blake, was in. Irvin was handed another rescue mission. Just as he was needed in 1940 to put the Canadiens franchise back on its feet, he was now called upon to steer the Blackhawks clear of total collapse. But Irvin's health was poor, and he would be dead of cancer in two years. Chicago's day would come, but it would come without Irvin.

If anyone could motivate the Canadiens and keep their fiery nature focused, particularly Richard's, it was the all-round talent who had played on the Rocket's opposite wing for six seasons and won two Stanley Cups with him. Toe Blake managed to combine a deep love (and knowledge) of the game and of the franchise with a genuine camaraderie with those who shared his commitment to the glory of the team. Though he always maintained some distance between himself and his players, they knew he was with them and believed in the possibility of their greatness. He was not unlike

Toronto's Hap Day in that he had enjoyed a long and fruitful career with the team he now coached, and was able to embody for the next generation of players the glory they sought to uphold. Other teams tried the same formula. Milt Schmidt of the Stanley Cup-winning teams of 1939 and 1941 coached the Bruins from 55/56 to 60/61; Sid Abel ran the Detroit bench from 58/59 to 67/68; and Neil Colville, Bill Cook, Phil Watson, Frank Boucher and Murray Patrick all had a go with the Rangers in the 1950s. But none of them had a manager as savvy (or as consistently successful) as Frank Selke behind him; none was able, in drawing on the triumphs of his own career, to bring forth triumphs as great as, even greater than, his own.

Montreal's record successes under Blake from 55/56 to 59/60 must be set in the context of the age. Without detracting from the accomplishments of the Canadiens' players and management, the team amassed its five consecutive Cup wins when the majority of the league's franchises were in varying degrees of disarray. Boston managed a few strong seasons at the end of the decade, but without a decent farm system the Bruins were built through trades for the present, not the future, and faded

badly after 58/59. New York continued to flounder, missing the playoffs altogether from 50/51 to 54/55, redeeming itself for three seasons, then missing the play-offs again from 58/59 to 60/61; its low point came in 59/60 when it won only 17 games. Toronto had begun to lose its way after its 50/51 win, making question-able trades as Conn Smythe's hockey smarts dulled. Detroit, having so dominated the game for the first half of the decade, broke up a winning team through erratic management. Always afraid of complacency in his players, general manager Jack Adams executed a nine-player deal with Boston after the 54/55 Cup win, including Terry Sawchuk, from which the team never completely recovered (not even after dealing to get Sawchuk back). He then exacerbated the situation by dumping the team's heart and soul, Ted Lindsay, and great new goaltending talent, Glenn Hall, in Chicago in 1957, because of their involvement in the failed players' associ-ation drive. The Leafs were similarly racked by manage-ment hysteria as captain Jim Thomson and fellow organizer Tod Sloan were sent to the Blackhawks.

While the Blackhawks ultimately benefited from these labour-related trades, until their lineup gelled they remained a house of hockey horrors, missing every playoff but one from 46/47 to 57/58. By the mid-1950s their circumstances were so dire that the league began bending its own rules to help them avoid total collapse. Although the lending of players to other teams was, technically, forbidden, the Blackhawks were able to borrow players from other teams through phony trades. Montreal participated in these player airlifts. Center Paul Masnick was sent to

Jacques Plante introduced the first functional goaltender's mask (left) to the NHL during a game against the New York Rangers on November 1, 1959 after being cut by an Andy Bathgate shot. He appears above wearing the mask in a home game against New York on December 19, 1959 that Montreal won 5-3. General manager Frank Selke made Plante undergo tests to see if the mask affected his vision. With no negative result, Plante kept wearing the mask. It took years for his fellow netminders to follow his example.

Chicago on November 9, 1954, for a player to be named later (Al Dewsbury), and was then returned to Montreal on December 10. Center Ken Mosdell was approaching the end of his career when he was sold to Chicago with left-winger Ed Mazur and veteran defenceman Bud McPherson for

$55,000 after the 55/56 Stanley Cup. Montreal retained the option to recall Mosdell at the end of the 56/57 season, and did so the following September. Other Canadiens went to Chicago in permanent deals for the 54/55 season as part of the league's rescue effort: center Johnny McCormack, utility left-winger Dick Gamble, right-wing prospect Eddie Litzenberger and defensive prospect Bucky Hollingworth.

The Canadiens ended Detroit's streak of seven regular-season championships in 55/56, relented to Detroit in 56/57, then took command again from 57/58 to 61/62. A glance at the lineup provides sufficient clues to its greatness. Montreal management had not been traumatized by the idea of a players' association to the degree Detroit and Toronto had, and declined to participate in the self-destructive behaviour of its league rivals as they dumped association organizers in Chicago. Selke could not see any hockey wisdom in banishing his most important defenceman, Doug Harvey, who was also an offensive spark, just because NHLers wanted to follow the lead of their baseball brethren. When the organization effort crumbled, Montreal's daunting lineup was left intact, while Detroit and Toronto had destabilized theirs and helped create a viable rival in Chicago.

As the Canadiens began their five-season reign in 55/56, their roster was unsurpassed. Jacques Plante had inherited the Canadiens goal from McNeil, who was available to relieve him (along with newcomer Charlie Hodge). The defence was a mix of experience and promising talent: Bouchard (who would

Maurice Richard had the honour of gracing the cover of the Forum's official program in 58/59 as the Canadiens franchise marked its 50th season. Richard aided the celebrations by leading the team to its fourth straight Stanley Cup win.

LA REVUE SPORTIVE du **Forum** SPORTS MAGAZINE 25¢

Maurice Richard

SAISON 1958-59 **CINQUANTENAIRE - GOLDEN ANNIVERSARY** SEASON

LA 50e SAISON CONSÉCUTIVE DES CANADIENS AU HOCKEY PROFESSIONNEL

LES CANADIENS' 50th CONSECUTIVE SEASON IN PROFESSIONAL HOCKEY

retire after 55/56), Harvey, Johnson and St. Laurent, with Bob Turner and Jean-Guy Talbot coming on stream. The lineup was going through an overhaul at center. Ken Mosdell was beginning his last full season, but was about to be lent to Chicago. Jean Béliveau was the team's lone experienced offensive anchor. Jackie LeClair was in his second season, Connie Broden was strictly a fill-in. The Rocket's younger brother, Henri, brought in that season initially as a sub on right wing for an injured Geoffrion, was converted profitably to center, and in the next two seasons Phil Goyette and Ralph Backstrom would join the team at the position. On right wing, the Canadiens were peerless, with Richard, Geoffrion and newcomer Claude Provost, as well as the veteran Curry in a supporting role. Left wing had Olmstead, Don Marshall (who had made the lineup in 54/55) and Moore.

Detroit players had won five consecutive scoring titles, beginning with Lindsay in 49/50 and carrying through with Howe from 50/51 to 53/54. From 54/55 to 58/59 Canadiens dominated the scoring race. Geoffrion, Richard and Béliveau swept the top three places in 54/55; Béliveau won it in 55/56, with Richard and Olmstead in third and fourth. After an interruption by Howe and Lindsay at the top in 56/57, Moore and Richard took the top two spots in 57/58, with Moore and Béliveau at the top again in 58/59. Overall, the Canadiens outscored every other team in every season from 53/54 to 61/62. From 57/58 to 59/60, when Montreal produced 250, 258 and 255 goals, its offensive output was simply overwhelming, despite the fact that Maurice Richard, hobbled by injuries, limped through those seasons with less than 20 goals in each of them. Boston, with the second-best offensive output in those years, trailed by 51 goals in 57/58, by 53 goals in 58/59, and by 35 goals in 59/60. The club's goals production was fueled by its awesome powerplay, quarter-backed by Doug Harvey, with Geoffrion, Béliveau and Richard providing the main scoring. It was a hat-trick by Béliveau in one powerplay against Boston that convinced the league, beginning in 56/57, to allow a penalized player to return to the ice once his team had been scored on. But that did not stop Montreal from continuing to score at a pace far ahead of the rest of the league.

All those goals would not have amounted to much without the Canadiens' superb defensive effort. From 55/56 to 59/60, the Vezina Trophy was the personal property of Jacques Plante. In 55/56 the Canadiens lost only 15 of 70 games and won 45, scoring 221 goals while allowing only 131. In 57/58 and 58/59, Plante's goals-against average was about 0.7 below the league scoring average, while Montreal's scoring was about 0.8 above it. In other words, a typical Montreal game had a net scoring advantage of 1.5. So dominant were the Canadiens that only two other teams—the Rangers and Bruins—scored more goals than they allowed in 57/58; every other team had a scoring deficit in 58/59 while Montreal had a scoring surplus of 100.

The Canadiens were prominent in All Star voting from 55/56 to 59/60, but did not monopolize it. Plante, despite his string of Vezinas, could not repeat the performance of Bill Durnan and dominate the first team— Glenn Hall of Chicago earned three appearances to Plante's two in these years. Doug Harvey, however, continued his streak of first-team appearances, which began in 51/52 and ran almost uninterrupted (he had to settle for the second team in 58/59) through 61/62. Fellow defenceman Tom Johnson made the second team in 55/56 and the first team in 58/59. Jean Béliveau was voted the top center in every season from 54/55 to 60/61 save one, 57/58, when Henri Richard displaced him to the second team. In his final seasons, plagued by injuries, Maurice Richard was no longer considered the dominant player at his position, although he was clearly the team leader, having taken over the captain's role from the retired Butch Bouchard in 56/57. His last All Star appearance was on the second team, in 56/57, and another Canadian right-winger would not make the first team until Geoffrion, in 60/61. The left-wing slot was Ted Lindsay's until 56/57, when Moore took it over for the two seasons in which he won the scoring race and then relinquished it to Bobby Hull.

During its run of five straight Stanley Cups, the Canadiens were rarely seriously challenged in the playoffs, winning 40 of 49 games as they encountered every other team in the league—eight of ten against New York, eight of nine against Detroit, eight of eleven against Boston, eight of ten against Chicago, and eight of nine against Toronto.

In 55/56 Montreal breezed past New York and then Detroit, losing only one game in each series as the team averaged 4.2 goals for and only 1.8 against. The 56/57 playoffs were another cakewalk, with the Rangers moved aside in five games and the Bruins downed in another five in the final; Montreal's goals-per-game average was 4.1, goals against 1.8. In 57/58 the Canadiens crushed Detroit in the semifinal, averaging 4.75 goals to Detroit's 1.5 in a four-game sweep. In the finals, though, the Canadiens met their first serious resistance in the Cup-winning streak when the Bruins had the series tied at two games apiece. Overtime was needed in game five for Montreal to manage a 3-2 win and resume control, and the defending champions almost blew game six when a 4-1 lead was whittled down to 4-3 by a determined Boston club. A late insurance goal by Doug Harvey gave Montreal its third straight Cup win, matching the NHL streak set by Toronto from 46/47 to 48/49.

The 58/59 playoffs brought two fresh challengers: the Leafs and the Blackhawks. Toronto was returning to its winning ways in its first season under the direction of Punch Imlach; the Blackhawks were emerging from their lengthy history of ineptitude with a club that featured: two Red Wings outcasts, goaltender Glenn Hall and left-winger Ted Lindsay; center Tod Sloan and defenceman Jim Thomson from the Leafs; right-

wingers Ken Wharram (brought up from the minors) and Ed Litzenberger (sent to Chicago by Montreal in 54/55); defenceman Dollard St. Laurent (acquired from Montreal that season); and sophomore left-winger Bobby Hull. (Stan Mikita also played his first three Blackhawk games in 58/59, although he wasn't with the club in the playoffs.)

A back injury in game two of the 58/59 semifinal knocked Béliveau out of the rest of the playoffs, and after four games, the series against the Blackhawks was tied at two apiece. Montreal took command with a chippy 4-2 win at home, then downed Chicago 5-4 in a controversial game in which referee Red Storey declined to call a penalty shot after Hull was hauled down on a breakaway by defenceman Al Langlois.

The semifinal win brought on the unlikely Leafs, who had squeezed into the playoffs on the last game of the season and were now playing inspired hockey for their new coach and general manager. Imlach's charges, who had eliminated Boston 4-3, pressed the champions in every match. Though the Leafs went down in five, their gritty performance, which included a lone win in overtime in game three, coupled with the credible performance of the resurrected Blackhawks in the semifinals, suggested that Montreal was no longer unassailable.

But the Canadiens were far from finished. In 59/60 season, the club won 40 games, one more than in 58/59. In the playoffs, Montreal matched the 51/52 performance of Detroit in taking the Cup without a single loss, amassing eight straight playoff victories, three of them shutouts. First Chicago went down in four, outscored 14-6, then fell Toronto, outscored 15-5. The Canadiens had averaged 3.6 goals to their opponents' 1.4.

With five straight Cup wins to its credit, six did not seem at all impossible, particularly after the club won its fourth straight regular-season title in 60/61. But for the first time in ten seasons, Montreal did not make the finals, as third-place Chicago—who had won only 29 games to Montreal's 41 and scored 56 fewer goals— downed them in six games in their semifinal.

Maurice Richard had retired after the 59/60 win, the only player to have participated in all the Canadiens' Cup victories since the revival of 43/44. Another five seasons would pass before the Canadiens made the finals again, and it would be a far different lineup that did so. Not only Richard, but a majority of players from the 59/60 club would no longer be on hand—just six members of the 64/65 Cup winning lineup, in fact, would be able to say they had been on the 59/60 winner.

In his final years as general manager, Frank Selke turned into a decisive deal-maker not afraid of the blockbuster trade. Toronto and Chicago had fashioned new championship lineups out of deal-making. Now Montreal, after years of relying on Selke's rebuilt amateur development system, was willing to make dramatic changes for immediate gains. Not even its most heralded players would be considered off-limits when trade talk began. ○

Cochrane
Smooth Rock Falls
Kapuskasing
Hearst
Kirkland Lake
Noranda-Rouyn
The Porcupine
Chapleau
Tri-Town
Nickel Belt
North Bay
MONTREAL
OTTAWA
TORONTO
DETROIT

MOTHERLODE

Small-town northern Ontario, touted as hockey's finest "breeding ground," provided a bonanza of postwar talent

"The territory between Sudbury and Timmins is one of the best breeding grounds in Canada—bar none." So proclaimed Hal Cotton, Boston Bruins scout, in 1946 as teams scrambled to secure the rights to fresh talents that would bring success in peacetime.

Before the arrival of the universal amateur draft in 1969, NHL scouts like Cotton barnstormed the Canadian hinterlands in search of teenagers with the proverbial "right stuff." As he freely noted, there were few if any better places to find them than the chunk of northern Ontario whose boundaries were roughly defined by Sudbury (the heart of the Nickel Belt) in the southwest, North Bay in the southeast, and Timmins (the heart of the Porcupine) in the north. That northern boundary was soon moved east to include Kirkland Lake and Noranda-Rouyn, just across the Ontario-

Quebec border. And a few players were offered up by more remote towns like Cochrane, Hearst, Smooth Rock Falls and Kapuskasing. (This territory was entirely distinct from other northern Ontario hotspots such as Sault Ste. Marie to the west and, far to the northwest, Port Arthur-Fort William.)

This was a land of lumber and mining, and it yielded to NHL scouts a bonanza of quality players born generally between 1925 and 1949, with a few pioneering spirits coming before them. (Those born after 1949 were subject to the universal draft and fall outside our survey.)

Boston scouts like Hal Cotton did find their share of players, such as Jerry Toppazzini, Doug Mohns, Larry Regan, Réal Chevrefils and Leo Labine. And the Bruins were especially attuned to the Ontario north, as the team's general manager, Art Ross, came out of Naughton, just west of Sudbury. But Toronto above all found a motherlode of talent hereabouts. Of 20 members of the 62/63 Stanley Cup-winning team, 11 were born in this fertile hockey terrain.

Methodology

Players are defined in three categories:
Pioneers: those who played or established themselves in the NHL before the postwar era.
Fresh Prospects: those who came into the NHL at the end of the Second World War or after, but before the arrival of the universal amateur draft in 1969.
Others: those who made minimal NHL appearances.

Players who have been inducted in the Hockey Hall of Fame carry the annotation **HHOF**. Career spans extend from the first to the last NHL or WHA game in which a player appeared. The spans thus may include seasons in which he made minimal or no appearances.

The Nickel Belt

With Sudbury as its main population area, the Nickel Belt was one of the most productive centers for young hockey talent. Players came either from Sudbury proper or from one of the company mining towns.

Pioneers

LARRY AURIE b. Sudbury 1905. Detroit right-winger 27/28 to 38/39. Won SC in 35/36, 36/37. 1st All Star 36/37. Number retired.
TOE BLAKE b. Victoria Mines, Ont. 1912. Sudbury amateur system product. Left-winger Montreal Maroons and Canadiens 32/33 to 47/48. Won SC with Canadiens 43/44, 45/46. SC finalist with Canadiens 46/47. Canadiens captain 40/41 to 47/48. Won Lady Byng 45/46, Art Ross 38/39, Hart 38/39. 1st All Star 38/39, 39/40, 44/45. 2nd All Star 37/38, 45/46. Canadiens coach 55/56 to 67/68. Won SC as coach 55/56, 56/57, 57/58, 58/59, 59/60, 64/65, 65/66, 67/68. HHOF
RED GREEN b. Sudbury [date unknown]. Left-winger with Hamilton Tigers, New York Americans, Boston Bruins, 23/24 to 28/29. Won 28/29 SC with Boston.
WILF (SHORTY) GREEN b. Sudbury 1896. Brother of Red. Starred on right wing with Hamilton Tigers, New York Americans, 23/24 to 26/27. Coached Americans. HHOF
ALEX McKINNON b. Sudbury [date unknown]. Played defence on Hamilton Tigers, New York Americans, Chicago Blackhawks, 24/25 to 28/29.
ART ROSS b. Naughton 1886. Won SC with Kenora Thistles, 06/07, with Montreal Wanderers 07/08. Played three games on defence with Montreal Wanderers in NHL, 17/18. Became general manager (and often coach) of Boston Bruins 24/25 to 53/54. Won 28/29, 38/39, 40/41 SC as GM. Won 38/39 SC as coach. HHOF
SAM ROTHSCHILD b. Sudbury 1899. Forward with Montreal Maroons, New York Americans, 24/25 to 27/28.

Fresh Prospects

AL ARBOUR b. Sudbury 1932. Defenceman, won SC with Detroit 53/54, Chicago 60/61, Toronto 61/62, 63/64. Also finalist with St. Louis 67/68, 68/69, 69/70. Coach of New York Islanders, Stanley Cup winners 79/80, 80/81, 81/82, 82/83. Jack Adams winner 79/80. HHOF
GEORGE ARMSTRONG b. Skead 1930. Toronto right-winger 49/50 to 70/71. Maple Leafs captain 57/58 to 68/69. SC winner 61/62, 62/63, 63/64, 66/67. SC finalist 58/59, 59/60. Maple Leafs coach 88/89. HHOF
CUMMY BURTON b. Sudbury 1936. Detroit right-winger 55/56 to 58/59.
GERRY DESJARDINS b. Sudbury 1944. NHL goaltender 68/69 to 77/78.
ED GIACOMIN b. Sudbury 1939. NHL goaltender, mainly with New York, 65/66 to 77/78. 1st All Star 66/67, 70/71. 2nd All Star 67/68, 68/69, 69/70. Won Vezina 70/71. Hart RU 66/67. HHOF

TIM HORTON
—see Cochrane
DOUG MOHNS *b. Capreol 1933*. Defenceman, played 1,390 regular-season games from 53/54 to 74/75, most with Boston, Chicago. Played in 56/57, 57/58 SC final with Boston, 64/65 final with Chicago.
JIM PAPPIN, *b. Copper Cliff 1939*. Right-winger from 63/64 to 76/77, mainly with Toronto and Chicago. Won 63/64, 66/67 SC with Toronto, played in 70/71, 72/73 final with Chicago.
EDDIE SHACK
b. Sudbury 1937. NHL right-winger 58/59 to 74/75. Won SC with Toronto 61/62, 62/63, 63/64 and 66/67.
TOD SLOAN *b. Vinton, Que. 1927, raised in Nickel Belt*. NHL center 47/48 to 60/61 with Toronto and Chicago. Won SC with Toronto 48/49, 50/51, with Chicago 60/61. 2nd All Star 55/56. Hart RU 55/56.
IRVIN SPENCER
b. Sudbury 1937. NHL defenceman, 59/60 to 73/74.
JERRY TOPPAZZINI *b. Copper Cliff 1931*. Brother of Jerry. NHL right-winger 52/53 to 63/64, mainly with Boston. Played in SC final with Boston 52/53, 56/57, 57/58.
ZELLIO TOPPAZZINI *b. Copper Cliff 1930*. NHL right-winger 48/49 to 56/57 with Boston, New York, Chicago. Played mainly in AHL, then coached Providence College.

Others

Sam Bettio (Copper Cliff), Clarence Bowcher (Sudbury), Bill Regan (Creighton), Bob Sabourin (Sudbury), Brian Smith (Creighton), Bob Wilson (Sudbury)

North Bay

Pioneers

LEO BOURGEAULT
b. Sturgeon Falls 1903. NHL defenceman 26/27 to 34/35. Won SC with New York Rangers 27/28.
STAN BROWN *b. 1898*. Defenceman with New York Rangers, Detroit, 26/27, 27/28.
AB DEMARCO *b. 1916*. NHL center 38/39 to 46/47. Father of Ab Jr., defenceman in NHL and WHA, 69/70 to 78/79.
BOB GRACIE *b. 1910*. NHL left-winger, 30/31 to 38/39. Won 31/32 SC with Toronto, 34/35 SC with Montreal Maroons.
PEP KELLY *b. 1914*. NHL forward 34/35 to 41/42, mainly with Toronto.
PETE PALANGIO *b. 1908*. NHL left-winger, 26/27 to 37/38. Won SC with Chicago 37/38.

Fresh Prospects

LARRY KEENAN *b. 1940*. NHL left-winger, 61/62 to 71/72. Played in SC final with St. Louis, 67/68, 68/69, 69/70.
HECTOR LALANDE *b. 1934*. NHL center, mainly with Chicago, 53/54 to 57/58.
GERRY ODROWSKI *b. Trout Creek 1938*. NHL and WHA defenceman, 60/61 to 75/76.
LARRY REGAN *b. 1930*. Left-winger with Boston and Toronto, 56/57 to 60/61. Played with Boston in 56/57 and 57/58 SC final, with Toronto in 58/59, 59/60 final. Won Calder 56/57.

Others

Gerry McNamara (Sturgeon Falls), Tony Poeta, Dalton and Carl Smith (Cache Bay)

Chapleau

Fresh Prospects

BUSHER CURRY *b. 1925*. Right-winger with Montreal Canadiens, 47/48 to 57/58. Won SC 52/53, 55/56, 56/57, 57/58. Lady Byng RU 55/56.
RON SCHOCK *b. 1943*. NHL center 63/64 to 77/78. Played in SC final with St. Louis 67/68, 68/69.

Others

Adie Lafrance

Tri-Town

The three settlements forming Tri-Town at the head of Lake Temiscaming are Cobalt, Haileybury and New Liskeard. The region has deep hockey roots. When railway construction touched off a silver boom in 1904, the game was established almost as soon as settlements were. By 1910, Cobalt and Haileybury had teams competing in the National Hockey Association, forerunner of the NHL.

Fresh Prospects

KENT DOUGLAS *b. Cobalt 1936*. NHL and WHA defenceman 62/63 to 72/73. Won SC with Toronto 62/63. Calder winner 62/63.
LEO LABINE *b. Haileybury 1931*. Right-winger, mainly with Boston, 51/52 to 61/62. Played in 52/53, 56/57, 57/58 SC final with Boston. Played in 60/61 SC final with Detroit.
TED LINDSAY *b. Renfrew 1925. Raised in New Liskeard*. Left-winger with Detroit and Chicago 44/45 to 64/65. Detroit captain 52/53 to 55/56. Won SC with Detroit 49/50, 51/52, 53/54, 54/55. In SC final with Detroit 44/45, 47/48, 48/49, 55/56. 1st All Star 47/48, 49/50, 50/51, 51/52, 52/53, 53/54, 55/56, 56/57. 2nd All Star 48/49. Won Art Ross 49/50, RU 51/52, 52/53, 56/57. Number retired by Detroit. HHOF

GUS MORTSON *b. New Liskeard 1925*. Defenceman with Toronto and Chicago 46/47 to 58/59. Won SC with Toronto 46/47, 47/48, 48/49, 50/51. 1st All Star 49/50. Chicago captain 54/55 to 56/57.

Others

Max Bennett, Hal Cooper, Joe Levandowski

The Porcupine

Perhaps the greatest source of hockey talent in the postwar years, the Porcupine was a thriving mining centre with Timmins serving as its main settlement. J.P Bickell, one of the original owners of Toronto's St. Patricks NHL franchise, made his fortune here in the Dome and McIntyre operations.

Pioneers

BILL CAMERON *b. Timmins 1904*. Right-winger with Montreal Canadiens 23/24, New York Americans 25/26. Won 23/24 SC with Montreal.

Cont'd p. 96

An angelic Gus Mortson of New Liskeard stars for the St. Michael's College Majors Junior A team, 1944. Mortson won four Stanley Cups with Toronto from 47/48 to 50/51, twice led the NHL in penalty minutes, then was traded to Chicago, where he served as captain from 54/55 to 56/57.

Cont'd from p. 95

TONY GRABOSKI *b. Timmins 1916.* Forward with Montreal 40/41 to 42/43.

Fresh Prospects

BILL BARILKO *b. Timmins 1927.* Toronto defenceman 46/47 to 50/51. Won SC with Toronto 46/47, 47/48, 48/49, 50/51. Number retired.

RÉAL CHEVREFILS *b. Timmins 1932.* Left-winger mainly with Boston 51/52 to 58/59. Played with Boston in 52/53, 56/57, 57/58 SC final. 2nd All Star 56/57.

LES COSTELLO *b. South Porcupine 1928.* Brother of Murray. Toronto left-winger 47/48 to 48/49. Won SC with Toronto 47/48.

MURRAY COSTELLO *b. South Porcupine 1934.* Brother of Les. Center with Chicago, Boston, Detroit 53/54 to 56/57. Played in 55/56 SC final with Detroit.

GORD HANNIGAN *b. Schumacher 1929.* Brother of Pat and Ray. Center with Toronto 52/53 to 55/56. Calder RU 52/53.

PAT HANNIGAN *b. Timmins 1936.* Brother of Gord and Ray. NHL right-winger 59/60 to 68/69 with Toronto, New York, Philadelphia.

FRANK MAHOVLICH *b. Timmins 1938.* Brother of Peter. NHL and WHA left-winger 56/57 to 77/78. Calder winner 57/58. 1st All Star 60/61, 62/63, 72/73. 2nd All Star 61/62, 63/64, 64/65, 65/66, 68/69, 69/70. Won SC with Toronto 61/62, 62/63, 63/64, 66/67, with Montreal 70/71, 72/73. HHOF

PETER MAHOVLICH *b. Timmins 1946.* Brother of Frank. NHL center 65/66 to 80/81. Won SC with Montreal 70/71, 72/73, 75/76, 76/77.

JOHN MCLELLAN *b. South Porcupine 1928.* Played two games at center with Toronto 51/52. Coached Toronto 69/70 to 71/72.

HOWARD MENARD *b. Timmins 1942.* NHL center 63/64 to 69/70.

BOB NEVIN *b. South Porcupine 1938. Moved to Toronto at 6.* NHL and WHA right-winger 57/58 to 76/77. Calder RU 60/61. Won SC with Toronto 61/62, 62/63. Captain of New York Rangers 64/65 to 70/71.

DEAN PRENTICE *b. Schumacher 1932.* NHL left-winger 52/53 to 73/74. More than ten seasons with New York. Played in 65/66 SC final with Detroit.

DALE ROLFE *b. Timmins 1940.* NHL defenceman 59/60 to 74/75. Played in 71/72 SC final with New York.

ALLAN STANLEY *b. Timmins 1926.* NHL defenceman 48/49 to 68/69. New York Rangers captain 52/53 to 53/54. Played in 49/50 SC final with New York, in 56/57, 57/58 SC final with Boston, in 58/59, 59/60 SC final with Toronto. Won 61/62, 62/63, 63/64, 66/67 SC with Toronto. 2nd All Star 59/60, 60/61, 65/66. Calder RU 48/49, Norris RU 59/60. HHOF

Others

Baz Bastien (Timmins), Daniel Belisle (South Porcupine), Dusty Blair (South Porcupine), Norm Defelice (Schumacher), Dutch Delmonte (Timmins), Red Doran (South Porcupine), Ray Hannigan (Schumacher), Ron Hudson (Timmins), Albert LeBrun (Timmins), Hill Menard (Timmins), Ray Powell (Timmins)

Hearst

Fresh Prospects

CLAUDE LAROSE *b. 1942.* NHL right-winger, mainly with Montreal Canadiens, 62/63 to 77/78. Won SC with Montreal 64/65, 65/66, 67/68, 68/69, 70/71, 72/73.

Smooth Rock Falls

Fresh Prospects

DICK MATTIUSSI *b. 1938.* NHL defenceman 67/68 to 70/71.

J.P. PARISE *b. 1941.* NHL left-winger 65/66 to 78/79.

Kapuskasing

Fresh Prospects

TED MCCASKILL *b. 1936.* NHL and WHA center 67/68 to 73/74.

Kirkland Lake

Prosperity and gainful employment could be found all along Kirkland Lake's "Mile of Gold." In 1938, just as a remarkable new generation of NHLers was being born, the Mile was thriving as seven major mines provided employment for more than 4,000.

Fresh Prospects

RALPH BACKSTROM *b. 1937.* NHL and WHA center 56/57 to 76/77. More than 12 seasons in Montreal. Won SC with Montreal 58/59, 59/60, 64/65, 65/66, 67/68, 68/69. Won Calder 58/59.

JOHN BLACKBURN *b. 1938.* NHL and WHA left-winger 62/63 to 75/76.

DICK DUFF *b. 1936.* NHL left-winger 54/55 to 71/72. Played in SC final with Toronto 58/59, 59/60. Won SC with Toronto 61/62, 62/63. Played in SC final with Montreal 66/67. Won SC with Montreal 64/65, 65/66, 67/68, 68/69.

MURRAY HALL *b. 1940.* NHL and WHA center 61/62 to 75/76.

LARRY HILLMAN *b. 1937.* Brother of Wayne. NHL and WHA defenceman 54/55 to 75/76. Won SC with Detroit 54/55. Played in SC final with Detroit 55/56. Played in SC final with Boston 57/58. Won SC with Toronto 61/62, 62/63,

63/64, 66/67. Won SC with Montreal 68/69.

WAYNE HILLMAN *b. 1938.* Brother of Larry. NHL and WHA defenceman 61/62 to 74/75.

WILLIE MARSHALL *b. 1931.* Center with Toronto (infrequently) 52/53 to 58/59. Set games-played and career scoring records after more than 20 seasons in AHL.

BOB MCCORD *b. Matheson 1934.* NHL defenceman 63/64 to 72/73.

BARCLAY PLAGER *b. 1941.* Brother of Bob and Bill. St. Louis defenceman 67/68 to 76/77. Played in 67/68, 68/69, 69/70 SC final.

BILL PLAGER *b. 1945.* Brother of Barclay and Bob. NHL defenceman with Minnesota, St. Louis and Atlanta 67/68 to 75/76. Played in 68/69, 69/70 SC final with St. Louis.

BOB PLAGER *b. 1943.* Brother of Barclay and Bill. NHL defenceman with New York and St. Louis 64/65 to 77/78. Played in 67/68, 68/69, 69/70 SC final with St. Louis.

DICK REDMOND *b. 1949.* Brother of Mickey. NHL defenceman 69/70 to 81/82. Played in SC final with Chicago 72/73.

MICKEY REDMOND *b. 1947.* Brother of Dick. NHL right-winger with Montreal and Detroit 67/68 to 75/76. Won SC with Montreal 67/68, 68/69. 1st All Star 72/73. 2nd All Star 73/74.

MIKE WALTON *b. 1945.* NHL and WHA center 65/66 to 78/79. Won SC with Toronto 66/67, with Boston 71/72.

Others

Buddy Boone, Chuck Hamilton

Cochrane

Fresh Prospects

TIM HORTON *b. 1930. Moved to Sudbury at 14.* NHL defenceman, mainly with Toronto, 49/50 to

73/74. Won SC with Toronto 61/62, 62/63, 63/64, 66/67. SC finalist with Toronto 58/59, 59/60. 1st All Star 63/64, 67/68, 68/69. 2nd All Star 53/54, 62/63, 66/67. Norris RU 63/64, 68/69. Number retired by Buffalo, Toronto. HHOF

Noranda-Rouyn

Fresh Prospects

BOB BLACKBURN *b. 1938.* Defenceman with New York, Pittsburgh, 68/69 to 70/71.

CHRISTIAN BORDELEAU *b. 1947.* Brother of J.P. and Paul. NHL and WHA center 68/69 to 78/79. Won SC with Montreal 68/69. (J.P. Chicago right-winger 71/72 to 79/80; Paul NHL and WHA right-winger with Vancouver and Quebec 73/74 to 78/79.)

JACQUES CARON *b. 1940.* NHL and WHA goaltender 67/68 to 76/77.

WAYNE CONNELLY *b. 1939.* NHL and WHA right-winger 60/61 to 76/77.

DAVE KEON *b. 1940.* NHL and WHA center 60/61 to 81/82. Fifteen seasons with Toronto Maple Leafs. Maple Leaf captain 69/70 to 74/75. Won SC with Toronto 61/62, 62/63, 63/64, 66/67. 2nd All Star 61/62, 70/71. Won Calder 60/61, Conn Smythe 66/67, Lady Byng 61/62, 62/63, 63/64 (RU), 66/67 (RU), 70/71 (RU). HHOF

JACQUES LAPERRIÈRE *b. 1941.* Montreal defenceman 62/63 to 73/74. Won SC 64/65, 65/66, 67/68, 68/69, 70/71, 72/73. In SC final 66/67. 1st All Star 64/65, 65/66. 2nd All Star 63/64, 69/70. Won Calder 63/64. Won Norris 65/66, RU 64/65. HHOF

PIT MARTIN *b. 1943.* NHL center 61/62 to 78/79; more than 10 seasons with Chicago. In 70/71, 72/73 SC final with Chicago. Won Bill Masterton 69/70.

Others

Bill McDonagh

THE ST. MIKE'S PIPELINE

A French order of priests that set out to educate Toronto's Irish underclass ran professional hockey's finest finishing school

Many northern Ontario teenagers during and after the Second World War advanced their hockey careers and furthered their education by attending Toronto's St. Michael's College on a hockey scholarship. Affiliated with the University of Toronto, the school was run by the Basilians, a French diocesan order of priests who originally set out in the mid-nineteenth century to educate the city's impoverished Irish underclass. The school developed a reputation for sporting excellence, at first in football, then in hockey, which earned its teams the nickname the "Fighting Irish of Bay Street." Its hockey successes—in particular early graduates to the NHL like the Leafs' own Joe Primeau and Detroit star Larry Aurie—attracted the attention of Conn Smythe and his partners in Maple Leaf Gardens, who established a sponsorship agreement with the school's hockey program, which consisted of the Junior A Majors and the Junior B Buzzers.

The school won its first Memorial Cup in 33/34, and four students from the early 1930s—Pep Kelly, Nick Metz, Reg Hamilton and Bobby Bauer—solidified St. Mike's' reputation as hockey finishing school *ne plus ultra*. Another Memorial Cup followed in 44/45, and the 45/46 team, featuring Tod Sloan and Red Kelly, lost a seven-game final to the Winnipeg Monarchs. So rich in talent was St. Mike's that the Leafs couldn't hoard every teenager playing hockey there, and two brilliant prospects in the mid-1940s, Red Kelly and Ted Lindsay, ended up in Red Wings uniforms.

In 1950 St. Mike's built its own separate school and hockey arena at Bathurst and St. Clair and renamed itself St. Michael's College School, separate from, though still affiliated with, the University of Toronto. It continued to take in many of the game's future stars under its sponsorship agreement with Maple Leaf Gardens, and in 60/61 won its third Memorial Cup, coached by Father David Bauer (brother of alumnus and Bruins star Bobby Bauer).

The school then abruptly cancelled the victorious Majors program, concluding that the school could no longer compete in a 60-game OHA Major Junior A schedule and still deliver a decent education to the players. Father Bauer established the Canadian national team program based on collegiate talent, and the school carried on with the Junior B Buzzers program.

The school continued to produce first-class players, and among the Buzzers alumni who went on to play in the NHL after the Majors program ended were Peter Mahovlich, Rod Seiling, Gary Monahan, Dave and Paul Gardner, Dave Maloney, Mike Gillis, Kevin and Gord Dineen, Rick Tocchet, Sean Burke and Eric Lindros. In 1996, school alumni saw a long-standing dream fulfilled when St. Mike's announced the return of the Majors in 97/98.

Ted Lindsay came down from New Liskeard with Gus Mortson (page 95) to play for St. Mike's in 1943. He left in 1944 at 19 to turn pro with the Red Wings.

Listed are alumni who played on either the Buzzers or the Majors during the original Majors years, which ended in 60/61, and went on to perform (for at least one game) in the NHL. They are listed according to their school years and annotated according to place of birth as follows:

N included in northern Ontario talents on pages 94 to 96
O born elsewhere in Ontario
Q born in Quebec
W born in western Canada
E born elsewhere
U unknown

Alumni who are known to have been Toronto properties while at St. Mike's, or were soon signed, appear in capital letters.

N Larry Aurie 21-22
O Dave Trottier 23-24
O JOE PRIMEAU 24-27
N Bill Regan mid-1920s
U D'Arcy Coulson 27-29
O Eddie Convey 27-29
O Bobby Bauer 29-33
N PEP KELLY 29-33
W NICK METZ 30-34
W DON METZ 31-36
O John O'Flaherty 32-35
O ART JACKSON 33-34
O REG HAMILTON 33-34
O Clare Drouillard 33-34
O Jack Crawford 33-35
O Harvey Teno 33-35
O Hal Jackson 35-36
W CHARLIE CORRIGAN 35-36
W BILLY TAYLOR 35-36
O Fred Hunt 35-37
U FRANK DUNLOP 35-38
O Frank Bennett 35-41
O TOM O'NEILL 39-42
U JEAN MAROIS 39-42
O Fran Harrison 40-46

O Ed Sandford 41-47
N Ted Lindsay 43-44
W JOHN McCORMACK 43-44
W JIMMY THOMSON 43-45
O Red Kelly 43-47
N GUS MORTSON 43-47
Q Leo Gravelle 44-45
W PHIL SAMIS 44-45
N TOD SLOAN 44-46
N LES COSTELLO 44-47
N JOHN McLELLAN 45-46
Q FLEMING MACKELL 45-47
N RAY HANNIGAN 45-47
O Norm Corcoran 46-49
O RUDY MIGAY 46-47
O Benny Woit 46-48
N Bill McDonagh 47-48
N TIM HORTON 47-49
N GORD HANNIGAN 47-49
O Tom McCarthy 47-51
U PAUL KNOX 47-53
N BOB SABOURIN 48-52
O JACK CAFFERY 48-54
N Leo Labine 49-50
N WILLIE MARSHALL 49-50

O Ron Murphy 49-50
E Charlie Burns 49-51
Q Bill Dineen 49-53
Q MARC REAUME 50-52
N MURRAY COSTELLO 50-53
N GERRY McNAMARA 50-54
O Howie Young 51-52
N DICK DUFF 51-55
O ED CHADWICK 52-53
O NOEL PRICE 53-56
N FRANK MAHOVLICH 53-57
O Lou Angotti 53-58
U Don Keenan 54-56
N PAT HANNIGAN 54-56
O BRUCE DRAPER 54-61
Q Reggie Fleming 55-56
O Gene Ubriaco 55-57
O GERRY CHEEVERS 55-60
N Gerry Odrowski 56-57
N Dick Mattiussi 56-58
O Michael Corbett 56-62
O JACK MARTIN 57-58
O DARRYL SLY 57-58
W CESARE MANIAGO 57-59
O ARNIE BROWN 57-61

N DAVE KEON 59-60
W LES KOZAK 59-60
N LARRY KEENAN 59-60
O ANDREW CHAMPAGNE 59-62
O Terry Clancy 59-62
O Tom Polanic 59-62
E BILLY MacMILLAN 59-62
O GARY SMITH 59-63
O DAVE DRYDEN 60-61
O MIKE WALTON 60-62
Q Gary Dineen 60-62
O Barry MacKenzie 60-62
O GERRY MEEHAN 60-65
O Mike Corrigan 61

The following alumni coached in the NHL:
Lou Angotti, Charlie Burns, Gerry Cheevers, Bill Dineen, Dick Duff, Red Kelly, Ted Lindsay, Billy MacMillan, John McLellan, Joe Primeau, Gene Ubriaco

TORONTO MAPLE LEAFS
The Sixties

PUNCH'S BUNCH

ONE OF THE MOST CELEBRATED TEAMS IN CANADIAN SPORTS HISTORY WAS ALSO THE FIRST TRULY ENGINEERED TEAM DYNASTY IN THE NHL. COACH AND GENERAL MANAGER PUNCH IMLACH KNEW HOW TO CUT A WINNING DEAL

F
or many older English-Canadian hockey fans—indeed, for many fans of the game who weren't even alive to see them play—the Toronto Maple Leafs of the 1960s epitomize dynastic greatness. The Leafs won four Stanley Cups in six seasons, including three in a row between 61/62 and 63/64. As sterling a record as that was, the team was even greater than the silverware it collected. It was the toast of a staunchly loyal hockey town that had suffered through the better part of a decade without a contender.

The players who brought the team its championships were adored long after they left the Leafs and the game altogether. Their successes marked the end of the Original Six era, with their final Cup win, in 66/67, coming in the spring that preceded the addition of six expansion teams. Expansion also swept away the old recruitment system that had tied some players to a club like the Leafs since their sixteenth birthday, and replaced it with a universal draft, introduced in 1969. The draft promised greater parity in the expanded league by dismantling the territorial and scouting systems of the Original Six clubs, and it helped free players from what many of them saw as indentured servitude.

In the process, however, teams like the Maple Leafs lost their roots. Players would no longer grow up, the way Tim Horton, George Armstrong, Bob Baun, Dick Duff, Frank Mahovlich, and so many other Leaf greats did, knowing that if they were destined to play at the highest professional level, the odds were that they would play as Maple Leafs. The great Leaf teams of the 1960s not only defined an era for many spectators, they closed it out as well.

RIGHT: Phil Esposito of the Chicago Blackhawks sees an opportunity as the Leafs' Terry Sawchuk kicks out a shot. Tim Horton is dumping Bobby Hull while Frank Mahovlich looks on. BELOW: the jacket of Leaf coach and general manager Punch Imlach.

CHAMPIONS

These Toronto teams were not regular-season power-houses; unlike the Red Wings and Canadiens of the 1950s, they were not regularly posting points percentages between 60 and 70 on their way to Cup victories. These Leafs posted some of the lowest win percentages of any NHL dynasty, mainly because of the exceptionally tight competition among top clubs in the 1960s (the appalling performances by the Bruins and poor showings by the Rangers during these final Original Six seasons notwith-standing). Certainly the league was much more competi-tive than it had been through much of the 1950s, when the Leafs were in steady decline, the Blackhawks a bad joke, the Rangers in perpetual disarray and the Bruins unevenly competitive. In many of those seasons, the NHL was essentially a two-team league—from 51/52 to 59/60, every Stanley Cup was won by Detroit or Montreal.

With the revival of Chicago and Toronto in the 1960s, competition was fierce. In 62/63, for example, the points percentage spread among the clubs qualifying for the playoffs was only 3.5, by far the lowest in NHL history, and the regular-season race among the four clubs making the playoffs remained close through the last few Original Six seasons. In five of seven Original Six seasons in the 1960s, the regular-season champion did not even reach the Cup finals.

In assembling a series of outwardly routine regular-season performances, the Leafs were also upholding the conviction of team founder Conn Smythe that the only important objectives in the regular season were to fill seats in Maple Leaf Gardens and make the play-offs. Smythe had been burned all through the 1930s by charismatic, league-leading Leaf teams that could not convert exemplary regular seasons into Cup victories. In the 1940s, the Leafs had shown a winning formula of solid, even so-so, regular seasons that served as preambles to playoff success. That formula was resurrected in the 1960s dynasty. In a nine-season stretch from 58/59 to 66/67, the Leafs played in six finals, winning four. Only once, in 62/63, did the Leafs win the regular season as well as the Cup—a consistent Maple Leaf trait, as in seven previous Cup victories, the Leafs won the regular season only once as well. Though never a pushover dur-ing the regular season, the great Maple Leaf teams blos-somed in springtime, just when they should.

They did it with a careful mix of promising young talents and proven veterans, and the architect of their success was Punch Imlach, a former Toronto Junior play-er who had managed and coached (and initially even played for) the Quebec Aces of the Quebec Senior league during its heady Jean Béliveau days and then the Springfield Indians of the American league for the 57/58 season. The Indians operation was affiliated with the Boston Bruins. Imlach's Aces had just won the minor-pro Edinburgh Cup in the spring of 1957 when Bruins gen-eral manager Lynn Patrick hired him as the Indians' gen-eral manager and coach. On hand to work with him as the new player-coach was Cal Gardner, who had won a

Stanley Cup with the Leafs in 50/51 and retired from the Bruins after they lost the 56/57 Stanley Cup final to the Canadiens.

Imlach was a fierce disciplinarian; during the war he had been a lieutenant and a player-coach with the Senior league team at the Cornwall army training base in eastern Ontario. His experience in ordering around enlisted men became a foundation for his lifelong auto-cratic style. In Springfield, Imlach ran up against Indians owner Eddie Shore; the former Bruins defensive great was perhaps the most autocratic figure in all of hockey, and halfway through the season they weren't even talking to each other. Imlach wasn't getting along all that well with the players, either. "He was really out-spoken," Gardner recalls. "He thought he was going to get more out of the players than he was getting." Gardner found him too vocal, too overbearing, too abusive in his language. "Players would come to me and say, 'What's going on?' I'd tell them, 'Play as well as you can. That's all they can ask.'"

Imlach asked a lot, and he got a lot. In 56/57, the Indians won only 19 of 64 games and finished last in the six-team league, missing the playoffs. With Imlach aboard (and to no small effect Gardner, who finished fourth in the scoring race), Springfield won 29 of 70 games and finished fourth. In the semifinals, the Indians upset the second-place Cleveland Barons in a seven-game struggle, then met the first-place Hershey Bears in the finals. Since its founding in 1936, the Springfield fran-chise had never made it to the league's Calder Cup series. In 57/58, the Indians fell just shy of winning it all, outscoring the Bears 20-18 but losing the series four games to two.

Imlach would remember Shore breaking his silence to offer grudging praise when it was all over: "I guess you've had yourself a pretty good year, son."

The Toronto Maple Leafs, meanwhile, had had a pretty awful year, perhaps the worst in the franchise's his-tory. The team won 21 of 70 games, finished last in the standings and missed the playoffs for the second straight year. Team impresario Conn Smythe had been compelled to step into the background in 1955, first turning over the general manager's duties to Hap Day, then (in 1957) allowing an executive committee chaired by his oldest son Stafford to run the team.

Toronto management had become a bewildering revolving door of famous hockey characters. Former Leaf great King Clancy, who had had a try at coaching the team from 53/54 to 55/56 after handling the American league farm team in Pittsburgh, was booted upstairs into a vice-presidency, making way for former Leaf right-winger Howie Meeker. Meeker lasted one season, 56/57, in which the Leafs finished fifth and missed the playoffs. In came former Canadien Billy Reay, under whom the Leafs finished dead last in 57/58.

In the summer of 1958, Stafford Smythe sought out Imlach as a new general manager. While speaking with Imlach in June during the league's annual meeting in Montreal, Stafford also drafted two players: Montreal

Toronto Maple Leafs

The Dynasty of the 1960s

Featuring the players and management who participated in Toronto's
Stanley Cup victories of 1961/62, 1962/63, 1963/64 and 1966/67

GENERAL MANAGER	COACH
1. Punch Imlach	1. Billy Reay and Punch Imlach
	2. Punch Imlach

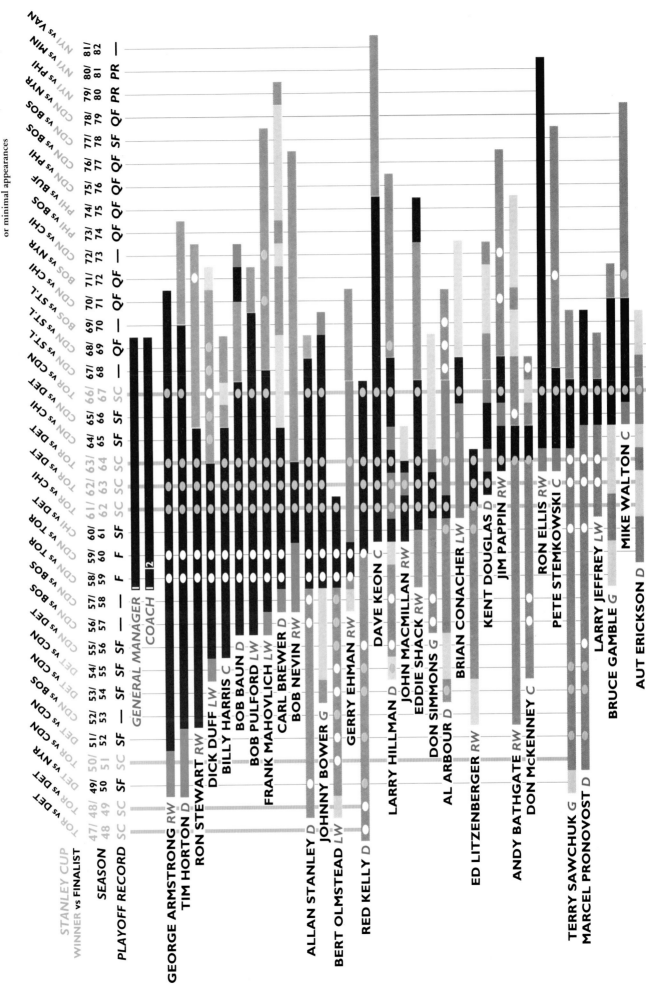

Canadiens veteran Bert Olmstead and Cleveland Barons goaltender Johnny Bower. Toronto had never before picked a player at the intraleague draft, which had been held since 1948.

The Leafs weren't entirely sold on Imlach as a full general manager, so they hired him as an assistant. But come September there was nobody around for Imlach to be an assistant to. Howie Meeker had been fired as coach, hired as GM, then fired again. And so Imlach became GM, and one month into the new season he fired Billy Reay and made himself the coach as well, using Olmstead, a pugnacious left-winger who had just won three Stanley Cups in a row, as an assistant playing-coach. Olmstead had been a tremendous motivator within the Canadiens ranks, and he fell into the same role with the Leafs. As a playing coach, he was supposed to run the practices, but in February 1959 he resigned his coaching role, pointing out that Imlach was doing everything and all he had was a title.

Whether or not Stafford Smythe discussed Bower with Imlach before drafting him that June, Imlach would have made no objection to the move. The veteran of twelve American league seasons had just won his third straight league MVP award and third straight first-team All Star berth. The seemingly ageless native of Prince Albert, Saskatchewan, had turned pro with Cleveland in 45/46, and had a very capable season as a New York Ranger in 53/54. But New York also held Gump Worsley's contract, and they decided to send Bower back to Cleveland and go with the barrel-shaped Montrealer instead. In the spring of 1958, Bower had been exemplary in the American league semifinal against Imlach's Indians. It took the Indians the full seven games to eliminate Bower and the Barons, and the impression on Imlach was still vivid when he went after Bower for the NHL.

Bower wasn't sure he wanted to join the Leafs—after 13 years, he was solidly established in Cleveland with his wife and children, and he wasn't prepared to uproot everyone to take another chance on the big time. He had a two-year no-trade contract with Cleveland, and he had already been approached by Toronto about coming up before the 1958 draft. Bower provided Imlach with a stiff set of demands. He wanted a two-year, one-way contract—the Leafs could not send him to the minors, and they could not trade him without his say-so. He was to be paid his two-year salary even if he was hurt at training camp that fall and never played a game. And he wanted moving expenses.

Imlach acceded, and Bower became a Leaf. In 58/59, Toronto's goals-against dropped from 226 to 201; over the next seven seasons, the Leafs would never allow more than 195. This was all to Bower's betterment, as a clause in his 60/61 contract stipulated a bonus of $500 for allowing fewer than 200 goals.

Imlach was no visionary strategist, no technocrat who brought complex playmaking to the resurrection of the Leaf franchise. Imlach's gift lay in assembling players who knew how to play, and combining them in lines and

Leaf defenceman Allan Stanley (in front of the net) and captain George Armstrong (10) have their hands full with a mid-1960s Canadiens attack by Henri Richard (16) and Yvan Cournoyer (12).

PUNCH'S BUNCH

pairings that let them play at their best. Most important, he understood the veteran player, and he had an uncanny ability to get quality mileage out of players other teams were prepared to give up on.

The Imlach revival was dramatic. In 57/58, the team's points percentage had slipped below 40 as it missed the playoffs for the second straight season. In 58/59, the first season under Imlach's direction, the Leafs improved total wins from 21 to 27, scraped into the playoffs and made it into the finals against Montreal. Though they lost that spring, and again to Montreal the following spring, the franchise was well on the road to revival.

The Toronto Maple Leafs of the Imlach era qualify as the first truly engineered championship dynasty. Other managers of successful teams had been willing to make big trades—no one more so than Detroit's Jack Adams in the 1950s, but Adams had as his team's foundation a superlative amateur development system that fed the club a steady supply of great talents, without which his periodic shake-up trades would not have been possible. The Canadiens of the 1950s were also built overwhelmingly from within. Though Toronto also had an extensive amateur talent system and scouting operation, by the late 1950s the right mix of players had not emerged.

"The Leafs had tried to build from within, but never seemed to have the luxury of not having to trade," says Dave Keon, who did come up through the Leaf development system to join the team in 1960. And so Imlach went out and made his own mix. The main ingredients in the Imlach-engineered revival were a handful of Leaf veterans awaiting a return to the franchise's glory days, a fresh crop of young Junior stars, and a group of established winners from elsewhere in the professional game, many of them with Stanley Cup experience. No dynastic team before ever assembled quite so many players from the roll calls of previous Cup winners.

Of twenty players who would have their name stamped on the Stanley Cup in 61/62, the first Leaf win since 50/51, ten were already playing for the Leafs when Imlach took over as coach and general manager in the fall of 1958. There were three long-standing veterans: Tim Horton, George Armstrong and Ron Stewart. Horton and Armstrong had played Junior hockey together in the Sudbury area and had become Leaf

properties as teenagers. They also both played for the club's American league farm team, the Pittsburgh Hornets, and were Calder Cup champions together in 51/52. Neither young man was with the Leafs for the 50/51 Cup drive, although both had seen some duty with Toronto since 49/50. Armstrong broke into the Leaf lineup playing 20 games in 51/52, and Horton joined him in 52/53. Both struggled in their early seasons. Armstrong was converted from center, where he had won two straight MVP awards with the Ontario Junior A league, to right wing, and the points would not come for him the way they had when the lanky Armstrong was a celebrated amateur.

Horton, though a bruising and brawling defencemen when he had starred for the St. Michael's College Majors in his last two Junior seasons, did not enthusiastically accept the enforcer's role expected of him when the Leafs called him up: he was viewed as a replacement for the late, great Bill Barilko, who was killed in a plane crash in August 1951 after scoring the winning goal in the deciding Stanley Cup game the previous April. While he earned a second-team All Star nomination in 53/54, a disastrous open-ice collision with Red Wings defenceman Bill Gadsby in March 1955 fractured his leg and jaw and nearly ended his career. The Leafs attempted to trade him away at least twice after that, and he was still trying to regain his form when Imlach came along.

The third Leaf veteran was journeyman right-winger Ron Stewart, a dependable 30-points-a-season man out of Calgary. Armstrong, Horton and Stewart were all there to stay, with varying degrees of success; Armstrong's career lasted 20 NHL seasons, Stewart's 21, Horton's 22.

For the past few seasons, the Leafs had been bringing new talent on stream from their amateur system, a battery of future stars who were suffering through the club's confusion of the late 1950s. The Toronto Marlboros won back-to-back Memorial Cups in 53/54 and 54/55, and from the 1950s Marlie ranks Imlach inherited a bevy of key talents: Bob Baun and Carl Brewer (Calder runner-up in 58/59) on defence, Bob Pulford on left wing, Billy Harris at center, Bob Nevin on right wing. From the Leafs' other Toronto-based source of Junior talent, the St. Mike's Majors, came left-winger Dick Duff, defenceman Marc Reaume and right-winger Frank Mahovlich. So celebrated a prospect was Mahovlich that the Leafs were obligated to pay the school a $2,000 bonus if the Leafs made the playoffs or Mahovlich won the Calder in his rookie season, 57/58, which he did.

In December 1958 Imlach acquired on waivers from Detroit right-winger Gerry Ehman, whom the Red Wings had just drafted from Boston the previous June. In exchange for Ehman, Imlach sent Detroit the rights to Tim Horton's former St. Mike's teammate, Willie Marshall, who ended up playing more than 20 seasons in the American league and set career regular-season and playoff scoring records that still stand today.

To these names Imlach began adding proven veter-

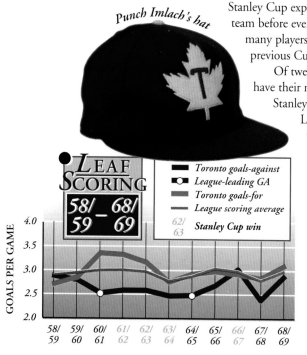

Punch Imlach's hat

LEAF SCORING 58/59 – 68/69

Legend	
▬	Toronto goals-against
◻	League-leading GA
▬	Toronto goals-for
▬	League scoring average
62/63	Stanley Cup win

GOALS PER GAME: 4.0 3.5 3.0 2.5 2.0

58/59 59/60 60/61 61/62 62/63 63/64 64/65 65/66 66/67 67/68 68/69

Toronto Maple Leafs 1958/59–66/67

Season	Finish	Record (W-L-T)	Points %	Awards (winners & runners-up)	All-Stars	Playoffs
58/59	4th	27-32-11	46.4	CALDER: Brewer RU VEZINA: Bower RU		Lost SC final 4-1 to Montreal
59/60	2nd	35-26-9	56.4	NORRIS: Stanley RU	2ND TEAM: Stanley (D)	Lost SC final 4-0 to Montreal
60/61	2nd	39-19-12	64.3	HART: Bower RU VEZINA: Bower CALDER: Keon, Nevin RU LADY BYNG: Kelly	1ST TEAM: Bower (G), Mahovlich (LW) 2ND TEAM: Stanley (D)	Lost SC semifinal 4-1 to Detroit
61/62	2nd	37-22-11	60.7	LADY BYNG: Keon VEZINA: Bower RU	2ND TEAM: Brewer (D), Keon (C), Mahovlich (LW)	Won SC final 4-2 over Chicago
62/63	1st	35-23-12	58.6	CALDER: Douglas LADY BYNG: Keon VEZINA: Bower RU NORRIS: Brewer RU	1ST TEAM: Brewer (D), Mahovlich (LW) 2ND TEAM: Horton (D)	Won SC final 4-1 over Detroit
63/64	3rd	33-25-12	55.7	LADY BYNG: Keon RU NORRIS: Horton RU	1ST TEAM: Horton (D) 2ND TEAM: Mahovlich (LW)	Won SC final 4-3 over Detroit
64/65	4th	30-26-14	52.9	CALDER: Ellis RU VEZINA: Sawchuk & Bower	2ND TEAM: Brewer (D), Mahovlich (LW)	Lost SC semifinal 4-2 to Montreal
65/66	3rd	34-25-11	56.4	CALDER: Selby	2ND TEAM: Stanley (D), Mahovlich (LW)	Lost SC semifinal 4-0 to Montreal
66/67	3rd	32-27-11	53.6	LADY BYNG: Keon RU CONN SMYTHE: Keon	2ND TEAM: Horton (D)	Won SC final 4-2 over Montreal

ans. In exchange for defenceman Jim Morrison and $7,500 Imlach acquired from Boston Allan Stanley, a blueliner who had broken in with the Rangers in 1948 and had been waiting with almost as much patience as Leaf fans for a Stanley Cup win. He came so close in 49/50, when the Rangers defied expectations and reached the finals against the Red Wings. The Rangers had been winning game seven 2-0 when the Red Wings scored twice to tie it up while Stanley was off serving a minor—at the time, the penalized player did not automatically return to the ice when the opposition scored. The game went into overtime, and Stanley was on the ice, blamelessly, when Detroit's Pete Babando blindly whacked a shot off a face-off into the Rangers net to end the miracle season. Stanley then served as New York's captain, but he was hounded out of town by the notoriously capricious and cruel fans of Madison Square Garden in 54/55. After a stint in Chicago (where his Uncle Barney had been in management and served briefly as coach in 27/28), Stanley landed in Boston, where Lynn Patrick was general manager. Patrick had been the Rangers coach when they reached the 49/50 finals, and he had always been impressed with Stanley's poise and ability. With Patrick's Bruins, Stanley played in back-to-back Cup finals against Montreal, losing both. When the Rangers reached the finals in 49/50, a conflict-

ing circus booking would not allow them to use Madison Square Garden as home ice, and the team went to Maple Leaf Gardens for its "home" games. Nine seasons later, Maple Leaf Gardens actually was home ice for Stanley, and it represented his last hope for a Cup win.

In his first season directing the Maple Leaf operation, Imlach had a defensive corps capable of winning the Cup: Baun paired with Brewer, Stanley paired with Horton, with Marc Reaume as a utility and Bower behind them. But the team as a whole wasn't ready; Toronto lost two consecutive finals to Montreal, 4-1 and 4-0.

Midway through the 59/60 season, Imlach added another veteran: Red Kelly. The defensive standout had played his Junior hockey for St. Mike's during the war, but Toronto had passed on his professional rights, doubting his ability to withstand the rigours of the professional game. The Red Wings thought otherwise and brought him into the lineup in 47/48, where he stayed for the next eleven-and-a-half seasons, a playmaking blueliner and regular Lady Byng winner who was on hand for four Red Wings Cup victories.

Imlach was watching and waiting when Detroit embarked on a youth movement in 59/60 and decided

to deal Kelly—to New York. Jack Adams put a four-play-er swap together with his Rangers counterpart Murray "Muzz" Patrick: Kelly and right-winger Billy McNeill for standout blueliner Bill Gadsby and a mighty thorn in Patrick's side, Eddie Shack. Patrick couldn't stand Shack, a crowd-pleasing showboater on right wing in his second season with the Rangers. Patrick felt Shack was all move-ment, no action and no discipline, making no real con-tribution to the team. Ivan saw hope for him, and was right to covet Gadsby, a first-team All Star in the previ-ous two seasons, with another first- and three second-team appearances before that.

But the deal wouldn't fly because the Red Wings players refused to go to New York. Both announced that they would rather retire than accept the trade. In 1959 Kelly had married figure-skating star Andra McLaughlin, and had growing business interests, including a bowling alley in his home town of Simcoe, Ontario, which lies between Detroit and Toronto. McNeill, a promising young talent, had lost his wife to polio in 1959, and had a two-year-old daughter; he had resolved that if a trade ever came, he would quit the game and remain in Canada.

And so the deal died, but both Detroit and New York had tipped their hands on players they were willing to part with. Within days, Imlach was engineering Kelly's trade to Toronto, which the celebrated rushing defence-man was more amenable to considering. It didn't hurt that Toronto was on its way to finishing second overall, whereas New York had been on its way to winning only 17 of 70 games and finishing last.

As much as Imlach coveted veterans, his interest in Kelly was unusual. The last thing the Leafs needed at the time was another quality defenceman. To get him, he gave up a defenceman—utility Marc Reaume, who had broken in with the Leafs in 1955, after Tim Horton broke his leg in the Gadsby collision. But Imlach didn't want Kelly on defence. He wanted him as a center (he had been used as a forward in a pinch in Detroit), so he could ignite the scoring genius of Frank Mahovlich.

It was one of the great one-for-one deals of all time. Reaume played only 38 games for Detroit in 60/61 before heading to the minors. (The Leafs reacquired him in the 1964 intraleague draft, but he never played for Toronto again.) In 59/60, Mahovlich had only 39 points, but in 60/61, with Kelly as his center, Mahovlich scored 48 times and registered 84 points, to finish second in league goal-scoring and third overall in points produc-tion. Kelly, in the process, set a Leaf record for assists, with 50. Kelly took so well to life in Toronto that he was elected as Liberal MP for the riding of York Centre in the 1962 federal election, and served his constituency while still playing for the Leafs.

The 60/61 season also brought three more notable additions to the Leafs. Bob Nevin came up full-time from Toronto's American league farm team, the Rochester Americans, and was a terrific newcomer on right wing. Out of the St. Mike's lineup came a genuine training-camp surprise, Dave Keon, one of the best all-round centers the game would ever see, both a great defensive forward and a scoring threat. Leaf scout Bob Davidson had been able to secure Keon's rights by using a spot on the Springfield Indians' negoti-ating list. The Leafs had all their spots occupied, but through a "friendship" agreement with Shore's Indians the Leafs were given use of Springfield space in exchange for the use of a player under contract to Toronto. Keon went to camp expecting to be assigned to Rochester—the previous spring he'd had a so-so tryout with the Sudbury Wolves of the Eastern Canadian Professional League, where former Canadiens star Murph Chamberlain was the coach—but ended up making the Leafs.

It was a toss-up between Keon and Nevin as to who would be named rookie of the year, and in the end the Calder went to Keon. Midway through the season, Eddie Shack, still on the Rangers' available-to-anyone list, was picked up for Johnny Wilson and Pat Hannigan, and from the Bruins came defenceman Larry Hillman, who had played for the Stanley Cup-winning Red Wings of 54/55 as an 18-year-old. Hillman replaced Reaume, but when injured he ended up going to Springfield to satisfy the loan demands of the Leafs-Indians friendship deal.

The 60/61 season was, on paper, the greatest in the Leaf rebirth under Imlach. The team's points percentage, at 64.3, was never higher as it won 39 of 70 games and finished just two points behind the Canadiens in the reg-ular season. Mahovlich vied for the scoring title, Bower won the Vezina and was runner-up for the Hart, Keon took the Calder, Kelly the Lady Byng, and three Leafs made the All Star team—Bower and Mahovlich the first team, Stanley the second team.

But there was another moribund franchise in ascent. The Blackhawks lineup included Glenn Hall in goal, Bobby Hull on left wing, Stan Mikita at center and Pierre Pilote on defence. Though the Blackhawks could not boast of any top-ten scorers (not yet, anyway) and finished 17 points behind the league-leading Canadiens, in third place, they upset Montreal 4-2 in the semifinals, while fourth-place Detroit, who had lagged 24 points behind Toronto on the season, was toppling the Leafs in only five games. In a battle of the also-rans, Chicago defeated Detroit in six games to win its first Cup since 37/38.

For 61/62, Imlach went shopping for veteran players. In June 1961 he drafted from Chicago defenceman Al Arbour, who had broken into the NHL with the Red Wings in 53/54 and had been drafted by the Blackhawks in June 1958. In December he picked up right-winger Ed Litzenberger, who had played his first NHL games with Montreal in 52/53. Litzenberger had just made the Canadiens full-time when he was sent to Chicago in December 1954 as part of the league's mercy airlift for the moribund franchise. He won the Calder that season, turned in outstanding seasons with the Blackhawks from 56/57 to 58/59 and served as team captain from 58/59 to 60/61.

In January 1959, during his first season in charge of the Leafs, Imlach had sought the approval of Stafford Smythe for a trade for Litzenberger that would mean giving up either Armstrong or Stewart. (Imlach was also willing to trade Armstrong to Boston for Jerry Toppazzini.) For whatever reason, the deal did not happen and Litzenberger stayed in Chicago, collecting a career-high 77 points. After Litzenberger's Hawks won the 60/61 Stanley Cup against Detroit, though, his team finally considered him expendable—he had lost his wife in a car crash a year earlier, and for the past two seasons his points production had been half of that of his glory years. Litzenberger was dealt to his 60/61 Cup opponents that June, for Gerry Melnyk and Brian Smith. But he didn't impress Detroit's Jack Adams, and in December 1961 Litzenberger was available on waivers. Imlach picked him up as a utility forward at center and right wing.

Imlach's only other significant change in 61/62 was the elevation of goaltender Don Simmons into a supporting role for Bower. In January 1961 Imlach had acquired Simmons in a one-for-one goaltender deal with Boston, giving up Ed Chadwick, who had been Toronto's starting goaltender in 56/57 and 57/58. Simmons had emerged as Boston's main netminder in the late 1950s, playing in the 56/57 and 57/58 Cup finals, but had been supplanted by Harry Lumley in the 58/59 semifinals against Toronto. Lumley, who had once starred for the Leafs (and every other NHL team except Montreal), was the main Bruins starter in 59/60. When Lumley retired at season's end, Simmons was back in charge for 60/61, but after a dreadful start to the season, in which Boston won only 3 of 18 games, Simmons was sent down to Providence of the American league, replaced by Bruce Gamble.

Simmons was unhappy with the demotion, feeling he was being unfairly singled out for the team's poor per-

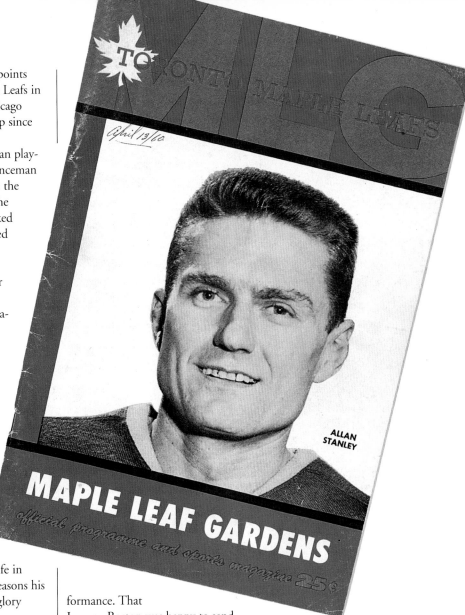

ALLAN STANLEY

MAPLE LEAF GARDENS
Official programme and sports magazine 25¢

Allan Stanley appears on the cover of a 1960 Maple Leaf Gardens programme. Acquired in a 1958 trade from the Bruins, Stanley became a stalwart Leaf defenceman in four Stanley Cup victories.

formance. That January Boston was happy to send him to Toronto for Chadwick. He didn't play at all for Toronto that season, but in 61/62 he spelled off Bower for nine regular-season games. (Gerry Cheevers, then a Leaf amateur prospect who won the 60/61 Memorial Cup with St. Mike's, also filled in for Bower for two games in 61/62.)

On November 8, 1961, Maple Leaf Gardens tried to generate a little publicity by celebrating Bower's birthday. At 37, he was then the oldest player in the league. Bower's exact age has always been a mystery; some say he was actually 41 at the time. Bower played 59 games that season, more than in any season for the rest of his career, as Imlach sought to preserve his ageless wonder.

Far more Leaf publicity was generated that November when it was revealed that Conn Smythe had sold about 45,000 of his 50,000 shares (a little more than one third of the common stock) in Maple Leaf Gardens to his son Stafford, who then revealed that he had two partners (of which his father insisted he was unaware): Harold Ballard and *Toronto Telegram* owner John Bassett. For the first time since 1927, the Leafs

Continued on page 109

THE PRICE OF SUCCESS

DID PUNCH IMLACH DEAL AWAY THE LEAFS' FUTURE WHEN HE SENT DICK DUFF AND BOB NEVIN TO NEW YORK?

Good deal or bad deal? The trade on February 22, 1964, that sent Dick Duff and Bob Nevin to New York and brought Andy Bathgate and Don McKenney to Toronto remains the most important deal of the Leafs' Imlach era because it remains the most controversial. Duff and Imlach were products of the Leaf amateur development system, and had been part of the 61/62 and 62/63 championship teams—Duff had even scored the winning goal of 61/62. Why Imlach made the trade, and why he should (or should not have), is an enduring issue.

When traded, Nevin hadn't reached the full potential promised in his rookie 60/61 season, in which he had finished second to Keon in Calder voting; he scored 12 goals in 62/63, and was on his way to another 12-goal performance in 63/64. Duff, who had been a solid Leaf since 55/56, was also in a scoring slump. Having scored more than 25 goals from 56/57 to 58/59, he hadn't produced more than 19 since then,

and this season would only produce 11, by far his lowest output since turning pro.

Imlach, his critics have maintained, made a deal to solve a short-term problem that would prove costly in the long run, for the careers of Duff and Nevin were far from over. But Imlach lived in the here and now, and when he made the deal he was less than two months away from the playoffs, in which he would be attempting to match the Maple Leafs' late-1940s feat of three straight Stanley Cups. He needed Bathgate and McKenney to do it. Who or what he needed next season, or what the Leafs would need three seasons from now, was not his major concern.

The Leafs of course won the 63/64 Stanley Cup, and the incoming former Rangers played an important role, picking up the offensive slack. Rookie right-winger Jim Pappin didn't get one point in 11 games, and Eddie Shack, while never prolific on right wing, was held to one assist in 13 games. McKenney was fourth on points; Bathgate was sixth, behind Dave Keon. In 10 games of the 62/63 playoffs, Duff had contributed four goals and one assist, Nevin three goals and no assists. While there is no way to say what Duff and Nevin might have contributed in the 63/64 playoffs had they still been around, there is no disputing the fact that McKenney and Bathgate made a far greater scoring contribution to the 63/64 win than Duff and Nevin did to the 62/63 win. Duff and Nevin combined for seven goals and one assist in 62/63—about 23 percent of team goals, with their assists accounting for 3 percent of team goals. McKenney and Bathgate contributed nine goals and 12 assists—25 percent of team goals, with their assists figuring in 33 percent of them.

After the 63/64 Cup win, doubts about the value of the trade nonetheless grew, and for good reason. It was questionable whether Toronto could have won in 63/64 without McKenney and Bathgate, but could they have won instead in, say, 64/65 or 65/66, had the trade not been made? And could costly trades subsequently made have been avoided if so much talent had not been surrendered?

Players discarded by Imlach regularly went on to bigger things elsewhere. Nevin became the captain of the Rangers in 64/65; Duff, traded to Montreal in 64/65, won four Stanley Cups with the Canadiens. In 11 seasons, Duff played in 9 Stanley Cup finals, winning 6 of them. It is doubtful that any player of his era saw more Stanley Cup action. And the three young prospects Imlach surrendered along with his starters in the trade—Bill Collins, Arnie Brown and Rod Seiling—all had solid futures in the

Bob Nevin (left) and Dick Duff celebrate their success in Toronto's Stanley Cup victory of 61/62. Nevin had tied the score in the deciding game against Chicago, and Duff had scored the winner.

league. Brown and Seiling were young defensive prospects, both with important roles to play in New York, while Collins, who was not yet 21, would begin an 11-season NHL career on right wing in 67/68 when drafted by the expansion Minnesota North Stars.

As for the two starters Imlach acquired, their contribution to the Leaf cause was shortlived. McKenney flopped in 64/65, his first full Leaf season, and Bathgate, ridden relentlessly by Imlach, also disappointed. Having produced 77 points in 63/64, Bathgate's output fell to 45 points as injuries limited him to 55 games. In the 64/65 playoffs Don McKenney didn't get a single point in six playoff games and Andy Bathgate contributed one goal. Dick Duff, meanwhile, who had been acquired from New York by Montreal that season, was having a tremendous playoffs, finishing fifth among the victorious Canadiens in scoring as they downed the Blackhawks in seven.

The consequences of the McKenney-Bathgate-Nevin-Duff deal kept reverberating. Feeling the loss of Duff on left wing before the 63/64 campaign was even over, Imlach was compelled to draft Dickie Moore from Montreal that June and haul him out of retirement as a Duff fill-in, with little effect. And it was unfortunate that with the trade for Detroit's Marcel Pronovost in 1965 the Leafs had to give up four players essentially to get one NHL-calibre defenceman, particularly when Imlach had dealt away Brown and Seiling to New York with Nevin and Duff. Seiling contributed 26 points to the Rangers in his first NHL season, 64/65, and became a cornerstone of the Rangers defence as the team rapidly improved; Arnie Brown began an 11-season career in 64/65 as well.

Imlach, meanwhile, was stranding defensive talent in the minors. He left Al Arbour in Rochester, calling him up for only 14 games from 62/63 to 65/66; once clear of the Leafs, Arbour played in three Stanley Cup finals with St. Louis. And then there was Larry Hillman, his circumstances exacerbated by injuries, who after being acquired in 1960 did not break through with the Leafs until 65/66. Rather than giving talent the chance to develop in the NHL, Imlach continued to opt through trades for proven old warriors who could get the job done the way he wanted.

No one can deny Imlach the glory of the four Stanley Cups his Leafs won, but the Duff-Nevin trade for some, even for some Leafs, signalled the beginning of the end to the last great Toronto dynasty. Shortly after Stafford Smythe fired Punch Imlach in 1969, the Montreal Canadiens met the St. Louis Blues in the Stanley Cup finals. The Canadiens won in four straight. In voting for the Conn Smythe Trophy to the playoff MVP, the league board of governors was near-unanimous: they chose the young Montreal defenceman Serge Savard. The only dissenting vote was cast by Stafford Smythe. His choice? Dick Duff.

Continued from page 107

were chasing the Stanley Cup without "King Conn" in firm control, although he continued for a time as chairman of the board.

The Leafs finished the 61/62 season in second place—comfortably ahead of third-place Chicago, and comfortably behind first-place Montreal. The team was also second to Montreal in goals for and against, and a close-fought Cup was promised between the two Canadian clubs. The Blackhawks, however, upset the Canadiens in six on the strength of Glenn Hall's outstanding goaltending, and that produced a final series between the Blackhawks and the Leafs, who had downed the Rangers in six, taking advantage of New York's long-standing inability to win at Maple Leaf Gardens.

The Leafs-Blackhawks series grew bitter as it grew longer. After the Leafs secured a 2-0 game lead, Chicago won convincingly 3-0 at home. Bower, who had been brilliant in the game three loss, pulled a leg muscle in the first period of game four and had to be replaced for the rest of the series by Simmons. Chicago had little trouble with him, assembling a 4-1 win in a fight-filled game that ended with game misconducts being awarded to Stan Mikita and Frank Mahovlich after a stick-swinging duel.

Back in Toronto, the Leafs offence erupted for eight goals, more than enough to cover the four the Blackhawks put behind Simmons. Game six in Chicago was a great goaltending duel without a single goal in the first two periods. Bobby Hull's goal at 8:56 of the third seemed to promise a seventh game, but Bob Nevin tied it up; the Cup was delivered to Toronto for the first time in 11 seasons when Tim Horton made a rink-length dash, sent the puck deep to Armstrong, got it back, then slipped it to Dick Duff who potted the winner. It was Horton's thirteenth assist of the playoffs as he led his teammates in playoff points, outperformed only by Chicago's Mikita. It was a playoff effort that would not be surpassed by another defenceman until Bobby Orr came along.

Simmons had performed well enough in the playoffs that Imlach now decided to use him in a tag-team pairing with Bower in 62/63, with the veteran star still playing the bulk of the games. The only significant changes to the winning roster were the arrival of rookie defenceman Kent Douglas, who replaced Al Arbour (sent to Rochester in the American league) and won the Calder, and the abrupt shipment of Bert Olmstead to New York.

Olmstead was being groomed by the Leaf brass for coaching duties somewhere in the Gardens system, maybe even right in the Gardens. Olmstead had been instrumental in having Shack benched in favour of Stewart during the 61/62 semifinal against New York. Toronto's 2-0 game lead had been erased by the Rangers when Olmstead's word (who did not play in the series) was heeded, and Toronto won the next two games to advance to and win the finals, with Olmstead playing in four of the six games. It came to be suspected that

109 | **PUNCH'S BUNCH**

Imlach, fearing for the coaching component of his job, dumped the old-school motivator before he could become a threat.

Olmstead had already been angered by the capricious way in which Frank Selke had left him unprotected in the 1958 draft, after all he had given to the Canadiens. Now bitter at being cut loose by Imlach, Olmstead refused to report to New York and retired. He was, however, brought into the Rangers system as director of player personnel in 1964.

The Leafs also came perilously close to making a monumental change when part-owner Harold Ballard agreed to sell Frank Mahovlich to Chicago for a cool million just before the start of the 62/63 season. Conn Smythe ordered his son Stafford to get the Leafs out of the sale; the deal, made in a cocktail-party encounter with Chicago owner Jimmy Norris, did not have the approval of the Gardens' board of directors. More important to the Leafs than losing Mahovlich was the prospect of team salary demands going through the roof if the Big M had such a lofty value attached to him.

In 62/63 Toronto won its first regular-season title since 47/48, edging Chicago by one point after losing its last two games of the season to Detroit. Again, Toronto produced the second highest number of goals and allowed the second fewest as the Vezina went to Chicago's Glenn Hall by a two-goal margin.

The regular-season victory counted for little in the playoffs, as this had been the most hotly contested season in league history. Only five points separated first-place Toronto from fourth-place Detroit. Paired with third-place Montreal in their semifinal, the Leafs nonetheless were 2-1 favourites to advance and did not disappoint as they confidently moved the Canadiens aside in five. Detroit had outlasted Chicago 4-2 in their series, and the 62/63 Cup final promised a great goaltending duel between two veterans, Sawchuk and Bower (who had appeared in every Toronto playoff game).

The series was closely played, but Toronto scored the key goals as Detroit went down in

Below is Red Kelly's Maple Leafs jersey. The Detroit defensive great was one of Punch Imlach's steals as he acquired him in February 1960 in a one-for-one trade for utility defenceman Marc Reaume. Imlach converted Kelly into a playmaking center, and in the process unlocked the scoring genius of left-winger Frank Mahovlich.

five, 4-2, 4-2, 2-3, 4-2, 3-1. Bower sparkled with a goals-against of 1.60, and while Frank Mahovlich went without a goal throughout the playoffs, Dave Keon turned in an outstanding effort, leading the team with 7 goals and 5 assists in 10 games. His final goal came at the end of the fifth game when Detroit, down 2-1 and enjoying a man advantage on a Leaf minor penalty, gambled by pulling Sawchuk to give them a two-man surplus. Keon, a master of the short-handed goal, deposited the puck in the empty Detroit net with five seconds to play to ensure the Cup victory. Keon had also made it all the way through the playoffs without incurring a single penalty—not surprising, as he had drawn only one minor penalty in each of the past two seasons, and had just won his second straight Lady Byng.

For 63/64, Imlach stayed with his winning lineup, the only significant change being the introduction of rookie right-winger Jim Pappin. In December, right-winger John MacMillan was sold to Detroit for $20,000, and defenceman Larry Hillman, who had been dragooned in and out of the minors ever since being acquired by the Leafs in 1960, was recalled from Rochester and joined the defence corps of Baun, Brewer, Horton and Stanley.

Injuries plagued the Leafs. Imlach was riding Mahovlich for his low goals production—having scored 36 in 62/63, he was on his way to 26 this season. The rumour surfaced in January that the Rangers were about to deal right-winger Andy Bathgate to Toronto. Bathgate had won the Hart in a 40-goal season in 58/59, and had been named the Rangers' captain in 1961. He had been turning into more of a playmaker than a sniper. He would produce only 19 goals this season, but 58 assists helped put him fourth in league scoring. Bathgate was 31, and had been playing for the Rangers since 52/53. New York saw an opportunity in Imlach's enthusiasm for veterans to move an ageing star while he was still worth something and pick up some younger blood that might help them climb out of the league cellar.

It was the first major deal Imlach cut after the Leafs had begun to win Stanley Cups again. On February 22, Bathgate came to Toronto with another veteran, center Don McKenney, who had broken into the NHL with Boston in 54/55 and had only been acquired by New York the previous season. In return, Imlach sent New York five players: Bob Nevin, Dick Duff, Arnie Brown, Rod Seiling and Bill Collins. The trade rocked the Leaf clubhouse and fans alike. Nevin and Duff were well-liked team players, and while both were in slumps, they would prove to have many strong seasons ahead of them. (See page 108.)

It was another tight regular season, with Montreal edging out Chicago for first place by one point, both teams having 36 wins. Toronto was in third with 33 wins, Detroit in fourth with 30. It would be Toronto's hardest-fought Cup win, and the fighting started in the opening game of their semifinal series with Montreal—a playoff record of 31 penalties was set as Montreal won

2-0. The series lead seesawed and Montreal won the critical fifth game to give them a 3-2 lead. To stave off elimination Toronto won convincingly at home 3-0, then advanced to the finals in a 3-1 win at the Forum in which Keon scored all three goals—the first on a breakaway, the second while killing a penalty, the third into the empty Canadiens net in the final minute.

Imlach could be satisfied with the results of his trade for Bathgate and McKenney in this series. Though not heard from in the first three games, Bathgate scored once in game four, McKenney twice in game five, and both ex-Rangers got one in game six.

Toronto now met Detroit, who had overcome second-place Chicago in seven games. Once again, Toronto trailed the series 3-2. Game six went into overtime and the winning goal on Terry Sawchuk came on a blueline blast from Bob Baun, who was playing on a broken ankle deadened by freezing. Game seven was anticlimactic as Toronto won confidently 4-0. Every playoff series that spring had gone the full seven games. Keon had led the team in playoff goals, with 7, while Frank Mahovlich led on points, with 15.

Imlach continued his fascination with veteran players, and as with Kelly, Detroit was the source. Detroit had found a new goaltending star in Roger Crozier, and at the intraleague draft in June 1964 general manager Sid Abel carried out a baffling juggling act with his netminding talent. Crozier was almost certain to be the Red Wings starter in 64/65, and Abel was facing the prospect of having to send Sawchuk to the minors. Abel was still looking for another NHL-quality goaltender, though, and as the draft approached, a deal was in the works between the Red Wings and the Canadiens that would see Montreal send Detroit Red Berenson and Gump Worsley for Larry Jeffrey and one or two minor prospects. Though Montreal had traded Jacques Plante to New York in the summer of 1963 to get Worsley, a hamstring injury had forced Worsley into the minors and opened the door for perennial Plante backup Charlie Hodge to shine (he won the Vezina in 63/64). But the Worsley deal did not come off, and Detroit went into the intraleague draft with its goaltending stable unresolved. As the draft began, Abel protected Crozier and Sawchuk, while Montreal left Worsley unprotected.

Imlach was in the market for a proven NHL goaltender to tag-team with Bower, to take more of the load off him than Simmons seemed able to. But even with Worsley available, in the first round Imlach went after another Canadien, surprising the gathering by choosing left-winger Dickie Moore, a star of the late 1950s Canadiens dynasty who had retired after 62/63 with bad knees. The Leafs were already feeling the loss of Duff on left wing; a right-winger, Gerry Ehman, had been tried on his opposite wing for four games but was no long-term solution. Imlach gambled the $20,000 fee due to Montreal that he could convince Moore to come out of retirement.

In the second round, Imlach almost took Worsley,

but something made him wait. The third round came, and with it a stunning move by Abel. He decided to draft from the Bruins goaltending prospect George Gardner, who was playing for its Central league affiliate in Minneapolis. With teams permitted to protect only two goaltenders, Abel had to dump either Crozier or Sawchuk, and there was no question of protecting Crozier. Abel would have to leave Sawchuk up for grabs and hope that at this late stage of the draft, nobody would be interested in a 35-year-old former Vezina winner and All Star. Picking right after Detroit, however, was Toronto. When asked if he had a choice, Imlach immediately shouted "Sawchuk!" and to make room for him dropped Gerry Cheevers. Montreal and Chicago still had to pick to close out the round. Both teams passed, and everyone passed in the fourth round. Imlach left the draft with two starting goaltenders whose combined age was somewhere in the mid-70s, and with Cheevers still in his back pocket.

King Clancy, Imlach's assistant, was ecstatic. He loved the veteran players as much if not more than Imlach. "This gives us the two goalies who fought it out for the Stanley Cup," he cheered. "What more could we ask?" And so the 64/65 season began with the Leafs' average age creeping ever higher.

Imlach convinced his draftee Moore to give the NHL another try. He was only a year older than Tim Horton, and had had a solid 50-point effort in his final season. In 38 games, though, Moore, struggling on his bad knees, contributed only 6 points. Sawchuk, however, was a more profitable gamble. Paired with Bower in a tag-team of genuine equals, Sawchuk showed winning form. And Imlach wasn't blinkered to the need for youth. Ed Litzenberger and Gerry Ehman were dropped, and into the lineup full-time came right-winger Ron Ellis and center Pete Stemkowski.

The 64/65 season began with Frank Mahovlich hospitalized in mid-November with a nervous breakdown. His mental equilibrium was shot from Punch Imlach's harping, public and private, about his failure to be as great as he should be. Mahovlich's dramatic crash-and-burn made many players and fans wonder just how important Punch Imlach was to the success of the Leafs. To some of them, he did as much, if not more, harm than good. "Imlach was never satisfied with anybody," Frank Mahovlich reflects. "He was a real queer kind of guy, a bit of a nut. He came out of the army, and he kind of ran the team like an army. You can't do that when guys have families. The thing was, the management let him do it, which made them stupid too."

Johnny Bower respected Imlach's abilities, but had

no illusions about his methodology and found his treatment of Mahovlich unforgivable. "I thought he was a very smart hockey man and manager. He was very, very strict. He was an army man. He always had the first word, and always the last word. If you listened to what he said, you were with the team. And if you worked hard, you were still with the team. But if you'd go your own way, you were in a lot of trouble."

Imlach worked the team hard in practices, sometimes scheduling two a day. Older players like Allan Stanley, who had been through and seen everything by then, had no problem with the Imlach regimen, but others did. Despite the exceptional closeness of this team, a rift developed between older veterans, who owed Imlach their second, even last, chance at greatness (and playoff bonus money to go with it), and the younger recruits, who chafed at his often overbearing, authoritarian style.

Imlach's ego knew no bounds. Most coaches or general managers naturally see the team as their team; Imlach tended to see himself as the team, slipping into the first person when discussing successes. "When I was winning Stanley Cups," was a telling sentence in his memoirs. "We" was a word that didn't occur to him. Players like Billy Harris would study those words and wonder where exactly *they* were when the goals were being scored. When his Toronto years were over, Tim Horton, who had a respectful relationship with Imlach and ended up playing for him in Buffalo, offered that the key to Imlach's success was that he was both coach and general manager. He had a control over the roster that predecessors like Joe Primeau, King Clancy, Billy Reay and Howie Meeker hadn't. With such power, Horton felt any one of them could have done just as well as Imlach.

Imlach's Leafs were perhaps the game's greatest playoff team. The Leafs got the job done where other equally if not more talented teams like Detroit, Chicago and Montreal failed to in the early 1960s. Imlach got the mix right, unafraid to cut deals and send players to the minors to shake up the lineup. If there was a weakness to his methods, it was that he had more faith in proven players than unproven recruits. "The Leafs were never very daring," says Keon. "They never felt confident enough to trade veterans and bring up people from the minors." Imlach and Stafford Smythe introduced few young talents from the Leafs' own development system as they preferred turning to veterans from other teams. At the beginning of the 65/66 season, Stafford Smythe was accused by Canadiens general manager Sam Pollock of tampering with Bernie Geoffrion, who had retired after the 63/64 season, by approaching him directly with a contract offer while he was on the Canadiens retiree reserve list. (Geoffrion ended up being picked up for a waiver fee in 1966 by New York.) And while a few young players like Ellis and Stemkowski were making it into the lineup, the Leafs under Imlach had a disturbing habit of placing their faith in prospects who did not turn into franchise

Tim Horton's stick from the 63/64 Stanley Cup.

players, while discarding or ignoring ones like Cheevers who were the game's emerging stars. The Leaf scouting system stumbled badly when it declined to secure the rights to Junior star Brad Park, playing right under their noses in Toronto. Park was having knee problems, and the Leafs dismissed his professional potential. New York thought otherwise and secured one of the great defensive stars of the expansion years, taking him second overall in the 1966 draft for unsecured amateur talent. Toronto also missed the chance to secure the rights to Ken Dryden, who was playing Junior B in Toronto, even though the Leafs had held the rights to his older brother Dave, now backing up Glenn Hall in Chicago.

Imlach should not be criticized too harshly for failing to build winning teams of the future when it was his job foremost to win in the present. His greatest problem was that the veterans refused to play badly, which would have made it easier to unload them in favour of younger legs. Bower and Sawchuk won the Vezina together in 64/65. Horton was runner-up for the Norris in 63/64 and a first-team All Star; he would make the second team in 66/67 and the first team again in 67/68 and 68/69 (when he was 39), while his defence partner Allan Stanley made the second team in 65/66 at age 40. Young prospects were stuck behind this bottleneck of savvy veterans, and profitable trades became more difficult for the Leafs as star performers aged.

The Leafs were also up against the impending expansion, which would take the league from six to twelve teams overnight after the 66/67 season. Each Original Six club would only be allowed to protect eleven players, and it was inevitable that veterans reaching the end of the line would be considered expendable. There would be compensation for drafted players, but the impending draft suppressed the veteran-player market. No one would make trades for a player they would end up choosing to leave unprotected in another season or two, particularly if it meant giving up young talent to get him. Only a team in need of a short-term fix would be in the hunt for an older, experienced player, and it would have to hope he didn't retire before the draft, which would mean the team couldn't collect on the fee it was entitled to if he had stayed around long enough to be selected by a beggars-can't-be-choosers expansion club.

Perversely, the Leafs, the club with the most veterans to unload, also happened to be the club most eager to deal for them.

The Leafs overall were ageing to such a degree that even the "younger" players were no longer so young. In 64/65 Billy Harris was about to turn 30, Bob Baun and Bob Pulford 29. Regular-season performances had been in steady decline since 60/61, when the club's points percentage was 64.3. In ensuing seasons it slipped to 60.7, 58.6 and 55.7. In 64/65 it slipped again, to 52.9, as the club won 30 of 70 games, nine fewer than in 60/61. Defensively, the club was never better, but offensively Toronto had come down about 25 goals per season since 61/62. From 64/65 to 66/67 the club didn't have one top-ten scorer.

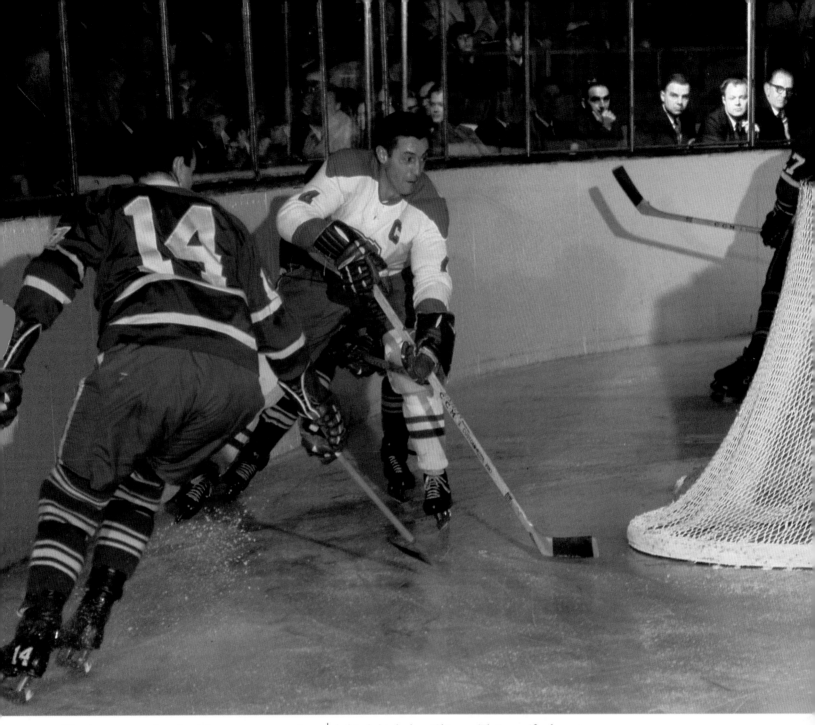

That is not to say that the club was a poor one. It was still a toss-up every spring who would reach the Cup finals from among Toronto, Montreal, Chicago and Detroit. But halfway through the 64/65 season the Leafs were in trouble. Mahovlich had been lost to a mental health holiday, both Bathgate and McKenney were having sub-par years, injuries were depleting the starting lineup, and Imlach was fuming. After 32 games Toronto was fourth with only 12 wins, having won only 4 of their last 15, and were just 5 points ahead of the traditionally inept Rangers. McKenney was demoted to Rochester in January, Imlach tried Horton as a forward with some success, and the Leafs regained some of their form, tying for second with the Canadiens in mid-February. At month's end McKenney was recalled from Rochester and Harris demoted; after ten seasons and three Cups he had played his last games as a Maple Leaf.

Toronto finished the season fourth, two points behind third-place Chicago. Their semifinal opponent was second-place Montreal. On February 10 the two teams had offered the fans at Maple Leaf Gardens an old-fashioned bench-clearing brawl, and the mood of the clubs was still ugly when the playoffs began. Frank Mahovlich, who had been assessed a ten-minute misconduct on February 10, knocked out Terry Harper with a cross-check, while Kent Douglas poleaxed Dave Balon, which earned him a one-game suspension. This hard-fought series was tied at two when Montreal won game five to take control. The Leafs led game six 3-1 after the first period but the Canadiens kept pressing and had the game tied 3-3 by the end of regulation time. The Leafs' quest for four straight Cups was ended at 16:33 of overtime by Claude Provost, whose goal sent Montreal into the finals.

In May, Imlach sent McKenney and Bathgate to Detroit with Harris and prospect Gary Jarrett for Marcel

Leaf center Dave Keon intercepts Canadiens captain Jean Béliveau. Keon was one of the finest checking forwards, a constant scoring threat when forechecking and a master of the shorthanded goal.

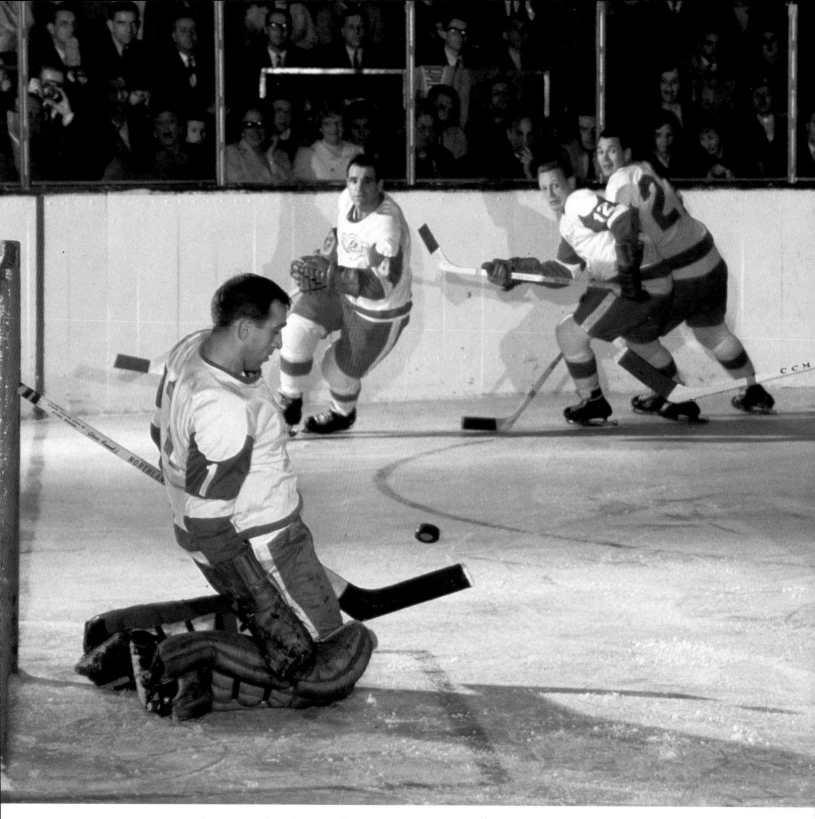

Pronovost, Ed Joyal, Larry Jeffrey, Lowell MacDonald and Aut Erickson. The deal netted Imlach yet another storied veteran in Pronovost. Now 35, the defenceman had turned pro with Detroit in 1950 with Sawchuk and had been through the Motor City's Stanley Cup reign of the early 1950s with him. Jeffrey, 25, was a left-winger who had been with Detroit for four seasons, never scoring more than ten goals, and was used in only 20 Leaf games in 65/66. Right-winger Lowell MacDonald, who had been used sparingly since 61/62 by Detroit, was dispatched to the minors and never did play as a Leaf; Los Angeles picked him in the expansion draft. Defenceman

Aut Erickson, who had bounced from Boston to Chicago to Detroit since 59/60, hadn't actually played for the Red Wings, and like MacDonald wouldn't play a regular-season game for the Leafs (although his appearance in one game of the 66/67 finals placed his name on the Stanley Cup). He too went to the minors and was selected by Oakland in the expansion draft, where he played one full season.

In the end, the Leafs had given up much essentially to get Pronovost. McKenney, to be sure, had played his best hockey by then; he gave Detroit 24 games in 65/66, and managed another 39 with St. Louis in 67/68. But

after winning the American league championship with Rochester in 64/65 before being shipped to Detroit, Billy Harris was able to play two and a half more NHL seasons. Jarrett, who had played one game as a Leaf in 60/61, began a nine-season NHL and WHA career in 67/68. Bathgate turned in four more steady seasons of NHL hockey, and after a three-season retirement had an 11-game return with Vancouver of the WHA.

Imlach's deal-making continued following the 64/65 playoffs and the Pronovost deal. The day before the annual intraleague draft in June, Imlach sent Ron Stewart to Boston for Orland Kurtenbach, Andy

Hebenton and Pat Stapleton; Hebenton and Stapleton were playing with the Portland Buckaroos of the WHL, and neither ever played with the Leafs.

In the intraleague draft that followed, the Leafs left unprotected three veterans who were debating retirement: Stanley, Kelly and Moore. No one touched the veterans, but Gerry Cheevers and Don Simmons, the goaltenders Toronto chose to leave unprotected in favour of their Vezina-winning duo of Bower and Sawchuk, were lost—Cheevers to the Bruins, Simmons to the Rangers. Cheevers was an especially tough loss, as he had just won the American league championship with the Rochester Americans and showed such obvious promise. After losing Cheevers, Imlach cut a deal with Springfield of the American league for goaltender Bruce Gamble, surrendering prospects Larry Johnston and Bill Smith. (Johnston played defence for Minnesota and California from 67/68 to 73/74.)

The Pronovost deal was Imlach's most significant move following 64/65, if only for the fact that it allowed him to deal with the Carl Brewer problem. The unpredictable star had threatened to quit to concentrate on studies at the University of Toronto at the beginning of 64/65, but had finally agreed to come out for another season. In October 1965, Brewer was holding out for more money with Horton, Keon, Pulford and Baun. Everyone eventually signed but Brewer, who made good on past threats and quit the game to go to school, an unimaginable act for a player on such a celebrated team who had been a second-team All Star in 64/65. And while Horton agreed to play, he did so with only a one-year contract as he felt the pull of his new donut-restaurant business. Pronovost, then, was Imlach's insurance against losing either Brewer or Horton (or Stanley, who had been contemplating retirement), and when Brewer indeed left, Pronovost's presence was a godsend.

Pronovost was a capable stay-at-homer who worked especially well with Sawchuk and came to be paired with Hillman, who had played with both Sawchuk and Pronovost as a teenager in the 54/55 Red Wings Cup win. But Pronovost was one more ageing player in an ageing roster. With expansion coming and the amateur development systems slated for demolition in favour of a universal draft, it now became a question of how long it would be before Imlach ran out of trading options and found there was no longer a development system fuelled by Marlies and St. Mike's players to turn to. Already the Leafs had lost the St. Mike's Majors when the school shut down its Junior A program in 1961. (See page 97.)

The Leafs reversed their downward regular-season trend in 65/66, winning 34 games to finish third, behind Montreal and Chicago. The club was fourth in scoring and goals against. Mike Walton played his first Leaf games at center, Bruce Gamble saw regular duty spelling off Sawchuk and Bower, and in a season lean on rookie talent, left-winger Brit Selby won the Calder—he would only play six games for Toronto in 66/67.

Before the playoffs could begin, Conn Smythe had an irate parting of the ways with Maple Leaf Gardens. Smythe was in Florida in March when he phoned John Bassett, who had succeeded him as chairman of the board, to tell him he was resigning his directorship. The reason: Harold Ballard had booked into the Gardens a boxing match between Cassius Clay (Muhammad Ali) and Ernie Terrell. "The fight had been kicked out of every place in the U.S. because Clay is a draft dodger and a disgrace to his country," Smythe would recall telling Bassett. "The Gardens was founded by men—sportsmen—who fought for their country. It is no place for those who want to evade conscription in their own country. The Gardens was built for many things, but not for picking up things that no one else wants."

The playoffs brought on first-place Montreal, and it was over quickly. Toronto went down in four straight. Eddie Shack, who had blossomed with 43 points in the regular season, led the club in playoff scoring with two goals and one assist.

Punch Imlach's reaction to the sweep was restrained. He tinkered on the margins of the roster but left the core of the team intact. Selby was out of the lineup, and so was center Ed Joyal, who had played only 14 regular-season games anyway. Left unprotected, Kurtenbach, who had contributed just 15 points in 65/66, was drafted by the Rangers that summer; Wally Boyer, who had played 46 games at center, was also left unprotected and was taken by Chicago. Brian Conacher, son of Lionel and nephew of Charlie, made the team on left wing. Otherwise untouched, the Leafs embarked on the last season of the Original Six era.

It was a strange campaign, as top teams blew hot and cold and struggled with injuries. The Rangers provided a welcome wild card to the league's long-standing predictability. No longer languishing in the cellar with Boston, New York had been reborn under new coach and general manager Emile Francis, and at mid-season was atop the standings.

In the new year Toronto hit the skids, losing ten straight; Kelly, Sawchuk and Mahovlich were injured, and Shack was riding the bench after playing so well the previous season. Imlach's heart threatened to give out under the strain of losing and he had to be hospitalized. With King Clancy behind the bench and the players taking matters into their own hands, the Leafs found their old form. Some felt they had been able to win in the past despite Imlach; now they were winning without him. For ten games, the Leafs could not be defeated. There were less than three weeks left in the season when Imlach returned to the bench on March 18. Toronto was assured of making the playoffs, and finished the season in third, behind Chicago and Montreal and ahead of the Rangers.

The 66/67 playoffs were in many ways the end of a hockey era. The Original Six was coming to a close after 25 seasons. A new players' association movement was in the works, organized by lawyer Alan Eagleson

with the support foremost of friends on the Leafs like Bob Pulford. The Leaf dynasty was obviously at an end. Too many players were getting too old, and the club had so little strength in youth. Montreal, by comparison, was making another elegant transition from one era of winning to another. A team with the likes of Jean Béliveau also had begun to introduce a new generation of stars like Yvan Cournoyer around 1965. While Detroit was about to collapse dramatically, Chicago was a powerful force with years of excellence left, New York had staged a dramatic resurgence, and Boston was on the cusp of a major turnaround.

The Leafs might have started the 66/67 season with minimal changes, but they would not be able to do the same in 67/68. The expansion draft and retirements would gut the team.

Thus the Maple Leafs of the 1960s embarked on one last post-season campaign with a crew of veterans who still knew how to win the big games. Chicago was their first opponent. The celebrated Blackhawks, who had run away with the regular season, succumbed in six games, its big guns like Bobby Hull stymied by Terry Sawchuk's spectacular netminding. Then came Montreal: after losing the opener 6-2, Toronto ground down the Canadiens in six for its fourth and final Cup of the decade. Dave Keon was a narrow choice over Sawchuk (who played 9 of 12 playoff games) for the series MVP award, the Conn Smythe trophy, based on his relentless two-way play.

In a matter of weeks, the great Leaf team was no more. Red Kelly retired and was hired by former Leaf Larry Regan, general manager with the expansion Los Angeles Kings, to serve as his coach. Al Arbour was drafted by St. Louis, Larry Jeffrey by Pittsburgh, Kent Douglas and Bob Baun by Oakland, Terry Sawchuk by Los Angeles. Eddie Shack was sold to Boston for the rights to Murray Oliver and $100,000—an undisclosed figure that today emphasizes how underpaid the Leafs of the 1960s were. Captain George Armstrong was left unprotected, but there were no takers, other clubs concluding that "Armie" would choose to retire rather than report to another club, having spent his entire career as a Leaf.

On March 3, a month before the end of the 67/68 season, Imlach made a major deal with Detroit, sending the Red Wings Frank Mahovlich, Pete Stemkowski, prospect Gary Unger and the rights to Carl Brewer for Paul Henderson, Norm Ullman and Floyd Smith. Mahovlich had been hospitalized a second time with shot nerves, and it was a trade that revitalized his career. After making the second All Star team in two straight seasons with Detroit, he was traded to Montreal, where he won two Stanley Cups with his younger brother Peter and was named to the first All Star team in 72/73. "It was a terrible, terrible situation," is how Mahovlich sums up his Leaf experiences, "and I was so relieved to get out of the place."

The Leafs finished fifth and missed the playoffs in 67/68, having been leapfrogged in one season by the Rangers and Bruins. On May 23, Jim Pappin, who had

refused a demotion to Rochester, was traded to Chicago for yet another old warrior, defenceman Pierre Pilote. Pilote played one season for Toronto and retired; Pappin played nine more NHL seasons, including a 92-point effort in 72/73, and played in two Cup finals with the Blackhawks. A few weeks after the Pilote-Pappin deal an unprotected Allan Stanley was drafted by the Philadelphia Flyers, with whom he played one season before retiring. Larry Hillman was also left unprotected: a flurry of deals moved him with blinding speed through the rosters of New York, Minnesota and Pittsburgh before he landed in Montreal that fall. He won a Stanley Cup—his sixth—with the Canadiens and played on through 75/76 in the NHL and WHA.

In 68/69, the Leafs were crushed four-straight by the rejuvenated Bruins. Punch Imlach was immediately fired by Stafford Smythe. By then, only a handful of players were left from the 66/67 Cup team: George Armstrong, who had less than two seasons remaining in his career; Tim Horton, who would be traded to New York the next season; Bob Pulford, who would be in L.A. in two more seasons; Johnny Bower, who promptly announced his retirement and became a team scout; Dave Keon, who took over as captain from Armstrong in the new season and stayed to 74/75, after which he jumped to the WHA; Ron Ellis, who played on as a

Leaf through 80/81; Marcel Pronovost, who played one more season; Bruce Gamble, who would be traded to Philadelphia in February 1971; and Mike Walton, who would be dealt to Philadelphia (which then flipped him to Boston) with Gamble.

In June 1969, following the quarterfinals lambasting by the Bruins, the Gardens board voted to remove Stafford Smythe as president and Harold Ballard as vice-president. An investigation by the provincial attorney general's office, ongoing since 1968, was closing in on the pair. They were suspected of siphoning off money from Maple Leaf Gardens, and while Smythe and Ballard were able to stage a counter-coup and regain control of the Gardens board, they couldn't do anything about the criminal investigation. In July 1971 both were charged with fraud; Ballard did time, while Smythe died on the operating table from a hemorrhaging ulcer just before he was scheduled to stand trial, in October 1971.

The great Leaf dynasty had died long before Stafford Smythe did—Billy Harris would insist it died on February 22, 1964, when Imlach, he contended, decided to make scapegoats of Nevin and Duff for his own shortcomings in dealing them away. For 30 years, Leaf fans have been waiting for a resurrection of this once-proud franchise. ◯

The last waltz: the 66/67 Toronto Maple Leafs celebrate their Stanley Cup victory after game six at Maple Leaf Gardens.

MONTREAL CANADIENS
The Sixties and Seventies

LES GLORIEUX

CONSTANT REBUILDING CARRIED THE CANADIENS TO TEN STANLEY CUP VICTORIES FROM 64/65 TO 78/79

That the Montreal Canadiens franchise could be considered to have entered a drought in the early 1960s is a testament to its longstanding excellence. Most clubs would have been thrilled with winning three regular-season titles in four outings, as Montreal did from 60/61 to 63/64. But for the Canadiens, these were difficult years that belied the club's proud image of invincibility. After appearing in every Stanley Cup final for ten straight seasons, and winning every Cup from 55/56 to 59/60, Montreal was eliminated in the semifinals four years running.

The club had become a post-season paradox. Statistically, the Canadiens had never appeared stronger. Montreal won 40 of 70 games in 59/60, its last Cup win in the five-victory streak; it won 41 in 60/61 and 42 in 61/62. Its regular-season titles in those latter two outings also gave it five such titles in a row, even though they did not produce more Cup wins. In 61/62 its goals-for (259) were the highest in team history; total losses (14) were its lowest in a 70-game season, with only two coming at home. But its inability to win playoff hockey in the new decade demanded change. The league was more competitive than it had been through most of the 1950s, and closer checking style was required. The club's ability to utterly dominate the league was gone, and it would not be back for more than a decade. The 1960s became an exercise in learning how to win again, and Montreal did win, with four Stanley Cup victories coming in the latter half of the decade. But these Canadiens were not invincible. They did not sweep confidently past opponents the way the late 1950s lineup did. These new wins required tremendous resolve and character above and beyond the talent at hand.

In the early 1960s Toronto showed how to win Stanley Cups after turning in mostly fair regular seasons. The Leafs were a playoff team, winning it all while rivals like Montreal and Chicago had to satisfy themselves with regular-season titles. After pulling off an upset win in 60/61, the Blackhawks were never again able to get their

RIGHT: A young Larry Robinson, who joined the Canadiens in 72/73, watches his captain, Henri Richard, be escorted from the ice of the Montreal Forum on a rough night against the Philadelphia Flyers. Richard played with the Canadiens from 55/56 to 74/75.
BELOW: The skates of Jean Béliveau, a Montreal Canadien from 53/54 to 70/71.

CHAMPIONS | 118

hands on the Cup, even after their regular-season performances improved dramatically and the lineup swelled with All Stars and scoring champions. Montreal was able to avoid Chicago's fate. It took several years, but as the team was methodically, at times traumatically, rebuilt, the Cup wins returned. And after a pause of only a handful of seasons, the rebuilding began anew. The foundations of the magnificent 1970s were laid while the club was amassing the successes of the 1960s. Montreal's modus operandi had become: draw on the past to win in the present while building for the future.

The impending change in Montreal's fortunes was telegraphed by the retirement of Maurice Richard after the 59/60 Cup win. The Rocket was living history; he was the only player in the Canadiens roster to have been on hand when the once-moribund franchise began its resurrection in 42/43, and he had played on every Canadiens Cup finalist and winner since then. Defencemen Doug Harvey and Tom Johnson had been around for all of the 1950s successes, and so had right-winger Bernie Geoffrion. Right-winger Dickie Moore came close, having missed only the 50/51 final, but he, as well as Jacques Plante, could say they had participated in every Montreal Cup win of the 1950s, which began with the 52/53 victory.

Richard, however, was rooted in the bedrock of the franchise's modern history. His career, beset by injuries, was clearly in its declining years when he chose to retire. His last All Star selection had come in 56/57, when he scored 33 goals. In his last three seasons, with his ice time cut back by infirmary appointments, he never produced more than 19 goals. He led the Canadiens in scoring in the 57/58 playoffs with 11 goals and 4 assists in 10 games after appearing in only 28 regular-season games, but it proved to be his last great playoff performance. In 58/59 he appeared in only four post-season games, producing no points at all, and his eight games in the 59/60 playoffs resulted in only one goal. It was his younger brother Henri, the Pocket Rocket, who led the team in playoff scoring that season, with three goals and nine assists.

Sam Pollock

The only member of the Canadiens organization with a greater weight of history behind him was Richard's old Punch Linemate, Toe Blake, whose team exploits reached back into the late 1930s and who had taken over as team coach in 1955. Richard outweighed

CANADIENS SCORING
1960/61–1968/69

GOALS PER GAME

4.0
3.5
3.0
2.5
2.0

60/ 61/ 62/ 63/ 64/ 65/ 66/ 67/ 68/
61 62 63 64 65 66 67 68 69

■ Montreal goals-against
□ League-leading GA
■ Montreal goals-for
□ League-leading scoring
— League scoring average
64/
65
● Stanley Cup win

general manager Frank Selke, who, as admired as he was for building the Canadiens powerhouse of the 1950s, wasn't hired until the summer of 1946, by which time Richard had been with the team for four seasons and was well established as its scoring star.

Richard was hurried into the Hockey Hall of Fame upon his retirement, and while he was given a vice-presidency with the team, he came to feel ignored, under-utilized and under-appreciated. Whether or not Richard was the key missing ingredient, once he was out of uniform, off the ice and the bench and out of the dressing room—and no longer team captain—Montreal stopped winning playoff hockey even as it continued to turn in strong regular seasons.

In Montreal, the team captaincy in 60/61 was put to a team vote (unlike Toronto, where it was a management appointment). Jean Béliveau narrowly outpolled Bernie Geoffrion, who had just won the Hart. Béliveau's leadership ability was unquestionable—before retiring after 70/71, he would win the Hart for the second time and be a runner-up another three times. The Béliveau years, from 60/61 to 70/71, provided a transition from the great Canadiens teams of the 1950s, of which Béliveau had been such a critical part, and the outstanding Canadiens teams of the 1970s, which in the last years of the decade dominated the NHL like no club has since. With Béliveau as team leader, Montreal played in six Stanley Cup finals and won five of them. While it would not match the feat of five-straight achieved by the club in the late 1950s, many of these Béliveau successes came when the Original Six clubs were at their most competitive, with four of the six teams regularly capable of winning it all.

Before these victories could be achieved, Montreal had to undergo a drastic rebuilding. Frank Selke had executed precious few trades of any consequence during the 1950s Cup streak; now, just as Punch Imlach rebuilt the Leafs with major deals, Frank Selke began shaking up the Canadiens as well. Some of the most treasured names in the Canadiens roster were ruthlessly discarded in the first seasons of the 1960s as the Cup streak ended and Chicago, Toronto and Detroit contested the championship in the four consecutive non-Canadiens finals.

Initially following the 59/60 victory, Selke made minimal changes. Left-wingers Ab McDonald and Reg Fleming were sent to Chicago for longstanding Red Wing and Blackhawk forward Glen Skov and right-winger Terry Gray. It was a poor deal for Montreal, as Gray was a fringe player and Skov played only three games as a Canadien while McDonald and Fleming had long careers ahead of them. Early in the season, Selke moved yet another left-winger, André Pronovost, to Boston, for one in return, Montrealer Guy Gendron, who had played five NHL seasons with the Rangers and Bruins.

Montreal eked out a season championship, two points ahead of Toronto, and met the third-place Blackhawks in the semifinal. Chicago had been steadily improving over the last three seasons, but had still

Montreal Canadiens

The Dynasty of the 1960s

Featuring the players and management who participated in Montreal's Stanley Cup victories of 1964/65, 1965/66, 1967/68, and 1968/69

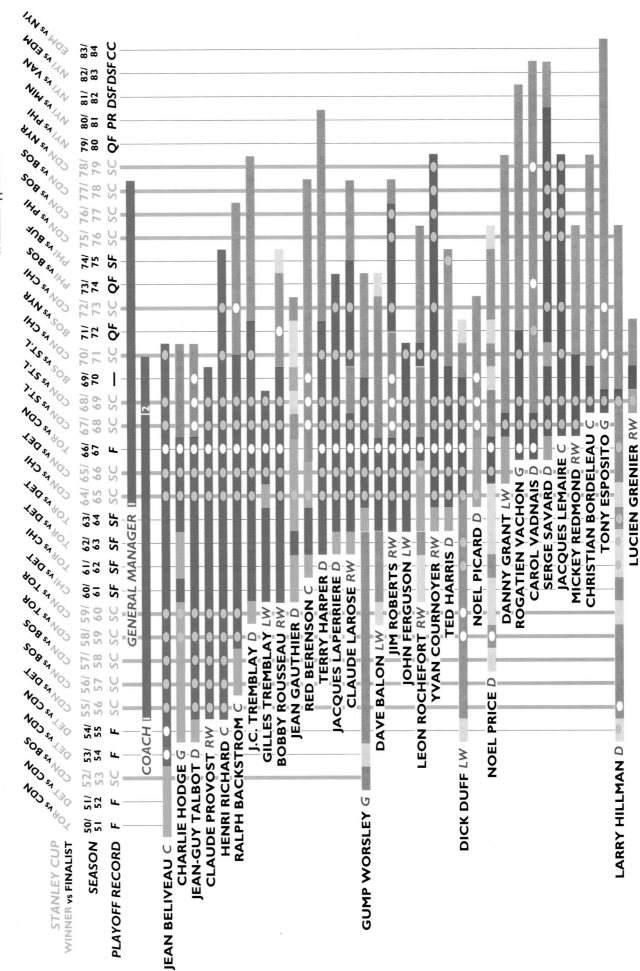

finished 17 points behind Montreal. The Canadiens won the opening game 6-2, then lost control of the series. Geoffrion, their Hart Trophy winner and the league's top scorer, was out for two games with injuries, and neither he nor Béliveau, who had finished second to him in the scoring race, dominated offensively: while Béliveau did register five assists, he did not get a goal, and Geoffrion was held to two in four games. The series was tied at two when the Hawks came into the Forum and blanked the Canadiens 3-0. Glenn Hall was exceptional in the Chicago net, and back in Chicago for game six he produced another 3-0 shutout as Montreal was eliminated—demonstrating why he, and not Plante, had been the first-team All Star in 59/60 and why he, and not Plante, was on the second team, behind Bower, in 60/61.

The 3-0 loss in game five at the Forum had propelled Selke to make noises about some player contracts needing to be renegotiated before the next season. After the semifinal loss, which was blamed in part on poor defence, Selke effected the worst humiliation a general manager could on a star by sending Doug Harvey to the minors. Harvey had won his sixth Norris Trophy as the league's top defenceman and earned his traditional posting to the first All Star team in 60/61. Selke's move struck Harvey as purely vindictive—a getting-even

move for his leading role in the players' association movement of 1957. Harvey had been too important to trade then, but now, with his career entering its final years, Selke (thought Harvey) could do whatever he wanted. When Harvey refused the demotion, Selke sold him that June to the Rangers, receiving tough-guy defenceman Lou Fontinato in the bargain.

Harvey's exile was just the start of a wholesale house-cleaning of the Canadiens defence corps. Bob Turner was sent packing to Chicago for Fred Hilts, who never played in the NHL, and Al Langlois went to New York to keep Harvey company in exchange for defenceman John Hanna. Hanna played only six games for Montreal, but Blake was able to ice a new defensive pairing of Fontinato and Al MacNeil (acquired from the Leafs for Stan Smrke) to spell off the experienced Tom Johnson and Jean-Guy Talbot. Also now in the defence full-time was 21-year-old J. C. Tremblay, who had steadily gained more exposure to the NHL, beginning with 11 games in 59/60 and 29 in 60/61. Tremblay had participated in the 60/61 semifinal debacle against Chicago, but had emerged with his reputation unscathed. He, Johnson and Talbot had survived Montreal's humiliation; Harvey, Turner and Langlois had not.

The Harvey sale began to look like one of Selke's

rare miscalculations when the veteran star earned another Norris and first-team All Star berth with the Rangers while serving as player-coach in 61/62. But Selke turned out to have judged Harvey's market value precisely. After one more season in New York, Harvey's NHL career appeared to be over. He was released by the Rangers after 14 games in 63/64 and headed for the minors, playing with the Quebec Aces of the American league. And getting rid of Harvey, along with Turner and Langlois, helped clear the path for new defensive talent in the Montreal system. Neither MacNeil nor Fontinato were longterm defensive considerations, and a young defence began to emerge as Tom Johnson's career wound down. By the time the Canadiens were back in a Stanley Cup final in 64/65, the team had an almost entirely new defence corps, Jean-Guy Talbot being the only 1950s veteran still on hand.

What was most striking about the Harvey sale was the ruthlessness with which Selke dumped a true franchise player. Harvey had been instrumental in the Canadiens' Cup victories of the 1950s, and he had come back from several injuries during 60/61 to play in the semifinal that earned him the trip to New York. Is this how a proud organization intended to treat all its ageing stars? Apparently it was. Already in 1958 Selke had allowed Bert Olmstead to be taken by Toronto in the intraleague draft, after the workhorse left-winger ignored injuries to help the team win another Cup. The Harvey deal emphasized the fact that the Canadiens were in business, and that the general stability of the lineup experienced at the height of the 1950s victories—when 12 players managed to participate in all 5 consecutive Cup victories—was over. Selke, too, was reaching the end of his career, but as he approached retirement he showed no tempering streak of sentimentality in his management of the celebrated team. If changes were necessary, changes would be made, and no one was immune from replacement or demotion.

The 61/62 season that followed the Harvey sale was one of the greatest in franchise history. The Canadiens won another regular season title with 42 wins and 14 losses—their fewest losses ever in a 70-game season, and the fewest since 44/45, when 8 were lost in a 50-game tour. Jacques Plante won the Vezina and Hart trophies, the last goaltender to date to be so honoured. Right-winger Bobby Rousseau, who had played his first 15 games with the Canadiens in 60/61, earned the Calder, while fellow right-winger Claude Provost, a checking specialist who had begun to collect points as well, was the Lady Byng runner-up.

In the semifinals they would face third-place Chicago, who had gone on to win the Cup in 60/61 after eliminating Montreal. Even without Henri Richard, who had a broken arm, Montreal was expected to win. The Canadiens did build a 2-0 series lead, but Chicago came back with four straight wins that culminated in a 2-0 victory on home ice.

Selke accepted this second-straight semifinal loss to Chicago without making any of the tempestuous

changes that had boiled up from the first. He could afford to be patient: fresh talent was coming up from the team's development system. During the new season Blake would try out prospects Claude Larose on left wing and Jacques Laperrière on defence, while Terry Harper joined the defence as Tom Johnson was injured and Al MacNeil was shipped to Chicago. Marcel Bonin, who had been with the team on left wing since 57/58, was retired with a formal farewell at the Forum on October 27—a move most certainly calculated to alleviate the bad taste the treatment of Doug Harvey had left in the mouths of fans.

The 62/63 season was one of the most closely contested in league history; no team could find a way to dominate. The Canadiens staggered from one crisis to another. Béliveau entered a scoring slump so disturbing that he openly discussed his retirement, and Geoffrion (among others) was hurt. At the end of the season, the top four clubs were separated by only five points. Though the Canadiens won only 28 of 70 games, by tying 23 they were able to finish third, three points back of the league-leading Leafs, whom they met in the semifinals. The defending Cup champions had little trouble with the Canadiens, taking the series 4-1. The last game, in Toronto, was a 5-0 shutout by Johnny Bower, and goaltending surely was on Selke's mind as the club's third regular season without an appearance in the Cup finals passed.

Selke was about to begin his final season as general manager before retiring in favour of his long-standing right-hand-man, Sam Pollock. He had never been one for blockbuster trades, but his club had stalled in its post-season performances. He made a passive change by leaving unprotected Tom Johnson, who had completed his thirteenth full season on defence. Boston drafted him in June, but Johnson never played another NHL game. Dickie Moore, hobbled by knee injuries, chose to retire.

When it came time for a deal, Selke looked to New York, where he had offloaded Harvey in 1961. New York had managed to make the playoffs in 61/62 under player-coach Harvey after a three-season absence, but had fallen back into bad habits again in 62/63 (without Harvey), finishing fifth, 21 points behind fourth-place Detroit. The Rangers were embarking on a roster shake-up and found Selke only too willing to help.

One of New York's most valuable players was goaltender Gump Worsley, a native Montrealer who had been toiling in the Rangers system since winning the Calder in 52/53. In the last three playoffs, Montreal had been outmatched in goaltending duels, first by Hall in 60/61 and 61/62, then by Bower in 62/63. Selke concluded Plante could not longer deliver the clutch playoff performances a Cup contender needed, and he didn't have enough confidence in backups like Charlie Hodge and Cesare Maniago to give them the job. So off to Madison Square Garden went Plante, accompanied by left-winger Don Marshall and center Phil Goyette, and into the Forum came Worsley, accompanied by left-wingers Dave Balon and Len Ronson and right-winger Leon Rochefort.

It was a strange deal all around, as neither team really got what it wanted—at least not right away. Plante did not take well to playing behind a team as sorry as the Rangers. After two seasons of losing, Plante quit rather than accept a demotion to Baltimore in the American league. And while Montreal was pleased to have Worsley, he immediately injured a hamstring and had to be sent to the Quebec Aces to recuperate. Montreal had no choice but to turn to Hodge, who'd been around as a backup since 54/55, and he turned out to be a first-class starter. Over the next two seasons, Worsley appeared in only 27 regular-season games, while Hodge carried the main load.

Montreal was back winning again in 63/64, aided by a tenacious new left-winger, John Ferguson, who took the place of Moore, and a strong two-way right-winger, Jimmy Roberts, who played his first 15 games. The club also had a four-game look at teenage defensive prospect Ted Harris. And from the Montreal Junior Canadiens another teenage prospect, right-winger Yvan Cournoyer, had a five-game tryout. The transformation of the Canadiens was almost complete.

In another close contest, Montreal won the 63/64 season championship on the strength of one tie, which gave them a one-point edge over the Blackhawks. The Hart Trophy went to Béliveau, Hodge won the Vezina by a two-goal margin over Hall, and Laperrière took the Calder (with Ferguson runner-up). The club prepared for its second consecutive semifinal against the Leafs, who had finished third, seven points back.

This was not the same club that Toronto had dispensed with in five games in 62/63. Montreal built a 3-2 series lead, but could not solve Johnny Bower, who was the centerpiece of a 3-0 shutout that tied the series, and who then allowed only one goal in game seven, as Toronto moved on to the finals with a 3-1 win.

The 64/65 season was Sam Pollock's first as general manager, and he took over just as Bernie Geoffrion retired. Boom-Boom's points production had been in decline since his 50-goal season of 60/61, as injuries limited his ice time. Geoffrion headed to Quebec to coach the Aces of the American league, where Doug Harvey played for him as a second-team All Star. Geoffrion's departure marked one more important break with the 1950s dynasty. Now only four players were left who had been with the Canadiens for all five consecutive Cup wins: Jean Béliveau, Jean-Guy Talbot, Henri Richard and Claude Provost. Talbot was the only veteran in a defence stocked with new talent: J. C. Tremblay, Terry Harper, Jacques Laperrière and Ted Harris, with Jean Gauthier also available. Béliveau, Ralph Backstrom (who had played on the 58/59 and 59/60 Cup teams) and Pocket Rocket Richard provided experienced playmaking and scoring at center that would be the envy of any team, with newcomer Red Berenson serving as a utility. Claude

Provost was the one old hand on right wing. Everyone else—Bobby Rousseau, Claude Larose, Jim Roberts and Yvan Cournoyer, with Leon Rochefort available—had come along after the 59/60 win.

Left wing was also populated by newcomers: Gilles Tremblay, Dave Balon and John Ferguson, whose sheer meanness was intended to give the Canadiens a better chance of winning. At mid-season the Canadiens acquired one more left-winger, an important last addition to a winning lineup. Pollock turned to the Rangers for yet another Canadiens deal, seeking out Dick Duff, a former Maple Leaf who had been part of a controversial trade between Toronto and New York in February 1964. (See page 108.) Pollock and Blake needed a replacement for Gilles Tremblay, who had broken his ankle and was lost for the season, and to get Duff they sent the Rangers right-winger Bill Hicke, who had been on the 58/59 and 59/60 Cup winners. Playing with Béliveau and Cournoyer, Duff got a second chance at winning after an unhappy sojourn in New York, and did not waste it, establishing a place for himself even after Gilles Tremblay returned.

The 64/65 All Star team illustrated just how much the Canadiens had changed in a few seasons. Playing defence on the first team was Laperrière, who had won the Calder only the year before and was runner-up in voting for the Norris. The veteran Claude Provost, emerging as the team's leading scorer in 64/65 after years as a checking specialist, made it on right wing, and Hodge, who hadn't been considered a candidate for starting goaltender the previous season, was named to the second team.

The emergence of Hodge as a starter and Provost as a scoring star demonstrated how much talent, some of it unrealized, lay in the Canadiens system. Certainly the Montreal organization showed no great desperation for fresh faces. It hardly ever used the intraleague draft to secure players. In fact, the Canadiens didn't draft a single player from another NHL team between 1959 and 1965.

For a team with a strong development system, the intraleague draft was an unnecessary and expensive way to fill gaps. While players left unprotected were far from useless, they were on the team lists every June because they were considered expendable, and the price for drafting one went from $15,000 to $20,000 in 1959 to $30,000 in 1965. These were years when a journeyman might be making $8,000 to $10,000. Far better to have your own low-salaried fringe players than to be paying another team big dollars for the right to sign theirs.

Finishing second overall in 64/65, the team was third in scoring and fourth in goals against, although play among the top four clubs remained tight. The team-scoring spread of playoff qualifiers was only 20 goals, their goals-against difference just 12, with Toronto, Chicago and Detroit's defensive effort separated by only 3 goals. It was another spring in which the Cup was entirely up for grabs.

The Canadiens continued their post-season rivalry with the Leafs, meeting them in a hard-fought semifinal

Montreal Canadiens 1960/61-68/69

Season	Finish	Record (W-L-T)	Points %	Awards (winners & runners-up)	All-Stars	Playoffs
60/61	1st	41-19-10	65.7	HART: Geoffrion ART ROSS: Geoffrion, Béliveau RU NORRIS: Harvey	1ST TEAM: Harvey (D), Béliveau (C), Geoffrion (RW) 2ND TEAM: Richard (C), Moore (LW)	Lost SC semifinal 4-2 to Chicago
61/62	1st	42-14-14	70.0	HART: Plante CALDER: Rousseau LADY BYNG: Provost RU VEZINA: Plante	1ST TEAM: Plante (G), Talbot (D)	Lost SC semifinal 4-2 to Chicago
62/63	3rd	28-19-23	56.4		2ND TEAM: Richard (C)	Lost SC semifinal 4-1 to Toronto
63/64	1st	36-21-13	60.7	HART: Béliveau CALDER: Laperrière, Ferguson RU VEZINA: Hodge	2ND TEAM: Hodge (G), Laperrière (D), Béliveau (C)	Lost SC semifinal 4-3 to Toronto
64/65	2nd	36-23-11	59.3	NORRIS: Laperrière RU CONN SMYTHE: Béliveau	1ST TEAM: Laperrière (D), Provost (RW) 2ND TEAM: Hodge (G)	Won SC final 4-3 over Chicago
65/66	1st	41-21-8	64.3	HART: Béliveau RU LADY BYNG: Rousseau RU VEZINA: Worsley & Hodge NORRIS: Laperrière	1ST TEAM: Laperrière (D) 2ND TEAM: Worsley (G), Béliveau (C), Rousseau (RW)	Won SC final 4-2 over Detroit
66/67	2nd	32-25-13	55.0	VEZINA: Hodge RU		Lost SC final 4-2 to Toronto
67/68	1st Div 1st OA	42-22-10	63.5	HART: Béliveau RU CALDER: Lemaire RU VEZINA: Worsley & Vachon NORRIS: Tremblay RU MASTERTON: Provost	1ST TEAM: Worsley (G) 2ND TEAM: Tremblay (D)	Won SC final 4-0 over St. Louis
68/69	1st Div 1st OA	46-19-11	67.8	HART: Béliveau RU CONN SMYTHE: Savard	2ND TEAM: Béliveau (C), Harris (D), Cournoyer (RW)	Won SC final 4-0 over St. Louis

for the third consecutive spring. The opening game was ugly, with Leaf defenceman Kent Douglas dropping Dave Balon in a fencing match and Frank Mahovlich knocking Terry Harper unconscious with a cross-check. The Canadiens survived the game with a 3-2 win, and went up by two on a 3-1 win. Blake then decided to switch goaltenders from Hodge to Worsley, who had played only 19 games that season. Toronto won game three 3-2 in overtime, and tied the series up with a 4-2 win at home, but Blake stuck with Worsley. Game five went to Montreal 3-1, and the Canadiens took the series 4-2 when Claude Provost scored in overtime in game six. After a four-season absence, the Canadiens were back in the finals, and their opponents this time were the Blackhawks, who had stopped them in the 60/61 and 61/62 semifinals.

Worsley had won Blake's confidence and drew the starting assignment over Hodge for the finals. In the first two games at the Forum, Montreal took command

with 3-2 and 2-0 wins. Moving to Chicago, the big slapshots and short ice surface served the Blackhawks well as Glenn Hall anchored a 3-1 win. The loss was costly for Montreal: Worsley tore a thigh muscle and had to be replaced by Hodge for game four. The Blackhawks ran wild, led by a two-goal effort from Bobby Hull, and tied the series with a 5-1 win.

Back in Montreal for game five, Montreal shocked Chicago with a 6-0 drubbing. In a rare turn of events, Hall was pulled while the Blackhawks were down 3-0 after two periods and replaced by backup Denis DeJordy. It was back to Chicago for game six, and the Blackhawks went back to Hall; the result was a 2-1 win that forced a seventh game.

Gump Worsley's career was never short of surprises. He got his biggest before game seven, when Toe Blake fingered him for the starting job, despite the fact that he had been out for the last three games with the torn muscle. The game was in Montreal on May 1, and

Henri Richard tees off against the St. Louis Blues while Yvan Cournoyer waits at the net and Jacques Lemaire turns to watch. Montreal met and defeated the Blues in the 67/68 and 68/69 Stanley Cup finals.

Worsley would turn 36 in two weeks. He had been playing professionally since 1949, in the NHL since 52/53, and he had never made it to the finals. Having at last made it, the weight of his own career and the pride of his home-town Canadiens rested on his shoulders. The outcome was never in doubt. Worsley shut out the Blackhawks as the veterans Béliveau and Richard were joined by team newcomers Duff and Cournoyer in putting four goals behind Hall.

The Canadiens drought was over. After five seasons of trying, Jean Béliveau had led the team to another Stanley Cup, and for his effort—a team-leading 8 goals and 8 assists in 13 games—he was awarded the league's new Conn Smythe Trophy as the most valuable player in the playoffs.

The Canadiens' checking game had been exceptional against the Blackhawks. In Chicago's seven-game semifinal against Detroit, Hull scored eight times. Against Montreal, he was held to just two goals, both in game four. Stan Mikita never scored at all against the Canadiens, after winning the scoring title for the second straight season.

Pollock cut a six-player deal with New York in June. Third-string goaltender Cesare Maniago was sent to the Rangers with fill-in center Garry Peters, who had played 13 games for Montreal in 64/65, and Pollock received in return four players: Gord Labossière, Earl Ingarfield, Dave McComb, and Noel Price. Of the four, only one, Price, played at all for the Canadiens, serving as an alternate defenceman for two seasons. Ingarfield,

left unprotected in the intraleague draft, was taken right back by the Rangers for a $30,000 draft fee. The trade had no real effect on the team beyond supplying Blake with Price as a substitute for Laperrière when his defensive star underwent knee surgery in early March 1966. Canadiens management could find no fault with their winning lineup; indeed, for the next two seasons it was virtually unchanged.

In 65/66 the Canadiens turned in a superb effort, winning the regular season title by an eight-point margin over Chicago. Its scoring touch was back—the team produced only one fewer goal than league-leading Chicago as Rousseau and Béliveau finished third and fourth in the scoring race. The defence was especially stingy: Worsley and Hodge combined to win the Vezina by a 14 goal margin and Laperrière won the Norris.

After a close 4-3 win in their opening game in the semifinal against Toronto, the Canadiens rolled off three more wins, parting ways in a fight-filled deciding game. Detroit had overcome the Blackhawks in six games, and that produced the first final series between the Red Wings and Canadiens since 55/56. Were it not for their rookie goaltender, Roger Crozier, Detroit would have been on summer vacation after four games. Instead, Detroit jumped to a 2-0 series lead in games at the Forum, and while Montreal then won four straight to take the Cup, an overtime goal by Henri Richard was required in the deciding game to wrap up the series. For his netminding heroics, Crozier was awarded the Conn Smythe Trophy, an honour that did not sit especially well with Gump Worsley, who had anchored the winning cause and helped the Canadiens get the necessary win in game six when they were outshot 30 to 22.

The team embarked on the 66/67 season with few changes required or undertaken. Rookie defenceman Carol Vadnais made his debut, and Red Berenson, who had not been able to crack a starting role at center after five seasons of trying, was sent to the Rangers.

It was the last season of the Original Six era, and it unfolded with injuries underpinning a hot-and-cold season for many teams. Only Chicago managed a steady campaign, finishing first with 41 wins. Montreal finished second with 32, just ahead of Toronto and New York. The semifinals brought on the Rangers, who were making their first trip to the playoffs in five seasons. They made a credible, scrappy effort, but Montreal moved them aside in four, advancing to meet the surprising, ageing Leafs, who had upset the Blackhawks in six in their semifinal.

The Canadiens were using a new goaltender, Rogatien Vachon, in the playoffs. The newcomer had stepped in when Worsley was injured in mid-February after already missing seven weeks with knee surgery. At 21, Vachon had made a rapid rise in the Canadiens system, skipping Junior A altogether as he went from the Thetford Mines Junior B team to the Quebec Aces of the American league, then to Houston of the Central league in 66/67. He played only 19 games with the Canadiens in 66/67, but was Blake's choice over Hodge to carry the Canadiens to a third straight Cup.

Leaf coach and general manager Punch Imlach made Vachon the brunt of a pre-series barb. Arriving in Montreal with his ancient duo of Terry Sawchuk and Johnny Bower, he asked, "Do they think they can win from us with a Junior B goalie in the net?" As it turned out, the Canadiens couldn't. It wasn't that Vachon wasn't good enough, only that Sawchuk was superhuman and the Leafs' checking relentless. The Canadiens went down in six.

After the 66/67 Cup loss, changes began—in part because of the failed Cup drive, in part because the expansion of the league from 6 to 12 teams limited the Original Six franchises' protected lists to just eleven players. Charlie Hodge was drafted by the Oakland Seals; Jim Roberts, Noel Picard and Jean-Guy Talbot by the St. Louis Blues; Noel Price by the Pittsburgh Penguins; Dave Balon by the Minnesota North Stars. Up from Houston came Serge Savard, a playmaking defenceman with huge potential, and Jacques Lemaire at center. Mickey Redmond moved in on right wing as Jim Roberts's replacement.

Montreal produced the best regular-season record, winning the East Division by four points over the vastly improved New York Rangers. It was an impressive all-round team performance: Worsley and Vachon shared the Vezina, and the team produced the third-highest number of goals without one top-ten scorer. They had

little trouble in the East playoffs, eliminating the Bruins in four and the Blackhawks in five. The tough games, surprisingly, were reserved for the finals against the West Division's St. Louis Blues. The expansion Blues had finished 24 points back of Montreal—if St. Louis had been in the East Division the club would not even have made the playoffs. But in the finals Glenn Hall was exceptional in the St. Louis net, and while Montreal won in four, every game carried a one-goal margin and two games ended in overtime. Hall won the Conn Smythe, giving Gump Worsley the unhappy distinction of having been the winning goaltender in the two series thus far in which the losing goaltender was named the most valuable player.

After the 67/68 win, the Canadiens appeared to be on a solid foundation. While 1950s veterans like Béliveau, Talbot, Provost and Henri Richard could not last forever, their careers were far from over, and the team exhibited a healthy mix of old hands, established players and emerging talents, with yet more talent available in the minor pro system and at the Junior level. The only off-season move of any note was the decision in June to trade new left-winger Danny Grant and veteran right-winger Claude Larose to Minnesota in exchange for Minnesota's first-round pick in the 1972 amateur draft and a player to be named at the end of the 70/71 season. Toe Blake took the opportunity to retire on a winning note, leaving Sam Pollock with the formidable challenge of finding someone who could fill Blake's skates and shoes.

Pollock arrived at a list of about ten candidates, and the leading one, at least to outsiders, seemed to be Busher Curry. The right-winger had made the Canadiens lineup in 47/48, in Blake's last playing season, and had been part of every Montreal playoff drive until his retirement in 1958. Curry had then moved into coaching, running the Quebec Aces of the American league from 61/62 to 63/64. He fit the profitable pattern set by Blake: a coach who could speak to the team with the experience of having won Stanley Cups as a Canadien himself.

But Pollock passed on Curry and made a selection that surprised even the new hiree himself. Pollock turned the team over to his director of player development, Claude Ruel, who had to be talked into taking the job.

Ruel's selection was one that wrote its own press copy. He was 29, the youngest coach in the NHL, and the only one to speak French. His English, for that matter, was haphazard. He was five-foot five and 230 pounds, a human cannonball. Pundits wondered whether, once behind the bench, he would even be able to see over the seated players.

Ruel had never played in the NHL. As a prospect with the Junior Canadiens in 1958, he had lost an eye in an exhibition game in Belleville. The career-ending injury had moved him into coaching within the Canadiens organization. After five seasons running the Junior Canadiens, he served as Montreal's chief scout for

MONTREAL CANADIENS

The Transitional Seventies

Featuring the players and management who participated in
Montreal's Stanley Cup victories of 1970/71 and 1972/73

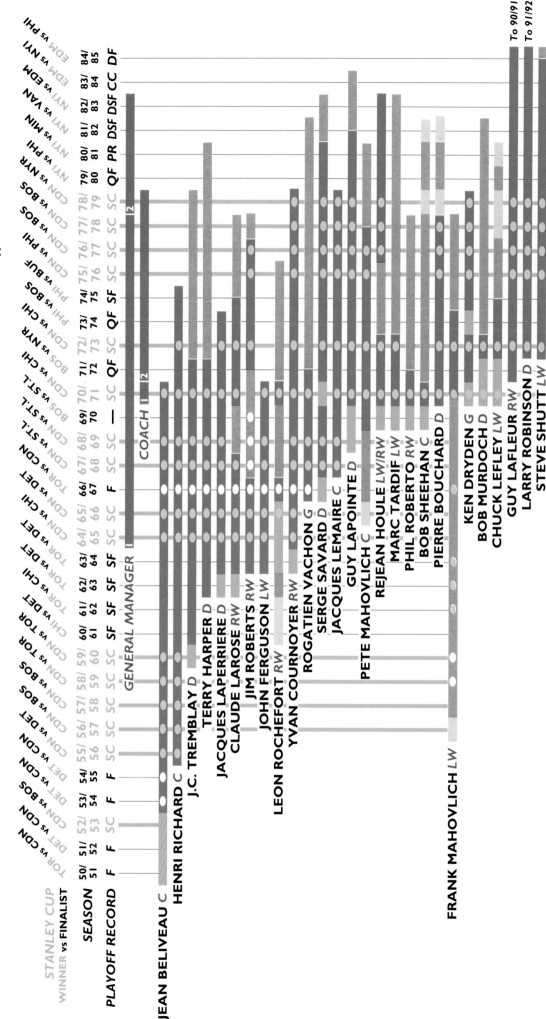

two years, then moved up to director of player development. After three years in the position, working at Pollock's side, Ruel was completely happy in the job, and had no great interest in running the Canadiens bench. But Pollock convinced him to accept the challenge.

The first season, 68/69, was a lengthy honeymoon between the coach and his team. His fractured English and his underdog persona kept him in the good books of his players. They fought off injuries to march steadily up the standings and won their second consecutive regular-season title, three points ahead of the Bruins. In the East Division semifinal, Montreal downed the Rangers in four straight. The West Division was still too weak for its finalist to put up a serious struggle in the Cup series, so everyone knew that the East Division finals between Montreal and Boston would determine the Stanley Cup champion. Western teams had won only 51 of 216 games against their Eastern counterparts in 68/69, and had been scored on 778 times. Boston and Montreal had the first- and third-best offences, producing 303 and 271 goals respectively. Every team in the East outscored the expansion teams of the West. The only edge the West had was in goaltending, as the veteran tag-team of Glenn Hall and Jacques Plante had won the Vezina with St. Louis by a wide margin.

The Montreal-Boston series was classic playoff hockey. It went six games, with three of them decided in overtime. Montreal took all three—the first two games, in Montreal, and the deciding game, in Boston, when Jean Béliveau scored in double overtime to give Montreal a 2-1 win. Serge Savard was outstanding, setting up all three goals in game one, then scoring the tying goal in game two and assisting on Mickey Redmond's overtime winner.

As expected, the final against the St. Louis Blues was a formality. The Blues weren't quite as dogged as they were in the 67/68 final. Plante started the first game for the Blues, which Montreal won 3-1. St. Louis then switched to Hall, its playoff hero of the previous spring, and the Montreal attack rolled on regardless. The Canadiens outscored the Blues 12-3 in the series as they put together four perfunctory wins and took the Cup.

Savard was the overwhelming choice of the league board of governors in Conn Smythe voting, and Claude Ruel became only the third coach in NHL history, after Blake and Detroit's Jimmy Skinner, to win the regular season and the Stanley Cup in his rookie season. The Canadiens players showed their affection by chipping in together to buy the horse-loving Ruel a four-year-old harness racer. But with four Cup wins in five seasons, it was Ruel's charges who were the true thoroughbreds.

Canadiens coach Claude Ruel and general manager Sam Pollock rewarded their champions of 68/69 by leaving the lineup near-intact for 69/70. Larry Hillman, the veteran defenceman who had first played for the Red Wings in 54/55, had been picked up from Minnesota in mid-68/69. After playing 25 regular-season games and making one playoff appearance, he

was let go by the Canadiens. Gary Monahan and Doug Piper were sent to Detroit in June for Pete Mahovlich and Bart Crashley. Montreal passed on goaltending prospect Tony Esposito; left unprotected, he was claimed by Chicago in the June intraleague draft.

That June saw the first full-fledged universal amateur draft in the NHL. It was also Montreal's last opportunity to exercise its right of first refusal for French Canadian talent from Quebec, granted to it in 1962 as a means of ensuring the uniquely Québécois nature of the franchise. Montreal was allowed to use its first two draft picks to secure young francophone Quebeckers ahead of any other team. While this provision would gain a mythic role in the creation of the Canadiens, it was never really exercised until the privilege was about to expire. In June 1969, Montreal exercised its right to take Réjean Houle and Marc Tardif from the Montreal Junior Canadiens.

Goaltending was the only aspect of the team that was truly unsettled. Rogatien Vachon had carried the Canadiens all the way through the playoffs after Gump Worsley dislocated his finger. However, even with Esposito let go, the Canadiens had a surplus of netminding talent. In addition to Vachon and Worsley, the Canadiens had the rights to two strong amateur prospects: Phil Myre, who had won the Memorial Cup with the Niagara Falls Flyers in 67/68, and Ken Dryden, who had graduated from Cornell University (where he had starred in U.S. collegiate hockey) in the spring of 1969 and was joining the Canadian national team program while he pursued a law degree.

The clutter in the Canadiens net was lessened when Worsley suffered a nervous breakdown in November 1969. Terrified of flying, the long travel schedules of the new expansion years kept him aloft far more than he could tolerate. When he refused to be demoted to Montreal's American league affiliate, the Nova Scotia Voyageurs, he was sold to the Minnesota North Stars on February 27, 1970.

By then, Ruel and his players were sliding into antagonism. Ruel was an excitable yeller by nature, and at the beginning of the 69/70 season he had begun to holler at defencemen like Harper, Tremblay and Savard, who he felt weren't doing their jobs behind the blueline. The team was beset with injuries: Richard, Béliveau, Ferguson, J. C. Tremblay and Provost all missed ice time. Early in the new year, with Montreal chasing the Rangers for the fourth and final playoff spot in the East, Ruel's prospects hit rock bottom as a hip check by Toronto's Bob Baun broke Serge Savard's leg—the same leg he had broken in five places the previous spring. "My best guy—gone," Ruel moaned in the press. "It's the worst man we could possibly lose now. He does two jobs for me, plays defence and kills penalties."

Montreal ended the season tied for the fourth place with the Rangers, only seven points out of first place. They had identical 38-22-16 records, and advancement was decided on the basis of goals scored. The Rangers, who had gone on a nine-goal binge in their final game,

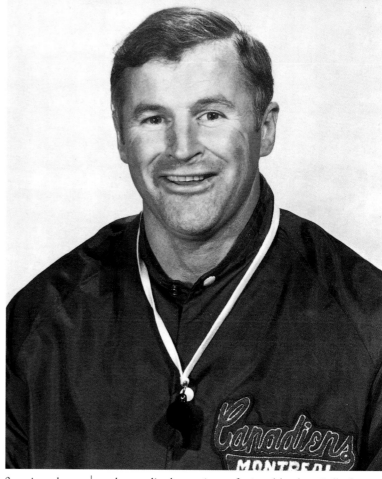

Claude Ruel (left) was Sam Pollock's surprise choice as the Canadiens coach when Toe Blake retired after the 67/68 Stanley Cup win. The team won another Cup under Ruel in 68/69, but in 69/70 Montreal missed the playoffs for the first time in 22 seasons. In December 1970 Ruel was replaced by Al MacNeil (right), who had been named his assistant that September. The Canadiens won the 70/71 Cup under MacNeil, but Henri Richard's public charge during the finals that MacNeil was favouring English Canadian players undermined his position. He was replaced two months later by Scotty Bowman.

edged the Canadiens by two. It was the first time the Canadiens had missed the playoffs in 22 seasons, and because the Leafs also failed to qualify, the 69/70 play-offs were the first in Stanley Cup history not to feature a Canadian team.

There was little consolation in the fact that the Canadiens had compiled a better record than every team in the West Division, including the Blues, who reached the Cup finals for the third straight season, losing this time to the Bruins. The Canadiens were in disgrace.

The roster shakeup began. On May 22, Pollock cut two deals, mainly with secondary properties. Center Christian Bordeleau was sold to St. Louis; right-wingers Lucien Grenier and Larry Mickey went to Los Angeles with goaltending property Jack Norris for right-winger Leon Rochefort (who had been with the Canadiens in the 66/67 final), defenceman Gregg Boddy and goal-tender Wayne Thomas. Veteran defenceman Ted Harris was dealt to Minnesota for a first-round draft pick. Also that month, right-winger Bobby Rousseau, who had been with the club since 60/61, was traded to Minnesota to retrieve Claude Larose. "There is no room for players who don't want to play and who blame everyone but themselves," Ruel announced after moving Rousseau. "They don't help Claude Ruel and this team." The tough talk continued at training camp in September. "Now the time has come for me to pick my men," he told the press. "The first year I am with the team, I take over the champions—no changes. We win. No changes, how can I change? Now this is different. We finish number five and I pick my own men."

Meanwhile, Sam Pollock was making some changes of his own. In a move unprecedented for the Canadiens,

and exceedingly rare in professional hockey, Pollock appointed an assistant coach for Ruel: Al MacNeil. A captain of the Memorial Cup-winning Toronto Marlboros in the mid-1950s, MacNeil had bounced around the NHL and minor leagues as a utility defence-man. After failing to crack the exemplary Leaf defence corps in the late 1950s, MacNeil had been traded to the Canadiens for Stan Smrke. MacNeil won the Eastern Professional league title as captain of the Hull-Ottawa Canadiens in 60/61, but after spending 61/62 as a full-fledged Canadien he was traded to the Blackhawks for Wayne Hicks. He put in four seasons with Chicago, then went back to Montreal when claimed in the June 1966 draft. The Rangers, though, immediately claimed him from Montreal, and after a season in New York he was taken by Pittsburgh in the expansion draft. Then it was back to Montreal yet again in a deal for Wally Boyer. He never did play for the Canadiens again. Pollock, whom MacNeil accepted as a mentor, moved him into coaching; he served as player-coach of the Voyageurs in 69/70, and in this new season, with the Voyageurs operation moving from Nova Scotia to Montreal to play right in the Forum, he was expected to run the Voyageurs as well as lend a hand to Ruel.

The inevitable came on December 3, 1970. Claude Ruel resigned as the Canadiens' coach, saying the team would not play for him. MacNeil immediately tendered his own resignation, considering it the appropriate thing to do, but rather than accept it Pollock gave him Ruel's job.

The changes continued as Pollock strove to find a winning formula in a clubhouse racked by internal dis-sension. A minor deal on the margins of the crisis

unfolded on December 11 as Michel Plasse, yet another goaltending prospect, was essentially lent to the Blues. Sold to them that day, he was bought back by Montreal the following August. A far more noteworthy deal came on January 13. Mickey Redmond, Guy Charron and Bill Collins were all sent to Detroit in exchange for Frank Mahovlich, older brother of Pete. The Big M's career had been revitalized with his trade from the Leafs to the Red Wings in 1968, and he brought to the Canadiens some badly needed firepower on left wing. Gilles Tremblay had retired after the 68/69 Cup win; John Ferguson was in the middle of his last season; and Mahovlich's old Leaf teammate, Dick Duff, so effective as a two-way player in the 68/69 Cup win, had been sold to Los Angeles the previous January. And on January 26, center Ralph Backstrom, who had feuded with Ruel, was sent to Los Angeles for Gord Labossière and Ray Fortin, neither of whom would have a role to play in the Canadiens' future.

The attacking arm of the Canadiens roster was undergoing a significant overhaul. Jean Béliveau and Henri Richard were still at center; both had played on Toe Blake's first Stanley Cup-winning lineup in 55/56. They had been joined at the pivotal position by Jacques Lemaire in 67/68, and by Pete Mahovlich and Bob Sheehan in 69/70. Six more new forwards were seeing ice time: Rochefort, back from Los Angeles; Réjean Houle and Marc Tardif, taken at the top of the 1969 amateur draft; Larose, retrieved from Minnesota; Chuck Lefley, drafted in 1970; and Phil Roberto. On defence, Guy Lapointe and Pierre Bouchard were playing their rookie seasons in the company of J. C.

Tremblay, Jacques Laperrière and Serge Savard.

The NHL had reconfigured its divisions for 70/71, to put an end to the anticlimactic Stanley Cup finals of the previous three seasons. Two new expansion clubs, Vancouver and Buffalo, were added to the awkwardly named East Division, and Chicago was moved to the West to give more strength to the expansion-club-dominated division. The Canadiens improved significantly over 69/70, finishing third in the East and fourth overall, and it was a tribute to their depth of talent that the team could finish second overall in scoring with only one top-ten scorer, Jean Béliveau, who was ninth.

Defensively, the team had a fair season. Boston, New York, Toronto, Chicago and St. Louis all allowed fewer goals. Rogie Vachon had been inconsistent in the Canadiens goal, and for the last six games of the regular season Sam Pollock tried out an untested talent: Ken Dryden.

Dryden had played one exhibition game for Montreal the previous fall, stopping 42 shots as the Canadiens defeated Boston 5-4. He had then begun legal studies at McGill, and didn't join the lineup of the Montreal Voyageurs until after MacNeil had been called up from his coaching duties there to take over the Canadiens from Ruel. In his first Voyageurs game on December 12, Dryden recorded a 4-0 shutout. He played 32 more games for the Voyageurs and added two more shutouts as he recorded a GA of 2.68.

The Canadiens had long been unafraid of putting netminders with no post-season NHL experience and relatively little regular-season preparation into the Stanley Cup playoff fray. They had done it with Jacques Plante in 52/53, and with Vachon in 66/67. Now, with

A former Junior player in the Canadiens system whose career had been cut short by injury, Scotty Bowman was proclaimed a coaching wizard as he took the St. Louis Blues to three consecutive Stanley Cup finals from 67/68 to 69/70. He gave up the general manager's job in St. Louis to coach the Canadiens in 1971. Under Bowman, Montreal won five Cups in eight seasons, including four in a row from 75/76 to 78/79.

Chosen first overall in the 1971 amateur draft, Guy Lafleur carried enormous expectations among fans as a successor to Jean Béliveau. Lafleur struggled so much in his first three Canadiens seasons that he considered jumping to the WHA. But he stayed, and won four Stanley Cups, three league scoring titles, three Lester Pearson Awards, two Hart Trophies and one Conn Smythe Trophy.

working wonders in goal. Down 3-2 in the championship series, Montreal forced a seventh game with a 4-3 win at the Forum, but it was a victory that caused much rancour to erupt. Henri Richard, benched by MacNeil in game six as he juggled lines, severely criticized his coach after the game, accusing him of not giving his French Canadians ice time and calling him the worst coach he'd ever had. The Canadiens were losing game seven in Chicago 2-0 when they fought back to take the game and the Cup with a 3-2 win.

MacNeil had won the battle and lost the war. Though Canadiens management was coy about his future, it was clear he was not coming back. For one thing, he spoke no French, a shortcoming the Canadiens could not abide. As a mid-season fill-in for Ruel, he had done admirably, but the franchise could not withstand a dressing-room split along the precarious language fault line. Dick Irvin had been an anglophone, and since his replacement by Blake in 55/56 the Canadiens had enjoyed bilingual coaching. Tensions between French and English had been avoided within the organization. But with Quebec in the thrall of the Quiet Revolution, with Montreal having just survived the trauma of the FLQ crisis and the imposition of the War Measures Act the previous October, the club could not endure a bitter divide within its roster along cultural lines. Ruel had complained that the team was unwilling to play for him when he stepped down in December, but the issue had never been his relationship with francophone players. Tellingly, MacNeil would recall that his only supporters in the team were Ken Dryden and Frank Mahovlich—both of them hailing from the anglophone side of the team and having been added to the roster only in the past few months.

As Ruel had, MacNeil remained within the Canadiens organization. He reverted to the Voyageurs as coach and general manager, and insisted that he was never actually fired from the Canadiens bench. Even during the playoffs, Pollock was evidently planning to replace him, whether the Cup was won or not. He had opened discussions with Scotty Bowman, another product of the Canadiens playing and management system who had moved away from Pollock in 1967 with league expansion.

Like Ruel, Scotty Bowman had had his playing career ended with an injury in his Junior days, in his case a skull fracture delivered by the stick of Jean-Guy Talbot in 1952. Born and raised in Montreal and fluently bilingual, Bowman had begun coaching in the Canadiens development system in 1954 when he was just 21. After rising to serve as coach and manager of the Hull-Ottawa Junior Canadiens, Bowman made his exit from the Canadiens system in 1967 when NHL expansion opened an opportunity for him in St. Louis. Lynn Patrick, who began the season as the Blues' coach and general manager, turned his coaching duties over to Bowman, and gave him the general manager's job as well in 1969.

Bowman was immediately hailed as a coaching

Vachon playing inconsistently, Pollock was prepared to bet the Canadiens' Cup chances on the gangly, cerebral Dryden. One can hardly blame him for searching out a magic bullet: Montreal's opening-round opponent was Boston, which had ruled the league in the regular season, outscoring Montreal by more than 100 goals as it won 57 of 78 games.

Initially, Pollock's gamble seemed a poor one. Montreal lost the first game 3-1 and was down 5-1 in the third period of game two when a six-goal burst by the Canadiens evened the series. The doubts were back after the Bruins stung the Canadiens 7-3 to take a 3-2 series lead, but Pollock stood by Dryden, and the newcomer came through for him. Of 260 shots fired at him by Boston's league-leading offence, only 26 got by as Montreal won the series in seven.

Despite having knocked off the overwhelming favourites in the opening series, Montreal did not find its way easily to a Cup win. Over three series, the Canadiens had to play 20 of 21 possible games. It took six games for them to move past the Minnesota North Stars in the semifinal round, and all seven final games to defeat the West Division champions, the Blackhawks, who had Montreal castoff Tony Esposito

wizard, guiding the Blues into three straight Cup finals. He showed an unabashed affection for Canadiens players of yore. He lured Jacques Plante out of retirement in 68/69 to share the Blues goal with Glenn Hall, and together the netminding veterans won the Vezina. Among the other Canadiens alumni to make their way onto Bowman's bench were Dickie Moore, Doug Harvey, Red Berenson, Noel Picard, Jimmy Roberts, Ab McDonald, Phil Goyette and even Jean-Guy Talbot, who had almost killed him in his Junior days.

In 70/71 Bowman turned over coaching duties to his seasoned defenceman, Al Arbour, who had won Stanley Cups with Detroit, Chicago and Toronto. The Blues were eliminated in the first round of the playoffs by the North Stars, thereby ending the string of trips to the Cup finals at three. Bowman wanted Arbour back as coach the next season, but it was said that the Blues ownership was balking; as a result, Bowman, who had three years left on a five-year contract as general manager, wanted out of town. While he wouldn't have general manager's duties in Montreal, there wasn't a team around that Bowman could have wanted to coach more than the Canadiens.

As Bowman arrived, the rebuilding of the lineup continued. Jean Béliveau retired after the 70/71 Cup win, his tenth in an 18-season Canadiens career. John Ferguson also retired, ending his eight-season Canadiens career with a fifth Cup. On May 25, following the Cup win, center Bobby Sheehan was sold to California, Leon Rochefort (who originally had been acquired from the Rangers back in the Plante deal of 1963) went to Detroit for defensive prospect Kerry Ketter and an undisclosed amount of cash. The 1968 deal that sent Danny Grant and Claude Larose to Minnesota had involved a player to be named at the end of the 70/71 season. The North Star player named was defenceman Marshall Johnston, but to square the deal Montreal gave the North Stars new defenceman Bob Murdoch, who had appeared in two playoff games. Johnston never played for the Canadiens, and two weeks after the swap Pollock got Murdoch back via the intraleague draft. Left-winger Yvon Lambert, who would not make the Canadiens lineup full-time until 73/74, was drafted from Detroit.

The Canadiens' major activity in June 1971 came at the amateur draft. The 1970 draft had been a disappointment for the club after its success in 1969, when it had used its right of refusal on French-Canadian talent to pick Houle and Tardif. The 1970 amateur class had been strong, but because it was an expansion year, newcomers Buffalo and Vancouver picked first and second, based on a

coin toss, and that was a right Pollock could not trade for. The Sabres were able to take Gilbert Perreault from the Montreal Junior Canadiens and the Canucks chose Dale Tallon from the Toronto Marlboros. Boston had traded its way into the third and fourth picks, and took Reggie Leach and Rick MacLeish, both of whom would end up starring for Philadelphia. The Canadiens picked fifth, and took goaltender Ray Martiniuk from the Flin Flon Bombers (the team that produced Leach and Bobby Clarke), then Chuck Lefley sixth from the Canadian Nationals. Martiniuk never made the NHL, and Lefley was strictly a journeyman. Toronto, on the other hand, did well in choosing Darryl Sittler (eighth) and Errol Thompson (twenty-second) after the Canadiens.

Pollock and Ruel had their eyes trained on the 1971 draft, as they were sure Guy Lafleur of the Quebec Remparts would be the top selection, although Marcel Dionne of the St. Catharines Blackhawks and Richard Martin of the Junior Canadiens were also highly touted. In 1970, Pollock sent left-wing prospect Ernie Hicke and a draft choice to California for the Seals' first-round pick in 1971. When California finished last in 70/71 with ten points to spare, behind Detroit, the selection order was set in Montreal's favour. The Canadiens took Lafleur, and right after them the Red Wings chose Dionne. Montreal then took Chuck Arnason seventh, Murray Wilson eleventh, and down in the second round, twentieth overall, Larry Robinson.

After winning the Conn Smythe as playoff MVP, Ken Dryden had the starting job in goal sewn up at the beginning of the 71/72 season. Rogie Vachon, seeing a lot of bench in his immediate future, went to Sam Pollock and asked to be traded to a team that needed a starter. Sympathetic, Pollock had him a deal in two days, sending him to Los Angeles on November 4 for backup Denis DeJordy, defenceman Noel Price (who had already been a Canadien in the mid-1960s) and left-winger Doug Robinson. None of the three players Pollock accepted for Vachon figured in his plans for the team. The deals continued into the season as Jimmy Roberts became a Canadien again as he was swapped

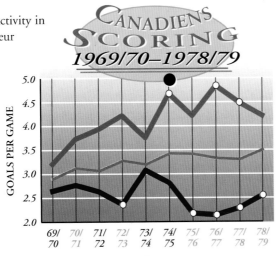

CANADIENS
SCORING
1969/70–1978/79

GOALS PER GAME

5.0
4.5
4.0
3.5
3.0
2.5
2.0

69/ 70/ 71/ 72/ 73/ 74/ 75/ 76/ 77/ 78/
70 71 72 73 74 75 76 77 78 79

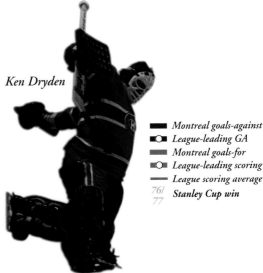

Ken Dryden

▬▬ *Montreal goals-against*
▭○ *League-leading GA*
▬▬ *Montreal goals-for*
▭○ *League-leading scoring*
── *League scoring average*
76/
77 *Stanley Cup win*

for Phil Roberto on December 13.

The Canadiens under Bowman finished third in the East and overall in 71/72, with the third-highest scoring record and fifth-best goals-against record. The miracle performance of the previous spring was not to be repeated, however. In the opening playoff round the Canadiens were eliminated by the Rangers in six, who went on to lose the finals against the Bruins.

The honeymoon between Bowman and many of his players was also over by season's end. He had offended some with his curfew bed-checks on road trips, and with his handling of their careers and egos. Ken Dryden, who admired Bowman's skill, also believed (as he wrote in *The Game*) that with marginal players—the young ones not yet established, the older ones on their way to retirement—he could be manipulative, and cruelly so. After the 71/72 season, defenceman Terry Harper wanted out. He had been with the team since his rookie season in 62/63, and he had been offered a three-year contract, but he dismissed it as three years of "high priced hell." In moving him to Los Angeles, Pollock received a bevy of draft goodies: the Kings' second pick in 1974, first and third pick in 1975, and the first pick in 1976. At the same time, another veteran defenceman was lost as J. C. Tremblay jumped to the Quebec Nordiques of the new World Hockey Association.

The 72/73 team was far removed from the lineup that had won the Canadiens the 68/69 Cup. Only five players were still around: Henri Richard (who had taken over as captain from the retired Béliveau), Jacques Laperrière, Yvan Cournoyer, Serge Savard and Jacques Lemaire, with Jimmy Roberts and Claude Larose from the mid-1960s Cup winners on hand as well. Pollock's trading continued to yield first-round draft picks, and in 1972 the Canadiens were able to choose left-wing sniper Steve Shutt fourth, goaltender Michel Larocque sixth, center Dave Gardner eighth (exercising the draft pick acquired from Minnesota back in 1968) and defenceman John Van Boxmeer fourteenth. The Canadiens didn't even pick in the second round.

In Buffalo, general manager Punch Imlach was accusing Pollock of underhandedness in the intraleague draft, charging he was cutting backroom deals to protect unprotected players. Imlach told *The Toronto Star* that Pollock made "obvious deals" with the Atlanta Flames and New York Islanders to prevent them from choosing either Bob Murdoch or Chuck Lefley. The Islanders instead had taken Bart Crashley and the Flames (who also grabbed goaltender Phil Myre) Terry Ketter. "The latter pair of defencemen are not in the same class as Lefley and Murdoch," Imlach protested. Some sort of deal with Islanders indeed seemed to have been made, as on June 26 Pollock sold the Islanders six players—goaltenders Chico Resch and Denis DeJordy, left-winger Germain Gagnon, right-winger Tony Featherstone, defenceman Murray Anderson and prospect Alex Campbell.

The 72/73 Canadiens were one of the strongest teams in franchise history, losing only 10 of 78 games as they finished first in the East and overall. They scored only one less goal than the league-leading Bruins, as Jacques Lemaire erupted with 44 goals and 51 assists and Frank Mahovlich contributed 38 goals and 55 assists. Ken Dryden won his first Vezina as the Canadiens were the only team to allow fewer than 200 goals, with 184. Dryden and Mahovlich were joined by defenceman Guy Lapointe on the first All Star team, with Yvan Cournoyer on the second team. Montreal had not been able to boast of so many first-team All Stars since 60/61.

In the playoffs, Montreal struggled with Imlach's young and talented Sabres before eliminating them in six. Two overtime games were then required to move past the emerging Philadelphia Flyers in the semifinals in five. The finals were a 70/71 Cup reunion, with the Blackhawks back for another try. Despite the fact that two of the best goaltenders (Dryden and Esposito) and defensive ensembles in the game were on hand, the series was a scoring bonanza. Game one was won by Montreal 8-3, and Chicago won game three 7-4 and game five 8-7. Chicago averaged 3.83 goals per game, Montreal 5.5—the Canadiens never scored fewer than four goals in a game. With a 6-4 win in Chicago, Montreal took the series in six. Yvan Cournoyer, who had scored the winning goals in games two and six, set a new playoff record of 15 goals as he won the Conn Smythe, while he and Lemaire matched Gordie Howe's record of 24 points in a final series.

Having reached new heights as a franchise, the Canadiens plunged into two seasons of adjustment. After winning the Vezina and the Stanley Cup in 72/73, Ken Dryden took a year off to complete his articling for his law degree. The arrival of the WHA had caused minimal damage to the roster in 72/73, but now it began to bite. Réjean Houle and Marc Tardif both made the jump—Tardif to Los Angeles, Houle to the Nordiques, and in 74/75 Tardif and Houle were playing on the Nordiques together with former Canadien J. C. Tremblay. In 73/74, Montreal's wins slipped from 52 to 45, scoring fell from 329 to 293, and goals-against ballooned from 184 to 240. After finishing second to Boston in the East, Montreal was eliminated in six by the Rangers in the opening playoff round. Jacques Laperrière retired; goaltender Michel Plasse was lost to Kansas City in the 1974 expansion draft, and Frank Mahovlich took his services to the WHA. He was almost joined in the rival league by Guy Lafleur, who had come into the Canadiens lineup right from the 1971 draft.

Lafleur arrived in Montreal in 1971 bearing the weight of enormous expectations. One of the greatest prospects the Quebec Junior league had ever produced, he was cast as the second coming of the just-retired Jean Béliveau. His arrival was heavy with portent; like Béliveau, Lafleur was coming out of the Quebec City amateur scene, where he had idolized Béliveau and even worn his signature number 4. Lafleur had the good sense not to wear it when he reached the Canadiens, choosing 10 instead, but the number on his back didn't matter to

Montreal Canadiens

The Dynasty of the late 1970s

Featuring the players and management who participated in Montreal's Stanley Cup victories of 1975/76, 1976/77, 1977/78 and 1978/79

GENERAL MANAGER
1. Sam Pollock
2. Irving Grundman

COACH
1. Scotty Bowman

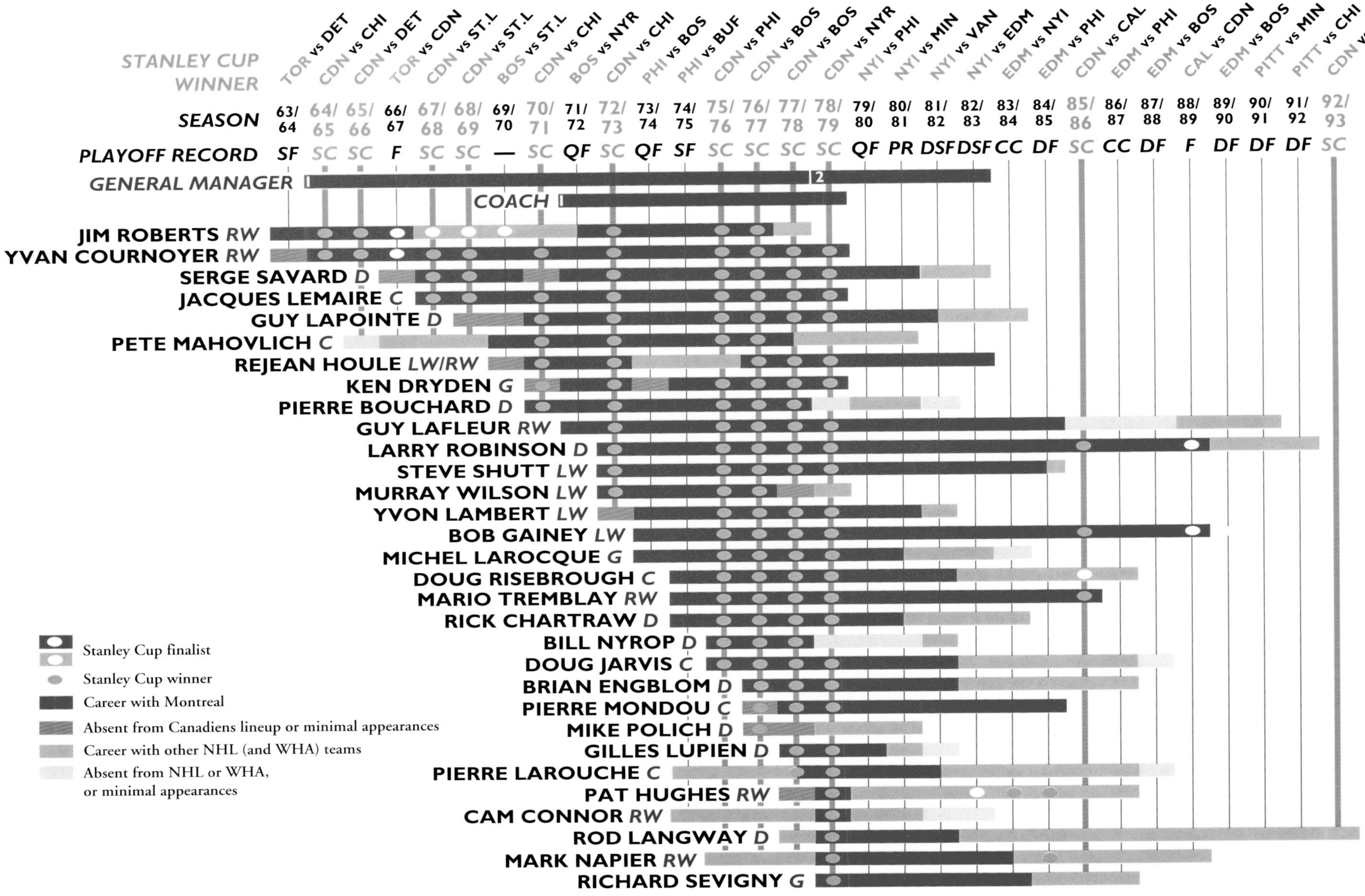

STANLEY CUP WINNER
TOR vs DET
CDN vs CHI
CDN vs DET
TOR vs CDN
CDN vs ST.L
CDN vs ST.L
BOS vs ST.L
CDN vs CHI
BOS vs NYR
CDN vs CHI
PHI vs BOS
PHI vs BUF
CDN vs PHI
CDN vs BOS
CDN vs BOS
CDN vs NYR
NYI vs PHI
NYI vs MIN
NYI vs VAN
NYI vs EDM
EDM vs NYI
EDM vs PHI
CDN vs CAL
EDM vs PHI
EDM vs BOS
CAL vs CDN
EDM vs BOS
PITT vs MIN
PITT vs CHI
CDN vs LA
SEASON
63/64
64/65
65/66
66/67
67/68
68/69
69/70
70/71
71/72
72/73
73/74
74/75
75/76
76/77
77/78
78/79
79/80
80/81
81/82
82/83
83/84
84/85
85/86
86/87
87/88
88/89
89/90
90/91
91/92
92/93
PLAYOFF RECORD
SF
SC
SC
F
SC
SC
—
SC
QF
SC
QF
SF
SC
SC
SC
SC
QF
PR
DSF
DSF
CC
DF
SC
CC
DF
F
DF
DF
DF
SC
GENERAL MANAGER
1
2
COACH
1
JIM ROBERTS RW
YVAN COURNOYER RW
SERGE SAVARD D
JACQUES LEMAIRE C
GUY LAPOINTE D
PETE MAHOVLICH C
REJEAN HOULE LW/RW
KEN DRYDEN G
PIERRE BOUCHARD D
GUY LAFLEUR RW
LARRY ROBINSON D
STEVE SHUTT LW
MURRAY WILSON LW
YVON LAMBERT LW
BOB GAINEY LW
MICHEL LAROCQUE G
DOUG RISEBROUGH C
MARIO TREMBLAY RW
RICK CHARTRAW D
BILL NYROP D
DOUG JARVIS C
BRIAN ENGBLOM D
PIERRE MONDOU C
MIKE POLICH D
GILLES LUPIEN D
PIERRE LAROUCHE C
PAT HUGHES RW
CAM CONNOR RW
ROD LANGWAY D
MARK NAPIER RW
RICHARD SEVIGNY G
Stanley Cup finalist
Stanley Cup winner
Career with Montreal
Absent from Canadiens lineup or minimal appearances
Career with other NHL (and WHA) teams
Absent from NHL or WHA, or minimal appearances

Larry "Big Bird" Robinson was a major reason the Philadelphia Flyers and Boston Bruins were unable to push around the Canadiens in the Stanley Cup finals. He won the Norris Trophy in 76/77 and 79/80 and the Conn Smythe Trophy in 77/78.

ond pick overall. Exactly how Pollock got this gem is uncertain. It was due to the California Golden Seals, and a clue to whatever deal was responsible is that Frank Selke's son, Frank Jr., was president of the Seals. The player Pollock most wanted was Bob Gainey, a superb defensive forward playing for Roger Neilson on the Peterborough Petes. He was unlikely, however, to be chosen early by any other team, and that gave Pollock some dealmaking room. The New York Islanders, choosing first, were going to take Denis Potvin, the best Junior defenceman since Bobby Orr. Atlanta, which was to pick fifth, was desperate for Tom Lysiak out of Medicine Hat as a scoring star. Flames general manager Cliff Fletcher wanted to pick higher than fifth to ensure getting Lysiak, and was offering a future first-round pick if Pollock would give up his second pick and go fifth. Pollock agreed, and the draft progressed with the Islanders taking Potvin, the Flames Lysiak, the Canucks Dennis Ververgaert, and the Leafs Lanny McDonald.

But there was another nervous general manager at the draft: Sid Abel of St. Louis. The Blues wanted goaltender John Davidson of the Calgary Centennials, but so did Boston, and the Bruins were set to pick sixth while the Blues were slotted eighth. For agreeing to swap spots with Abel, Pollock bagged another future first-round pick. St. Louis got Davidson, the Bruins settled for André Savard, Pittsburgh took Blaine Stoughton with the seventh pick, and in eighth, Montreal chose Bob Gainey—the player nobody else was in a hurry to have. By gambling that he could give up the second and then the fifth pick without losing him, Pollock was able to get the player he wanted and bank two future first-round picks in the process.

In five seasons since 1969, the Canadiens had won two Stanley Cups, had earned or dealt their way into holding 14 first-round picks, and had used those picks for the most part cleverly and profitably. Drafting had brought the club the likes of Lafleur, Tardif, Houle, Shutt, Wilson, Murdoch and now Gainey. Pollock's trades were rarely used to gain stars. Time and again he was able to move veterans or talents marginalized by the sheer depth of the Canadiens roster on to skill-hungry teams and accumulate valuable draft picks in the process. After the 72/73 Cup win, for example, Pollock was able to send Bob Murdoch and Randy Rota to Los Angeles for the Kings' first pick in the 1974 draft and cash. That got the Canadiens Mario Tremblay, selected twelfth. (The Terry Harper deal of 1972 had yielded three other picks from the Kings, in 1974, 1975 and 1976, from which came center Pierre Mondou.) Before the Canadiens had secured Tremblay in the 1974 draft, they had already chosen Doug Risebrough seventh and Rick Chartraw tenth. They were able to pick Risebrough because in March they had sent Dave Gardner to St. Louis in exchange for the Blues' first-round pick. It was no accident that the three teams who would rule the NHL from 75/76 to 89/90, the Canadiens, then the Islanders, then the Oilers, built

fans, who expected immediate stardom.

Lafleur had just turned 20 when he came to the Canadiens, and his first three seasons showed steadily less promise: he scored 29, 28 and then 21 goals while his points production slipped from 64 to 55 and stalled at 56. He was sorely tempted to head back to Quebec City to play with the Nordiques, but resolved to stick it out and not be seen as a quitter. Besides, to him the NHL was indisputably the pinnacle of the professional game.

In the meantime, Sam Pollock had turned in a masterful performance at the 1973 amateur draft. He had dealt his way into holding 7 of 20 first-round picks in a draft held two months after his team won the Stanley Cup; even at that, the story of the 1973 draft was not how many picks Montreal had, but how many more picks Pollock turned them into as it made off with one of the game's great, and largely overlooked, new talents.

Montreal went into the 1973 draft holding the sec-

Montreal Canadiens 1969/70–78/79

Season	Finish	Record (W-L-T)	Points %	Awards (winners & runners-up)	All-Stars	Playoffs
69/70	5th Div 5th OA	38-22-16	60.5		2ND TEAM: Laperrière (D)	Missed playoffs
70/71	3rd Div 4th OA	42-23-13	62.2	CONN SMYTHE: Dryden	1ST TEAM: Tremblay (D) 2ND TEAM: Cournoyer (RW)	Won SC final 4-3 over Chicago
71/72	3rd Div 3rd OA	46-16-16	69.2	HART: Dryden RU CALDER: Dryden	2ND TEAM: Dryden (G), Cournoyer (RW)	Lost SC quarterfinal 4-2 to New York
72/73	1st Div 1st OA	52-10-16	76.9	NORRIS: Lapointe RU VEZINA: Dryden CONN SMYTHE: Cournoyer	1ST TEAM: F. Mahovlich (LW) Dryden (G), Lapointe (D) 2ND TEAM: Cournoyer (RW)	Won SC final 4-2 over Chicago
73/74	2nd Div 4th OA	45-24-9	63.5	MASTERTON: Richard		Lost SC quarterfinal 4-2 to New York
74/75	1st Div 1st Conf 1st OA	47-14-19	70.6		1ST TEAM: Lafleur (RW) 2ND TEAM: Lapointe (D)	Lost SC semifinal 4-2 to Buffalo
75/76	1st Div 1st Conf 1st OA	58-11-11	79.4	ART ROSS: Lafleur VEZINA: Dryden PEARSON: Lafleur	1ST TEAM: Dryden (G), Lafleur (RW) 2ND TEAM: Lapointe (D)	Won SC final 4-0 over Philadelphia
76/77	1st Div 1st Conf 1st OA	60-8-12	82.5	HART: Lafleur ART ROSS: Lafleur VEZINA: Dryden & Larocque NORRIS: Robinson CONN SMYTHE: Lafleur PEARSON: Lafleur ADAMS: Bowman	1ST TEAM: Dryden (G), Robinson (D), Lafleur (RW), Shutt (LW) 2ND TEAM: Lapointe (D)	Won SC final 4-0 over Boston
77/78	1st Div 1st Conf 1st OA	59-10-11	80.6	HART: Lafleur ART ROSS: Lafleur VEZINA: Dryden & Larocque CONN SMYTHE: Robinson PEARSON: Lafleur SELKE: Gainey	1ST TEAM: Dryden (G), Lafleur (RW) 2ND TEAM: Robinson (D), Shutt (LW)	Won SC final 4-2 over Boston
78/79	1st Div 1st Conf 2nd OA	52-17-11	71.9	HART: Lafleur RU VEZINA: Dryden & Larocque NORRIS: Robinson RU CONN SMYTHE: Gainey MASTERTON: Savard SELKE: Gainey	1ST TEAM: Dryden (G), Robinson (D), Lafleur (RW) 2ND TEAM: Savard (D)	Won SC final 4-1 over New York

the cores of their winning lineups through shrewd drafting, not blockbuster trades.

By 74/75, the Canadiens were almost completely remade, stocked with an array of cultivated talent. One of the last links with the old Canadiens dynasty came with the retirement of Henri Richard in the 74/75 season. Only right-wingers Jimmy Roberts and Yvan Cournoyer were left from the 64/65 championship team, and defenceman Serge Savard and center Jacques Lemaire were the only other players who were on the 67/68 and 68/69 winners. Most important, Guy Lafleur had made a spectacular turnaround in his sputtering career in 74/75. Doffing his helmet to let his blond locks stream, Lafleur scored 53 goals and added 66 assists to finish fourth in the scoring race, two points

ahead of Pete Mahovlich. Lafleur would not be a team leader in the manner of Béliveau—the captaincy moved to Cournoyer after Henri Richard's retirement—but he became an indispensible part of the Canadiens offence, playing with linemates Jacques Lemaire and Steve Shutt.

In 73/74 and 74/75, the Stanley Cup was won by the Broad Street Bullies of Philadelphia. The Canadiens hated everything they stood for, but had to wait until 75/76 to challenge their thuggery. The Canadiens had finished in a three-way tie atop the 74/75 standings with the Sabres and the Flyers, but had been stopped by the Sabres in the semifinals in six games; Buffalo had then lost to Philadelphia in six.

In 75/76, the Canadiens had Ken Dryden (back from his articling in 74/75), as well as newcomers Bill

Nyrop on defence and Doug Jarvis at center. Montreal dominated the regular season, losing only 11 of 80 games. Lafleur won the scoring race and Dryden the Vezina. In the playoffs the club was overwhelming, losing only one game in three best-of-seven series. Chicago was swept in four in the quarterfinal, the Islanders in five in the semifinal. The sweetest win came against the Flyers in the final. Philadelphia went down in four in a methodical and unflappable performance.

The Canadiens were hailed for their finesse, but it was their mastery of the close-checking defensive game that derailed the Philadelphia bid for a third consecutive Cup. Montreal's defencemen were too big, too fast, and too skilful for the Flyers' forwards to scare off the puck, and the forward lines had both scoring power and checking ability. "During the regular season, the big scorers did a lot of the work," said Steve Shutt. "But in the playoffs it was the people I like to call the plumbers—the ones that did all the dirty work—who carried the club. Guys like Jim Roberts, Bob Gainey, Bouchard and Doug Jarvis. They never get much recognition, but they're the backbone of the team."

Savard was ebullient. "This is not only a victory for the Canadiens; it is a victory for hockey. I hope that this era of intimidation and violence that is hurting our national sport is coming to an end. Young people have seen that a team can play electrifying, fascinating hockey while still behaving like gentlemen."

With the return of Réjean Houle from the WHA for 76/77, Montreal's ability to dominate the game was not a matter of if, but of how long. The core of the team changed little. The only major trades came after the next Cup win, in 76/77. In August Jimmy Roberts made another trip to St. Louis in exchange for the Blues' third-round pick in 1979. And on November 29, 1977 Pollock made an old-fashioned shake-up trade, sending Pete Mahovlich to Pittsburgh, packaged with Peter Lee for Pierre Larouche and Peter Marsh, and sending to the team the message that positions on the club were not permanent.

After winning 12 of 13 games in the 75/76 playoffs, the Canadiens made it look easy again in 76/77, winning 12 of 14 as they moved by the Blues in four and the Islanders in six before downing the Bruins in four in the final. It was a little harder in 77/78, but nonetheless impressive as the team won 12 of 15—taking Detroit in five, Toronto in four and Boston in six in the final.

From 75/76 to 78/79, individual accolades for Canadiens based on regular-season performance were impressive. Dryden won every Vezina and took over the first-team All Star berth in those years. Lafleur also made the first team in every season (as well as in 79/80), in addition to winning the Hart Trophy in 76/77 and 77/78 and the Art Ross as the league's leading scorer from 75/76 to 77/78. The Frank J. Selke Trophy was introduced in 77/78 to honour defensive forwards, and Bob Gainey won it for four straight seasons. Larry Robinson won the Norris as the league's top

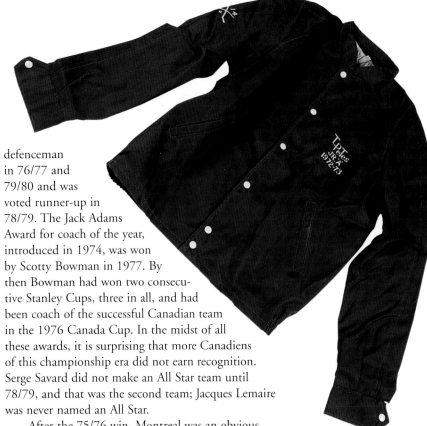

defenceman in 76/77 and 79/80 and was voted runner-up in 78/79. The Jack Adams Award for coach of the year, introduced in 1974, was won by Scotty Bowman in 1977. By then Bowman had won two consecutive Stanley Cups, three in all, and had been coach of the successful Canadian team in the 1976 Canada Cup. In the midst of all these awards, it is surprising that more Canadiens of this championship era did not earn recognition. Serge Savard did not make an All Star team until 78/79, and that was the second team; Jacques Lemaire was never named an All Star.

After the 75/76 win, Montreal was an obvious choice to repeat their successes, and lost only eight and ten games respectively in the 76/77 and 77/78 season. In 78/79, though, a "four-peat" was far from a given. The New York Islanders were steadily improving, and the grinding Bruins of Don Cherry, Cup finalists in 76/77 and 77/78, were still game.

Just as important was a sense that the Canadiens organization was undergoing an uncomfortable transformation. In the summer of 1978, Edward and Peter Bronfman sold the Canadiens franchise to the Molsons, of brewing fame. General manager Sam Pollock retired, and Irv Grundman arrived as managing director, while the director of player personnel role was given to Al MacNeil. It was a shuffle of responsibilities that left Scotty Bowman locked out of any hope of promotion. Only a month before the sale, he had signed a new two-year coaching contract, understanding that Pollock's job would become open to him when he retired. The sale of the franchise had compelled Pollock to move on with the Bronfmans and left Bowman answering to a new boss chosen by the Molsons. Irked, Bowman began negotiating with the Buffalo Sabres for a new job with a larger role, while continuing to coach the Canadiens.

Even in the midst of their 1970s reign, the Canadiens management did not take their eyes off the future. The club drafted relentlessly, determined to build and to rebuild from within. In 1978 the club drafted 27 players, the biggest fishing expedition in the league. But the club's own successes were hampering it. Prospective talents knew there was a logjam of quality players blocking their way to a starting position in Montreal. The WHA was still alive then, and it made sense to many to take their services to the rival league, where they could get ice time and a starter's salary. In

Sam Pollock's acquisition of Bob Gainey (opposite page) was a masterpiece of dealmaking. The Canadiens' general manager began by securing the second pick overall in the 1973 amateur draft. He wanted Gainey of the Peterborough Petes (whose team jacket appears above), but he was sure the defensive forward wouldn't be a first choice for other teams. As a result, he dealt his way down to holding the eighth pick, collecting two future first-round draft picks as he went, then selected Gainey.

Gainey was one of the game's most complete players. He won the Conn Smythe Trophy in 78/79 and owned the Frank J. Selke Trophy as the league's top defensive forward from 77/78 to 80/81.

1978, the Canadiens were unable to sign their first four draft choices to a contract as they opted instead for WHA careers. Their first pick, Danny Geoffrion, who was chosen eighth, signed instead with the Quebec Nordiques; their second pick, Dave Hunter, who went eighteenth, joined the Edmonton Oilers, as did their fourth pick, Ron Carter, who went thirty-sixth. (Their third choice, Dale Yakiwchuk, never made the tier-one pros.)

Pollock had one success against the WHA in securing Mark Napier. In 1975 at age 18, which was underage for the NHL (and even, technically, the WHA), he had been signed to play for the WHA's Toronto Toros, which moved to Birmingham. As a Birmingham Bull he scored 60 goals in 76/77, and in 1978 he turned 20 and became eligible for the NHL draft. Pollock chose him and was able to sign him away from the WHA.

The Canadiens' 78/79 season wasn't quite as spectacular as the preceding ones. Total wins fell from 59 to 52, scoring dropped by 22 goals and goals against rose by 21, moving above 200 (at 204) for the first time in four 80-game seasons. The Canadiens nonetheless finished with the league's second-best record, one point behind the Islanders.

The playoffs were more of a struggle than the team had known since 74/75. While the Canadiens were able to eliminate the Maple Leafs in four straight in the quarterfinal, the last two games were decided in overtime. In the semifinals the Bruins recovered from 2-0 and 3-2 series deficits to force a seventh game in Montreal. Boston appeared to have the series won in the closing minutes, holding a 4-3 lead. Then came a bench minor for too many men on the ice—in their quest to hold back Guy Lafleur, an excess of Bruins left-wingers had grabbed ice time. With little more than a minute of play remaining, Lafleur scored on the powerplay to force overtime. The Canadiens did not waste their reprieve, winning the game at 9:33 on an Yvon Lambert goal to move on to the finals against the Rangers.

Montreal lost the opening game to New York at home 4-1, then settled down to run up four straight wins and secure their fourth straight Cup. The victory was scarcely theirs when the dynasty began to come apart.

Three key players—Ken Dryden, Jacques Lemaire and Yvan Cournoyer—all announced their retirements. In June, Al MacNeil revealed he was leaving as director of player personnel to become coach of the Atlanta Flames. One week later, Scotty Bowman declared that he was through as the Canadiens' coach. He was becoming coach, general manager and managing director of the Buffalo Sabres. His time in Montreal

had been enormously productive. In the four consecutive Stanley Cup seasons, his Canadiens had won 320 regular-season games while losing 46; in those playoffs, they had won 48 of 58 games.

In Bowman's stead Irv Grundman hired former Canadiens great Bernie Geoffrion, but Boom-Boom lasted only 33 games before being replaced by a reluctant Claude Ruel. The team finished third overall and encountered the Minnesota North Stars in the quarterfinals. The young and eager North Stars rocked the Canadiens with 3-0 and 4-1 defeats at the Forum to open the series, but Montreal responded with 5-0, 5-1 and 6-2 wins. With the North Stars on the ropes, the Canadiens faltered. Minnesota pushed the series to a seventh game with a 5-2 win at home.

Game seven was in Montreal. When the Canadiens won the Stanley Cup at the Forum on May 21, 1979, it was the first home-ice Cup win Canadiens fans had enjoyed since May 11, 1968. On April 27, 1980, those fans watched with stunned silence as North Stars defenceman Al MacAdam beat Denis Herron with less than 90 seconds to play to give Minnesota a 3-2 win and thwart the Canadiens' quest to match their 1950s record of five straight Cup wins.

Most uncharacteristic about the Canadiens defeat in the 79/80 quarterfinals was that a dynasty had ended without a proper showdown between king and conqueror. In the 1960s and 1970s, Montreal had had to prove itself in playoffs against Toronto and then Boston and then Philadelphia as it sought league supremacy. In 79/80, the Canadiens were felled by a squad of inspired upstarts who were then eliminated in five games in the semifinals. The New York Islanders won the next four Stanley Cups, and they moved into the champion's role with only semifinal confrontations back in 75/76 and 76/77 as thin evidence that two of the game's greatest dynasties, which came back-to-back, ever truly confronted one another.

Montreal did not suffer a collapse quite to the degree that Toronto did after the 66/67 win, but the seasons that followed the 78/79 win were not unlike the drought that beset the team after 59/60. From 79/80 to 82/83, the Canadiens were knocked out in the opening round by Minnesota, Edmonton, Quebec and Buffalo. It was not until 83/84, when the Canadiens and the Islanders met in the conference finals, that there was another playoff confrontation between these great clubs. The Islanders won that series 4-2, but it proved to be their own playoff swan song, as the Edmonton Oilers defeated them 4-1 in the finals to begin another dynastic reign. By then, the Canadiens club had been entirely transformed. When Montreal won another Cup in 85/86, it did so with only three players from the 1970s reign: Larry Robinson, Bob Gainey and Mario

Tremblay. (Doug Risebrough opposed them in the finals as a Calgary Flame.) When the Canadiens again reached the finals in 88/89, Robinson and Gainey were still with them. They lost this rematch with the Flames in six.

The excellence of the 1970s Canadiens continued in other avenues. Serge Savard was general manager of the Canadiens when they won the Cup in 85/86 and 92/93 and lost the 88/89 final. Bob Gainey was hired as the coach of the Minnesota North Stars (now Dallas Stars) in 1990 and named general manager in 1992; Doug Jarvis became an assistant coach there. In 1993 Jacques Lemaire became coach of the New Jersey Devils and Larry Robinson his assistant. After the Devils won the Stanley Cup in 94/95, Robinson was hired to coach the Los Angeles Kings. And when Serge Savard was fired along with coach Jacques Demers as the

Canadiens struggled at the beginning of the 95/96 season, Mario Tremblay became one more name from the club's winning past to assume the coach's role, while Réjean Houle replaced Savard as general manager. The assistant coaches were Steve Shutt, Yvan Cournoyer and Jacques Lemaire.

The greatest years of the Montreal Canadiens might be behind the club, but even with only two Cup victories since 78/79, the team continues to stand out among Original Six franchises. Only Boston and New York have also won Stanley Cups since the first major expansion in 1967: the Bruins in 69/70 and 71/72, the Rangers in 93/94. But with so much about the business and structure of the NHL having changed, Montreal fans no longer dream about matching the Cup streaks of the 1950s, 1960s and 1970s. They dream simply about winning another one. ○

Larry Robinson and Serge Savard parade the Stanley Cup around Boston Garden on May 14, 1977. Jacques Lemaire scored his third game-winner of the series to defeat the Bruins 2-1 in overtime, allowing Montreal to sweep Boston in the Cup final.

THE GAME THEY PLAYED

THE GAME THEY PLAYED

The parity dilemma of the Seventies

When the NHL expanded in 67/68 by adding six new teams—the St. Louis Blues, Philadelphia Flyers, Minnesota North Stars, Pittsburgh Penguins, Oakland Seals and Los Angeles Kings—it took steps to ensure that the new clubs would have a fighting chance. The old development system was phased out, replaced with a universal amateur draft in 1969. The new teams were placed in their own division, with its champion guaranteed a berth in the Stanley Cup final. But after St. Louis made it to three straight finals and lost all 12 games, the league divisions and playoff format were reorganized for 70/71, just as new expansion franchises were added in Vancouver and Buffalo. More new teams followed—the Atlanta Flames and New York Islanders in 72/73, the Washington Capitals and Kansas City Scouts in 74/75.

After the changes of 70/71, it took until 73/74 for an expansion club to reach the Cup finals again. The Philadelphia Flyers won, and defended their title in 74/75 against the Buffalo Sabres in the first Cup series between expansion clubs. It would appear that the expansion teams had come into their own, but in truth they continued to underperform. Philadelphia was the only club from the 67/68 expansion ranks to make the finals in the decade. No other member of that initial expansion made it until 80/81, when the North Stars did. As it happened, they lost to the New York Islanders, the

72/73 expansion team which had won its first Stanley Cup in 79/80. As a group the initial expansion teams lagged behind the Original Six clubs throughout the decade in average goals for and against, briefly erasing a consistent scoring deficit in 74/75 and 75/76 before falling into arrears again. Oakland didn't even survive the decade. After changing its name to the California Golden Seals in 70/71, the franchise was moved to Cleveland in 76/77, then merged with Minnesota.

The Philadelphia Flyers, led by captain Bobby Clarke, were the first expansion team to win the Stanley Cup.

What went wrong with the 67/68 expansion clubs? By gaining the finals in 74/75, the Buffalo Sabres showed it was possible to build a contender quickly. Too many 67/68 expansion clubs traded away their futures, giving up draft choices to Original Six clubs in exchange for veteran players, in hopes of short-term success. The New York Islanders, on the other hand, consistently drafted high and well, and won their first of four straight Stanley Cups in 79/80. Four of the six 67/68 newcomers have yet to win the Cup.

Successes of the Philadelphia Flyers and Los Angeles Kings helped neutralize the scoring deficit problem shared by the 67/68 expansion clubs in their first seven seasons. But by the end of the decade the performance gap between the Original Sixers and the first expansion clubs was widening again. Ironically, many of these expansion clubs were being overtaken by those that followed, such as the Buffalo Sabres and the New York Islanders.

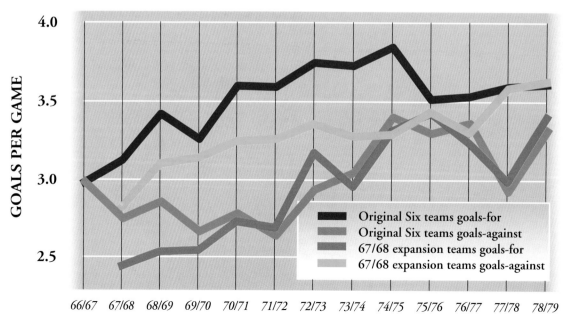

GOALS PER GAME

4.0

3.5

3.0

2.5

Legend:
- Original Six teams goals-for
- Original Six teams goals-against
- 67/68 expansion teams goals-for
- 67/68 expansion teams goals-against

66/67 67/68 68/69 69/70 70/71 71/72 72/73 73/74 74/75 75/76 76/77 77/78 78/79

The expansion franchises of 67/68 began their NHL careers much weaker than the Original Six teams. Over the next decade, that weakness was never entirely erased, as this chart showing regular-season points percentages illustrates. With the Philadelphia Flyers' Stanley Cup wins of 73/74 and 74/75 and good showings from the Los Angeles Kings, by mid-decade the league was on the brink of regular-season parity between the Original Six and 67/68 teams. In the meantime, the league had placed franchises in Buffalo (the 74/75 Cup finalist), Vancouver, Washington, Long Island, Atlanta and Kansas City. Most 67/68 teams could not keep pace with the successes of the Original Sixers, led by Boston and Montreal, or even with subsequent expansion teams like the Sabres and the Islanders. All five surviving 67/68 teams had win percentages of less than 60 at the end of the decade, while Montreal had played above 60 in every season since 67/68. The next 67/68 team to win the Stanley Cup was Pittsburgh, in 90/91. Los Angeles did not reach the finals until 92/93.

ORIGINAL SIX

Montreal	*Canadiens*
New York	*Rangers*
Boston	*Bruins*
Chicago	*Blackhawks*
Toronto	*Maple Leafs*
Detroit	*Red Wings*

67/68 EXPANSION

Philadelphia	*Flyers*
Los Angeles	*Kings*
Pittsburgh	*Penguins*
St. Louis	*Blues*
Minnesota	*North Stars*
Oakland	*Seals**

*Became California Golden Seals in 70/71
Played as Cleveland Barons 76/77–77/78*

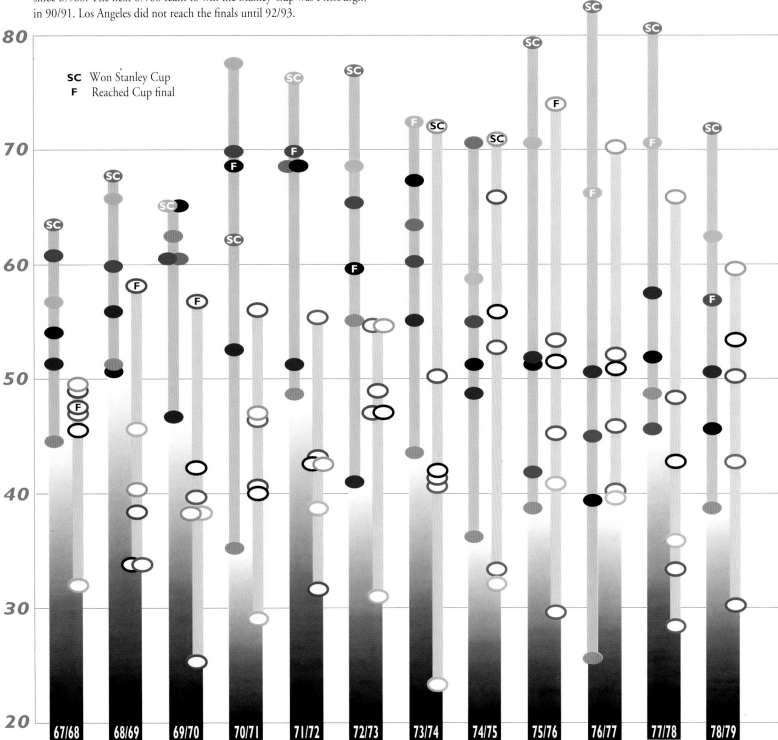

SC Won Stanley Cup
F Reached Cup final

BOSTON BRUINS
The Late Sixties / Early Seventies

BIG, BAD

**WITH BOBBY ORR AND PHIL ESPOSITO AT
THE HEART OF THE TEAM, THE BOSTON BRUINS
WERE A FORCE TO BE RECKONED WITH**

*RIGHT: Phil Esposito was
dealt from Chicago to
Boston in 1967. He won
five scoring titles, two
Hart Trophies and two
Pearson Awards as a
Bruin before being
traded to the New York
Rangers in 1975.
BELOW: A Boston Garden
Stanley Cup programme
from 1972, when the
revived Bruins won their
second Cup.*

A once-proud franchise, the Boston Bruins endured one of the NHL's worst performance streaks before executing one of its most dramatic revivals. In 66/67, the Bruins won 17 of 70 games and finished last, missing the playoffs for the eighth consecutive season. In 67/68, the Bruins won 37 of 74 games, and while they were defeated in the quarterfinals, the Boston franchise was clearly back on its feet and ready to challenge for the Stanley Cup again, not having been in the finals since 57/58. In one season scoring had increased 42 percent, goals against had dropped 17 percent, and total points had almost doubled, from 44 to 84.

What had brought on such a dramatic improvement in a long-standing league laughingstock? The simplest answer would be: expansion. In 67/68 the NHL jumped from 6 to 12 franchises, and in the resulting diluted talent pool, even a sad-sack Original Six outfit like Boston would find easy pickings in games against the expansion clubs gathered in the new West Division. After all, every Original Six franchise except Detroit had a better regular season than the newcomers in 67/68.

But expansion alone does not come close to accounting for Boston's resurgence. This was a dramatically different Bruins club, on the ice and in management, and the proof was in its unfolding ascent. Boston just kept getting better, becoming one of the most powerful clubs of the early 1970s and most consistently dangerous of the new decade. From 69/70 to 77/78, the Bruins played in five Cup finals and won two of them; the club also won seven division and three regular-season titles that decade.

During the 1950s, the Bruins were the only team to consistently challenge the mighty Red Wings and Canadiens in the playoffs. But after reaching the finals twice, in 56/57 and 57/58, by 59/60 the Bruins were in the league cellar with the Rangers, as veteran players passed their peak years and youth failed to

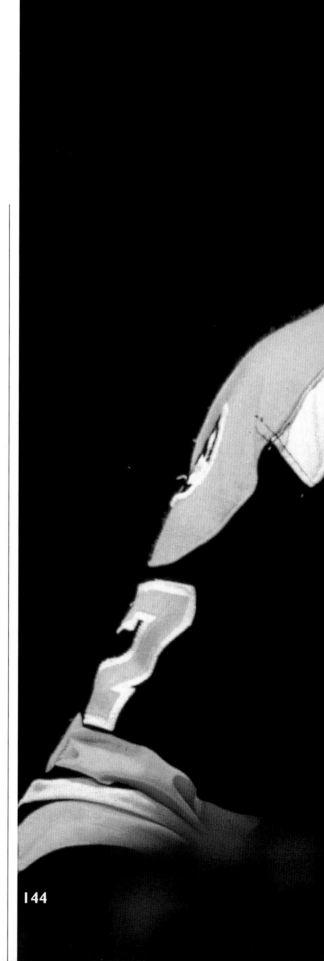

CHAMPIONS

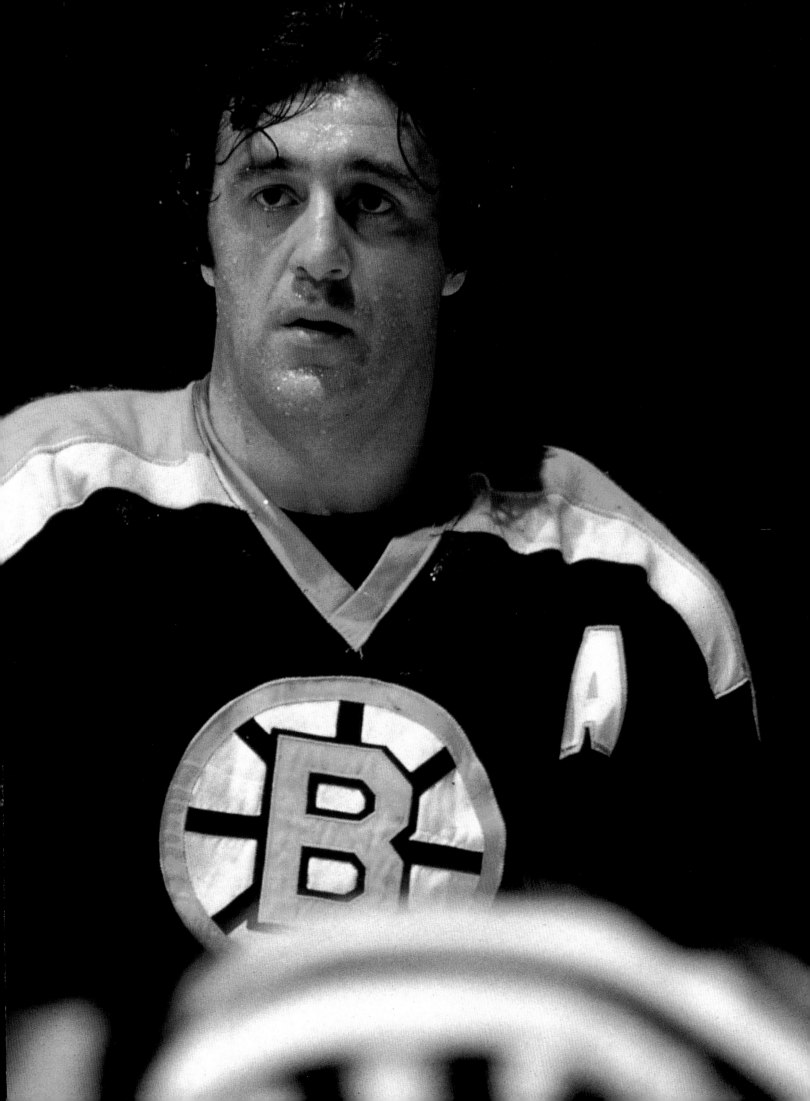

save them. Up front Boston had been powered by such standouts as centers Don McKenney and Bronco Horvath, right-wingers Jerry Toppazzini and Leo Labine, and left-winger Vic Stasiuk. As well, the Bruins had enjoyed the experience of veteran defencemen Allan Stanley and Fern Flaman. All of them were soon out of the lineup—Stanley traded to Toronto in 1958, Flaman retiring after 60/61, Labine and Stasiuk traded to Detroit in 60/61, Toppazzini retiring after 63/64, Horvath sent to Chicago in 61/62, McKenney heading to New York in 62/63. Franchise players were rare as these men moved on. One exception was left-winger Johnny Bucyk, a fearless scorer who had come up through the Detroit development system, played in the 55/56 finals with the Red Wings, and probably would have made a career there had Detroit not traded Terry Sawchuk to Boston after the 54/55 Cup win and then decided it needed him back. Sawchuk returned to Detroit in a deal for defenceman Larry Hillman and Bucyk, who played in the 57/58 final for Boston against Montreal as part of its celebrated Uke Line with Stasiuk and Horvath, and was the only player with personal memories of Bruins excellence when the team recovered its form in the late 1960s.

During the early 1960s, Bucyk was joined by a few players who would aid in the franchise's resurgence. Defenceman Ted Green made the team at age 21 in 61/62, and became perhaps the team's most popular player that decade. That same season, another 21-year-old defenceman, Ed Westfall, made the cut. But as bad as the Bruins were in these years (in 61/62 they finished last with only 15 wins), the team was not so hopeless that every young talent could find a starting position. Dallas Smith, who played a full season in 60/61, was judged too green and sent to the minors, spending the next five seasons in the Western, Eastern Professional, American and Central leagues. And the Philadelphia Flyers of the 1970s would be built with a host of castoffs from the Bruins development system of the mid-1960s. If nothing else, the subsequent success of once-marginal Bruins players showed that, even on a team as poor as the Bruins, it

Harry Sinden

Bruins SCORING 1967/68-1977/78

	Boston goals-against
	Boston goals-for
O	League-leading scoring
	League scoring average
69/70	**Stanley Cup win**

GOALS PER GAME

5.5
5.0
4.5
4.0
3.5
3.0
2.5
2.0

67/68 68/69 69/70 70/71 71/72 72/73 73/74 74/75 75/76 76/77 77/78

was not easy for new faces to break into the NHL of the 1960s.

In January 1961 the Bruins acquired a new goaltender, importing Ed Chadwick from Toronto in exchange for Don Simmons. In 61/62, Boston allowed 306 goals, becoming the first NHL team to allow more than 300 goals in a 70-game season. Defensively, Boston was in a league of its own—the next worst performance of 61/62 was Detroit, with 219 goals against. Chadwick only played four games for Boston that season; the rest were shouldered by Bruce Gamble and Don Head.

While Gamble and Head weren't solely responsible for Boston's awful GA, the Bruins knew they needed stronger netminding, and in 1962 they drafted Eddie Johnston from Montreal. Johnston had yet to play a game with the Canadiens, and he came to Boston the year before Montreal cut the blockbuster deal that sent Jacques Plante to New York in exchange for Gump Worsley. The Canadiens also had Charlie Hodge in reserve; thus, as horrendous an assignment as Boston was for an aspiring netminder, at least the struggling club could provide regular ice time. In 62/63, Johnston played 49 games (relieved by Bob Perreault) and posted the league's worst GA, 4.00, but he could not be faulted as the overall weak Bruins wins slipped to 14. (In 63/64 Johnston got all the ice time a goaltender could ask for when he became the last netminder to carry his team for an entire 70-game season.) The team was marginally better in 62/63—goals against were down (to 281), goal production was up (from 177 to 198), and while wins were down a surge in ties improved total points from 38 to 45. Still, Boston missed the playoffs by 32 gaping points, and early in the season Milt Schmidt, who had been part of the glorious Bruins teams at the start of the Second World War and coached the club from 54/55 to 60/61, took over coaching from Phil Watson.

Defensively, Boston kept improving—goals against fell to 212 in 63/64—but offensively the team lagged badly. By 64/65, team scoring was down to 166 goals while Detroit and Chicago were leading the league with 224. The Bruins were producing fewer goals than were allowed by every NHL team but one, the Rangers. Apart from Bucyk, the only other offensive bright spot was center Murray Oliver, acquired from Detroit in 60/61.

In the intraleague draft of June 1964, the Bruins participated in a major shuffling of netminding talent. It all happened in the closing moments, when Detroit general manager Sid Abel shocked the gathering by dropping Terry Sawchuk from his protected list and selecting from the Bruins' unprotected ranks George Gardner, who was minding net with the Bruins' Central league farm club in Minneapolis. Abel was gambling that no one would go after Sawchuk at this late stage—after all, Montreal had left Gump Worsley unprotected since the first round and no one had touched him—but Punch Imlach swept in and snagged Sawchuk for the Leafs. Once he had Sawchuk, though, Imlach had to leave unprotected either Johnny Bower or prospect Gerry Cheevers, who had won the Memorial Cup with the St. Mike's Majors in 60/61,

BOSTON BRUINS

The Champions of the early 1970s

Featuring the players and management who participated in Boston's
Stanley Cup victories of 1969/70 and 1971/72

GENERAL MANAGER
1. Milt Schmidt

COACH
1. Harry Sinden
2. Tom Johnson

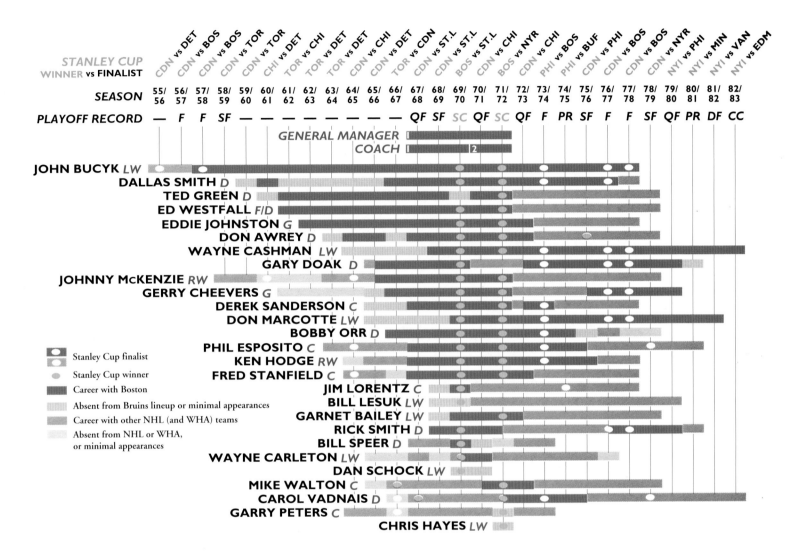

STANLEY CUP WINNER vs FINALIST

CDN vs DET / CDN vs BOS / CDN vs BOS / CDN vs TOR / CDN vs TOR / CHI vs TOR / TOR vs DET / TOR vs DET / TOR vs DET / CDN vs CHI / CDN vs DET / TOR vs CDN / CDN vs ST.L / CDN vs ST.L / BOS vs ST.L / CDN vs CHI / BOS vs NYR / CDN vs CHI / PHI vs BOS / PHI vs BUF / CDN vs PHI / CDN vs BOS / CDN vs BOS / CDN vs NYR / NYI vs PHI / NYI vs MIN / NYI vs VAN / NYI vs EDM

SEASON	55/56	56/57	57/58	58/59	59/60	60/61	61/62	62/63	63/64	64/65	65/66	66/67	67/68	68/69	69/70	70/71	71/72	72/73	73/74	74/75	75/76	76/77	77/78	78/79	79/80	80/81	81/82	82/83
PLAYOFF RECORD	—	F	F	SF	—	—	—	—	—	—	—	—	QF	SF	SC	QF	SC	QF	F	PR	SF	F	F	SF	QF	PR	DF	CC

GENERAL MANAGER
COACH (2)

JOHN BUCYK LW
DALLAS SMITH D
TED GREEN D
ED WESTFALL F/D
EDDIE JOHNSTON G
DON AWREY D
WAYNE CASHMAN LW
GARY DOAK D
JOHNNY McKENZIE RW
GERRY CHEEVERS G
DEREK SANDERSON C
DON MARCOTTE LW
BOBBY ORR D
PHIL ESPOSITO C
KEN HODGE RW
FRED STANFIELD C
JIM LORENTZ C
BILL LESUK LW
GARNET BAILEY LW
RICK SMITH D
BILL SPEER D
WAYNE CARLETON LW
DAN SCHOCK LW
MIKE WALTON C
CAROL VADNAIS D
GARRY PETERS C
CHRIS HAYES LW

Legend:
- Stanley Cup finalist
- Stanley Cup winner
- Career with Boston
- Absent from Bruins lineup or minimal appearances
- Career with other NHL (and WHA) teams
- Absent from NHL or WHA, or minimal appearances

as there was room for only two goaltenders on the list. Imlach stayed with Bower and left Cheevers available. Chicago and Montreal passed to close out the round, and that is how the the draft ended, with Imlach in the catbird seat holding Sawchuk, Bower and Cheevers.

At the draft of unsecured amateur talent that June, Boston, choosing fourteenth, secured the rights to Ken Dryden, not yet 17, who was playing Junior B in Toronto, but immediately dealt his rights away to Montreal in a four-player swap. Boston sent Montreal Dryden and Alex Campbell, whom they had picked second, in exchange for Guy Allen and Paul Reid, whom Montreal had picked twelfth and eighteenth. It was a costly deal for the Bruins. Of the four players involved, only Dryden ever made the NHL, and he became the dominant goaltender of the 1970s.

The 64/65 season proved to be the end of the line for general manager Lynn Patrick, the former Rangers great who had been in the job since 54/55. The Bruins

had finished last for the fifth straight season. Hap Emms, an NHL left-winger of the 1930s who had played briefly for the Bruins in 34/35, stepped in as Schmidt continued as coach.

The day before the intraleague draft in June 1965, Emms made a deal with Punch Imlach, acquiring right-winger Ron Stewart, a veteran of 13 Toronto seasons, in exchange for right-winger Andy Hebenton (a long-standing Ranger before coming to Boston for 63/64), center Orland Kurtenbach and 25-year-old defenceman Pat Stapleton, who had not been able to secure a starting job in Boston. Stapleton and Hebenton had spent 64/65 playing for the Portland Buckaroos of the Western Hockey League. They were the only players on the Buckaroos roster not under contract to Portland, and Buckaroos management was so annoyed with Boston having traded them that they broke off their farm-team relationship as a result.

At the intraleague draft, goaltending was again in

the spotlight. The Leafs' Sawchuk and Bower had won the Vezina together, and Cheevers had made the American league's first All Star team in 64/65 as the Rochester Americans won the American league championship. Imlach could not bring himself to leave unprotected either of his veteran starters to shield Cheevers. Hap Emms moved in and made Cheevers a Bruin. Rochester coach Joe Crozier lamented the loss. "Cheevers is the most exciting goalie you'll ever see," he reportedly told the Bruins. "He'll have your fans on the edge of their seats all night."

Cheevers wouldn't do it right away. He was assigned to the Oklahoma City Blazers of the Central league, to work with player-coach Harry Sinden, and appeared in only seven Boston games. Eddie Johnston shared the Bruins net with another new talent, Bernie Parent, who had starred with the Niagara Falls Flyers of the Ontario Junior A.

The Bruins' goals-against began to balloon after 63/64, reaching 275 in 65/66. As the Bruins headed for one of their worst performances ever that season, Emms started cutting mid-season deals. Left-winger Parker MacDonald, who had just been acquired from Detroit, went back to the Red Wings for center Pit Martin. Left-winger Reggie Fleming went to New York for right-winger Johnny McKenzie, who had already played in Detroit and Chicago in his five-and-a-half-season NHL career. As a final shake-up, captain Leo Boivin, a Bruins defenceman since 54/55, was sent to Detroit for three young players: defenceman Gary Doak, left-winger Bill Lesuk, and an amateur draft pick, which would be used to acquire right-winger Steve Atkinson, whose NHL career would come with the expansion Buffalo Sabres.

The Bruins finished 26 points out of the playoffs in 65/66, the season redeemed only by the even poorer showing of the Rangers. When it was over, team management was shaken up. Milt Schmidt was promoted to assistant manager as part of his grooming to replace Emms in two years. Schmidt elected to take himself off the bench, hiring as his own replacement 33-year-old Harry Sinden, who at the time became the youngest NHL coach.

Sinden continued the trend begun in Detroit in 47/48, when Tommy Ivan became the first league coach not to have been an NHL player. Twenty seasons after Ivan's landmark appearance, other Original Six teams still had veteran players behind the bench— Sid Abel in Detroit, Billy Reay in Chicago, Toe Blake in Montreal. But coaches were emerging from the minor-pro development system, where they had demonstrated their abilities as strategists and motivators. Toronto had opted for a non-veteran, Punch Imlach, in 58/59, and in 64/65 New York had hired as general manager and then coach Emile Francis, who had played goal for only 95 games over six NHL seasons, 73 of them in two seasons with Chicago. Blake was soon to retire in Montreal, and he would be replaced by a non-veteran, Claude Ruel, who at 29 was even younger than Sinden when he got

the Boston job. The expansion clubs of 67/68 would continue the trend. In St. Louis, non-veteran Scotty Bowman would take charge in the first season; Philadelphia hired Keith Allen, who had played 28 games with the Red Wings in the mid-1950s before making his mark as a coach and general manager in the Western league; and Minnesota would have non-veteran Wren Blair.

Sinden was a former Senior league player who had won an Allan Cup and a world title for Canada in 1958 with the Whitby Dunlops. He had spent four years in the minors as a player-coach, leading Kingston to the old Eastern Canadian Professional Hockey League title before moving on to Minneapolis and then Oklahoma City, where he coached the Bruins' Central league farm clubs.

"I like a team that skates like Montreal, checks like Detroit, is as mean as Toronto," he said when hired to coach the Bruins. He was a proponent of the close-checking game, arguing that Montreal wasn't able to break through (the Canadiens had been shut out of the finals from 60/61 to 63/64 before winning in 64/65 and 65/66) until they had begun to play Detroit's style of checking game.

Sinden's arrival made no immediate difference in the Bruins' fortunes. The 66/67 season, in fact, was even worse than its predecessors, as wins slumped from 21 to 17, points from 48 to 44. Before the season started, Hap Emms listed eight Bruins players as "untouchables": goaltenders Eddie Johnston and Bernie Parent, defencemen Gil Marotte, Gary Doak and Ted Green, and forwards Pit Martin, Murray Oliver, Johnny Bucyk and Johnny McKenzie. But as the team continued to slump, and as Emms made way for Schmidt, who took over as general manager after 66/67, the untouchable list came in for some vigorous handling.

As horrible as the 66/67 season was, there was a glimmer of hope in Beantown. Gerry Cheevers came up from Oklahoma for 22 games; while his GA was a steep 3.27, he compared very favourably with Parent (3.65 over 17 games) and Johnston (3.74 over 31 games).

Overwhelmingly the most important lineup addition in 66/67 was defenceman Bobby Orr. First scouted by Boston at age 14 in 1962, Orr's rights were snared by the Bruins and he was brought along as an Oshawa General in the Ontario Junior A. Orr was as celebrated a future star as Jean Béliveau had been in the early 1950s and Wayne Gretzky would be in the 1970s. He was brilliant both offensively and defensively, and while defence-men before him like Red Kelly and Bill Gadsby (and the Bruins' own Eddie Shore before the Second World War) had shown rushing ability, Orr was playing a whole new end-to-end, scoring, playmaking and rush-thwarting game. In the throes of 65/66's misery, assistant-GM Schmidt had hoped to be able to call up Orr, but the superstar in waiting wasn't yet 18, and so was ineligible. Once up in Boston in 66/67 (with a two-year contract that paid him an unprecedented $75,000 signing bonus), Orr went to work reshaping the defensive role. He won the Calder as Boston struggled through another awful

Bobby Orr arrived in the NHL at age 18 in 66/67 as a full-fledged star, winning the Calder and earning a second-team All Star berth. Beginning in 67/68, he won the Norris Trophy and made the first All Star team for eight straight seasons. The Hart Trophy winner for three straight seasons, he also became the first defenceman to win the Art Ross Trophy as the league's leading scorer in 69/70. He won it again in 74/75, and was runner-up three times.

effort, but it was the last in the team's eight-season slump. Harry Howell of the Rangers won the Norris Trophy as the league's top defenceman. "I'm glad I won it now," he quipped, "because it's going to belong to Orr from now on." Howell had seen the future with 20/20 clarity: Orr won the next eight straight Norris Trophies.

In 66/67, Boston was solid defensively. It had Johnston and Cheevers (and the about-to-be-unloaded Parent) sharing the goal, and Green, Orr, Doak, Marotte and (at last) Dallas Smith on defence, with Don Awrey also in the system. Up front, however, little was happening as the team continued to trail the league in scoring. The Bruins had broken up the Uke Line by trading Stasiuk in 60/61 and Horvath in 61/62 because the unit was felt to be too offensive-minded. But no high-producing forward line had emerged to replace the scoring might of the Uke trio.

Boston's salvation, as it happened, came in the collapse of the Chicago Blackhawks in the 66/67 playoffs. Chicago had been the league's runaway success that season. The club finished 17 points ahead of second-place Montreal, allowed 18 fewer goals than Montreal (which earned Glenn Hall and Denis DeJordy the Vezina), and outscored all other clubs by a wide margin as Stan Mikita, Bobby Hull and Ken Wharram finished first, second and fourth in scoring. In their semifinal against third-place Toronto, though, the Hawks were out-hustled and out-muscled, going down in six.

Blackhawks management opted for an immediate house-cleaning. Particularly disappointing had been the playoff performance of center Phil Esposito, who had been the league's third-best center, and seventh overall, in scoring during the season. In six playoff games against Toronto, Esposito hadn't contributed a single point. On May 15, Chicago sent Esposito, right-winger Ken Hodge and center Fred Stanfield to Boston for two of Emms' untouchables, center Pit Martin and defenceman Gil Marotte, as well as minor-pro goaltender Jack Norris. The next untouchable to go was Murray Oliver, who on the same day was sent to Toronto with $100,000 for Eddie Shack, who stayed two seasons before moving on to Los Angeles. Another untouchable left town when Bernie Parent was left unprotected in the expansion draft three weeks later and was claimed by Philadelphia.

The Bruins won the big deal with the Blackhawks hands down. Esposito's 66/67 playoff slump was an aberration in an otherwise outstanding career, and Hodge and Stanfield would play key roles in the upcoming Bruins resurgence. Chicago did receive a quality forward in Martin, and Marotte had eleven more dependable seasons ahead of him in the NHL and WHA, but Norris played only ten games over two seasons with Chicago before going to Los Angeles and then the WHA.

The Esposito trade was just the beginning of major changes in the Bruins as they prepared for the first NHL expansion season. The team began the 67/68 season with a completely new slate of centers, with ex-Blackhawks Esposito and Stanfield joined by rookie Derek Sanderson. Ed Westfall, an outstanding checker

and penalty-killer, was converted from defence to right wing (although he played other forward positions as well). With strong defence and goaltending now augmented by scoring ability, Sinden's lineup erased eight seasons of misery with one solid effort, moving from sixth to third with 40 more points than in 66/67. There would be no turning back.

No Bruin had made an All Star team since Bronco Horvath in 59/60 when Bobby Orr gained the second team in 66/67. In 67/68 Orr graduated to the first team, staying there for eight straight seasons, and Phil Esposito (who finished second in the scoring race) and Johnny Bucyk (ninth in scoring) made the second team—there hadn't been three Bruins All Stars in one season since 47/48. For the first time since 57/58, the Bruins scored more goals than they allowed as they won 37 of 74 games. But the quarterfinals showed how far the team had yet to go, as first-place Montreal easily disposed of them in four games.

It was experience this team needed more than anything; the winning lineup was essentially established in 67/68. Presciently, Esposito told Sinden when he arrived in 1967 that the team would win the Stanley Cup in three years. Only the left-wing position was much in question. Johnny Bucyk, who became captain after Leo Boivin was traded, was the lone fixture on that wing. In 68/69 Wayne Cashman found a regular starting position, and in 69/70 so did Don Marcotte; Wayne Carleton joined them when he was acquired from Toronto on December 10, 1969 for new center Jim Harrison.

The new Bruins of Harry Sinden were also the Big Bad Bruins: physically tough, intimidating, not likely to be pushed around—especially on home ice, the ancient barn known as Boston Garden. Its ice surface was nine feet shorter and two feet narrower than the standard NHL rink. These cramped conditions were perfect for Boston's close-checking, hard-hitting game. It also didn't hurt that Esposito, Hodge and Stanfield came from Chicago, home of the league's other undersized Original Six rink (a full 15 feet shorter than standard). The Garden ice surface also suited a rushing defenceman like Orr, who could get down the ice and get back quicker than on a normal rink.

In 68/69 the Bruins were capable of winning the Cup. They finished second in the East Division, three points behind Montreal. Phil Esposito won the Hart Trophy—the first Bruin to do so since Milt Schmidt in 50/51—and the Art Ross as the league's leading scorer with a record 126 points—the first Bruin to earn the trophy since Herb Cain in 43/44. The team splurged on goals, becoming the first NHL club to score more than 300 (303). In the quarterfinals the Bruins massacred the Leafs, outscoring them 17-0 in the opening two games at Boston Garden, then winning 4-3 and 3-2 in Toronto to advance to meet the Canadiens, the defending Stanley Cup champions, in the semifinals.

This was the series everyone acknowledged to be

BOSTON BRUINS 1967/68–74/75

Season	Finish	Record (W-L-T)	Points %	Awards (winners & runners-up)	All-Stars	Playoffs
67/68	3rd Div 3rd OA	37-27-10	56.8	ART ROSS: Esposito RU LADY BYNG: Bucyk RU CALDER: Sanderson NORRIS: Orr	1ST TEAM: Orr (D) 2ND TEAM: Esposito (C), Bucyk (LW)	Lost SC quarterfinal 4-0 to Montreal
68/69	2nd Div 2nd OA	42-18-16	65.8	ART ROSS: Esposito HART: Esposito NORRIS: Orr	1ST TEAM: Orr (D), Esposito (C) 2ND TEAM: Green (D)	Lost SC semifinal 4-2 to Montreal
69/70	2nd Div 2nd OA	40-17-19	65.1	ART ROSS: Orr, Esposito RU HART: Orr LADY BYNG: Bucyk RU CONN SMYTHE: Orr NORRIS: Orr	1ST TEAM: Orr (D), Esposito (C) 2ND TEAM: McKenzie (RW)	Won SC final 4-0 over St. Louis
70/71	1st Div 1st OA	57-14-7	77.6	ART ROSS: Esposito, Orr RU HART: Orr, Esposito RU LADY BYNG: Bucyk NORRIS: Orr PEARSON: Esposito	1ST TEAM: Esposito (C), Hodge (RW), Orr (D), Bucyk (LW)	Lost SC quarterfinal 4-3 to Montreal
71/72	1st Div 1st OA	54-13-11	76.3	ART ROSS: Esposito, Orr RU HART: Orr LADY BYNG: Bucyk RU CONN SMYTHE: Orr NORRIS: Orr	1ST TEAM: Orr (D), Esposito (C)	Won SC final 4-2 over New York
72/73	2nd Div 2nd OA	51-22-5	68.6	ART ROSS: Esposito HART: Esposito RU NORRIS: Orr	1ST TEAM: Orr (D), Esposito (C)	Lost SC quarterfinal 4-1 to New York
73/74	1st Div 1st OA	52-17-9	72.4	ART ROSS: Esposito, Orr RU HART: Esposito LADY BYNG: Bucyk VEZINA: Gilbert RU NORRIS: Orr PEARSON: Esposito	1ST TEAM: Orr (D), Esposito (C), Hodge (RW) 2ND TEAM: Cashman (LW)	Lost SC final 4-2 to Philadelphia
74/75	2nd Div 4th Conf 5th OA	40-26-14	58.8	ART ROSS: Orr, Esposito RU LADY BYNG: Bucyk RU NORRIS: Orr PEARSON: Orr	1ST TEAM: Orr (D) 2ND TEAM: Esposito (C)	Lost preliminary round 2-1 to Chicago

the "real" Stanley Cup contest. The league was divided into East and West Divisions, with the more powerful Original Six clubs in the East and the expansion franchises quarantined in the West. Montreal (103 points) was tilting with Boston (100) as the Los Angeles Kings (58) were taking on St. Louis (88). Whoever emerged from the Montreal-Boston set-to was going to crush the finalist from the West Division. And the pundits proved correct in that the Montreal-Boston series was the most exciting of the spring of 1969. Three of six games, including the deciding one, went into overtime. Experience was the difference in the two clubs, as Montreal won all three overtime games to advance to meet and defeat St. Louis in four straight.

The series frustrated Sinden, who believed his Bruins to be the equal of the Canadiens. The difference was that Montreal had been in every final in the previous four seasons, and had won three of them. The Bruins didn't have a single "franchise" player who could boast of any Stanley Cup success. Only four of these had ever been to the finals, and none had won. Johnny Bucyk had lost with Detroit in 55/56 and with Boston in 57/58; McKenzie, Esposito and Stanfield had lost with Chicago in 64/65 to some of those same Canadiens who mastered them in the 68/69 semifinal.

All the same, Boston's playoff effort of 68/69 was a big improvement over 67/68. And in 69/70, the Bruins held their own as the Canadiens struggled, missing the playoffs for the first time in 22 seasons. Phil Esposito's old team, the Blackhawks, had leapt from last to first in the East in one season, propelled by the success of their rookie goaltender, Phil's brother Tony, who had been cut loose in the intraleague draft by Montreal in June. Tony Esposito won the Vezina and the Calder and made the first All Star team, the first goaltender to sweep all three honours since the Bruins' Frank Brimsek in 38/39.

Boston had its own silverware collectors. Bobby Orr, in addition to winning his second consecutive Norris Trophy, earned his first Hart Trophy and his first Art Ross. These were monumental milestones in the game. No defenceman had ever won the NHL scoring race, and his points production was only six shy of teammate Phil Esposito's league record, set the previous season. He would win three Harts in a row, another record performance (Eddie Shore won three in four seasons from 34/35 to 37/38).

The teams of the Esposito brothers finished the 69/70 season tied on points. Chicago, having won more games, was awarded first in the East and overall. The Bruins opened their playoffs confidently with an 8-2 pasting of the Rangers at home, but New York regrouped in time to take the Bruins to six games. A 4-1 win in the final game iced the Rangers and sent the Bruins up against the Blackhawks in the division finals.

The showdown between the Esposito teams failed to provide the sparks hoped for. The Bruins handled the Blackhawks confidently, 6-3, 4-1, 5-2 and 5-4, and headed for the Cup finals against the Blues, who were in their third consecutive Cup series after downing the Pittsburgh Penguins in six.

The West Division champion was not expected to be quite the walkover it was in the previous two Cup finals. After all, St. Louis had won 37 games to Boston's 40 in 69/70. But the Blues could not handle these Bruins. Boston raced to three straight wins of 6-1, 6-2 and 4-1. Having been outscored 16 to 4 thus far, the Blues took the Bruins into overtime in game four. Bobby Orr took a pass from behind the net that Blues goaltender Glenn Hall stabbed at in vain with a poke check, and flicked it in the net. As he was tripped up and the goal light flashed, Orr threw his arms in the air and soared horizontally past the cameras, celebrating the first Bruins Stanley Cup win since 40/41. It was his first goal of the final series;

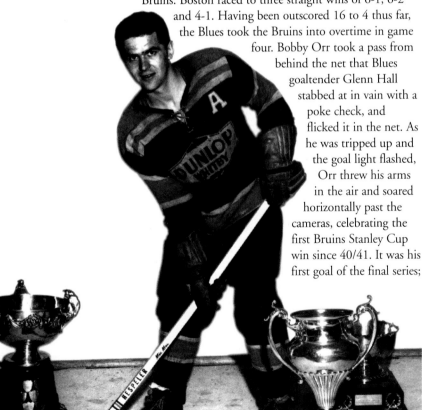

Harry Sinden starred with the Whitby Dunlops in Canadian Senior league competition, winning the Allan Cup and a world championship for Canada in 1958. He was a player-coach in the Bruins' minor professional system when hired to coach Boston in 1966.

he had four assists to go with it, and was awarded the Conn Smythe Trophy as playoff MVP. Esposito had paced the team with eight points on two goals and six assists; captain Johnny Bucyk, after 15 seasons of disappointment, had won the Cup with a team-leading six goals in the series.

Harry Sinden, who was earning a pittance as the Bruins' coach, took the Cup victory as a sign that it was now time to do something more profitable with his life; he quit the job to try making a living outside of hockey. He was back, however, as general manager in 72/73. In the meantime, the Bruins' coaching duties were assumed by Tom Johnson.

The 69/70 season felt like a warm-up when the next campaign got rolling. The lineup was little changed—notable was the loss of defenceman Gary Doak to the Vancouver Canucks in the 1970 expansion draft. The remaining Bruins ran roughshod over the league, winning 57 games and tying 7 for a points percentage of 77.6. The team scored 399 goals— the next best effort, from the Canadiens, was 108 goals back. Esposito, Orr, Bucyk and Hodge took the top four places in the scoring race, all with more than 100 points, with Cashman, McKenzie and Stanfield joining them in the top ten. Esposito shattered all known standards of offensive production as he logged 76 goals and 76 assists, just shy of the goal-a-game pace last seen from Maurice Richard when he produced 50 in 50 in 44/45.

It was a performance freighted with omens. The last season that anyone or any team would wish to emulate would be that of Richard and the Canadiens of 44/45, who also ran away with the regular season, with a points percentage of 80. And those Canadiens had been upset in their Stanley Cup semifinal, downed in six by an inspired, close-checking bunch of Maple Leafs who went on to win the Cup against Detroit.

The history of the NHL, in fact, was littered with teams who dominated the regular season, only to fall in the playoffs, often before reaching the finals. It had happened to Phil Esposito and the Blackhawks in 66/67, when they won the regular season with an impressive points percentage of 67.1. But there had been far larger flops in the league's past, and the greatest of all had been the Bruins of 29/30, whose points percentage of 87.5 did not sway the determination of the Canadiens who defeated them in the Cup final that year.

The Bruins of 70/71 did not get to the Cup final. They did not even get past the quarterfinals. Matched against the Canadiens in the opening round, they should have had little trouble. The Bruins had won five of their six-regular season meetings, and in their last encounter just before the playoffs began they had all but run the Canadiens out of the rink in winning 7-2. In the last six games of the season, however, the Canadiens had been trying out a new goaltender: Ken Dryden, the 1964 draft pick the Bruins had traded away to Montreal. He was finally making his NHL debut, and the big guns of the Bruins could not level him. It took all seven games, but the Canadiens downed the supposedly indomitable Boston squad.

The playoff loss did not provoke any major changes to the lineup. It had been a tough series, but the Canadiens had shown themselves worthy by winning the Cup in a seven-game final against the Blackhawks. In recent personnel changes, center Mike Walton had been acquired from Toronto via Philadelphia on February 1, 1971, in a deal that saw the Bruins give up their top draft pick of 1970, Rick MacLeish, and left-winger Dan Schock. The Bruins had drafted extremely well in 1970. In addition to taking MacLeish third, they had also selected Reggie Leach fourth. Neither could find a place in the Bruins lineup, though, and in a few seasons they ended up becoming major stars with the Flyers.

In the 1971 draft, the Bruins used their first pick to take defenceman Ron Jones, who never had much of an NHL career and only played eight games with the Bruins. Their second pick, taken fourteenth overall, was more profitable, as they chose right-winger Terry O'Reilly of the Oshawa Generals. O'Reilly would make the team in 72/73 and play all 13 of his NHL seasons for the Bruins, two of them as captain, before going on to coach them.

For the 71/72 campaign, the Bruins stayed with the lineup that had delivered such a sparkling regular season in 70/71. One adjustment was made, on February 13, as defencemen Rick Smith and Bob Stewart were packaged with Reggie Leach and sent to the California Golden Seals for a tough, points-producing defenceman, Carol Vadnais, and right-winger Don O'Donoghue.

The 71/72 season didn't see quite as overwhelming a performance from the Bruins as 70/71, but there was hardly shame in it. The Bruins were the only team to win more than 50 games (54) in the 78-game season, just two points off their 70/71 performance. Esposito and Orr topped the scoring race for the second straight season; Esposito's 66 goals were down from his stupendous 76-goal output of 70/71, but were still 16 more than the next best performance of 50 by Vic Hadfield of the Rangers and Bobby Hull of the Blackhawks. And Orr's 80 assists were 13 more than the next-best effort, which came from Esposito. (The high number of assists accorded to Bruins stars was a source of carping elsewhere in the league. Critics complained that the scorer at Boston Garden would give Esposito or Orr an assist if they were on the same sheet of ice when the puck went in the net.)

These playoffs would hold no repeat of the shocker delivered by Ken Dryden and the Canadiens in 70/71. The Bruins recorded two shutouts in eliminating Toronto 4-1 in the quarterfinals. In the semifinals, St. Louis was powerless as the Bruins swept them in four by scores of 6-1, 10-2, 7-2 and 5-3. The finals against the Rangers were not so straightforward. Four games were decided by one goal, but the Bruins came through with a 3-0 win in New York to take the series in six. Orr, with four goals and four assists in the final series, won his second Conn Smythe Trophy.

How long Boston could have continued to rule the league had the World Hockey Association not appeared in 72/73 is a great unknown. All that is known is that the Bruins' Stanley Cup victories stopped on May 11, 1972, at Madison Square Garden. The debut of the rival league ripped through the Bruins starting lineup, costing them Gerry Cheevers, Ted Green and Derek Sanderson.

Cheevers was by far the greatest loss— Green's on-ice role had diminished since a near-fatal head injury in 1969 (the result of a horrifying pre-season stick-swinging duel with Chicago's Wayne Maki), and Sanderson's flamboyant lifestyle was going to sink one of the era's more promising careers. Cheevers, on the other hand, was a consummate team player who was more concerned with the team's overall performance than his goals-against average. "Cheesie" never won a Vezina, or, remarkably, any kind of accolade in the NHL—not even an All Star team appearance. The Russian netminding star Vladsilav Tretiak would call him the greatest goaltender he had ever seen. Cheevers and Eddie Johnston shared the Boston netminding job and got along famously, but in the 71/72 finals Cheevers had carried the Bruins through all six games against the Rangers. His jump to the Cleveland Crusaders was a big loss, and was also not the sort of temporary move that players like Sanderson indulged in. After signing a 10-year contract worth more than $2 million, Sanderson played only eight games for the Philadelphia Blazers before heading back to the Bruins. Cheevers stayed with Cleveland for three and a half seasons before a falling-out with the team ownership brought him back to the Bruins in mid-75/76.

By then, the championship Bruins team of 71/72 was for the most part dismantled. Johnny McKenzie, who was sold to the Philadelphia Flyers in August 1972, chose to play for the WHA Blazers instead. Mike Walton jumped to the Minnesota Fighting Saints of the WHA in 1973. Fred Stanfield, who had come from Chicago with Esposito in 1967, was sent to the Minnesota North Stars for goaltender Gilles Gilbert in May 1973. Derek Sanderson, after returning to the team from his WHA adventure, was offloaded to the Rangers in June 1974 for center Walt McKechnie. Cheevers' netminding partner, Eddie Johnston, was sent to Toronto in May 1973 to complete a deal in which the Bruins had received the ancient netminder Jacques Plante and Toronto's third choice in the 1973 draft for Boston's first-round choice in the same draft. Toronto did well by the deal, selecting defenceman Ian Turnbull fifteenth overall.

Bobby Orr was all but lost to the team, his knees a

The Bruins are a franchise with a storied past. Boston was one of the first American teams in the NHL, joining in 24/25 and winning its first Stanley Cup in 28/29. An early star was center Cooney Weiland, whose jersey appears above. As the pivot point of the "Dynamite Line," Weiland scored 43 goals in 44 games in 29/30. He later scouted for and coached the Bruins, then ran the hockey program at Harvard.

Continued on page 157

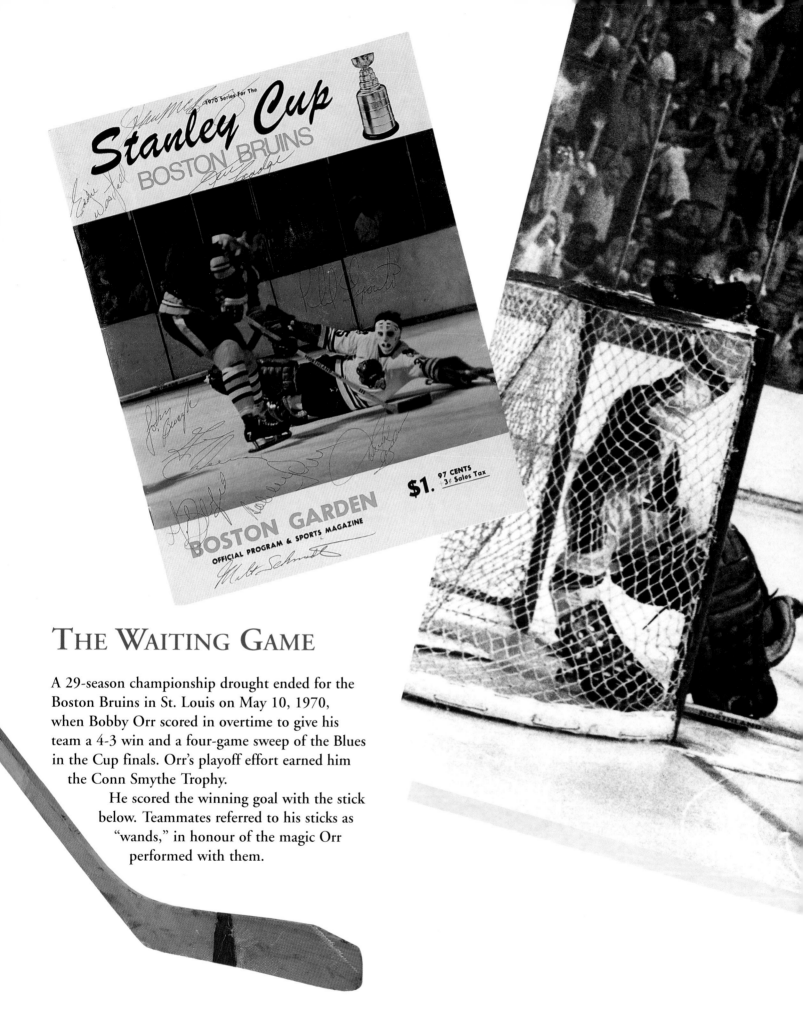

The Waiting Game

A 29-season championship drought ended for the Boston Bruins in St. Louis on May 10, 1970, when Bobby Orr scored in overtime to give his team a 4-3 win and a four-game sweep of the Blues in the Cup finals. Orr's playoff effort earned him the Conn Smythe Trophy.

He scored the winning goal with the stick below. Teammates referred to his sticks as "wands," in honour of the magic Orr performed with them.

Continued from page 153

ruin; he would sign as a free agent with the Blackhawks in June 1976. Already lost was Phil Esposito. On November 7, 1975, Esposito was sent to the Rangers with Carol Vadnais for defensive star (and captain) Brad Park and the high-scoring, gentlemanly center Jean Ratelle. But one of the team's biggest losses was also one of its most overlooked. Ed Westfall had been left unprotected after the 71/72 Cup win and was taken by the New York Islanders in the expansion draft that followed. The Islanders moved the versatile player (who was also one of the most decent human beings in the game) to defence and made him their captain.

Former defensive great Bob Goldham, writing in the Maple Leaf Gardens program of 1970, had this to say of Westfall's importance: "When you get right down to it, these are the type of fellows a team needs when it aims at a championship. I remember playing with the Red Wings when we had those powerful and classy clubs, but it was players such as Glen Skov and Marty Pavelich and Tony Leswick who were the hidden backbone of our team. They not only did a great job keeping the opposition scoreless, but they came up with the big goals themselves. A club simply couldn't function without such players."

The Bruins did make the 73/74 finals without Westfall and the other players who were either shed or jumped after the 71/72 win. The season, in fact, was one of the club's best, with four All Stars chosen from the team, a points percentage of 72.4, and a slew of silverware for its stars. Gerry Cheevers' replacement, Gilles Gilbert, also did well in finishing second in the Vezina race. But the league had an even tougher gang on the block by then. The Philadelphia Flyers, stocked with a legion of former Bruins properties and with an uglier attitude than the Bruins on their baddest day, downed Boston in six.

The previous season, Flyers captain Bobby Clarke had won the Hart Trophy, ending Orr's streak at three. Phil Esposito supplanted Clarke in 73/74, then it was back to Clarke for two seasons. The Norris, however, remained Orr's property indisputably through 74/75.

When Cheevers returned in mid-75/76, more changes were still to come. Ken Hodge was sent to the Rangers in exchange for right-winger Rick Middleton on May 26, 1976, after Boston lost 4-1 to the Flyers in the semifinals. First Stanfield, then Esposito, now Hodge: the last of the three Blackhawks who had come over to the Bruins in 1967 was gone.

The Bruins themselves were not through. The team was being rebuilt rather than dismantled, and a disciplined, grinding team emerged, with Don Cherry arriving as coach in 74/75 and staying through 78/79. Seven players from the champions of 69/70 and 71/72 were still with the team when Cherry guided them into the 76/77 finals against the Canadiens. They were captain Johnny Bucyk on left wing; defencemen Dallas Smith, Gary Doak (who had come back to the team in a trade with Detroit for left-winger Garnet Bailey and

defenceman Murray Wing on March 1, 1973) and Rick Smith (who returned to the Bruins through a trade for Joe Zanussi with St. Louis on December 20, 1976); left-wingers Wayne Cashman and Don Marcotte; and goaltender Gerry Cheevers, who was brilliant in his playoff appearances.

Cherry's Bruins were the only team to consistently harass the mighty Canadiens franchise of the late 1970s. After losing to Montreal in the finals of 76/77 and 77/78, Boston fell one bench penalty short of eliminating the Canadiens in the 78/79 semifinals and advancing to its third consecutive Cup finals appearance. Boston was leading 4-3 in the closing moments of game seven when the checking assignment on Guy Lafleur caused confusion in the ranks. Six Boston skaters were on the ice for at least 30 seconds before the officials noticed. After a bench penalty was assessed, Guy Lafleur tied the score on the powerplay; Yvon Lambert won the game and the series for Montreal in overtime.

Cherry then took the coaching job with the Colorado Rockies, an assignment that did not work out. The Bruins of the late 1970s may have been grinders, but they were talented grinders, and Cherry's bluster had no influence on an unfulfilled expansion lineup (the team had started out as the Kansas City Scouts in 74/75) as the Rockies won only 19 of 80 games in 79/80. Gerry Cheevers came in as the Bruins coach in 80/81, and had some regular-season and playoff successes, but when the team dropped to fourth in the Adams Division in 84/85 he was fired by Sinden. His old netminding partner, Eddie Johnston, coached the Pittsburgh Penguins from 79/80 to 82/83, and served as the Penguins general manager from 1983 to 1988. After a demotion to assistant general manager, he left the Penguins to serve as vice president and general manager of the Hartford Whalers in 1989. He returned to the Penguins bench in 1993.

The Bruins of the 1970s rank among the great teams of NHL history, but fell shy of reaching the plateaus of success earlier achieved by Detroit, Toronto and Montreal. Like the Bruins team that came 30 years before them, they were hampered in part by circumstances beyond their control. The Bruins who won the Stanley Cups of 38/39 and 40/41 were derailed by a world war and never recovered their momentum. The Bruins of the 1970s were hobbled by the arrival of the WHA and, perhaps more than anything, by the hobbling of Bobby Orr, who may have been the greatest player in the history of the game. When his deteriorating knees took him out of the lineup in 75/76, there was no one of his calibre to take his place, not even a player as great as Brad Park.

The team regularly finished at or near the top of its division, even regaining the Cup finals in 87/88 and 89/90 as they found a new rushing defenceman, Ray Bourque, to echo the exploits of Orr. But another Cup win has eluded the team since 71/72. And with the closing of the cramped, humid and utterly unique Boston Garden in 1995, the Bruins, for better or worse, put their past behind them. ○

Secured from Toronto in the 1965 intraleague draft, Gerry Cheevers anchored the Bruins' Stanley Cup wins of 69/70 and 71/72. His decision to jump to the WHA in 1972 was a blow to Boston, and his return to the Bruins in the middle of 75/76 was crucial to the team's competitiveness against Montreal in the 76/77 and 77/78 Cup finals. Though he was never singled out for any NHL award or All Star appearance, the Russian netminding great Vladislav Tretiak called Cheevers the greatest goaltender he had ever seen.

PHILADELPHIA FLYERS
The Seventies

SHERO'S HEROES

A TEAM THAT FOUGHT TO THE FINISH, FREDDIE THE FOG'S BROAD STREET BULLIES WERE THE TOAST OF THE CITY OF BROTHERLY LOVE

Right: Reggie Leach was the consummate sniper, a former Junior teammate of Bobby Clarke who was sprung from the lowly California Golden Seals in 1974.
Below: A statue honours singer Kate Smith, who virtually guaranteed a Flyers win whenever she belted out "God Bless America" before a game at the Philadelphia Spectrum.

The Philadelphia Flyers do not command such a significant place in the history of hockey simply because they won two Stanley Cups. Most important to the Flyers' notoriety—and it is more notoriety than fame—is how they won, not what they won.

They were the self-proclaimed "Broad Street Bullies," who made three straight Stanley Cup finals, and won two of them. They were a team of grinders, snipers and brawlers who terrorized professional hockey and both excited and horrified fans. Two decades after they ruled the NHL, it may be difficult for fans who never saw them in action to buy into their notoriety. After all, the most penalized editions of the championship Flyers are not among the top five of the league's biggest rule-breaking teams. With total minutes in the 1,700 range, the 73/74 and 74/75 teams pale beside the 80/81 Flyers, who incurred 2,621 minutes, or the Sabres of 91/92, who were assessed 2,713 minutes. And for all the brawling they did, the Flyers' antics wouldn't have raised an eyebrow amid the on-ice histrionics of the NHL of the 1940s and 1950s, when referees were punched by both players and management and sticks were regularly cracked over opponents' heads. Nonetheless, the Flyers were, to their critics, everything that was wrong with the professional North American game in the NHL's initial expansion years, a team that put thuggery at the core of its game plan. Old-time NHLers might have fought and spilled blood, but they did it because they lost their tempers, not because it was the team's winning strategy.

The charges brought against the Flyers are among the blackest in the game's history. To wit: they brought to the NHL the sideshow brutality of minor pro loops (which inspired the antics of the film *Slapshot*), thereby setting off an arms race in goons

among all NHL clubs and throwing the entire amateur development system out of kilter. In placing such an emphasis on physical intimidation, they led the game away from finesse skills and into the humiliations the Canadian game suffered at the hands of the Soviet in the Summit Series of 1979 and the Canada Cup of 1981. Criticism spilled over onto the league itself, which was accused of turning a blind eye to the goonery because it sold tickets when the league was in a battle for market share with the World Hockey Association. The Flyers were the antithesis of the stylish and skilful Canadiens team taking shape in that decade, and when Montreal ended the Philadelphia reign of terror in brutally efficient fashion in the 75/76 finals, fans who felt the North American game was falling Flyers-first into a behavioral sinkhole breathed a sigh of relief.

It wasn't quite that cut-and-dried. The Flyers could never have been as successful as they were through intimidation alone. They brought skills to their victories that cannot be overlooked. Most important, they were one of the most team-focused outfits the Stanley Cup has ever seen, an all-for-one, one-for-all operation masterminded by a mild-mannered minor-pro veteran, Fred Shero.

Their successes as individual players were contained almost exclusively within their Flyers careers. Only the veteran defenceman Ted Harris, who had won four championships with Montreal, had sipped champagne from the Cup before; the only other player to have reached the Cup finals before becoming a Flyer was defenceman Terry Crisp, who soldiered through three losing efforts as a St. Louis Blue. And only one player, Al MacAdam, ever reached a Cup final again after leaving the Flyers, and that was in a losing effort as a Minnesota North Star against the New York Islanders in 80/81.

The fan support for the team was ferocious; enforcer Dave Schultz had his own private following known as Schultz's Army. And in

the age that begat disco, white three-piece suits and blow-dried hairstyles for men, athletes included, there was something irresistible to fans about a team whose members carried *noms de glace* like The Hammer, Moose, Cowboy and Hound Dog. To their rabid supporters, the Flyers were hockey redux, real men who cursed and punched people and stuck up for each other.

If the Maple Leafs of the 1960s were the first truly engineered dynasty, the first club to be built out of both farm-system talent and trades that brought in players who had already won Stanley Cups, then the Flyers of the 1970s were the first dynasty to be engineered from the professional game's spare parts. Expansion of the NHL in 1967 and the arrival of the WHA in 1972 stretched player resources to the limit. Players who before 1967 would have toiled exclusively in tier-two leagues now had tier-one careers in the NHL. It was inevitable that a coach who knew how to make the most of the skills of fair-to-middling players could create a champion. While Harry Sinden did come out of the minor leagues to coach and manage the great Bruins team of the early expansion years, he was able to work for the most part with tier-one talents. It was left to two other minor-league wizards, Keith Allen and Fred Shero, to create a winner out of players whom other top clubs wouldn't even give a chance to play.

Shero didn't arrive on the scene until the fall of 1971, four years after the Flyers first took shape. Entering the league in the 67/68 expansion, the Flyers, under general manager Bud Poile and coach Keith Allen, initially stocked their roster in an expansion draft held June 6, 1967 which allowed them to pick and choose among contracted players the Original Six teams left off their protected lists. These were essentially players the established teams considered expendable—not always second-rate, but deemed non-essential to their own futures. Of the original Flyers draftees, four players—defencemen Ed Van Impe and Joe Watson, right-winger Gary Dornhoefer and goaltender Bernie Parent—would participate in both Flyers' Cup wins. Right-winger Simon Nolet, acquired that first season, would also play on the 73/74 team.

Boston was the league's success story in

Flyers scoring
71/72 to 79/80

Philadelphia goals-against
League-leading GA
Philadelphia goals-for
League-leading scoring
League scoring average
74/75 Stanley Cup win

Bernie Parent

PHILADELPHIA FLYERS

The Champions of the mid-1970s

Featuring the players and management who participated in Philadelphia's
Stanley Cup victories of 1973/74 and 1974/75

GENERAL MANAGER
1. Keith Allen

COACH
1. Fred Shero

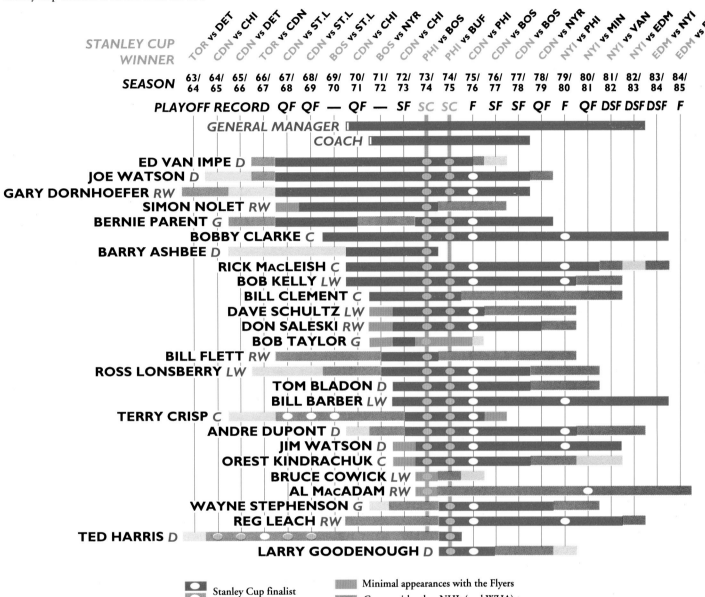

STANLEY CUP WINNER: TOR vs DET, CDN vs CHI, CDN vs DET, TOR vs CDN, CDN vs ST.L, CDN vs ST.L, BOS vs ST.L, CDN vs CHI, BOS vs NYR, CDN vs CHI, PHI vs BOS, PHI vs BUF, CDN vs PHI, CDN vs BOS, CDN vs BOS, CDN vs NYR, NYI vs PHI, NYI vs MIN, NYI vs VAN, NYI vs EDM, EDM vs NYI, EDM vs PHI

SEASON	63/64	64/65	65/66	66/67	67/68	68/69	69/70	70/71	71/72	72/73	73/74	74/75	75/76	76/77	77/78	78/79	79/80	80/81	81/82	82/83	83/84	84/85
PLAYOFF RECORD	QF	QF	—	QF	—	SF	SC	SC	F	SF	SF	QF	F	QF	DSF	DSF	DSF	F				

GENERAL MANAGER
COACH
ED VAN IMPE D
JOE WATSON D
GARY DORNHOEFER RW
SIMON NOLET RW
BERNIE PARENT G
BOBBY CLARKE C
BARRY ASHBEE D
RICK MacLEISH C
BOB KELLY LW
BILL CLEMENT C
DAVE SCHULTZ LW
DON SALESKI RW
BOB TAYLOR G
BILL FLETT RW
ROSS LONSBERRY LW
TOM BLADON D
BILL BARBER LW
TERRY CRISP C
ANDRE DUPONT D
JIM WATSON D
OREST KINDRACHUK C
BRUCE COWICK LW
AL MacADAM RW
WAYNE STEPHENSON G
REG LEACH RW
TED HARRIS D
LARRY GOODENOUGH D

Legend:
- Stanley Cup finalist
- Stanley Cup winner
- Career with Philadelphia
- Minimal appearances with the Flyers
- Career with other NHL (and WHA) teams
- Absent from NHL or WHA, or minimal appearances

---

the seasons immediately preceding the Flyers' ascent, and in winning two Stanley Cups at the start of the decade, the Big Bad Bruins' revitalized Original Six franchise foreshadowed Philadelphia's own winning formula of scoring and brawling. It should not be surprising that nine championship Flyers at some point in their careers had been in the Bruins' talent pool, mainly at its margins.

And three of the four original Philadelphia draftees to play on a Cup winner came from the Bruins' system—Joe Watson, Gary Dornhoefer and Bernie Parent. Of the three, Parent was the greatest catch. Like Dornhoefer, Parent had been an amateur Bruins proper-

ty, starring with the Niagara Falls Flyers in 63/64 and 64/65. He was named the Ontario Major Junior A's top goaltender in both seasons, and anchored the Flyers' Memorial Cup win in the latter season. He performed indifferently as a Bruin, and when the 1967 expansion draft came along, Boston wisely decided to protect as its netminders Eddie Johnston and a 1965 acquisition from the Maple Leafs' farm system, Gerry Cheevers. The Flyers also drafted another goaltender, Doug Favell, who was a buddy of Cheevers from St. Catharines, Ontario.

The fourth original draftee, defenceman Ed Van Impe, had just finished his first NHL season with the hugely disappointing Blackhawks. After ruling the league

SHERO'S HEROES

in the regular season, Chicago had folded in the playoffs, going down in six games to the Leafs in the semifinals. In a rebuilding that saw the Hawks trade sniper Phil Esposito to the Bruins, Chicago general manager Tommy Ivan left Van Impe unprotected. Flyers GM Bud Poile, who had won a Stanley Cup as a Maple Leaf in 46/47, snapped up Van Impe and made him team captain in his second Philadelphia season.

Though not a Bruins alumnus, Van Impe had two other qualities shared by many of the Cup-winning Flyers—he was a product of the western Canadian amateur system, and he racked up penalty minutes. Fourteen Stanley-Cup winning Flyers came out of the rough-and-tumble western game. Van Impe was from Saskatoon, home town of original Flyer coach Keith Allen, and had led the Saskatchewan Junior league in infractions in 1958/59, recording 150 penalty minutes in 48 games while playing for his hometown Quakers. Van Impe's fellow Flyer original Joe Watson was from Smithers, B.C. Furthermore, Fred Shero was from Winnipeg and Gerry Melnyk, who became the Flyers' chief scout after his playing days ended due to heart problems following the 67/68 season in St. Louis, was from Edmonton.

Keith Allen would assert he was fed up with the way the the Flyers had been manhandled by the Blues in their first two playoff outings. St. Louis downed Philadelphia in a tough quarterfinal series in 67/68 that twice went into overtime and required all seven games. In 68/69, the Blues overwhelmed them in the quarterfinals, winning 5-2, 5-0, 3-0 and 4-1. Allen wanted bigger, tougher players.

At the amateur draft in June 1969, the Flyers squandered their first-round pick on Bob Currier, who was taken sixth overall but never played in the NHL or WHA. The Flyers chose more wisely in the second round, taking center Bobby Clarke seventeenth overall. Had it not been for his diabetes, which scared off other teams, Clarke almost certainly would have gone in the first round. Flyers scout Gerry Melnyk was sold on him and convinced the team to pick him.

Clarke had played for his home town Flin Flon Bombers in the Western Junior league, leading the league in assists and points in 67/68 and 68/69 and setting records for assists and points in 67/68. He was a two-way player who could take care of himself and was one of the league's most penalized players with 148 minutes in 59 games in 67/68 and 123 minutes in 59 games in 68/69.

In the fifth round the Flyers took left-winger Dave Schultz of the Sorel Blackhawks of the Quebec Junior league. Born in Waldheim, Saskatchewan, Schultz had played for the Swift Current Broncos of the Western Junior league in 67/68 and 68/69. In the sixth round the Flyers took Don Saleski, a right-winger from Moose Jaw, Saskatchewan.

Of the Flyers' 1969 draft picks, only Clarke, who turned 20 in August, graduated directly to the NHL. He had a very capable rookie season, producing 46 points in 76 games, but the team won only 17 of 76 games—only

6 on the road—and finished fifth in the West, missing the playoffs. Keith Allen had moved up from coaching to take over as general manager from Bud Poile during the season; Vic Stasiuk, a veteran Original Sixer from Lethbridge, Alberta, who had played with Detroit, Chicago and Boston, came from coaching the Quebec Aces farm club to run the Flyers bench.

On February 1, 1971, Allen cut two critical player deals. He sent Bernie Parent to Toronto, packaged with Philadelphia's second-round pick in the upcoming amateur draft (which the Leafs used to net defenceman Rick Kehoe) in exchange for goaltender Bruce Gamble, defenceman Mike Walton and Toronto's first-round pick in the same draft. With Walton as trade bait, Allen went after Rick MacLeish that same day. Boston had assigned MacLeish, their first-round draftee of 1970, to Oklahoma, as MacLeish was only 21 and the defending Stanley Cup champions were not hurting for quality centers. With starting centers like Phil Esposito, Derek Sanderson and Fred Stanfield, Boston decided MacLeish was expendable, and agreed to move him and Danny Schock to Philadelphia for Walton.

The Flyers were much improved in 70/71, winning 28 of 78 and finishing third in the realigned West Division. But the playoffs matched them with the division-leading Blackhawks. Four games later, another year passed with another early exit from the playoffs.

The most important change in the Flyers in 71/72 came not on the bench, but behind it. In November 1971 Allen replaced Vic Stasiuk with Fred "The Fog" Shero, a strategist who knew how to deploy the unique talents Allen had been assembling. Born in Winnipeg in 1925, Shero had graduated from the defensive corps of the St. James Canadiens of the Winnipeg Junior league to enter the New York Rangers' system in 1946. In 48/49 Shero was a full-time Ranger, and he was with the team in its Cinderella season of 49/50, when the underdog club, largely on the strength of Chuck Rayner's goaltending, made it to the Stanley Cup finals against the Red Wings. The dream season ended in overtime of the seventh game when a fluke shot eluded Rayner. Shero would recall that he spent all seven games of the finals riding the bench.

It was his last appearance in the NHL. He moved to the Cincinnati Mohawks of the American league, and in 1951 was part of a multi-player package that the Rangers sent to the Cleveland Barons of the American league in exchange for defenceman Hy Buller.

Shero spent three seasons with the Barons, and in 52/53 and 53/54 he was a key figure in their championship seasons. His best professional season as a player

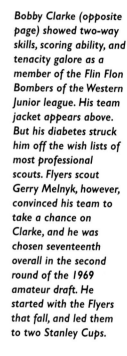

Bobby Clarke (opposite page) showed two-way skills, scoring ability, and tenacity galore as a member of the Flin Flon Bombers of the Western Junior league. His team jacket appears above. But his diabetes struck him off the wish lists of most professional scouts. Flyers scout Gerry Melnyk, however, convinced his team to take a chance on Clarke, and he was chosen seventeenth overall in the second round of the 1969 amateur draft. He started with the Flyers that fall, and led them to two Stanley Cups.

came in 53/54, when he was named to the second All Star team as he contributed an impressive 21 goals and 32 assists from the blueline, sixth best on the Barons club.

"He was a very fine competitor," recalls Johnny Bower, the Barons' star goaltender in those years. "He was one of the better defencemen in the American league at hip-checking, lining people up with his rear end and taking them into the boards. He didn't go around cross-checking people. He wasn't a fast skater, but he was a good guy in his own end, in clearing the front of the net for the goaltender. He hated to lose, just hated it. And he was a good team leader in the dressing room."

It surprises Bower to learn that Shero once boxed. "He was tough enough to be a good, solid defenceman. He didn't have to go looking for trouble, and I can't remember him ever being in a fight." Concludes Bower, "He was well liked, but quiet. It was pretty hard to get him fired up and mad at anything."

After Shero's 54/55 season was cut short at 37 games, probably by injury, Shero went home to Winnipeg to play for the Warriors of the minor-pro Western league in 55/56. Shero found the Western league game a bit rough, and blamed lax officiating.

A regular opponent of Shero in these years was defenceman Keith "Bingo" Allen, who as a Detroit Red Wing property earned two glances at the NHL. In 53/54 he appeared in 10 regular-season games, and

then dressed as a substitute forward for the Detroit playoff drive; his five games on the ice placed his name on the Stanley Cup. In 54/55 he was called up for 18 games, but wasn't used in the playoffs when Detroit won its second straight Cup.

Like Shero, Allen moved over from the American league to the Western league, playing in Edmonton and Brandon before settling in Seattle, where he became player-coach of the Totems in 56/57. In 57/58 Allen stopped playing to concentrate on coaching and was promoted to the general manager's job as well. He almost single-handedly revived the Totems franchise, making it a winner and hockey a priority among Seattle sports fans.

W hile Allen was making a career for himself in Western league management, Shero was moving into coaching. In 57/58 he and the Winnipeg Warriors' goaltender of 56/57, future Boston Bruin Eddie Johnston, lit out for Shawinigan Falls, Quebec, to join the minor-pro Cataracts of the Quebec league. The Cataracts finished second overall and won the league championship, but the team was unable to secure a sponsorship agreement with an NHL club and folded at the end of the season. Shero was on the road again—back west, to Moose Jaw, where the Canucks were entering play in the Saskatchewan Junior league. The Canucks had hoped to hire Shero's former

Season	Finish	Record (W-L-T)	Points %	Awards (winners & runners-up)	All-Stars	Playoffs
72/73	2nd Div 7th OA	37-30-11	54.5	ART ROSS: Clarke RU HART: Clarke CALDER: Barber RU PEARSON: Clarke	2ND TEAM: Clarke (C)	Lost SC semifinal 4-1 to Montreal
73/74	1st Div 2nd OA	50-16-12	71.8	HART: Parent RU CONN SMYTHE: Parent VEZINA: Parent JACK ADAMS: Shero	1ST TEAM: Parent (G) 2ND TEAM: Ashbee (D), Clarke (C)	Won SC final 4-2 over Boston
74/75	1st Div 1st Conf 1st OA	51-18-11	70.6	HART: Clarke CONN SMYTHE: Parent VEZINA: Parent	1ST TEAM: Parent (G), Clarke (C)	Won SC final 4-2 over Buffalo
75/76	1st Div 1st Conf 2nd OA	51-13-16	73.8	ART ROSS: Clarke RU HART: Clarke CONN SMYTHE: Leach	1ST TEAM: Clarke (C), Barber (LW) 2ND TEAM: Leach (RW)	Lost SC final 4-0 to Montreal

Ranger teammate Chuck Rayner (a Saskatchewan native) as their coach, but the deal fell through, and so they turned to Shero.

The team finished last, and Shero was again on the move. The Rangers assigned him to their International league farm club in Minnesota, the St. Paul Saints, for 59/60, and there he did a splendid job with an odds-and-sods bunch, winning the league championship. The assignment brought a hint of his NHL future, as the team picked up the nickname "Fighting Saints," and a story in the November 6, 1960, issue of *The Hockey News* described them as a "rough and tumble" outfit.

Shero settled in as the Rangers' man in Minneapolis/St. Paul, which he had first haunted as a player with the Twin-Cities' American league club in 48/49. He coached the Saints through 62/63; when the Central Professional league was formed in 63/64 as an NHL development loop, the Saints departed the International league as the New York Rangers established a CPHL affiliate in town, the St. Paul Rangers. Shero became its coach; across town, Harry Sinden was serving as player-coach of Boston's Central league farm operation, the Minneapolis Bruins.

In 64/65, Shero guided the St. Paul Rangers to the league championship, despite financial difficulties which saw New York step in at mid-season to keep the club afloat. Shero's team, renamed the Minnesota Rangers, compiled the best regular-season record in 65/66 and lost the best-of-seven final 4-3 to the Tulsa Oilers.

The Rangers moved their sponsorship to the Omaha Knights, and Shero went along with the deal. After the Knights lost the Central League finals 4-1 to the Oklahoma City Blazers, the Rangers then sent Shero to Buffalo, to coach their Bisons farm club. Shero was there for three seasons, winning the league championship in the last Bison campaign, 69/70, before the club was folded in favour of the new NHL franchise, the Sabres.

Despite his Central league and American league successes, Shero garnered no invitations to coach in the NHL. There appeared to be no chance of him graduating to the Rangers. Emile Francis was solidly established as coach and general manager, and NHL teams then didn't have assistant coaches. When Shero's Bisons folded after their championship season, the job of coach and general manager for the new Sabres team went to Punch Imlach, who had been dumped by the Maple Leafs in the spring of 1969. Shero moved back to the Central league and the Omaha Knights, the league's defending champions. He guided them to another championship and was named the league's coach of the year. Finally, Philadelphia and the NHL came calling. Stasiuk was out and Shero was in. He had just turned 46 when the 71/72 season began. Shero's new job put him in contact with a number of familiar faces from his minor-pro days, and the circle would grow larger.

On January 28, 1972, Keith Allen made a seven-player trade with the Los Angeles Kings. The main prizes for the Flyers were right-winger Bill "Cowboy" Flett and left-winger Ross Lonsberry. Flett, who hailed from Vermilion, Alberta, had been hobbled by injuries throughout his career, which he began as a Maple Leaf property in the 1960s. The Kings had acquired Flett from Toronto in the 1967 expansion draft, and *The Sporting News* had named him its rookie of the year in the West Division in 67/68, when he scored 26 goals. Though he hadn't scored that many in a season since, when he was healthy he was worth having. Lonsberry, who had enjoyed a 53-point season in L.A. in 70/71, was yet another westerner, and another alumnus of the Bruins' development system, to come into the Flyers lineup. The deal also gave the Flyers veteran center Ed Joyal, an Edmontonian who had broken into the NHL with Detroit in 62/63, and rookie defenceman Jean Potvin, older brother of Denis.

The 71/72 season was a setback for the Flyers. Total

wins dropped to 26 and the Flyers fell to fifth in the West, missing the playoffs. At the amateur draft in June 1972, the Flyers picked Bill Barber in the first round and Tom Bladon in the second round. A star center with the Kitchener Rangers of the Ontario Junior league, Barber had an older brother, John, who had played 19 games for Shero on the championship 69/70 Bisons. Once in the Flyers family, Bill Barber was converted to left wing by Shero. Defenceman Bladon was a 20-year-old star of Edmonton Junior hockey when picked by the Flyers.

In 72/73, the Flyers began to gel as a powerhouse and a phenomenon. Shero became the first NHL coach to hire his own assistant. He brought aboard Mike Nykoluk, a former American league star who had been league MVP while with Hershey in 66/67, to tend to the club's offensive weaknesses. Dave Schultz and Don Saleski, who had each appeared in one regular-season game with the team in 71/72, joined the lineup. Playing for the Salem Rebels in 69/70 with Saleski after being drafted by the Flyers, Schultz had amassed an Eastern-league record of 356 penalty minutes in 67 games (along with 32 goals and 37 assists). In 71 games with the Richmond Robins in 71/72, Schultz set an American league penalty record: 392 minutes.

On December 14, 1972, the Flyers cut a key deal with St. Louis to get Shero a prized pupil, André "Moose" Dupont, a six-foot, 200-pound defenceman from Trois-Rivières. Dupont was with the Montreal Junior Canadiens when drafted by the New York Rangers in 1969. He was assigned to Omaha in the Central league, where he was named rookie of the year. In 70/71 Shero was Omaha's coach, and Dupont recorded 15 goals and 24 assists, seventh best on the team, in 54 games. He also led the league in penalty minutes in the regular season (308) and in the playoffs (75). Dupont was named the league's top defenceman and co-winner of the MVP award as he and Shero won a league championship together.

Shero admired Dupont's work ethic, his determination to keep learning and make the most of his limited ability at a time when free-wheeling playmakers like Bobby Orr and Brad Park were the models of defensive greatness. New York, however, decided they could do without him and traded him to St. Louis. To get him for Shero, the Flyers packaged defenceman Brent Hughes and right-winger Pierre Plante and received in return Dupont and the Blues' third-round 1973 draft pick.

On March 5, 1973, with the playoffs approaching, the Flyers acquired center Terry Crisp. As a Boston property, Crisp had played on the Niagara Falls Flyers Junior club with Dornhoefer, and had been with Dornhoefer on the Minneapolis Bruins, playing against Shero's St. Paul Rangers, in the early 1960s. In 65/66 and 66/67, Crisp had been with the Oklahoma City Blazers, making him a teammate of Lonsberry, Favell and Parent when the Blazers defeated Shero's Omaha Knights for the Central league title.

Crisp was taken from Boston by St. Louis in the 1967 expansion draft, but played for Shero's Buffalo Bisons when they won the American league title in 69/70. Having been with the Blues for the three seasons they reached the finals, Crisp was one of the few Flyers with any Stanley Cup experience. Drafted by the New York Islanders in the 1972 expansion draft, Crisp was sprung from Long Island by the Flyers, who surrendered defenceman Jean Potvin and a player to be named—Glen Irwin, who never played in the majors.

In 72/73 the Flyers took their great leap forward. Wins jumped from 26 to 37, which allowed them to leapfrog over Minnesota, St. Louis and Pittsburgh into second place in the West Division, eight points behind Chicago. Goal production went from 200 to 296, fourth best in the league, behind Montreal, Boston and New York. The Flyers became the first NHL club to have two centers with more than 100 points. Clarke finished second in the scoring race behind Phil Esposito with 37 goals and 67 assists and won the Hart Trophy as the player most valuable to his team. MacLeish, the Bruins' castoff, had a tremendous season, finishing fourth in league scoring with 50 goals and 50 assists; like Maurice Richard in 44/45, MacLeish was only 23 and just getting started on his NHL career when he reached the 50-goal mark. The Flyers became the fourth team in league history, after Chicago in 68/69, Boston in 70/71 and Montreal in 71/72, to have five 30-goal scorers in one season. In addition to Clarke and MacLeish, Flett tallied 43, and Barber and Dornhoefer 30.

But these milestones paled in comparison to what was seen as a more noteworthy accomplishment: the Flyers set a new team penalty mark of 1,754 minutes. Schultz led the way with 259, and close behind were Kelly (236), Dupont (215) and Saleski (205).

The 72/73 season was when the Flyers became the scourge of professional hockey, when they became Exhibit A in any discussion of how the game was lurching into the gutter. The low point of the Flyers' season came in Vancouver on December 29, when a swarm of Flyers went into the stands after a fan who had grabbed Don Saleski's hair in the middle of a fight. The Flyer stampede brought down criminal convictions on several Flyers for causing a disturbance, fighting, and assaulting a police officer.

The 72/73 season ended with the Flyers losing in the semifinals 4-1 to Montreal, although the first two games ended in overtime. Shero had virtually the entire team lineup that would win him Stanley Cups. He had Van Impe, Joe Watson, Barry Ashbee, Andre Dupont and Tom Bladon on defence. In the 1972 draft the Flyers had taken Joe Watson's brother Jim, who had been named the top defenceman in the Western Junior league as a Calgary Centennial in 71/72. Jim Watson had come up from Richmond for four games in 72/73, and was ready to join the lineup full-time.

At center Shero had Bobby Clarke, Rick MacLeish, Terry Crisp and Bill Clement. Coming on stream was Orest Kindrachuk, a captain of the Saskatoon Blades of

Brawling his way to the top, Dave "The Hammer" Schultz set penalty-minute records in the Eastern, American and National leagues. In 74/75 he accounted for more than one-quarter of all Philadelphia penalty minutes as he set a new league record of 472 minutes.

the Western Junior league in 70/71 who was playing for the San Diego Gulls of the Western Hockey League in 71/72 when the Flyers picked him up. He became one of Shero's favourite Flyers, along with Clarke, Parent and Dupont, admired by his coach for his willingness to take a hit in the corner to make a play, leaving the glory of scoring to linemates.

On left wing, the Flyers had Ross Lonsberry, Bill Barber, Dave Schultz and Bob Kelly; on right wing, Simon Nolet, Don Saleski and Bill Flett. Forward positions weren't carved in stone, as Shero liked to experiment with players' roles, but the team had the right number of bodies with the right mix of talent. Except in goal.

In 72/73, the Flyers allowed 256 goals, the most in the franchise's history. It was a mediocre performance—at 3.28 goals per game, it was the same as the league's average team GA mark. The Flyers' offence, at 3.79 goals per game, was about half a goal better than both the team and league GA. A championship team as a rule needs a much higher margin between the average number of goals it scores per game and the average number it allows.

Doug Favell had turned in a respectable season, with a personal GA of 2.83, but he had only played 44 games. Shero and Allen needed a goaltender who could carry the bulk of the season and give the team more breathing room in its goal margin. And they knew just where to get one.

Shero had been watching his team's netminding future struggling all season across town, with the Philadelphia Blazers of the WHA. He was former Flyer original Bernie Parent, who had played with Favell on the Oklahoma City Blazers team that denied Shero's Omaha Knights the 66/67 Central league championship.

Parent had jumped to the WHA from the Leafs in 1972, lured by a promise from the Miami Screaming Eagles of a five-year $750,000 contract that would also provide him with a new house, boat and car every year; in Toronto, Parent had been making about $40,000. The Miami franchise folded before the first WHA season could begin, and Parent signed instead in June 1972 with the WHA's Philadelphia franchise. He struggled with the Blazers; his GA went from 2.56 with the Leafs to 3.61 with the Blazers. "I used to watch poor Bernie in a WHA game," Shero would recall. "And hell, he had to stop 45 shots a game. Rather than hurting him, the WHA made him a better goalie. He'd never seen so many shots in an NHL game."

In the playoffs against the Cleveland Crusaders (who had the Bruins' two-time Stanley Cup hero Gerry Cheevers in goal) in the spring of 1973, Parent refused to play any more after losing the series' opening game in overtime. Having washed his hands of the WHA, Parent was ready to return to the NHL, and Shero wanted him back in a Flyers uniform. On May 15, 1973, after the Flyers had lost their semifinal series,

they sent their first pick in the upcoming amateur draft to Toronto, with future considerations, in exchange for the Leafs' NHL rights to Parent and their second-round pick. The Flyers used the second-round pick to secure defenceman Larry Goodenough. The Parent deal was finalized on July 27, when Doug Favell was shipped to Toronto as the future consideration.

In his first game back as a Flyer, Parent let in seven goals in 12 minutes, and Shero had to pull him. From then on, however, Parent was a defensive mainstay and goaltending ironman. He appeared in 74 of the Flyers' 80 games in 73/74 and recorded a 1.89 average with 12 shutouts. He made the first All Star team and shared the Vezina with Tony Esposito after the Flyers and the Blackhawks both allowed only 164 goals.

Penalty-wise, it was the same old Flyers. The team amassed 1,750 minutes, 600 more than any other club. Schultz led the way, brawling to a league-record 348 minutes. But the Flyers didn't need to rely on a single player like Schultz to maintain their reputation as the toughest outfit in the league. If you fought one Flyer, went their motto, you fought the whole team.

The 73/74 finals were a fitting confrontation between the Big Bad Bruins and the Broad Street Bullies—the Original Six team that had defined toughness in the first expansion years versus the expansion team that emulated their basic style, using many players who had once been part of their own system.

The Bruins set the league's offensive benchmark, leading all teams with 349 goals, 76 more than the Flyers, and sweeping the top four places in the scoring race. (Clarke was fifth.) Defensively, though, the Flyers were a much tighter team than Boston, allowing 57 fewer goals.

Shero's game strategy honed in on Bobby Orr. Before the first game he wrote on the dressing-room chalkboard, "One man cannot beat 17." He had his players take the game to Orr, make him carry and handle the puck. Shero already felt that the Bruins asked too much of Orr, who had finished second in scoring to Esposito with 32 goals and 90 assists. If he had been coaching him, Shero would note, he would have limited Orr's role to about 40 assists. The idea was to wear Orr down, not by pounding him senseless (Orr had a pugnacity that deterred the strategy, anyway) but by making him play a bigger role in the game than he should.

The Flyers lost the opener 3-2 and were losing the second game 2-0 after one period when they rebounded to win 3-2 in overtime. Shero's strategy of keying on Orr appeared to work. After winning game two, the Flyers took control, earning 4-1 and 4-2 victories that put them a game away from becoming the first expansion club to win the Cup. Boston got back in the series with a 5-1 win. In game six Rick MacLeish scored at 14:48 of the first period to give him 13 goals, the best effort of the playoffs, and that was all the scoring the 73/74 post-season would see. The Flyers hung on to win 1-0 and the series four games to two.

The Flyers had defeated an offensive machine by limiting them to 2.17 goals per game while scoring 2.5 in response. Parent, who posted a 2.02 GA with two shutouts over 17 playoff games, won the Conn Smythe Trophy as the series MVP. *Sport Magazine*, in naming him the league MVP, presented him with an AMC Matador. Taking pity on his parsimonious coach, who was creaking around in a junker Maverick, Parent instructed his agent to give the car to Shero.

It was a strange world, Shero himself realized, in which a player gave a car to his coach. Parent's gesture was understandable; his return to Philadelphia under Shero had made him a champion and a star. But the ges-

ture also served to acknowledge Shero's importance to the success of the team. Beyond key players like Parent and Clarke, Shero was the reason for the Flyers' success.

Shero was loquacious, funny and indifferent to giving offence when volunteering opinions. He was also a wellspring of contradictions. "Don't you say you understand me," Shero said to his wife Mariette in the presence of reporter Dan Proudfoot in 1974. "I don't understand myself, so how in the world are you supposed to understand me?"

He was both a gregarious conversationalist and a lone wolf. In the late 1950s, he was an instructor at a respected hockey clinic run by the University of North

Drafted seventh overall by Philadelphia in 1972, Bill Barber won the Calder Trophy in 72/73. From 72/73 to 81/82, he scored 30 or more goals in every season but one. Barber reached the 50-goal plateau in 75/76, when he was named to the first All Star team.

In 1970, the Boston Bruins chose Reg Leach and Rick MacLeish (above) third and fourth overall in the amateur draft. Neither could find a place in the Bruins' championship roster, and both ended up in Philadelphia. In 72/73, his first full season with the Flyers, MacLeish produced 50 goals and 50 assists.

Dakota. Glenn Hall was one of his fellow instructors. "He was always quiet," the Hall of Fame goaltender recalls. "Freddie was somewhat of a loner. He'd be sitting right with you talking, and then all of a sudden he'd just be gone. You wouldn't even see him until the next morning."

He appeared to be engaged in a fundamental internal struggle over the style of hockey his team played and the style he wanted to be known for. His relationship with violence was confounding. He volunteered that he had boxed as a youth (a profile during his minor-pro coaching days stated he had once held Manitoba's bantam and flyweight titles), but happily gave it up for hockey at age 20. He avowed that one of his big problems as a player was that he wasn't physical enough.

Shero had come out of Winnipeg with fellow defenceman Jackie Gordon (who went on to coach and manage the Minnesota North Stars in the 1970s) to play in the Rangers' system, and he recalled how "Jackie used to drive me crazy telling me to be more aggressive. That just wasn't my nature. I never could hit a guy unless he hit me first."

Shero admitted to picking a fight with Gordie Howe, a foolish move as Howe almost pounded him

senseless. After being knocked down for the third time, Shero was advised by the Wings' Sid Abel to stay down, otherwise Howe was going to kill him.

Shero was loath to give much credit to the physical aspect of the Flyers' game plan, and sometimes went to absurd lengths to deny it. He did once allow that the Flyers style was "controlled mayhem," and in an interview with Billy Libby of *The Hockey News*, published in February 1975, admitted, "If we can, we'll intimidate our rivals. We try to soften them up, then pounce on them. If they can stand up to us, fine. If not, that's their trouble. I don't see it as dirty tactics. There are lots of ways to play this game. This is our way. It's a rough game. Our way works. But I swear I have never told a player to attack another player. In fact I have told my players if they ever hear me saying something like this, they can break a stick over my skull. I ask only that they play aggressively."

Most galling to Shero's critics were his assertions that he was a student and admirer of the Russian game, considered the antithesis of Flyers goonery. Depending on when he was making the claim, Shero had read either hundreds or millions of times the strategy book written by Anatoli Tarasov, the architect of the Soviet system.

Shero was in fact a devoted student of the Russian game, and had been since about 1960. During the 73/74 Stanley Cup finals against Boston, Shero experienced an outburst of Tarasov worship. After the Flyers won game two to tie the series, Shero contacted Loyola College in Montreal and booked himself into a three-week course in the Soviet Union on sport and physical education. It was as if, while driving a bulldozer, Shero had been gripped by the urge to learn to handle a Maserati. The Flyers won three of the next four games to take the Stanley Cup, and in late May Shero and 99 other students of the game were studying at the feet of the master, Tarasov. Shero admired the creativity of Russian playmaking, though he thought their system was weak defensively, and in preparing to play Boston that spring he had studied films of the 1972 Canada-Russia series to come up with a successful penalty-killing strategy. (His strategy: shifts of no more than 60 seconds to keep legs fresh.)

Shero was fully prepared to criticize the North American style of play. "I do not believe in hockey as it's been played in North America the past 20 years," he pronounced after winning the Stanley Cup, a few days before leaving on his trip to the Soviet Union. "To me, it's based on all sorts of unsound theories. We give up possession of the puck too much. A man gets to center and if he has no play, he dumps it into the other team's zone and hopes to get it back by forechecking. By next season I want my team to be using the Russian system, which is to retreat and try to form another play, rather than give the puck away."

Shero might have wanted to do that, but his own basic set of 16 do's and don'ts for his players had none of the flair of the Russian system he admired. It was no-nonsense lunch-bucket hockey, molded to the skills of tier-two players who needed to follow a disciplined game plan. Don't think, just do, was the method behind his strategies. Don't go offside on a three-on-two or a two-on-one. Don't make a diagonal pass in your own end, unless you're 100 percent certain. Never throw a puck blindly out from behind your opponent's net. And though he had nothing good to say about dump-and-chase hockey while on his way to Russia, it remained a cornerstone of the Flyers' game. Shero rule number nine directed that a puck carrier who finds himself across center ice with no room to skate and no one to pass to "must shoot it in." No stylish retreating and regrouping was allowed in the Shero playbook. If people want to see fancy skating, he once said, they should go to the Ice Capades.

There were a few important rules missing from Shero's list, rules best described as the unwritten ones. Unwritten rule number one: intimidate the opposition. Shero knew he didn't have enough talent for his players to prevail in one-on-one situations, much less play in the tightly choreographed Russian passing style. He could, in fact, be disarmingly frank about their individual mediocrity. Approaching the end of the 73/74 season, Shero turned his attention to the Canadiens and offered to Jim Proudfoot of *The Toronto Star*, "Talentwise this team doesn't compare to Montreal. Aside from Bobby Clarke and Bernie Parent, we don't have a man who could make their squad. But when we have to beat them, we do." Montreal, he explained, relied too much on individual talent. The Flyers' system required and received self-sacrifice from its players.

To win a game, the Flyers needed to create man-advantage situations, and one way to do that was to win the battles in the corners and around the crease. Opponents had to be afraid to go into a corner after the puck with a Flyer. By the same token, Flyers players had to be unafraid to go into the corner and take the hits in order to create opportunities. Shero understood that stickhandling was not to be confused with puck control, that playmaking was not just about slick passing. It was about creating situations in which the Flyers momentarily had a numerical advantage on which they could capitalize.

Unwritten Shero rule number two: fight to earn your opponent's respect, because in hockey respect is fear, and fear leads to puck control. In the Flyers' heyday there were definite advantages to using fighting to establish control of the ice and the game. Most important, it takes two to fight, and in the days before the instigator rule was introduced to rein in *provocateurs*, a brawl usually resulted in a pair of penalized players. Hence, the Flyers suffered no disadvantages in manpower after Schultz pounded on an opponent. And if a Flyer happened to take a quality player into the penalty box with him, so much the better. Of course, on a team that amassed 3,351 penalty minutes in its two championship seasons, there were going to be times when it played short-handed. Like the Bruins, the Flyers were going to have to be outstanding penalty-killers, and in studying the Bruins system Shero made them masters of the art of short-handed goals.

For all the talk, much of it from Shero himself, about tactical sophistication, the Flyers' game was built on desire and discipline. Shero's greatest achievement was as a motivator. He wrote daily aphorisms on the dressing-room chalkboard that often had players scratching their heads, but the messages got through. A typical one read: "A winner says, 'There ought to be a better way to do it.' A loser says, 'That's the way it has always been done around here.'" And so Shero got across the idea of a system, a team-focused concept in an era when players looking for scoring bonuses wanted to go solo. Other teams with as much or more talent than the Flyers were floundering while "Shero's Heroes" were getting their pictures taken with the Stanley Cup.

In many ways, the Shero of Philadelphia was the Shero of St. Paul 15 years earlier. Having come out of a two-season playing spell in the Western league in which he saw aggressive teams excel in an atmosphere of *laissez-faire* officiating, Shero had taken a mixed bag of St. Paul players, turned them into the "Fighting Saints" and won a league championship. When brought to Philadelphia, Shero was handed the ingredients needed

Bernie Parent (who wore this jersey) was a Boston Bruins cast-off who polished his craft playing with Jacques Plante in Toronto. After a traumatic season with the Philadelphia Blazers of the WHA, he joined the Flyers for the 73/74 season. He won two consecutive Vezinas, was named to two consecutive first All Star teams, and was awarded two consecutive Conn Smythe Trophies as playoff MVP. Without his goaltending, Philadelphia's Stanley Cup wins would have been impossible.

for a return of those Fighting Saints: a general manager who had learned the ropes in the Western league and had selected players accordingly, a group of players who could be sold a team concept, and a league whose regulations (or more accurately, its enforcement of them) tolerated an intimidating style.

A large part of the credit for Philadelphia's success was due to its captain, Bobby Clarke. He was talented, inspiring, indefatigable and, when he had to be, nasty. As a Flin Flon Bomber, Clarke had played at a chaotic time in western Junior hockey, when NHL expansion and the elimination of sponsored amateur teams had created a schism in the Canadian Junior hockey scene. For several seasons, fractiousness within the Canadian amateur hockey system meant that western Junior teams were ineligible to compete for the national championship, the Memorial Cup. In 68/69 Flin Flon had to settle for a championship series of sorts with the St. Thomas Barons of the Western Ontario Junior league under the auspices of the shortlived Canadian Hockey Association. The play of Clarke and his teammates, however, was so aggressive that, trailing three games to one in the best-of-seven series, St. Thomas refused to play them any more. The series was awarded by default to the Bombers.

In the championship season of 73/74, Clarke was joined on the second All Star team by defenceman Barry Ashbee, while Parent made the first team. There wasn't much to do in the way of improving the Flyers for 74/75. Ashbee, however, had had his career ended during the 73/74 season by an accidental injury that cost him the sight in one eye. Shero added him to the coaching staff (and the Flyers retired his number) and

brought Larry Goodenough up from Richmond. Bill Flett was dealt to Toronto after the 73/74 Cup win, but the big deal for the Flyers following the victory was for Bobby Clarke's old Flin Flon Bombers linemate, Reggie Leach, who led the Western Junior league in goals in 67/68 and, after missing most of 68/69 with injuries, in goals and points in 69/70. After being named the league MVP in 69/70, Leach was drafted third overall by Boston. He seemed to have just what the Bruins were looking for—lots of points, and penalty minutes to go with them: 208 minutes in 59 games in 67/68, 168 in 57 games in 69/70. But in 23 games with the Bruins in 70/71, Leach produced only 6 points and stayed entirely clear of the penalty box. In February 1972 the Bruins dealt him to the lowly California Golden Seals, along with defencemen Rick Smith and Bob Stewart, to get the tough, high-scoring defenceman Carol Vadnais and right-winger Don O'Donoghue.

Leach still wasn't playing up to the potential of his Junior days, and while he would never collect penalty minutes quite like he did in Flin Flon, he was a sniper whose best NHL effort to date was only 23 goals with the Seals in 72/73. On May 24, 1974, Leach became a Flyer. Philadelphia gave up Larry Wright, a center out of Regina who had played only 9 games for the Flyers in 72/73 and none in the championship season, their first pick in the summer's draft, and a promising right-winger, Al MacAdam. MacAdam had a long NHL career ahead of him, but the Flyers guessed correctly that he was worth giving up to see if reuniting Leach with Clarke could help the Flyers make the leap into the four goal-per-game realm of the most powerful offensive teams.

Leach was an instant success in Philadelphia, contributing 45 goals and 33 assists, but the Flyers' offence didn't leap to new heights. Goals production increased, from 3.5 to 3.66, as the league overall scored more goals, up from 3.2 to 3.43. With 293 total goals, though, the Flyers weren't close to the league's most offensively dangerous teams. Five other clubs—Montreal (374), Pittsburgh (326), Buffalo (354), Boston (345) and the Rangers (319)—outscored them. But the Flyers still had Bernie. Playing 68 of 80 games, Parent recorded a GA of 2.03 with 12 shutouts to win another Vezina. "When Parent is out there," Shero once said, "we know we can win games we have no business winning."

The 74/75 Stanley Cup was the first all-expansion final, pitting the Flyers against the Buffalo Sabres. A 1970 expansion club, the Sabres had improved wins from 32 to 49 in 74/75 as they tied with the Flyers and the Canadiens for the overall regular-season lead. The Sabres were a stylish, fast-breaking young outfit that played a wide-open game, scoring 354 goals while allowing 240. Their signature line was "The French Connection" of Richard Martin, Gilbert Perreault and

René Robert. Where the 73/74 final between the Bruins and Flyers had been a contest between like-minded clubs, the 74/75 final was a confrontation of two entirely different styles: a grinding, disciplined, dump-and-chase game versus a fleet-footed, explosive offensive system. For Flyers detractors, it was a contest that could determine which style would rule: whether might would continue to be right in the professional game.

The outcome, 4-2 for Philadelphia, does not tell how close the young Sabres came to winning. Philadelphia took the opening games 4-1 and 2-1 at home, then the Sabres won both their home games, 5-4 and 4-2. A 5-1 defeat at the Spectrum in Philadelphia put the Sabres to the wall, and they came up short in game six at home, losing 2-0. The star of the series was Parent, without whom the Flyers could not have won. His goaltending during Buffalo powerplays was electrifying, and there was no question he deserved his second straight Conn Smythe Trophy after recording a GA of 1.89 (as in 73/74) and producing 4 shutouts in 17 playoff games.

The Flyers looked perfectly capable of making it three Cups in a row in 75/76. Leach got even better, scoring 61 goals, and Clarke finished second in scoring, 6 points behind Guy Lafleur, with Barber in fourth, with 50 goals and 62 assists. The team's goals-against was bested only by the Canadiens' Ken Dryden and the Islanders' Billy Smith and Chico Resch. In scoring, the team led the league for the first time. Its scoring margin was very healthy, about the same as in 74/75—1.74, with goals-for of 4.35 and goals-against of 2.61. Minimal changes were made to the lineup.

The Flyers showed their championship form in an exhibition match against the Soviet Red Army in January 1976, billed as the ultimate clash of hockey styles. Halfway through the first period, Ed Van Impe nailed Valery Kharlamov with a body check that sent the entire Soviet team to the dressing room in protest. They returned when league president Clarence Campbell explained if they didn't play, they wouldn't get paid, and lost 4-1. Far from a showcase for goonery, the game showed the Flyers to be a first-rate hockey club.

The triumph of finesse promised but not delivered by the Sabres in the spring of 1975 and the Soviet Red Army in January 1976 came from the Canadiens in the spring of 1976. No game was a rout—the scores were 4-3, 2-1, 3-2 and 5-3—but in sweeping the Flyers the Canadiens were firmly in control. Their defence, players like Larry Robinson, Guy Lapointe and Serge Savard, were too big and too strong to fight or knock around, and their front line players were too fast and too good to throw off their game. Most important, with Dryden in goal and Parent sidelined, replaced by Wayne Stephenson, the 75/76 final was no contest, and for the next four seasons this team would rule the league.

The Flyers did not vanish. They remained a strong and dangerous club, but by the time they again reached the finals, in 79/80, they were completely transformed. After the Flyers lost to Boston in the 77/78 semifinal Fred Shero quit and was immediately hired as coach and general manager of the Rangers, almost 20 years after first becoming a coach in the New York system. Bobby Clarke was publicly angry with Shero, accusing him of having been dishonest with his players, of plotting a move to New York while coaching them in the semifinals against the Bruins.

Shero appeared to have been at the end of his rope with the club. He would grouse about Flyers owner Ed Snider meddling in player affairs, about not having true control of the team, which was what the Rangers deal gave him as general manager. In May 1978, with the Flyers on the way to dropping their semifinal series with the Bruins 4-1, Shero passed out a message to players after a practice. His inspirational tone had given way to the sarcasm of a condescending superior:

> There are six kinds of athletes:
> A—con man athlete
> B—the hyper-anxious athlete
> C—the athlete who resists coaching
> D—the success phobic athlete
> E—the injury-prone athlete
> F—the depression-prone athlete
> Dear fellow workers, please circle the appropriate letter so that I may be better able to serve you.

Shero showed that his coaching ability wasn't limited to the particular mix of talents the Flyers presented. In his debut season in New York, he got the Rangers into their first finals since 71/72. New York won the first game, only to have Montreal sweep the next four. Shero's coaching efforts bookended the Canadiens four-year reign of the NHL. The first win had come against Shero's Flyers, the last against Shero's Rangers.

The Rangers stumbled in 79/80, while the Flyers made the finals, against the Islanders. Seven players were left from the Flyers' championship days: Bobby Clarke, Rick MacLeish, Bob Kelly, Bill Barber, André Dupont, Jim Watson and Reg Leach. Bernie Parent certainly would have been there, but an accidental stick in the eye from a Shero Ranger during a Flyers home game on February 17, 1979, had ended his career. The Flyers lost the 79/80 final to the Islanders on an overtime goal in game six by Bob Nystrom. By the time the Flyers made another return to the finals, in 84/85 against the Edmonton Oilers, no one was left from the mid-1970s championship teams, Clarke having retired at the end of the 83/84 season.

By then Shero was finished as a coaching force. He had stepped down in November 1980 from his Rangers job, admitting to a drinking problem, but his main problem was stomach cancer, which had gone undetected during his Flyers years.

A man who once avowed he hated to fight, Fred Shero fought it until his death in 1990. ○

NEW YORK ISLANDERS
The Eighties

BUILT FOR SPEED

DRAFTING CAREFULLY, WAITING PATIENTLY, BILL TORREY ASSEMBLED A CUP-WINNING MACHINE FOR NASSAU COUNTY

he architect of the New York Islanders, winners of four straight Stanley Cups in the early 1980s and one of the classiest, most disciplined and most exciting clubs ever to win or lose in the NHL, was a fellow in a bow tie named Bill Torrey.

As a kid growing up near Montreal's Forum, Torrey would sneak into the hockey palace to watch the Canadiens practise during their string of marvellous seasons in the 1950s. These were the Canadiens managed by Frank Selke and coached by Toe Blake, the Canadiens who played in ten straight Cup finals and won six of them. There wasn't a better hockey operation around to spy on, or to be inspired by.

After graduating from St. Lawrence University in upstate New York, during which he played hockey on the school team, the business and psychology major took a job with NBC in New York. His dad was urging him to come back to Montreal when he announced that he had a new job—he was going to work as the business manager and promotions czar for the American league's Pittsburgh Hornets hockey franchise. The Hornets had closed down in 1956 when the rickety Duquesne Garden, a converted streetcar barn, was torn down; now they were being revived for the 61/62 season.

The senior Torrey was dumfounded. He demanded: You call that a job?

It was a job that kept him working in hockey's managerial back rooms until the NHL expanded in 67/68. One of the blessed new franchise sites was Oakland, California, and Torrey became the Oakland Seals' executive vice president in 68/69. The Seals had a good second season, then went into a tailspin. Torrey would remember having to deal with about half a dozen different owners in his brief spell with the team. The cream of the crop was the flamboyant Charles Finley, who took over in 1970. "Charlie O" had exciting new ideas about running a hockey franchise in the Bay

RIGHT: Mike Bossy (left) looks on as linemate Bryan Trottier hoists the Stanley Cup in celebration of the Islanders' third consecutive win in 1982. This victory was a four-game sweep of the Vancouver Canucks. BELOW: General manager Bill Torrey's trademark bow tie. "The thing I liked about them was that they were small. You can fold them up and put them in your pocket. You can't spill on them."

area. "He had us trying out white skates, then green and gold skates," Torrey recalled. "And he wanted a mascot, a seal. Not a guy in a costume, a live seal out on the ice." After nine months of Finley, Torrey quit, and set up an advertising and PR company, located in the Pittsburgh Civic Arena.

Expansion rolled bravely on in the NHL, and in a bid to give the new WHA a hard time in the coveted New York market, the league awarded to Roy Boe a Long Island franchise that would begin playing in 72/73, just as the WHA was beginning operations with a team of its own, the New York Raiders. Torrey was 37 when hired by Boe as his general manager.

The pressure on expansion franchises to find a shortcut to success was enormous, and no franchise felt more pressure than Long Island. The new team would be competing for fans with the WHA's Raiders and the established New York Rangers, Stanley Cup finalists in 71/72. When he showed up, Torrey was reminded by a member of the press that the Rangers hadn't won the Cup in more than 30 years. "My timetable for winning doesn't extend quite that long," Torrey replied.

Not that he showed himself to be in a hurry. Many of the NHL franchises that had arrived since 67/68 had sought quick gains by trading away draft choices to get veteran players who could ensure a few wins and put fans in the seats. Over the long term, however, it was a disastrous strategy. A savvy dealmaker like Montreal's Sam Pollock, who had learned the ropes at Frank Selke's right hand, seeded the new clubs with castoffs, gathering in return first-round draft picks; when the clubs with which he traded still finished deep in the standings, the draft pick he had secured from them allowed him to choose high and

Al Arbour

ISLANDERS SCORING
74/75 to 83/84

- ■ **Islanders goals-against**
- ◨ **League-leading goals-against**
- ▬ **Islanders goals-for**
- ◨ **League-leading scoring**
- **League scoring average**
- 80/ 81 **Stanley Cup win**

well. After winning the 70/71 Stanley Cup, for example, Pollock was still able to draft first overall that June, securing Guy Lafleur.

The Islanders began by taking from the expansion draft a grab-bag of league spare parts that served to fill the roster. Torrey's first pick was goaltender Billy Smith of Los Angeles. Smith had been drafted by the Kings in 1970 and had won the American league championship in 70/71 when assigned to Springfield. When the Kings acquired Rogatien Vachon from Montreal in November 1971, Smith was made expendable. A surprise acquisition was the classy and versatile checker Ed Westfall, whom the Bruins had decided to leave unprotected after their Stanley Cup win that spring. Torrey made Westfall his captain, gaining a quality player who could lead by example on and off the ice. Westfall would retire after the 78/79 season. Of the original Islanders acquired in the expansion draft, only Torrey's first selection, Billy Smith, would still be around when the Islanders started winning Stanley Cups in eight seasons.

In their first season, 72/73, the Islanders set a new league standard for ineptitude, winning only 12 of 78 games, with just 2 of those coming on the road. Torrey would not forget how it seemed that the newspaper in every town they pulled into carried a headline announcing the arrival of the "hapless New York Islanders." He began to think that "hapless" was part of the team's actual name.

Torrey bit his lip and resisted the temptation to deal away the future for the present. Boe bit along with him. "I knew I had to be patient," the team owner reflected in 1975 after Torrey was named NHL executive of the year in a _Sporting News_ poll of his managerial peers. "It was like raising children. Bill's philosophy was to go with the youngsters, and I agreed that was where our future would be."

At the club's first amateur draft in 1972, Torrey had selected Billy Harris, Lorne Henning, Bob Nystrom and Garry Howatt. His sense of player potential was solid: all became starters, and three of the four would be Cup winners. And by finishing last in 72/73, the Islanders owned the first pick overall in the 1973 amateur draft.

It was widely acknowledged that the first prospect to go would be Denis Potvin of the Ottawa 67s, a smart rushing defenceman who had the makings of a new Bobby Orr or Brad Park. As the draft approached, Torrey was besieged by overtures from fellow general managers eager to cut deals to get their hands on the first pick. Torrey turned them aside, but he still had no guarantee of actually landing Potvin. The WHA was up and running, and as a rogue league without a territorial agreement it was free to go after any player not under contract with an NHL club. The Islanders had already lost a number of their original expansion-draft selections to the short-lived New York Raiders. Torrey knew that he might expend his precious first pick on Potvin and see him sign with a WHA club.

It seemed no small coincidence, then, that on March 5, three months before the draft, Torrey dealt

The Dynasty of the early 1980s

Featuring the players and management who participated in the Islanders' Stanley Cup victories of 1979/80, 1980/81, 1981/82 and 1982/83.

GENERAL MANAGER
1. Bill Torrey

COACH
1. Al Arbour
(73/74–85/86, 89/90–93/94)

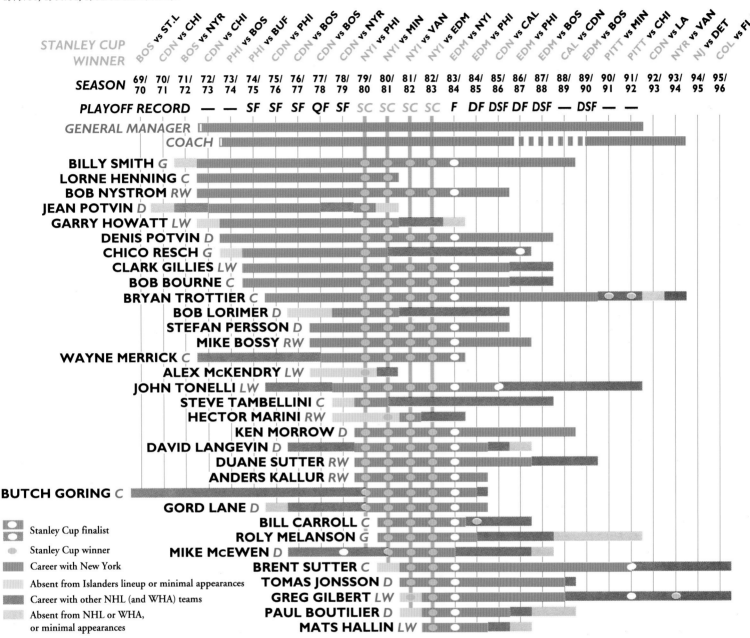

Legend:
- Stanley Cup finalist
- Stanley Cup winner
- Career with New York
- Absent from Islanders lineup or minimal appearances
- Career with other NHL (and WHA) teams
- Absent from NHL or WHA, or minimal appearances

away Terry Crisp to Philadelphia to get Jean Potvin, older brother of Denis. The Potvin brothers, both defencemen, were very close—their dad, Armand Potvin, was a textbook hockey parent, staying up all night flooding a rink in the yard for his boys when they were growing up in Overbrooke, Quebec, across the river from Ottawa. Now, if Denis were to sign with the Islanders, he could play with his brother Jean. At least, that is the way onlookers saw Torrey's scheme playing out. If it was a scheme, it worked. Potvin was drafted and signed, and he emerged almost immediately as a star.

After the first terrible season, Torrey needed more than new players. He also needed a new coach, as former NHLer Phil Goyette had not lived up to expectations.

But who would even want the job? After that first season, Roy Boe would remember, "Bill took much more mental abuse than I did. Our first coach didn't work out and it was hard to get another one. No one really wanted to come with us because of the way the team looked."

Torrey found the man he wanted—unwanted in St. Louis. Blues defenceman Al Arbour had moved to coaching the team under general manager Scotty Bowman at the end of the 70/71 season. Bowman had a falling out with the Blues' ownership when they balked at allowing him to hire Arbour for 71/72, and he quit to take the coaching job in Montreal. Arbour was then given the chance to coach the Blues in 71/72, but he wound up sacked.

Arbour was a studious, even-keeled fellow who had ridden the professional-hockey roller-coaster for 18 years, moving from Detroit to Chicago to Toronto to St. Louis, in and out of the minors, along the way winning Stanley Cups with the Red Wings, the Blackhawks and the Leafs and finishing his career with three straight Cup final appearances with the Blues. Arbour had been a near-permanent fifth defensive wheel, until expansion arrived and saved him from a cold-storage existence with the Leafs' minor system.

He was a defenceman's defenceman, and that was important to Torrey, who would explain, "The first job of every inexperienced team is to cut down on the goals allowed. After that, you can start building more offence." By hiring Arbour, Torrey had a coach who could teach an entire team the importance of taking care of their own end. Torrey had also landed a first-class stable of netminders before the Islanders had even played their first game. From the ranks of Billy Smith and Gerry Desjardins, taken in the expansion draft, and Glenn "Chico" Resch and Denis DeJordy, purchased from Montreal soon after, Smith and Resch emerged as one of the best tag-team pairs in the league.

Bill Torrey broke into hockey management with the Pittsburgh Hornets of the American league in the early 1960s. After a chaotic term as executive vice-president of the Oakland Seals, he was hired as general manager of the new Islanders franchise in 1972. When the club's majority owner encountered financial trouble in 1978, Torrey was instrumental in arranging a bailout, and became franchise president.

The team's second season, 73/74, wasn't much better than the first, as the Islanders won only 19 games. Defensively, though, the team was much improved, as it allowed 100 fewer goals over the same 78-game schedule. The breakthrough came in 74/75, when the Islanders won more games (33) than they had in the first two seasons combined. Denis Potvin became the club's first All Star, named to the first team. Scoring rose from 182 goals to 264; goals against dropped from 247 to 221 as Resch and Smith played their first tag-team season. While their offensive production was still indifferent, their defensive game was the league's third best, behind Philadelphia and Los Angeles. The Islanders struggled for every possible point, recording more ties (22) than any other club, which allowed them to finish third in the Patrick Division, tied on points with the Rangers.

The Islanders then gave their fans an exhilarating playoff run. The preliminary round was a "subway series" between the Rangers and the Islanders. An overtime win in game three at Madison Square Garden sent the Islanders into the quarterfinals against Pittsburgh. The Penguins jumped to a three-game lead, setting the stage for a thrilling Islanders comeback. By winning four straight, the Islanders became the first NHL team since the Maple Leafs of

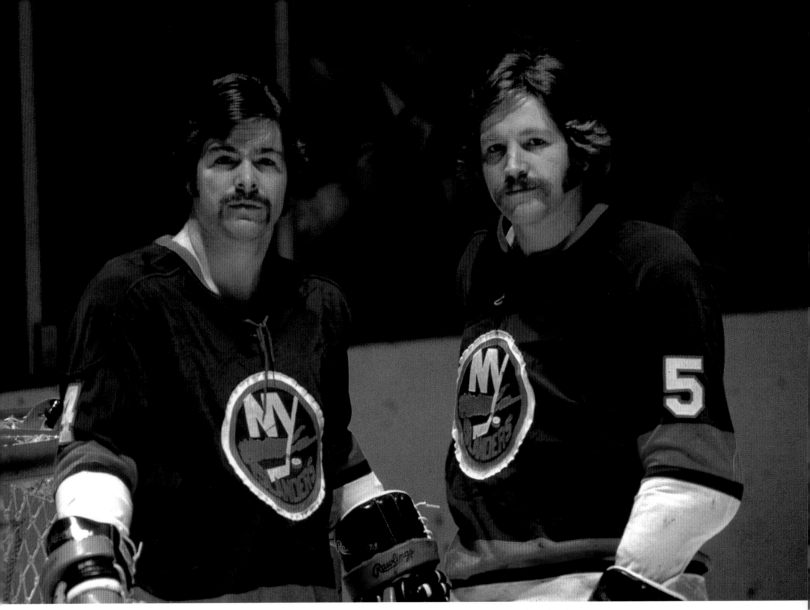

41/42 to win a best-of-seven playoff series after being down three games to none. In the semifinals against the Philadelphia Flyers, the Islanders tried it again. Down three games to none to the defending Cup champions, Arbour's team rallied to win three straight and force a seventh game. There the campaign ended, with a 4-1 loss to the Flyers in Philadelphia.

There, too, the Islanders' ascent stalled. The team improved in every season that followed, winning 42 games in 75/76, 47 in 76/77, 48 in 77/78 and 51 in 78/79, but it could not reach the finals. They were stopped in five in the 75/76 semifinals by Montreal, in six in the 76/77 semifinals by Montreal, in seven in the 77/78 quarterfinals by Toronto, and in six in the 78/79 semifinals by the Rangers.

The Islanders appeared to lack for little. After the 73/74 season (the Islanders' last middling effort), the team held the third pick overall in a strong draft year and used it to select a hulking left-winger from Moose Jaw, Saskatchewan named Clark Gillies, who would be a cornerstone of the Islanders franchise. Down in the second round, they did even better when they took another Saskatchewan prospect, Bryan Trottier, twenty-second overall. Trottier was only 17 when selected, and he stayed in Junior hockey for another season playing

for Lethbridge. When he came up to the Islanders in 75/76, Trottier was an immediate star, contributing 95 points and winning the Calder, outpolling teammate Chico Resch. Trottier was a model of the Islanders' future greatness. He was a center who could score, make plays and check relentlessly and cleanly. He went through the 100-point barrier in 77/78 and stayed above it for five consecutive seasons.

Once the Islanders began winning, their draft choices came lower, but the team continued to pick well. In 1977, coming off a strong season, they had the fifteenth of 18 first-round picks. There were some strong candidates in the draft pool that year: Detroit took Dale McCourt first overall, and Colorado chose Barry Beck second. After that, some ill-fated selections were made, players who never had more than journeyman careers. With their lowly pick, the Islanders were considering a lanky sharpshooter from Laval, Quebec named Michel (Mike) Bossy. Torrey had to choose between Bossy, a scorer who couldn't hit or check, and another player, a checker who couldn't score. Take the scorer, Arbour told him. He could always be taught to check. Teaching a checker to score was another matter. Down in the second round, after other teams had selected prospects like Miles Zaharko, Daniel Chicoine and Neil Labatte, who

Three months before the 1973 amateur draft, in which the Islanders would choose first overall, general manager Bill Torrey traded Terry Crisp to Philadelphia for Jean Potvin (left). At the draft, Torrey used his first pick to take the highly touted Denis Potvin (right), younger brother of Jean. Acquiring Jean Potvin was seen as Torrey's way of making sure Denis signed with the Islanders instead of a WHA team.

had little future in the NHL, the Islanders, choosing thirty-third overall, took Toronto's John Tonelli. The solid left-winger, who could both score and hit, had already turned pro with the Houston Aeros of the WHA at 18 in 1975, but the Islanders now had his NHL rights, and he would join the team in 78/79.

Mike Bossy was 20 years old when he arrived in Long Island in the fall of 1977, a new bride temporarily left behind. Arbour gave the right-winger Bryan Trottier as his center. Bossy responded by scoring 53 goals, a record for a rookie, and won the Calder. In 80/81, he became the first player to match Rocket Richard's record of scoring 50 goals in 50 games, and finished the season with 68. He scored more than 50 goals in every season he played but his last, 86/87, when chronic back problems forced his retirement.

In 77/78, Bossy's first season, the

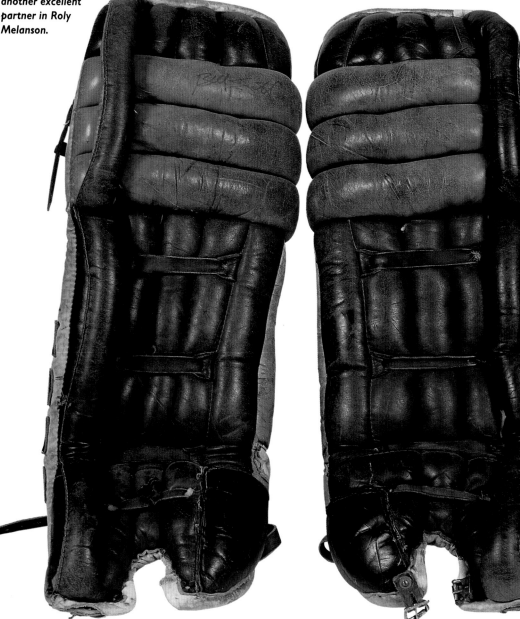

Islanders had six players who scored 30 or more goals: Bossy (53), Trottier (46), Gillies (35), and Denis Potvin, Bob Nystrom and Bob Bourne (30 each). Only the Canadiens scored more as a team, and the Islanders' goals-against average was bettered only by the Canadiens and the Flyers. But when the Leafs' Lanny McDonald scored in overtime of game seven of their quarterfinal series, the Islanders, who had been expected to challenge the reigning Canadiens in the Cup finals, came up shockingly short.

It was almost their last shot at Stanley Cup success, for the Islanders ownership was in trouble. The team was $22 million in debt—majority owner Roy Boe was taking a beating from his basketball franchise, the New York Nets, and was still labouring under the initial $10 million franchise cost for the Islanders. Bill Torrey took a front-line role in arranging a bail-out. Working with minority owner John O. Pickett, Torrey pulled the operation back from the brink of bankruptcy and became team president as well as general manager.

Then came the loss in the 78/79 semifinals to the Rangers. The season had showered the club with individual awards. Trottier and Bossy finished first and fourth in the scoring race; Trottier won the Hart, Potvin his third Norris in four seasons and Arbour the Jack Adams Award. Five Islanders made the All Star team—Trottier, Potvin and Gillies on the first team, Resch and Bossy on the second team. The Canadiens had four All Stars, and only two regular-season individual awards, the Vezina and the Selke. But the Canadiens had another Stanley Cup. The Islanders' 78/79 season made it clear that this was a team of stars who could not come through in the playoffs. The stars the Islanders had were fine—it was "character" players the team most needed. Billy Smith, for one, felt the team wasn't tough enough to win playoff hockey, and took on the enforcer role himself, hacking away at any opposing player who wandered too near his crease.

Season	Finish	Record (W-L-T)	Points %	Awards (winners & runners-up)	All-Stars	Playoffs
74/75	3rd Div 3rd Conf 8th OA	33-25-22	55.0	NORRIS: D. Potvin RU	1ST TEAM: D. Potvin (D)	Lost SC semifinal 4-3 to Philadelphia
75/76	2nd Div 2nd Conf 5th OA	42-21-17	63.1	HART: D. Potvin RU VEZINA: Resch & Smith RU CALDER: Trottier, Resch RU NORRIS: D. Potvin	1ST TEAM: D. Potvin (D) 2ND TEAM: Resch (G)	Lost SC semifinal 4-1 to Montreal
76/77	2nd Div 2nd Conf 4th OA	47-21-12	63.5	VEZINA: Resch & Smith RU MASTERTON: Westfall	2ND TEAM: D. Potvin (D)	Lost SC semifinal 4-2 to Montreal
77/78	1st Div 1st Conf 3rd OA	48-17-15	69.4	ART ROSS: Trottier RU HART: Trottier RU CALDER: Bossy NORRIS: D. Potvin	1ST TEAM: D. Potvin (D), Trottier (C), Gillies (LW) 2ND TEAM: Bossy (RW)	Lost SC quarterfinal 4-3 to Toronto
78/79	1st Div 1st Conf 1st OA	51-15-14	72.5	ART ROSS: Trottier HART: Trottier NORRIS: D. Potvin VEZINA: Resch & Smith RU ADAMS: Arbour	1ST TEAM: D. Potvin (D), Trottier (C), Gillies (LW) 2ND TEAM: Resch (G), Bossy (RW)	Lost SC semifinal 4-2 to Rangers
79/80	2nd Div 2nd Conf 5th OA	39-28-13	56.9	CONN SMYTHE: Trottier		Won SC final 4-2 over Philadelphia
80/81	1st Div 1st Conf 1st OA	48-18-14	68.8	CONN SMYTHE: Goring NORRIS: D. Potvin RU	1ST TEAM: D. Potvin (D), Bossy (RW)	Won SC final 4-1 over Minnesota
81/82	1st Div 1st Conf 1st OA	54-16-10	73.8	ART ROSS: Bossy RU HART: Trottier RU LADY BYNG: Bossy RU VEZINA: Smith JENNINGS: Smith & Melanson RU CONN SMYTHE: Bossy	1ST TEAM: Smith (G), Bossy (RW) 2ND TEAM: Trottier (C), Tonelli (LW)	Won SC final 4-0 over Vancouver
82/83	2nd Div 4th Conf 6th OA	42-26-12	60.0	LADY BYNG: Bossy VEZINA: Melanson RU JENNINGS: Smith & Melanson CONN SMYTHE: Smith PATRICK: Torrey	1ST TEAM: Bossy (RW) 2ND TEAM: Melanson (G)	Won SC final 4-0 over Edmonton
83/84	1st Div 1st Conf 2nd OA	50-26-4	65.0	LADY BYNG: Bossy SELKE: Trottier RU	1ST TEAM: Bossy (RW) 2ND TEAM: D. Potvin (D), Trottier (C)	Lost SC final 4-1 to Edmonton

Torrey and Arbour launched an extensive rebuild of the club roster. Back in January 1978, they had made the unhappy decision to trade Jean Potvin to the Minnesota North Stars. The elder Potvin had been far more than a lure to get Denis to sign in 1973. In 75/76 Jean Potvin had produced 72 points, an outstanding effort that few NHL defenceman ever manage, and he was still a key member of the defence corps in 77/78. But the Islanders needed another center, and so, with enough regret to cause Arbour to shed tears with

Potvin, Jean was traded to the Cleveland Barons along with veteran left-winger J.P. Parise for center Wayne Merrick and defenceman Darcy Regier, who only ever played 11 games for the Islanders.

In 1978, the Barons operation merged with the Minnesota North Stars. In the dispersal draft that followed, Potvin was judged a keeper and placed on the Minnesota protected list. After the disappointment of the 78/79 season, Al Arbour wanted Jean Potvin back, foremost because he had just lost defencemen Gerry

Hart and Pat Price to the Edmonton Oilers in the expansion draft held to bring the Oilers and three other WHA teams into the NHL. Luckily for the Islanders, a good friend of Torrey's, Lou Nanne, had retired as a North Stars defenceman and taken over as general manager in 77/78. The two men spoke almost daily, with Torrey instructing Nanne in the nuances of running an NHL team. After Hart and Price were lost to the Oilers, Nanne did Torrey a big personal favour: he sold him Jean Potvin's rights, accepting Ritchie Hansen, an off-and-on center with the Islanders, as compensation. On June 10, 1979, Jean Potvin was signed as a free agent by the Islanders.

The day before Jean Potvin was signed, the Islanders plucked defenceman Dave "The Bammer" Langevin from Edmonton in the reclamation draft that allowed NHL clubs to take back players whose rights they held from the four WHA teams joining the NHL. After his summer of dealing, Torrey was beginning to feel satisfied with the emerging shape of the Islanders' defence. Although he regretted losing Hart to Edmonton, the defenceman was 30 and fighting injuries. "We'll have the youngest Islander team in history next season," Torrey said. "Making Hart available was one of the toughest things I have ever had to do, but when we reclaimed Dave Langevin from Edmonton, we gained seven and one half years right away."

The Islanders were also gaining defensive muscle. In December the trend continued with center Mike Kaszyki sent to Washington for Gord Lane, who would accrue 205 penalty minutes that season. Still another defenceman was added that season when Ken Morrow of the "Miracle on Ice" U.S. Olympic team joined the lineup after the gold-medal victory in Lake Placid in February. More strength arrived up front in the form of the club's 1979 first-round pick, right-winger Duane Sutter, one of six brothers from Viking, Alberta who made the NHL. Torrey then took his brother Brent, a center, as his first-round pick in 1980.

Not all the Islanders personnel changes were made with brawn as the priority. In August 1979, right-winger Anders Kallur, the most valuable player in the Swedish professional league, was signed as a free agent. And as the playoffs approached, Torrey slipped under the trading deadline with a deal designed to give the club another effective center. In exchange for right-winger Billy Harris, an Islanders original, and defenceman Dave Lewis, who had been with the team since its second season, Torrey secured one of the game's stylish workhorses, Butch Goring. The native Manitoban had spent his entire professional career in Los Angeles, producing plenty of points since arriving in 1969 and getting nowhere near the Stanley Cup.

It was a masterful trade that gave the the Islanders a lineup of experienced, productive centers. In addition to Goring there was Lorne Henning, an Islanders original whose ice time would decrease dramatically with the new acquisitions. Bob Bourne had been with the team

At age 17, Bryan Trottier was drafted by the Islanders twenty-second overall in the second round of the 1974 draft. He joined the Islanders after another season of Junior hockey, and became its most feted player, winning the Hart, the Art Ross and the Conn Smythe trophies, and was also named to four All Star teams. The fact that he could win a league scoring title in one season and be voted runner-up for its defensive forward honour, the Selke award, in another, demonstrates the completeness of Trottier's game.

since September 1974 when he was acquired from the Kansas City Scouts in exchange for Bart Crashley and the rights to Larry Hornung, an original Islanders expansion draft choice who had jumped to the WHA. Bryan Trottier was the league's most valuable player and highest scorer in 78/79. Wayne Merrick, who had been labeled a floater earlier in his career, had come to the Islanders in the 77/78 Jean Potvin deal and was there to stay. Finally, there was Steve Tambellini, the Islanders' first-round draft pick in 1978.

The 79/80 regular season nonetheless appeared to be a major step backwards for the Islanders. Wins dropped from 51 to 39; All Star selections went from five to nil; top-ten scorers went from four to one (Trottier, who was sixth) as team scoring plunged from 358 to 281. The team finished second in the Patrick Division, 25 points behind Philadelphia, fifth overall. But the overwhelming difference between 78/79 and 79/80 was that the Islanders played playoff hockey. They played seven overtime games and won six of them.

In the preliminary round they moved past Goring's former teammates in Los Angeles 3-1, then produced two overtime wins in five games to down the Bruins, who had made the 76/77 and 77/78 finals (and came within a bench penalty of eliminating the Canadiens in the 78/79 semifinals). The win over the Bruins was vital; it showed that the Islanders could beat a tough club that had playoff experience. The Sabres were next, and Buffalo was taken in six. The Islanders were at last in the finals, and their opponents were their division rivals, the Philadelphia Flyers.

The first game began badly for the Islanders when Denis Potvin accidentally put the puck in his own net trying to stuff it under Billy Smith. Potvin redeemed himself at 4:07 of overtime when he scored the goal that gave the Islanders a 4-3 win in Philadelphia. Game two in Philadelphia was a Flyers swarming as Paul Holmgren contributed a hat-trick to an 8-3 win. In game three, though, the Flyers' penalty-prone style got the better of them. All six Islanders goals came on powerplays. The first one, remarkably, was on a Flyers powerplay in the opening minutes of the game, when Lorne Henning put the Islanders ahead on a short-handed effort. That 6-2 win at Nassau Coliseum was followed by a 5-2 win that gave the Islanders a 3-1 series lead. In game five back in Philadelphia, Bryan Trottier matched the playoff record of 27 points set by Phil Esposito in 69/70 and Frank Mahovlich in 70/71. The Flyers won, however, 6-3, and it was back to Long Island for game six.

The consensus after the deciding game, which the Islanders won 5-4 in overtime, was that the Flyers were jobbed. One of the Islanders' goals was questionable—Denis Potvin redirected the puck with what was probably a high stick—and another goal, by Duane Sutter, came on a blatant offside. Clark Gillies had carried the puck into the Flyers end and made a drop pass that was two feet on the wrong side of the blueline when Butch Goring collected it. After Sutter scored on the play, Flyers protests made no difference. But the Flyers

Defenceman Dave "The Bammer" Langevin was one reason the get-physical game plan of the Vancouver Canucks did not work in the 81/82 finals. The Islanders won in four.

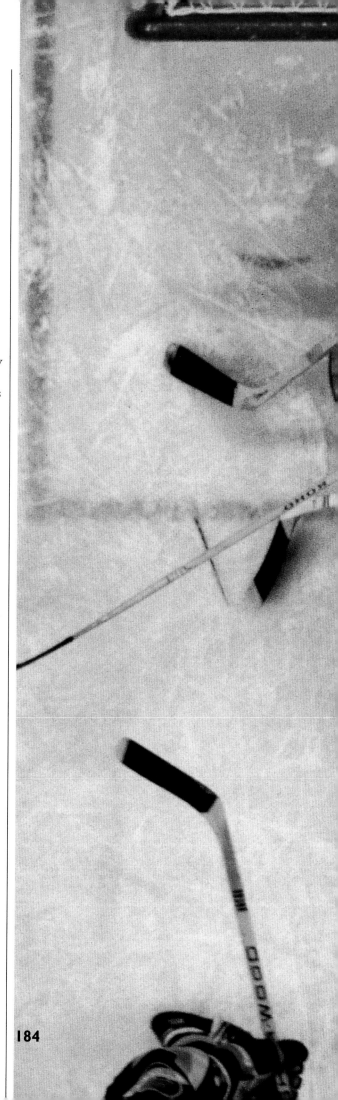

rallied from a 4-2 deficit in the third period to force overtime. "I was panicking. It was Scared City. They were really pounding on us in the third period," Smith would say. At 7:11 of overtime, the Islanders concluded their Cup quest stylishly when John Tonelli fed a perfect pass to a streaking Bob Nystrom, who redirected it past Pete Peeters.

For all the sour grapes about missed calls in game six, the Flyers had been harmed most by their penalties, which led to 14 Islanders powerplay goals. In all, the Islanders scored a record 25 powerplay goals in the 79/80 playoffs. Bryan Trottier, with a record 29 playoff points, won the Conn Smythe.

An impromptu celebratory parade wound down the Hempstead Turnpike as Long Island celebrated its new-found sporting fame. The Stanley Cup spent the night on Bill Torrey's porch as guests watched a videotape of the deciding game—pondering, no doubt, Duane Sutter's critical and controversial goal. When a reporter tried to suggest to Billy Smith that the Islanders were the first New York team to win a Stanley Cup in 40 years, he carefully corrected him. "The Cup wasn't won in New York City. It belongs on Long Island."

Many of hockey's great general managers have believed that one of the biggest enemies of a dynasty is complacency. It doesn't hurt to make a shake-up trade with a star player now and then, they'd say, to remind everyone that they were running a hockey club, not a country club—no lifetime memberships available. Torrey refused to give anyone a no-trade contract, which did not interfere with keeping his major stars signed and satisfied. Now, he let most of the 80/81 season pass before making his shake-up deal. On March 10 he sent Chico Resch and Steve Tambellini to the Colorado Rockies for defenceman Mike McEwen and goaltending prospect Jari Kaarela.

Torrey certainly wasn't desperate for defensive talent and had no real need for a goaltender. Kaarela, who had played five games for the Rockies, never played for the Islanders. In 1979 he had drafted Roly Melanson fifty-ninth overall and in 1980 Kelly Hrudey thirty-eighth. Melanson became Smith's new tag-team partner, although Smith was the acknowledged playoff goaltender, an unsurpassed "money" player who had set a new league record of 14 consecutive playoff wins in 79/80. It was a simple calculation for Torrey after that Stanley Cup season: when Smith was in net, the Islanders won playoff games.

In 80/81 the Islanders were back on top of the league with 48 wins and a points percentage of 68.8. The club led in scoring and was fourth in goals against. They avenged their 77/78 semifinal upset at the hands of the Leafs by demolishing Toronto 9-2, 5-1, 6-1 in the preliminary round. The quarterfinals brought a pesky effort from the emerging Edmonton Oilers, but the Islanders won in six. The semifinals resurrected the "subway series" of 74/75, but the Rangers failed to make much of a stand as the Islanders rolled up wins of 5-2, 7-3, 5-1 and 5-2.

The Islanders' fourth Stanley Cup was a playoff masterpiece. Their opponents were the fast-rising Edmonton Oilers, who had averaged 7 goals per game against the Calgary Flames in the division finals. Billy Smith held Gretzky and company to just 1.6 goals per game as the Islanders swept the Oilers in four.

Defenceman Ken Morrow had a storybook 79/80 season. After participating in the U.S. Olympic team's "Miracle On Ice" gold-medal performance at Lake Placid in February 1980, he joined the Islanders lineup in time to participate in its first Stanley Cup win. Morrow was a defensive mainstay of the team for ten seasons.

The finals produced a strange match: the poised, powerful defending champions versus a bunch of kids, which is what the Minnesota North Stars were. Goaltender Don Beaupré, for one, was only 19, and Lou Nanne quipped, "We're so young that if we don't win the Stanley Cup, we're going to challenge for the Memorial Cup because we have nine players who are eligible."

The North Stars had finished third in the Adams Division with 35 wins, but in the playoffs had thus far been able to master the Bruins, the Sabres and the Flames.

In game one in Long Island, though, Nanne's youngsters were taught a dispiriting hockey lesson. Trailing 1-0 halfway through the first period, the North Stars got a break when Bob Bourne was assessed a five-minute major for spearing. But in the course of the Minnesota powerplay, Bryan Trottier and Anders Kallur each scored shorthanded goals. The Islanders won the opener 6-3, and except for a win in game four, the North Stars were largely star-struck as they went down 6-3, 6-3, 7-5, 2-4, 5-1.

The Islanders set or matched 22 records in the 80/81 playoffs. Among them were Mike Bossy's most goals in one season and one playoffs (85, with 68 during the season and 17 during the playoffs) and most power-play goals (9) in the playoffs. Billy Smith matched his 79/80 record of most consecutive wins (14). The team broke its 79/80 record by scoring 31 powerplay goals in the playoffs. It also broke its 79/80 record of 7 shorthanded goals by producing 9. Denis Potvin broke Bobby Orr's record of 24 playoff points, with 25.

The 81/82 Islanders were little changed from 80/81 in roster or performance. They produced the best finish of the regular season with a franchise-high 54 wins and a points percentage of 73.8. But the team was delivered a scare in the division semifinals by the Pittsburgh Penguins, who, after losing the first two games of the best-of-five 8-1 and 7-2, forced a fifth game and took the Islanders into overtime. After a 4-3 win moved the Penguins aside, the Islanders entered another subway series with the Rangers. This year, New York put up more of a fight but still went down 4-2.

And that, unfortunately for fans in general, was the last serious threat to the Islanders in the 81/82 playoffs. In the conference finals the Quebec Nordiques lost in four straight, and in the finals the Vancouver Canucks, under rookie coach Roger Neilson, made the mistake of challenging the Islanders with a physical game plan. Billy Smith flailed his stick at opponents and set them on edge and off their game. Vancouver enforcer Tiger Williams ventured how he would be pleased to "punch Smith in the esophagus so hard he has to eat out of a blender for six months." The Canucks took the Islanders into overtime in game one, losing 6-5, but thereafter the Islanders were never in danger, reeling off three more victories of 6-4, 3-0 and 3-1.

If there was a disappointment in the emerging Islanders dynasty, it was that it had come without a classic showdown between the old champion and the new. While Montreal and the Islanders had met in the 75/76 and 76/77 playoffs, the two clubs had never met when they were at their peak. After four consecutive Stanley Cups, Montreal had bowed out dramatically with an opening-round loss to the North Stars in 79/80. The Islanders had won their last two Cups in unsatisfying final series against upstart clubs. Finally, in 82/83, a reckoning between a king and a pretender was found.

The Edmonton Oilers had begun hinting at greatness as a team, rather than being merely an operating base for superstar Wayne Gretzky, as early as 80/81 when they took the Islanders to six games in the quarterfinals. Edmonton faltered in 81/82, squandering a fine regular season with a 3-2 upset in the division semifinals at the hands of Los Angeles. In 82/83, Edmonton drove over its playoff opponents, winning 11 of 12 matches as it reached the finals. The team was young, fast and dazzling. The Islanders were getting old, and they finished 10 points behind the Oilers in the regular season.

The league played an unbalanced schedule, however, and while Edmonton had been punishing weak rivals in the Smythe Division, the Islanders were playing tough, close-checking opponents like the Flyers (who won the division), the Rangers and the Washington Capitals. The Islanders had to move aside the Capitals (3-1), the Rangers (4-2) and the grinding Bruins (4-2) before meeting the Oilers. Arbour's team then produced its most impressive Stanley Cup win, out-checking, out-hustling and out-scoring Gretzky and company in a four-game sweep. While Mike Bossy had impressed with five game-winning playoff goals, Billy Smith was the obvious choice for the Conn Smythe. In the four-game final series he allowed only 1.6 goals per game against a team that had outscored its opponents 74-33 in its previous 12 playoff games.

The Islanders now had four consecutive Stanley Cup wins. Could they possibly make it five, and match the record set by the Canadiens in the 1950s? The doubts were considerable. The team was another year older, and the Oilers, their evident successors, were still young and still learning. The Islanders won an impressive 50 of 80 games in 83/84 as they regained the

Patrick Division title, but Edmonton won 57. The two clubs moved toward each other through the playoffs.

Fittingly, the Islanders had a conference-final encounter with the team whose reign it had supplanted, the Montreal Canadiens, before it met the next dynasty in the finals. This was a far different Montreal club than the one that had ruled the late 1970s, and the Islanders advanced in six. But this was also a far different Islanders club from the one that had won the last four Cups. The lineup was much the same, but it was tired, and hurting. Edmonton came off a nine-day layoff to shut out the Islanders 1-0 in Nassau County. While the Islanders fought back with a 6-1 win in game two, after that it was an Edmonton final. At times ugly, the series went Edmonton's way with convincing 7-2, 7-2 and 5-2 victories. Leg cramps caused by dehydration had driven Denis Potvin from game three, and Mike Bossy, nursing a viral infection, didn't get a single shot on goal in the last two games. To keep a lineup patched together, the Islanders had kept 27 players on hand.

After the loss, Bill Torrey gibed, "I was telling Al that in five years we had one bad week. Unfortunately, it came at the wrong time. The Oilers were very well

prepared. They were fresh, they were young. They had every motivational thing going for them, and when we didn't cash in on our opportunities, they took off. Give them credit for that." But the ill will between the two clubs, mainly directed at the Oilers by the Islanders, was so great that it almost tore apart Team Canada when their star players were thrown together for the Canada Cup series that fall.

It was the final encounter between the dynasties, one closing out its championship run, one just embarking on one. During Edmonton's streak of five Stanley Cups in seven seasons, the Islanders could not move past their division finals. In 88/89, the Islanders were last in the Patrick Division, most of their championship players now retired.

Bryan Trottier, however, got another chance at winning when he joined the Pittsburgh Penguins in 90/91. "I wish everyone who played hockey could know the feeling of winning the Stanley Cup," he said after earning his second Cup, against Minnesota, in 80/81. "You win it once and you get greedy. You want to keep on winning it." As a Pittsburgh Penguin he kept on winning it, in 90/91 and 91/92. ○

Billy Smith tastes Stanley Cup victory. He was a focal point of all four Islanders wins, and was awarded the Conn Smythe Trophy for his performance against the Oilers in the 82/83 finals. Along with Denis Potvin, Bob Nystrom and Mike Bossy, his number has been retired by the Islanders. He is the first goaltender who played in the 1980s to be elected to the Hockey Hall of Fame.

EDMONTON OILERS
The Eighties

WAYNE'S WORLD

THE EDMONTON OILERS WENT FROM LOSING IN THE WHA TO WINNING BIG IN THE NHL— THE DIFFERENCE WAS A KID NAMED GRETZKY

RIGHT: Wayne Gretzky warms up Oilers goaltender Ron Low in 1982. After coaching the Oilers' American league farm club in Nova Scotia, Low became Edmonton's head coach in 1994.
BELOW: Wayne Gretzky's first pair of skates.

A s one of four WHA teams to join the NHL for the 79/80 season, the Edmonton Oilers seemed to have so little going for them, aside from a teenage phenomenon named Wayne Gretzky. The first miracle of the Oilers was that, just four seasons later, they were in the Stanley Cup finals. The second miracle was that, after winning the Cup four times over five seasons with Gretzky, they would win a fifth one without him. Edmonton, though, will always be Wayne's World; the Oilers would never have gotten into the NHL without him.

The National Hockey League's absorption in 1979 of four of six teams left in the World Hockey Association experiment was one of the great swindles of professional sport. The terms of the conditional surrender of the league that had driven the NHL to distraction for seven seasons were grimly one-sided.

Talks between the NHL and the WHA to end the rivalry, and above all the skyrocketing player salaries that went along with it, had been ongoing since 1977. The NHL had expanded too quickly in an attempt to keep the WHA out of key or potential markets, and at the beginning of the 78/79 season as many as one-third of the NHL's 17 teams were in financial trouble. The WHA meanwhile had slipped from 15 teams in 75/76 to 7. The war between the leagues had to end.

The retirement of Clarence Campbell as NHL president in 1978 helped move the merger talks along; his successor, former Detroit Red Wings executive John Ziegler, saw more sense in a truce or a negotiated surrender than a protracted war. And of all the WHA teams still operating, the Edmonton Oilers topped the list of clubs that would be welcomed in the NHL. It would be welcomed because it was a solid operation in an enthusiastic market, and because it had what the NHL needed: professional hockey's future star, an 18-year-old phenomenon named Wayne Gretzky.

CHAMPIONS

The Oilers club was one of ten founding WHA operations. When the franchise was awarded to promoter Bill Hunter in 1972, it was called the Oil Kings. A franchise had also been awarded to Calgary, but when it failed to materialize the Edmonton team played its first season as the Alberta Oilers.

The team was renamed the Edmonton Oilers for the 73/74 season. After surviving its first two seasons in Bill Hunter's 5,200-seat Edmonton Gardens, the club moved into the city's first-class new Northlands Coliseum for 74/75. In the summer of 1975, the team was bought by real estate flip-master Nelson Skalbania. Two years later, Skalbania sold the Oilers to Peter Pocklington, who had parlayed a teenage genius for car sales back in London, Ontario, into an Edmonton-based business empire that included a Ford dealership and meat packing and trust companies.

Skalbania went south, buying a majority share of the WHA's Indianapolis Racers franchise. It was the league's weakest team in 77/78, losing 51 of 80 games. The WHA overall was beginning to lose its battle for players with the NHL. The New York Rangers, for example, stole away Swedish stars Ulf Nilsson and Anders Hedberg from the Winnipeg Jets for 78/79. The solution arrived at by some WHA teams was to beat the NHL to the best young players by signing them as underage Juniors. Officially, the WHA, like the NHL, pledged not to draft or sign Canadian Junior players younger than 20. But the Birmingham Bulls, owned by Toronto's John Bassett, ignored the regulation and began signing so many teenagers that the team became known as the "Baby Bulls."

Skalbania, with an ailing operation in Indianapolis, went after the greatest Junior prospect three years before he was eligible for the draft. Wayne Gretzky of Brantford, Ontario, had been a national figure in Canada since the age of 12. He was the next big thing, as big as or bigger than Bobby Orr or Gordie Howe. His style was unmistakable: an almost slight figure with a bent-over skating style who had a rare gift for sensing the ebb and flow of the game, and whose scoring ability was exceeded only by his playmaking skill. Playing center for the Sault Ste. Marie Greyhounds of the OHA Junior A in 77/78, he produced 70 goals and 112 assists. He was 17 years old in June 1978

when his agent Gus Badali negotiated a personal-services contract between Gretzky and Skalbania; the seven-year deal was estimated to be worth $1.75 million to the Great One, the kid who couldn't miss.

The way Skalbania saw it, the personal-services contract got around the WHA's rules about underage players, since technically Gretzky was employed by him, not by the team. But it really didn't matter, because the WHA was coming apart anyway. It was speculated that Skalbania only wanted to keep the Racers running long enough to cash in on the inevitable merger with/surrender to the NHL. Indianapolis couldn't hope to be one of the WHA clubs to make the switch to the NHL, but so long as the Racers were still operating when the deal was done, the franchise would be eligible for a compensation payment from the surviving teams as the league was shut down.

Gretzky's fourth professional game was a match at home against the Edmonton Oilers on October 20, 1978. It was the first time Oilers coach and director of hockey operations Glen Sather saw him in action. "I thought Wayne must be a stick boy or some kid who hung around with the team," he told *The Toronto Star*'s Milt Dunnell in 1984. "Then, the game started and he went around one of our veterans like he was a lamp post." At 6:02 of the second period, Gretzky scored; 39 seconds later, he scored again.

The Racers were in financial trouble, and Skalbania desperately needed cash. Back in Edmonton, Sather urged Pocklington to buy Gretzky and anyone else they could get. After eight games as an Indianapolis Racer, Gretzky, along with goaltender Ed Mio and defenceman John Hughes, became an Edmonton Oiler; Nelson Skalbania became $850,000 richer. But that money was soon gone, and in December the Racers operation folded.

"Now, when I look back," Sather reflected in 1984, "I ask myself, where would the Oilers be, where would my coaching career be, if I had been wrong about Gretzky. But I was sure I was right. He had that sparkle in his eyes where others have glass."

Sather was a former journeyman player who had already made a personal fortune in real estate developments in and around Banff, Alberta, when he went to work for Pocklington. Originally signed by the Red Wings in the 1960s, he made it a condition of his contract that Detroit pay for his university education in the off-season. (Sather never did play as a Red Wing.) His NHL career kept bringing him within striking distance of a Stanley Cup win, but the win never came. He played for the Bruins in 67/68 and 68/69; after the Bruins sent him to the Pittsburgh Penguins, they won the Cup in 69/70. He reached the 71/72 finals with the New York Rangers, losing to the Bruins in six. He was with the Canadiens in 74/75 when they lost 4-2 in the semifinals to Buffalo. The next season, Montreal began its run of four straight Cup wins, but by then Sather was playing in Minnesota. He jumped to the WHA in 76/77 to play for the Oilers as a utility forward.

Oilers Scoring
82/83–89/90

GOALS PER GAME

6.0
5.5
5.0
4.5
4.0
3.5
3.0

82/83 83/84 84/85 85/86 86/87 87/88 88/89 89/90

■ Edmonton goals-against
■ Edmonton goals-for
○ League-leading scoring
League scoring average
83/84 **Stanley Cup win**

EDMONTON OILERS

The Dynasty of the 1980s

Featuring the players and management who participated in the Oilers' Stanley Cup victories of 1983/84, 1984/85, 1986/87, 1987/88 and 1989/90

GENERAL MANAGER
1. Glen Sather

COACH
1. Glen Sather
2. Bryan Watson, Glen Sather
3. Glen Sather
4. John Muckler

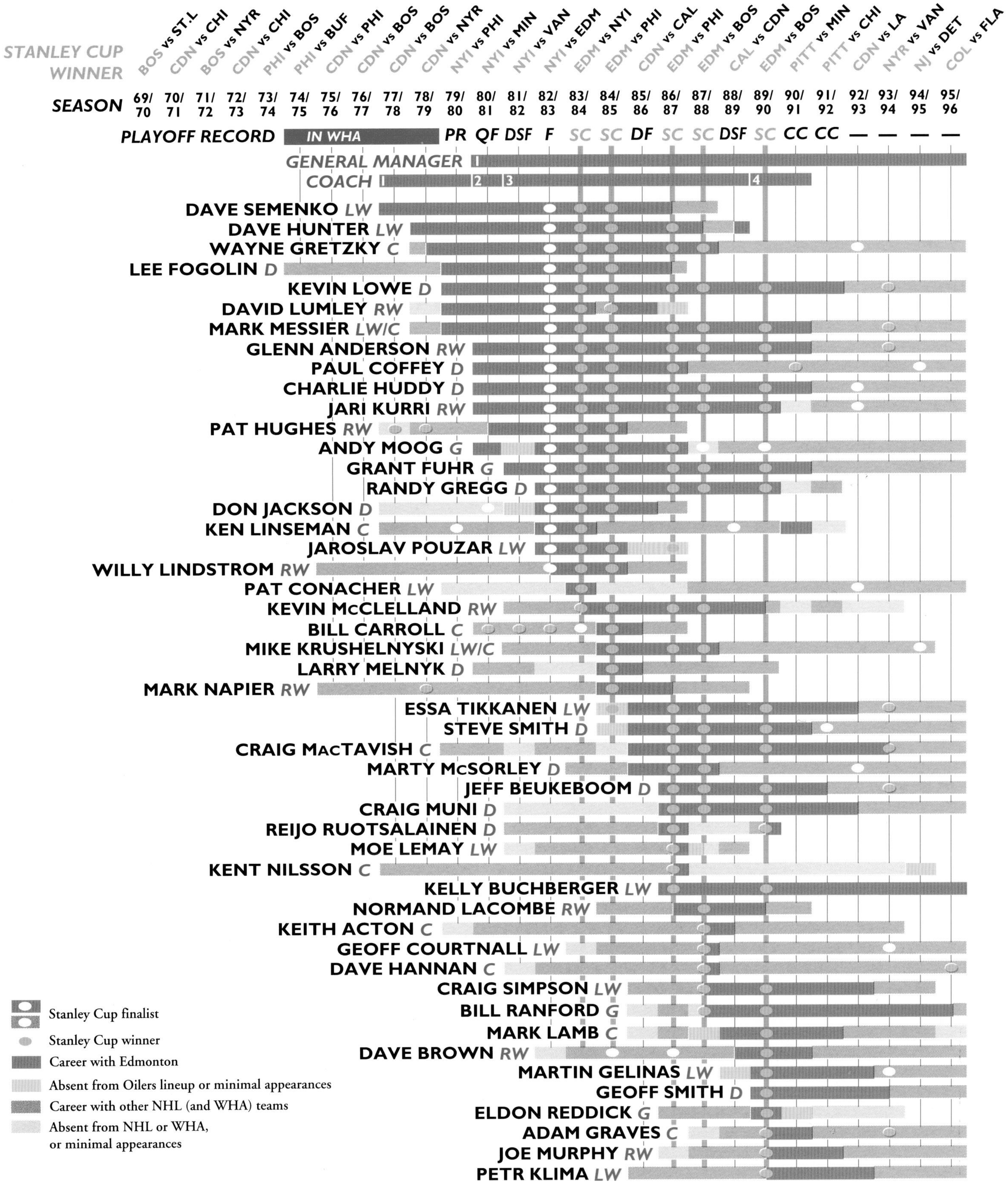

STANLEY CUP WINNER

BOS vs ST.L · CDN vs CHI · BOS vs NYR · CDN vs CHI · PHI vs BOS · PHI vs BUF · CDN vs PHI · CDN vs BOS · CDN vs BOS · CDN vs NYR · NYI vs PHI · NYI vs MIN · NYI vs VAN · NYI vs EDM · EDM vs NYI · EDM vs PHI · EDM vs CAL · EDM vs PHI · EDM vs BOS · CAL vs CDN · EDM vs BOS · PITT vs MIN · PITT vs CHI · CDN vs LA · NYR vs VAN · NJ vs DET · COL vs FLA

SEASON

69/70 · 70/71 · 71/72 · 72/73 · 73/74 · 74/75 · 75/76 · 76/77 · 77/78 · 78/79 · 79/80 · 80/81 · 81/82 · 82/83 · 83/84 · 84/85 · 85/86 · 86/87 · 87/88 · 88/89 · 89/90 · 90/91 · 91/92 · 92/93 · 93/94 · 94/95 · 95/96

PLAYOFF RECORD — IN WHA — PR · QF · DSF · F · SC · SC · DF · SC · SC · DSF · SC · CC · CC · — · — · — · — · —

GENERAL MANAGER 1

COACH 1 · 2 · 3 · 4

DAVE SEMENKO LW
DAVE HUNTER LW
WAYNE GRETZKY C
LEE FOGOLIN D
KEVIN LOWE D
DAVID LUMLEY RW
MARK MESSIER LW/C
GLENN ANDERSON RW
PAUL COFFEY D
CHARLIE HUDDY D
JARI KURRI RW
PAT HUGHES RW
ANDY MOOG G
GRANT FUHR G
RANDY GREGG D
DON JACKSON D
KEN LINSEMAN C
JAROSLAV POUZAR LW
WILLY LINDSTROM RW
PAT CONACHER LW
KEVIN McCLELLAND RW
BILL CARROLL C
MIKE KRUSHELNYSKI LW/C
LARRY MELNYK D
MARK NAPIER RW
ESSA TIKKANEN LW
STEVE SMITH D
CRAIG MacTAVISH C
MARTY McSORLEY D
JEFF BEUKEBOOM D
CRAIG MUNI D
REIJO RUOTSALAINEN D
MOE LEMAY LW
KENT NILSSON C
KELLY BUCHBERGER LW
NORMAND LACOMBE RW
KEITH ACTON C
GEOFF COURTNALL LW
DAVE HANNAN C
CRAIG SIMPSON LW
BILL RANFORD G
MARK LAMB C
DAVE BROWN RW
MARTIN GELINAS LW
GEOFF SMITH D
ELDON REDDICK G
ADAM GRAVES C
JOE MURPHY RW
PETR KLIMA LW

Legend:
- Stanley Cup finalist
- Stanley Cup winner
- Career with Edmonton
- Absent from Oilers lineup or minimal appearances
- Career with other NHL (and WHA) teams
- Absent from NHL or WHA, or minimal appearances

Sather's career had come full circle. Back in 1963, Sather won the Memorial Cup as captain of the Edmonton Oil Kings; he was born about 120 miles southeast of the city, in Wainright. For the last ten years, he had been running a hockey school in Banff in the off-season. He was 34 years old at the start of the 77/78 season when Oilers general manager Bep Guidolin took him out of the lineup and installed him behind the bench. "I entertained my first thoughts about becoming a coach the day Guidolin told me I was either going to coach or sit in the crowd," is how Sather would recall his promotion. After Pocklington bought the Oilers, Sather assumed the general managership in 1980 and then the club presidency.

Wayne Gretzky, the kid who had skated around Sather's Oilers like they were lamp posts, compiled 46 goals and 64 assists in the WHA in 78/79. On January 26, 1979, his eighteenth birthday, Gretzky appeared at center ice of Northlands Coliseum before a game against the Cincinnati Stingers to sign a personal-services contract that bound him to Peter Pocklington until 1999. Its value was estimated at $4 to $5 million, with a built-in renegotiation schedule.

Getting Gretzky may have been the largest single motivation within NHL ranks for merging with the WHA. The best league was supposed to have the best players, and Gretzky was obviously destined for greatness. His presence alone was giving the failing WHA continuing legitimacy. The NHL needed Gretzky the way the Montreal Canadiens had once needed Jean Béliveau.

The parallels between Béliveau and Gretzky are intriguing. In the early 1950s, Béliveau had a contractual obligation to play for Montreal whenever he chose to turn professional, but he was making an unheard-of salary playing as a so-called amateur with the Quebec Aces of the Quebec Senior league. To get him, the Canadiens ultimately bought the entire Senior league, turned it into a minor-pro loop and so made it contractually imperative for Béliveau to become a Canadien.

In Gretzky's case, though, the NHL was not going to have to buy the whole WHA. The NHL was going to make the WHA buy into the NHL, and the teams that did so would pay dearly.

The NHL was agreeable to having three strong WHA clubs join up: the Winnipeg Jets, New England Whalers and Edmonton Oilers. The WHA insisted that a fourth team, the Quebec Nordiques, also be included. The deal needed the approval of 14 of 17 NHL teams, and at a board of governors meeting in Key Largo on March 8, 1979, the proposal to end the WHA failed to pass by two votes.

One of the endless laments heard in Canada is that hockey, "Canada's game," has been usurped by American dollars. Few people seem to recall that when the opportunity was first presented for three Canadian WHA teams to be added to the NHL, all three existing Canadian NHL clubs voted against it.

The five dissenting NHL clubs were the Los Angeles Kings, Vancouver Canucks, Toronto Maple Leafs, Montreal Canadiens and Boston Bruins. Boston's objections were territorial, as the team didn't relish having the Whalers, who played in Hartford, Connecticut, operating in their back yard. Los Angeles and Vancouver shared concerns over an expanded NHL leaving them isolated on the west coast, with few home games against crowd-pleasing eastern NHL teams. In Montreal and Toronto, the concerns were measured in television dollars. Molson Breweries had just bought the Montreal Canadiens franchise in 1978 and was a co-producer with the Canadian Broadcasting Corporation of "Hockey Night in Canada." Having five Canadian NHL teams instead of three would divide the television revenue pie into thinner slices, and the Toronto and Montreal franchises were not happy.

Just as unhappy, though, were consumers in Edmonton, Winnipeg and Quebec when they learned the brewery was standing in the way of their future as professional hockey towns. A boycott of Molson brands arose, and an embarrassed Canadiens operation had to backtrack. Toronto was intransigent on approving the NHL-WHA deal, but two weeks after the Key Largo meeting Montreal and Vancouver changed their positions when a second vote was held in Chicago. Vancouver was won over with the assurance that a balanced schedule would be adopted, with all clubs playing each other four times, two at home, two away.

The terms under which the four WHA clubs agreed to enter the NHL were the harshest imaginable. The NHL insisted on treating their arrival not as a merger but as an expansion. Thus, the WHA clubs were required to pay an expansion franchise fee of $6 million on their arrival. But these clubs also had to wind up the WHA, which meant paying a $1.5-million compensation payment to each of the two franchises, in Cincinnati and Birmingham, that were being left behind. The WHA then held a dispersal draft to redistribute the players under contract to Cincinnati and Birmingham, with more money changing hands as a result. In the end, it was estimated that it cost each of the four WHA teams about $10 million (U.S.) to move to the NHL, a huge sum for a sports franchise at the time.

To make matters worse, the WHA clubs were left with almost no players, as the NHL decreed that NHL rights to players its clubs had drafted, only to see them sign with WHA teams, would be asserted through a reclamation draft. In this way the Oilers lost much of the lineup that had got the team into the last WHA championship in the spring of 1979, which Edmonton lost 4-2 to Winnipeg. Ironically, Edmonton was the only club among the four WHA teams to enter the NHL never to have won the WHA's Avco Cup.

The expansion draft held to stock the rosters of the new clubs allowed each club to draft 15 players and two goaltenders from the unprotected lists of the existing NHL clubs, with no club to lose more than four. The draft was a farce. Much dealing went on beforehand, as

Mark Messier makes full contact with a St. Louis Blue in 1982. He first played professionally at age 17 with the Indianapolis Racers of the WHA, filling in for Wayne Gretzky, who had been sold to Edmonton. In 81/82 Messier blossomed, scoring 50 goals and making the first All Star team with Gretzky.

defence for Detroit and Chicago in the 1950s. The younger Fogolin had been Buffalo's first pick in the 1974 amateur draft, going eleventh overall, and had turned in five strong seasons with the Sabres. With Scotty Bowman just arriving from the Canadiens to run the Sabres hockey operation, Fogolin apparently was lost in the shuffle and left unprotected, much to Buffalo's regret.

Edmonton had chosen 9 players in the WHA dispersal draft and 16 in the NHL expansion draft. Of these 25 selections, hardly anyone had a role to play in the NHL Oilers. None of the dispersal draft picks made their way into the starting lineup. Goaltender Mike Liut was a major talent, but he chose to sign with St. Louis. Bryan "Bugsy" Watson, an old friend of Sather's taken from the Cincinnati list, quit playing to become an Oilers assistant coach. From the 16 players drafted off the NHL lists, only four made the team, all defencemen: Fogolin; Pat Price from the New York Islanders; Colin Campbell from the Pittsburgh Penguins; and Doug Hicks from the Chicago Blackhawks. And of those, only one, Fogolin (who served as captain from 80/81 to 82/83), would still be with the team in the spring of 1983 when the Oilers reached the Stanley Cup finals for the first time.

The Oilers' strategy during the draft was to concentrate on free agents. That way, if the player chose to sign with a team other than Edmonton, the Oilers would receive compensation. The Oilers estimated that the policy saved them anywhere from $350,000 to $500,000 when the draft was over, which was money they could use for signing Juniors in the amateur draft.

There were more hazards in store for the WHA clubs. The amateur entry draft was to include teenagers who had been playing for WHA clubs. The Oilers, however, were not going to surrender Gretzky. His name was on a personal-services contract that bound him to Pocklington. Pocklington had a lock on Gretzky's contract; if he hadn't, the WHA-NHL "merger" would never have happened in the first place.

existing NHL teams made agreements with the arriving ones to supply them with other players or future draft picks to ensure that many unprotected players remained de facto protected. Those players that were truly available didn't inspire much enthusiasm.

The day before the expansion draft, a nonplussed Glen Sather noted, "At one time, there were 761 names up for grabs. After poring over the names, only 53 excited us a little. Too many of the players have huge, out-of-sight contracts, problems with their present coach or GM, a drinking problem or are already retired, like Bobby Orr. And that doesn't include the guys who aren't very good, period."

Like the other former WHA teams, the Oilers were seen going through the motions of selecting players they either didn't want or had no hope of signing, simply because there was a draft and they were expected to participate. Among Edmonton's picks were two unlikely prospects from the Pittsburgh Penguins: Tom Edur, who had retired before the 78/79 season because, as a Jehovah's Witness, he took exception to the violence in hockey, and Wayne Bianchin, who missed all of 78/79 after spinal surgery. Bianchin played 11 games for the Oilers in 79/80; Edur could not be induced to return to the game. The Oilers also drafted left-winger Inge Hammarstrom, who after four seasons with the Leafs had been traded to St. Louis in 77/78. Hammarstrom went home to Sweden after 78/79 with no interest in returning to the NHL. The Oilers were unable to change his mind.

Edmonton did come away with one gem, defenceman Lee Fogolin, whose father Lidio (Lee) had played

For the WHA teams joining the NHL, the 1979 amateur entry draft promised little gold. All of the existing NHL teams picked first, and were then followed by the new clubs from the WHA in the reverse order of their finish in the last WHA season. This meant Edmonton had the last first-round pick, twenty-first overall.

Fortunately, the Oilers had a shrewd chief scout working for them. Barry Fraser had begun scouting for the Kitchener Rangers Junior team as a hobby before turning it into a full-time job in the WHA, first with the Cleveland Crusaders, then the Houston Aeros and finally the Oilers. He convinced Sather to take defenceman Kevin Lowe of the Quebec Remparts as his first-round pick. Edmonton's next pick was forty-eighth overall in the third round; the Oilers took a teenaged enigma named Mark Messier. And sixty-ninth overall, Glenn Anderson was chosen.

Anderson, who was from Vancouver, was playing at

Season	Finish	Record (W-L-T)	Points %	Awards (winners & runners-up)	All-Stars	Playoffs
79/80	4th Div 8th Conf 16th OA	28-39-13	43.1	ART ROSS: Gretzky RU HART: Gretzky LADY BYNG: Gretzky	2ND TEAM: Gretzky (C)	Lost preliminary round 3-0 to Philadelphia
80/81	4th Div 8th Conf 14th OA	29-35-16	46.3	ART ROSS: Gretzky HART: Gretzky LADY BYNG: Gretzky RU	1ST TEAM: Gretzky (C)	Lost SC quarterfinal 4-2 to Islanders
81/82	1st Div 1st Conf 2nd OA	48-17-15	68.8	ART ROSS: Gretzky HART: Gretzky PEARSON: Gretzky VEZINA: Fuhr RU	1ST TEAM: Gretzky (C), Messier (LW) 2ND TEAM: Fuhr (G), Coffey (D)	Lost division semifinal 3-2 to Los Angeles
82/83	1st Div 1st Conf 3rd OA	47-21-12	63.5	ART ROSS: Gretzky HART: Gretzky PEARSON: Gretzky SELKE: Kurri RU	1ST TEAM: Gretzky (C), Messier (LW) 2ND TEAM: Coffey (D)	Lost SC final 4-0 to Islanders
83/84	1st Div 1st Conf 1st OA	57-18-5	74.4	ART ROSS: Gretzky, Coffey RU HART: Gretzky PEARSON: Gretzky NORRIS: Coffey RU CONN SMYTHE: Messier	1ST TEAM: Gretzky (C) 2ND TEAM: Coffey (D), Messier (LW), Kurri (RW)	Won SC final 4-1 over Islanders
84/85	1st Div 1st Conf 2nd OA	49-20-11	68.1	ART ROSS: Gretzky, Kurri RU HART: Gretzky PEARSON: Gretzky LADY BYNG: Kurri NORRIS: Coffey CONN SMYTHE: Gretzky	1ST TEAM: Gretzky (C) Coffey (D), Kurri (RW)	Won SC final 4-1 over Philadelphia

the University of Denver, and U.S. collegiate hockey was not considered a prime source of professional recruits—for one thing, the teams only played about once a week, and the schedule wasn't considered intense enough to develop first-class skills. But when Fraser saw Anderson working out with the Canadian national team, he was sure the 19-year-old had the ability to play major-league hockey.

Messier's hockey bloodlines were pure. His father, Doug, had been one of the more penalized defencemen in the Western Hockey League. After retiring, Doug Messier had become a high school teacher and Junior coach. Mark Messier had played briefly for his father on the St. Albert Saints of the Alberta Junior league before jumping to the WHA's Indianapolis Racers. He was only 17, and he had never even played tier-one Junior hockey before making the leap. Nelson Skalbania brought him in to plug a hole at center that had just been created by the sale of Wayne Gretzky to the Oilers. When the Racers folded in December, Messier returned to the St. Albert Saints, but was quickly back in the WHA, playing for Cincinnati. That put Messier in Northlands Coliseum as a Stinger on January 26, 1979, when Gretzky celebrated his eighteenth birthday by signing his 21-year, multi-million-dollar contract with

Pocklington. Eight days earlier, Messier too had turned 18, but no one had made a megabucks public fuss over him. In 52 WHA games in 78/79, Messier scored once, on a long fluke shot, and produced ten assists. NHL teams were not clamouring for his services, but Sather and Fraser liked his determination and raw skill.

They also learned that he went his own way. Sather was annoyed with Messier when he was late for training camp that fall, holding out until he signed an escalating contract worth about $70,000. When he missed a plane to St. Louis in late October, Sather sent him down to the Houston Apollos in the Central league as a disciplinary measure. If nothing else, the trip demonstrated just how good Messier was. He outclassed his teammates and the competition in Houston and was retrieved after only two weeks.

But he still had a long way to go. "Sometimes you'd see him on the ice and you'd think his mind was at Newport Beach watching the waves come in," is how Sather would describe Messier in his first NHL seasons. He scored 12 goals in 79/80, 23 in 80/81. Then, in 81/82, Mark Messier scored 50.

As Messier went, it seemed, so went the Oilers. For their first two NHL seasons, Edmonton was in the lower ranks of the weak Smythe Division, winning 28

of 80 games in 79/80, 29 in 80/81. The offence was daring, inventive and undisciplined; one school of thought held that the Oilers hadn't the faintest idea what they were doing on the ice.

At the 1980 draft, the Oilers struck it rich with three well-chosen picks. Rushing defenceman Paul Coffey was their first selection, taken sixth overall. Their third pick, taken sixty-ninth, was 20-year-old right-winger Jari Kurri of Finland.

Oilers scout Barry Fraser had first seen Kurri play at age 17 in 1978 when he was scouting overseas for the Houston Aeros. Already starring in the Finnish Elite League, Kurri was a member of the Finnish team that competed in the world Junior championships in Montreal that year. Gretzky played for the Canadians, and both were named to the tournament All Star team. Kurri, however, became the most celebrated player of the tournament when he scored in the second overtime period to upset the USSR in the championship game.

Fraser visited with Kurri over Christmas 1979 and asked him to keep his playing options open. The Finns were beginning to assemble their team for the 1980 Olympics, and Kurri was a natural candidate. Fraser wanted to draft him that summer, though, and bring him to North America, which would mean Kurri having to pass on the Olympic opportunity. Kurri decided the NHL was worth it. "We could never have waited until the fourth round [of the 1980 draft] if everybody had known what we knew, that he'd come to the NHL right away," Fraser reflected in 1983. "He'd have gone real high."

Kurri's dad was part-owner of an Esso station in Helsinki, so it was fitting that he was going to play professional hockey in a Canadian oil town. Thinking he would give the NHL two years, he signed a one-year contract with an option year. Kurri hardly spoke a word of English when he arrived, but he learned quickly. He became an Oilers starter in the fall of 1980. The Oilers tried one right-winger after another with Gretzky until turning to Kurri just before Christmas. They clicked immediately. Kurri was the defensive forward and creative playmaker Gretzky needed. In March 1983, as the

Oilers homed in on their first trip to the Cup finals, Fraser proclaimed, "Kurri is by far our most complete player. If he doesn't win that Selke Trophy, they should throw it in the garbage." He didn't—Bobby Clarke earned the honour as the league's top defensive forward that season. Kurri never did win the trophy. He was destined to be one of the NHL's most underrated talents, overshadowed by his celebrated center, his skills downplayed because of his proximity to the Great One.

Barry Fraser made another inspired draft pick in 1980. The Oilers' sixth selection, down at 132nd, was Andy Moog, a goaltender from Penticton, B.C., who was playing for Billings in the Western Junior league. Moog had been scouted by former Oilers netminder Dave Dryden, who had become an assistant coach. Goaltenders are notoriously unpredictable as draft picks. Top selections often do not pan out, while choices made deep in the draft—sometimes not even drafted at all but signed as free agents—can turn into stars. Moog was one of those finds that reinforces the role of solid scouting in building a championship club.

Moog was outstanding in the 80/81 playoffs after appearing in just seven regular-season games. The Oilers took the defending-champion New York Islanders to six games in the quarterfinals, and Islanders captain Bryan Trottier saw a team of the future over his shoulder as the Islanders moved on to win their second title. (The Oilers had already showed moxie in the 79/80 playoffs, eliminating the Canadiens three straight in the preliminary round. Though downed in three straight in the next round by the Philadelphia Flyers, two games went into overtime, and the Flyers went all the way to the finals.)

As outstanding as Moog had been, however, the Oilers weren't standing pat on their goaltending roster. Edmonton held the eighth pick overall in that summer's amateur draft, and the club made a rare move in using it to select a goaltender. There was thought to be a jinx on using a first pick to choose a netminder, which went back to Montreal using its first pick (fifth overall) in 1970 to take Ray Martiniuk of the Flin Flon Bombers, who never made the NHL. But the Oilers had scouted Grant Fuhr to death. He was born and raised in Spruce Grove, about 20 miles west of Edmonton, and in Pee Wee had been coached by former great Glenn Hall. At 17, Fuhr had moved to Victoria, B.C., to play for the Cougars of the Western Junior league; in his first season scouts called him the greatest Junior netminding prospect since Bernie Parent in the mid-1960s. The Cougars had just won the league championship when the Oilers used their first pick to take him. At training camp that fall, Fuhr wrested the starting job away from Moog, who was sent to Wichita in the WHL.

With Fuhr picked in the opening round of the 1981 draft, the nucleus of the championship Oilers club of the 1980s was complete: Gretzky, Messier, Lowe, Coffey, Anderson and Fuhr. But one of the most important additions to the Oilers was one of the most overlooked. In September 1981, Ted Green was hired as the team's defensive coach.

Oilers coaching was a a revolving door of faces in the first few seasons. Sather tried Dave Dryden, Billy Harris and Bugsy Watson as assistant coaches. He replaced himself with Watson as head coach in 80/81, then fired his old friend early in the season and took over again. Green's arrival, which was followed by the hiring of John Muckler as offensive coach in 1983, gave the Oilers stable, methodical coaching, something a roster of creative youngsters badly needed. "John Muckler and Teddy Green are the masters with the videotape," Kevin Lowe would write. "They'll point out aspects of a team's game plan or discuss ways of adapting. That's the key: rather than honing on to one game plan, like a bully clinging to a club, Muck and Greenie will work on showing us how to adapt, to change."

Green had been a defensive anchor of the Boston Bruins through

In 82/83 the Oilers were stunned by a four game sweep in the Stanley Cup finals at the hands of the New York Islanders. In 83/84, a more seasoned, better prepared Oilers club was back in the finals against the Islanders, and this time got the job done masterfully, winning in five and outscoring the four-time champions 19 to 6 in the last three games.

Harassed by Dick Beddoes in a 1979 television interview over the sorry state of his team, Oilers owner Peter Pocklington (above) blurted out that they would win the Stanley Cup in five years. The team delivered right on schedule, in the spring of 1984.

its fruitless 1960s campaigns. He was playing a leading role in its late-1960s revival when a terrible stick-swinging incident between him and Blackhawk Wayne Maki in a 1969 pre-season game almost cost him his life. His fractured skull had to be repaired with a steel plate, and while he returned to the game and participated in the Bruins' 71/72 Stanley Cup win, he no longer held a front-line position. In 1972 he jumped to the new WHA and played with the New England Whalers for three seasons. It was his move to the Winnipeg Jets in 1975 that was most important to his coaching future. In 75/76 the Jets had nine elite Europeans in the line-up, seven Swedes and two Finns, and for four seasons the stay-at-home Ted Green provided defensive insurance to the Jets' creative attack. The club won four Avco Cups, including the last one, against the Oilers.

Glen Sather greatly admired the panache of the Jets and modeled his NHL Oilers after them. (In 82/83, right-winger Willy Lindstrom, a Swedish star who had spent four seasons in the WHA with the Jets, was acquired by Sather from Winnipeg.) Like general manager Bill Torrey of the New York Islanders, Sather believed in youth, and in his trading (he traded so relentlessly that he was nicknamed Montey, after Montey Hall, Canadian-born host of the game show "Let's Make a Deal") he consistently moved older players to get at youngsters. But unlike Torrey, who built his club on the premise that any weak team had to start with defence and go from there, Sather was enchanted by the shoot-'em-up offence. It was hard not to be with Wayne Gretzky, the most exciting player in the league, at center. As a result, the team was unbalanced. Defence was never a high priority for the Oilers, who routinely allowed four goals per game. Even as the team began to win it was dogged by its defensive weakness.

In 81/82 the Oilers rocketed up the standings, finishing second overall to the Islanders. They scored 417 goals—92 by Gretzky alone—which was 32 more than the second-best effort, by the Islanders. But they also allowed 295 goals, 72 more than Montreal, which had the best defensive record, and 45 more than the

Islanders. The division semifinals held a nasty surprise. The Oilers were matched with the Los Angeles Kings, who had finished fourth in the Oilers' Smythe Division with half as many wins. The Kings won the opening game in a 10-8 offensive-free-for-all, and upset Edmonton 3-2 in the best-of-five series.

In 82/83 Edmonton scored more goals (424) and allowed more goals (315) than in 81/82 and posted the third-best overall record. This time the Oilers made it all the way to the finals, but the Islanders, who had won the last three Cups, were waiting. Against the Winnipeg Jets in the division semifinals, the Oilers had averaged 4.7 goals per game. Against the Calgary Flames in the division finals, the Oilers' output was a staggering 7 goals per game. They had ousted the Flames with a 9-1 rout in game five on April 20. But in the opening game of the final series in Edmonton on May 10, Oilers fans watched in shock as the Islanders took an early 1-0 lead and held it all the way to the end of the game, when an empty-net goal gave them a 2-0 opening win. The Oilers had not been shut out at home in two seasons, 189 games earlier. That shutout loss, too, had been delivered by the Islanders' Billy Smith.

Smith deservedly won the Conn Smythe as the Islanders swept the Oilers in four. His maniac-with-a-stick act, which he punctuated with slashes of Gretzky and Anderson in the opening games, unhinged Sather and got the Oilers in a distracted lather. The series ultimately went the Islanders' way because the older, more experienced, more poised defending champions showed that they could play great offensive and defensive hockey. Edmonton lost the last three games 6-3, 5-1 and 4-2. After scoring 71 goals in 80 regular-season games, after breaking Islander Mike Bossy's 35-point playoff record with a 38-point showing, Gretzky could not be happy with a final-series performance that contributed only 4 assists on the 6 Edmonton goals.

As with many wayward kids, the Oilers' failure in the 82/83 finals was blamed on environment. The league had moved to an unbalanced schedule, meaning the Oilers played a preponderance of games against fellow members of the weak Smythe Division. The Oilers were the only Smythe team to win more than half of its games, and every Smythe team had allowed more than 300 goals. "I'm not shooting down the teams in our division because we had some very entertaining games with them," John Muckler said after the loss. "But I wish we played more times during the season against the Islanders, Boston, Buffalo, Montreal and Philadelphia because they're the strong checking teams."

Ted Green saw hope in the loss. "The Islanders had 11 regulars between the ages of 28 and 32. Of guys we had playing the final series, three are 28 [Fogolin, Lumley and Hughes], and one is 32 [Lindstrom]. That makes a difference. Take three years off those figures and what age were the Islander guys? 26, 27, 28. At a young age, our guys gained one hell of an experience in these playoffs. They should progress at an earlier stage

EDMONTON OILERS 1985/86–89/90

Season	Finish	Record (W-L-T)	Points %	Awards (winners & runners-up)	All-Stars	Playoffs
85/86	1st Div 1st Conf 1st OA	56-17-7	74.4	ART ROSS: Gretzky HART: Gretzky LADY BYNG: Kurri RU NORRIS: Coffey ADAMS: Sather	1ST TEAM: Gretzky (C), Coffey (D) 2ND TEAM: Kurri (RW)	Lost division final 4-3 to Calgary
86/87	1st Div 1st Conf 1st OA	50-24-6	66.3	ART ROSS: Gretzky, Kurri RU HART: Gretzky PEARSON: Gretzky LADY BYNG: Gretzky RU	1ST TEAM: Gretzky (C), Kurri (RW)	Won SC final 4-3 over Philadelphia
87/88	2nd Div 2nd Conf 3rd OA	44-25-11	61.9	ART ROSS: Gretzky RU HART: Fuhr RU LADY BYNG: Gretzky RU VEZINA: Fuhr CONN SMYTHE: Gretzky	1ST TEAM: Fuhr (G) 2ND TEAM: Gretzky (C)	Won SC final 4-0 over Boston
88/89	3rd Div 3rd Conf 7th OA	38-34-8	52.5	SELKE: Tikkanen RU	2ND TEAM: Kurri (RW)	Lost division semifinal 4-3 to Los Angeles
89/90	2nd Div 2nd Conf 5th OA	38-28-14	56.3	ART ROSS: Messier RU HART: Messier PEARSON: Messier CLANCY: Lowe CONN SMYTHE: Ranford	1ST TEAM: Messier (C)	Won SC final 4-1 over Boston

in their lives than the Islanders did."

In 83/84 the Oilers were far better prepared for their rematch with the Islanders in the finals, although they almost didn't make it there. After scoring 18 goals against Winnipeg and sweeping them in three in their division semifinals, the Oilers ran into the Calgary Flames, who were not going to go down under a hail of pucks the way they had in the spring of 1983. Calgary won two overtime games in a protracted and nasty seven-game series that ended with a 7-4 Oilers win. It was an ordeal by fire the Oilers came to feel they needed to improve their playoff discipline. In the conference finals, Minnesota provided little resistance as the Oilers scored 22 times in a four-game sweep.

The Oilers had nine days in which to prepare for the finals against the Islanders, who were in the midst of a 4-2 series win against the Canadiens when Edmonton won the clinching game against Minnesota. The Oilers coaching staff went to work, bringing in Roger Neilson (who had coached Vancouver in the 81/82 finals against the Islanders) to review game films. They reviewed how the Oilers had lost to the Islanders in the 82/83 finals, and how the Islanders had beaten the Rangers, Washington and Montreal in this year's playoffs.

The Oilers hadn't beaten the Islanders in ten games when they met in the first game of the finals in Long Island. Fuhr drew the starting assignment and was impermeable, turning away 38 shots. The lone goal of the game came from a "character" player, the hard-nosed right-winger Kevin McClelland, who had 189

penalty minutes that season. When acquired by the Oilers early in the season, McClelland was bouncing between the Pittsburgh Penguins and their American league farm team in Baltimore. At 1:55 of the third period, McClelland converted a giveaway by Islanders right-winger Duane Sutter into the only goal the Oilers needed to defeat the defending champions at home.

Roly Melanson replaced Billy Smith in the Islanders goal for game two, and New York came away with a 6-1 win as the Oilers' discipline broke down in a brawling contest.

The Oilers, however, did not fold. Back in Edmonton for game three, the teams were tied at two in the final minute of the second period when Glenn Anderson and Paul Coffey scored 17 seconds apart while the teams were playing four-on-four. Outshot 40-26 in the game, the Islanders surrendered three more goals in the third as they lost 7-2.

Game four was another 7-2 Oilers rout as Edmonton punished Billy Smith with 38 shots. Four minutes into the game, the Oilers were up 2-0. The turning point came when the Oilers successfully killed a five-minute major assessed to Ken Linseman for high-sticking Bryan Trottier. Moog, who had replaced Fuhr in goal in game three when Fuhr suffered a bruised shoulder, was solid as the Oilers ran up the score. Gretzky got his first goals of the series, opening and closing the Edmonton scoring. Smith was pulled after the sixth goal in favour of Melanson. The Islanders were in full retreat.

Game five brought the Oilers a Cup victory on

The Oilers celebrate a goal against the Philadelphia Flyers in the 86/87 finals. Edmonton built a 3-1 series lead, but rookie goaltender Ron Hextall anchored a Flyers comeback that forced a seventh game. While the Oilers won their third Stanley Cup with a 3-1 win at home, Hextall was awarded the Conn Smythe Trophy.

home ice. Though outshot 25-22, Edmonton pulled off a 5-2 win as Moog continued to deliver great playoff goaltending. At one point the Oilers led 4-0, and Smith was again replaced by Melanson. The Islanders mounted a terrific counter-offensive in the third period, but the Oilers' lead held. The Islanders' quest to match the 1950s Montreal Canadiens' record of five consecutive Cup wins was thwarted with the 4-1 series loss. It was now Edmonton's turn to challenge the record.

The Oilers began their quest by breaking one long-standing Canadiens record. They went 15 games without a loss (13 wins and 2 ties) at the start of the 84/85 season, bettering the record performance of Montreal in 43/44. The season overall wasn't quite as spectacular as 83/84—the team won 49 of 80 games, 8 fewer than the previous season—but the Oilers were the only club to score more than 400 goals (401) as Gretzky and Kurri finished first and second in the scoring race. Gretzky had 73 goals, while Kurri, with 71, set an NHL record for right-wingers. Gretzky recorded his one-thousandth NHL point on December 19, reaching the plateau faster than any player in league history. He had already set a record in 81/82 by reaching the 50-goal mark in 39 regular-season games.

Gretzky and Kurri were also playing with a new linemate, Mike Krushelnyski, acquired from Boston for Ken Linseman. Mark Messier and Glenn Anderson also had a new winger, Mark Napier, picked up from Minnesota for Gord Sherven and Terry Martin. And

the season brought a maturation of wildman Messier. Off the ice, he kept finding trouble behind the wheels of fast cars, tangling with breathalyzers and other vehicles and attracting unwelcome press attention. In February 1984 he was suspended for six games for breaking his stick over the head of Vancouver's Thomas Gradin, and he attracted a career-high 165 penalty minutes in 83/84. His receipt of the Conn Smythe Trophy for his performance in the 83/84 playoffs underlined his importance to the team, and in 84/85 his penalty minutes fell dramatically, to 57, albeit a total aided by a ten-game absence as he served a suspension for cracking the cheekbone of Calgary's Jamie Macoun in another high-sticking incident.

The Oilers were susceptible to playoff jitters, and they began the 84/85 post-season with a near-disastrous outing against the lowly Los Angeles Kings. Andy Moog was injured on March 1 in a collision with J. P. Kelly of the Kings, and Grant Fuhr was called upon to carry the Oilers through the playoffs. Fuhr came out of a slump and sharpened up just when he was needed. Though the Oilers swept the Kings in three, two games ended in overtime and Fuhr had to turn away a penalty shot in each of the last two games. Edmonton then produced another four-game sweep of Winnipeg in the division finals, and while Chicago took them to six games in the conference finals the Oilers offence was running full tilt, scoring 44 times.

The Cup finals matched the Oilers with a Philadelphia club being rebuilt under coach Mike Keenan. The young Flyers surprised the Oilers 4-1 in the opening game, but from then on Edmonton was in complete control, winning the next four games. In their clinching 8-3 win at home, the Oilers set a record for the most goals scored in a winning Stanley Cup game. Other records fell. Jari Kurri's 19 goals was the most of any playoff season, and Grant Fuhr's 15 wins matched Billy Smith's record for the most wins by a goaltender in a playoff season. Paul Coffey had been outstanding on defence. His three goals and two assists in game two of the Winnipeg series matched the league record for most points in a playoff game by a defenceman. Gretzky won the Conn Smythe, but there were many who felt Coffey, who had won his first Norris Trophy that season, deserved it. "I've never seen anyone play any better, including Himself," said Ted Green. And in Green's lexicon "Himself" meant not Gretzky but former Bruins teammate Bobby Orr.

The 85/86 season was the turning point in the Oilers dynasty. It was the season everything seemed to be going so right, then ended up going so wrong. The day before the final game of the 84/85 Cup series, John Muckler signed a three-year contract to serve as Sather's co-coach. Under Muckler and Sather, the team won a franchise-high 56 games, and Gretzky, Coffey and Kurri were first, third and fourth in the scoring race. Kurri and Gretzky had a new linemate, Essa Tikkanen. Coffey won another Norris, Gretzky his seventh consecutive Hart, Sather his first Jack Adams Award as the league's top coach. The Oilers were bound for a Stanley Cup "three-peat," and after that, the five-straight record of the 1950s Canadiens beckoned. Notably absent, however, was Ted Green, who had taken a leave of absence from the organization to concentrate on a computerized skate-sharpening business.

Edmonton warmed up its Cup drive with a demolition of Vancouver in their division semifinals, winning 7-3, 5-1 and 5-1. That produced another divisional final against their now mortal enemies down the road in Calgary. The Flames battled to a 3-2 series lead, forcing Edmonton to come up with a 5-2 win in Calgary to bring on a decisive seventh game. In the closing moments of game seven the game was tied 2-2 and apparently headed for overtime when Oilers defenceman Steve Smith gathered the puck behind his goal and prepared to launch a rush. He moved out to the side of the goal to send the puck up ice ... and banked the puck into his own net off Grant Fuhr's skate. The astonished Flames celebrated in front of a stunned Northlands Coliseum crowd and Oilers bench. The game ended soon after with the Edmonton dream of a record run of Cup wins over. Calgary went on to lose in the finals to Montreal.

Banking the puck into their own net was not the way the Oilers wanted their reign to end, or to be remembered. The Oilers were on a mission to reassert their claim to league supremacy. While Steve Smith was the goat of game seven, the mishap did not stain him. Far more affected was Jari Kurri, who was held to one goal in the seven games with the Flames. Kurri bore the brunt of the usual argument weighed against European stars: not tough enough to deliver in a physical series.

Sather listed six "untouchables" on the Oilers' roster in 1986: Gretzky, Messier, Fuhr, Kurri, Coffey and Anderson. With Ted Green back as an assistant coach in 86/87, Sather tinkered with the margins of the roster. Tough-guy left-winger Dave Semenko went to Hartford, original defenceman Lee Fogolin and right-winger Mark Napier to Buffalo. Jeff Beukeboom, Craig Muni and Reijo Ruotsalainen all started on defence, and Kent Nilsson, who had played with the WHA Jets in the late 1970s, was acquired from Minnesota.

Kurri rebounded from the criticisms heaped on him after the 85/86 playoff debacle, finishing second to Gretzky in the scoring race; Mark Messier was fourth. The team produced the best record for the fourth straight season.

The Cup drive began with a straightforward five-game elimination of Los Angeles in the division semifinals that included a 13-3 pasting. Winnipeg fell in four straight in the division finals, and that brought on Edmonton's second Cup finals against the Philadelphia Flyers. The biggest difference between the Flyers of 84/85 and 86/87 was rookie goaltender Ron Hextall. The Oilers built a 3-1 series lead, but Hextall's play brought the Flyers back into the series, and a seventh game was required for the Oilers to win their third Cup. The Conn Smythe went to Hextall, who was only the fourth player on a losing team to win the playoff MVP award (and the second losing Flyer in a row, after Reggie Leach in 75/76, to be so honoured).

The Oilers dynasty was still alive, but fighting scandals and internal dissent. Paul Coffey was fed up with Glen Sather and Peter Pocklington. He had been angry with Sather ever since he was publicly criticized for his play at the start of the 86/87 season, and now he wanted a raise or a trade. Coffey alleged that the team observed a double standard in its treatment of players—some were coddled while others were dumped on. He was making $320,000 (Canadian) at the time while Denis Potvin and Rod Langway were bringing in about $500,000 (U.S.). Unable to reach an agreement with Pocklington and Sather, Coffey was dealt to Pittsburgh on November 24 with left-wingers Dave Hunter and Wayne Van Dorp for left-winger Craig Simpson, center Dave Hannan and defencemen Moe Mantha and Chris Joseph.

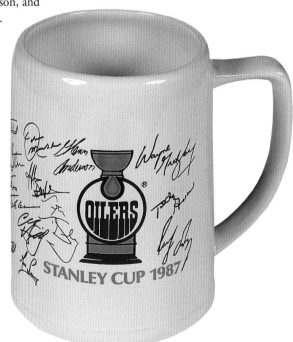

Grant Fuhr's finest season was 87/88, when he won the Vezina, was named to the first All Star team, and was outstanding in the playoffs as the Oilers won their fourth Stanley Cup with a four-game sweep of Boston.

Another unhappy Oiler was Andy Moog, who had lost the first-string goaltending job to Grant Fuhr. He had decided to join the Canadian Olympic team program rather than play another season as an Oiler, and on March 7, 1988, Moog's rights were dealt to Boston for left-winger Geoff Courtnall, goaltender Bill Ranford and a second-round draft pick.

Fuhr carried the Oilers for a record 75 of 80 regular-season games, winning 40 of them. He was touted for the Hart Trophy, made the first All Star team for the first time in his career, and won his first Vezina. His middling goals-against average would have kept him far from the trophy in earlier seasons, but the Vezina had switched to a vote format in 1982. At last, Fuhr's role as the dependable backstop on an offensive-minded team was properly recognized. In the playoffs he won a record 16 of 18 games as the Oilers marched past Winnipeg in five, Calgary in four, Detroit in five and Boston (with Moog in goal) in four in the finals.

The Oilers had raced through the 87/88 playoffs with an ease that suggested they could still mount five straight Cup victories. Unfortunately for the dynasty the outside world had intervened in the form of Peter Pocklington's ongoing financial misadventures. In 1983 his Fidelity Trust Co. had failed, costing the Canadian Deposit Insurance Corp. $359 million to rescue depositors. In 1986 his

Gainers Inc. meat-packing operation experienced a truly nasty strike, and in 1989 the province of Alberta would seize the company after it defaulted on government loans.

The day after the Oilers had won their fourth Cup, Wayne Gretzky was told by Pocklington about an offer for him from the Vancouver Canucks. The point man of the deal was Nelson Skalbania, who had signed Gretzky to his original personal-services contract. Apparently, Skalbania was willing to pay Pocklington $20 million for Gretzky's contract. Skalbania would then parlay Gretzky's playing rights to the Canucks and his marketing rights to Vancouver businessman Jim Pattison, who had masterminded Expo 86. According to Gretzky's fiancée, Janet Jones, Gretzky's response to Pocklington was, "I can't believe you coming to me with this the day after we won the Cup."

The rumours persisted that Pocklington had Gretzky in play. Phil Esposito, general manager of the New York Rangers, would confirm that Sather approached him at the June draft, offering Gretzky.

On July 16, Gretzky and Jones were married in a fairy-tale wedding in Edmonton. Paul Coffey, who served as an usher, would say that Gretzky told him at the wedding that Pocklington was trying to trade him. Five days after the wedding, Gretzky received a call from Bruce McNall, owner of the Los Angeles Kings. As Gretzky told *The Toronto Sun*, McNall said he had

Pocklington's permission to contact him. "Peter had told him, 'If you can swing him over, you've got him,' " is how Janet Jones put it. The McNall call was the first serious indication that Pocklington was actually going to unload him.

The motivations of both Pocklington and Gretzky would be called into question as the deal unfolded. Gretzky's position was that, when it became clear that Pocklington was going to deal him, it was in his best interests to engineer a deal he could live with, and that was a trade to Los Angeles. Gretzky allegedly got the deal he wanted by agreeing to state at the press conference that it was all his idea; and that they were happy to be moving to Janet's home town (she was a film actress, although she would stop working once they were married).

The deal between McNall and Pocklington saw Gretzky packaged with defencemen Marty McSorley (Gretzky's enforcer of choice) and Mike Krushelnyski for center Jimmy Carson, draft pick Martin Gélinas of the Hull Olympiques, first-round picks in 1989, 1991 and 1993 and $15 million. Gretzky would also get $5 million for coming to L.A.

One press report described the Pocklington-Gretzky press conference on August 9 as an exhibition worthy of the World Wrestling Federation. It featured Gretzky revealing that Janet was expecting, and the Great One shedding tears over leaving Edmonton. Some observers could not contain their cynicism: after all, Gretzky was on his way to Lotus Land, where he would be a lot richer and more famous than he could ever be in Edmonton. Pocklington did not help the mood when he told *The Edmonton Journal* that Gretzky had "an ego the size of Manhattan.... He's a great actor, I thought he pulled it off beautifully when he showed how upset he was. I think he was upset, but he wants the big dream."

Gretzky, however, did appear genuinely distraught at leaving the Oilers. There was much circumstantial evidence that he'd had no intention of leaving Edmonton for L.A. He and Janet Jones had chosen Edmonton for their wedding just a few weeks before the trade announcement, even though neither of them owned a house there. Jones also didn't own a house in L.A., and she had recently moved her car and clothing to Edmonton.

It appears that Gretzky's Edmonton career was cut short by his fateful decision in the summer of 1987 to replace his unusual personal-services contract with a more conventional player contract. According to sports reporter Al Strachan, Gretzky had pushed for a new five-year deal with Pocklington that gave him the option of retiring after three years. The contract did not carry a no-trade provision, however, and if Pocklington wanted to cash in on Gretzky, he would have to move him before the approaching retirement clause depleted his market value. One year after signing the new contract, Gretzky was sent packing.

The trade ushered in a nightmare Oilers season. Grant Fuhr slumped and had to be spelled off by Ranford for 29 games. Edmonton dropped to third in the Smythe Division, seven points behind Gretzky's Kings, and in the opening round of the playoffs the Kings won a seven-game series that culminated with a 6-3 defeat of the Oilers in Los Angeles.

It was not yet time to write the Oilers epitaph. John Muckler took over as head coach for 89/90 and set forth on a campaign with a sturdy core of players who had been with the club since the 82/83 finals: defencemen Kevin Lowe, Randy Gregg and Charlie Huddy, center Mark Messier, left-winger Glenn Anderson and right-winger Jari Kurri. With Bill Ranford providing exceptional playoff netminding and captain Mark Messier an effective motivational spark, the Oilers struggled to down the Jets in seven, dropped Gretzky's Kings in four, then mastered the Bruins in five in the finals.

There would be no happy ending to the story, however. Grant Fuhr ended up being suspended after it was revealed that he had undergone treatment for cocaine use—a notorious *Sports Illustrated* story back in 1986 had printed assertions that unnamed Oilers were using the drug. The sell-off of big-ticket Oilers by Pocklington continued, and in his battle over the terms of his lease with the city-owned Northlands Coliseum, he won few friends by threatening to move the Oilers out of Edmonton. By 91/92, the only core Oiler left was Kevin Lowe, and he was sent to New York in December 1992.

"Can you imagine what that team might have done in a market like Toronto or Montreal or New York that could have afforded to keep it together?" Sather speculated in November 1993. The following spring, the New York Rangers won their first Stanley Cup since 39/40. In the lineup were seven former Cup-winning Oilers—Kevin Lowe, Mark Messier, Glenn Anderson, Essa Tikkanen, Craig McTavish, Jeff Beukeboom and Adam Graves. It was the largest airlift of talent from one championship team to another in NHL history, and it made Sather's "can you imagine" not hard to imagine at all.

The Oilers went four consecutive seasons, from 92/93 to 95/96, without making the playoffs as Sather's youth drive failed to produce a winning lineup. Kevin Lowe was brought back from New York to play with this young team, and in 96/97 it began to show promise. Ticket sales went up, and Peter Pocklington moved to sell 45 percent of the Oilers in a public share offering that would allow him to pay down his debts to the Alberta Treasury Branches. As always, Peter's Principles were the talk of Edmonton, but for the first time in too many dry seasons, the hopeful Oilers were as well. ○

The 89/90 season was Mark Messier's turn to shine. Key players like Wayne Gretzky and Paul Coffey had been traded away and the Oilers no longer dominated the regular season. Messier, with a core team of about a half-dozen veteran Oilers, led Edmonton into the finals against Boston. The 4-1 series victory was convincing, and Messier won the Hart and Pearson Trophies in addition to making the first All Star team that season. His championship jersey appears above.

INDEX

Indexed are people who appear in this book. Not included are text references in "Motherlode" (page 94), "The St. Mike's Pipeline" (page 97) and charts. Photographic citations are in italics.

continued on page 208

IMAGE SOURCES

All equipment and memorabilia in this book appears courtesy of the Hockey Hall of Fame, except for Wayne Gretzky's skates on page 190, which were on temporary loan to the HHOF when photographed and belong to the Gretzky family. Photographs of these items, including the Gretzky skates, are by Bruce MacLellan.

Hockey Hall of Fame Archives
11, 16, 20, 24, 25, 26, 27, 28, 29, 30, 44, 75 (top, bottom), 78, 120, 130, 146, 158 (photo: Craig Campbell)

London Life–Lewis Portnoy/ Hockey Hall of Fame
126, 132, 133, 136, 138, 142, 145, 156, 159, 160, 162, 179, 191, 194

Fred Kennan/Hockey Hall of Fame
154-55 (Orr image)

Graphic Artists/Hockey Hall of Fame
99, 113, 114, 122, 131, 164, 166, 169, 170, 176, 178

Imperial Oil–Turfosky/ Hockey Hall of Fame
Contents, 22 (left), 41, 42, 51, 52, 74 (all), 75 (middle), 82, 106, 152

Frank Prazak/Hockey Hall of Fame
102, 117, 119, 148, 196

Bruce Bennett Studios
175, 182, 185, 186, 189, 198, 200, 204

Reuters/Corbis-Bettmann
9, 13

UPI/Corbis-Bettmann
18, 22 (right), 38, 45, 56-57, 58, 62-63, 66-67, 68, 71, 76-77, 90, 141

Corbis-Bettmann
202

National Archives of Canada
72 Montreal Gazette/PA197448
80 (top) Montreal Gazette/PA108233
80 (bottom) Montreal Gazette/PA142655
81 (bottom) Montreal Gazette/PA142658
84 Montreal Gazette/PA142656
88 Montreal Gazette/PA142654
91 Montreal Gazette/PA197451
95 PA053806
97 PA053809

MAKING THIS BOOK

This book uses the typefaces Adobe Garamond and Gill Sans in the interior design. It was produced on a Mac platform using Quark XPress 3.32, Adobe Photoshop 3.0 and Adobe Illustrator 5.5

Jacket design: Martin Gould
Editor: Meg Masters
Copy editor: Catherine Marjoribanks
Production director: Dianne Craig
Production editor: Lori Ledingham
Interior design, photo research, illustrations, occasional image scans: Douglas Hunter
POODLE COUNTRY

Printed and bound in Singapore on acid neutral paper by arrangement with Imago Sales USA Inc.